Jeff,

I have really enjoyed working with you and getting to know you over the past 3 years. I appreciate all the insights you have shared and your friendship. Hope you enjoy this book.

Dick Thompson

About This Book

Why is this topic important?

Emotionally effective behavior is the magic wand that opens—not the future—but the present moment NOW to the fullest influence of our passion, creativity and determination. It is the texture and intensity and direction of the emotional energy we transmit that lets other people know what we want and how to work with us. It tells them how urgent our message is in terms of timeliness, how valuable it is in terms of the results we are seeking to achieve, and how pleased or displeased we are with the progress currently being made toward achieving that goal. This is the essence of emotional effectiveness, and it is the bottom line in all leadership and teamwork.

What can you achieve with this book?

Groundbreaking work has resulted in excellent emotional intelligence assessments, as well as authoritative books and articles on Emotional and Social Intelligence (ESI). This *Handbook* adds the much-needed element of practical applications so you can take this great thinking straight to your clients or staff to make a long-term difference. With contributions from ESI leaders across the world, you can tap directly into any of the seventeen chapters that best match your facilitation, coaching, or training needs. The wide variety of content enables you to explore your focus areas as well as learn about new ones. You can achieve an exceptionally high and well-founded level of confidence in the value of emotional intelligence from exploring these case studies, the developmental strategies, and the research this volume proffers and take that learning into your work with clients and staff.

How is this book organized?

The *Handbook* is organized into four sections designed to help you select the chapters that best match your needs. The first part focuses on leader and individual development through coaching. Chapters address ESI coaching strategies, working with high achievers, a case example based on extensive leadership work in South Africa and Cambodia, leadership derailment, interpretation techniques for working with the EQ-i® and EI and catastrophic failure. The second part of the book provides guidance for teams, organizations, and cultures with chapters on team conflict resolution skills, bridging your ESI application from individuals to organizations, understanding star performers' ESI attributes, and perspectives and strategies in ESI development in South Africa. Part Three combines wisdom by demonstrating ESI connections with personality type profiles, by combining the EQ-i® and the MSCEIT, and by the powerful combination of ESI with Appreciative Inquiry. It also includes a look at the social aspects within emotional intelligence. Part Four focuses on education, including a sustainable, skill-based approach to building emotional literacy in schools, developing emotional, social, and cognitive skills in MBA programs, and research on building leadership in schools. There is plenty to support your current interests and to take you into new areas.

About Pfeiffer

Pfeiffer serves the professional development and hands-on resource needs of training and human resource practitioners and gives them products to do their jobs better. We deliver proven ideas and solutions from experts in HR development and HR management, and we offer effective and customizable tools to improve workplace performance. From novice to seasoned professional, Pfeiffer is the source you can trust to make yourself and your organization more successful.

Essential Knowledge Pfeiffer produces insightful, practical, and comprehensive materials on topics that matter the most to training and HR professionals. Our Essential Knowledge resources translate the expertise of seasoned professionals into practical, how-to guidance on critical workplace issues and problems. These resources are supported by case studies, worksheets, and job aids and are frequently supplemented with CD-ROMs, websites, and other means of making the content easier to read, understand, and use.

Essential Tools Pfeiffer's Essential Tools resources save time and expense by offering proven, ready-to-use materials—including exercises, activities, games, instruments, and assessments—for use during a training or team-learning event. These resources are frequently offered in looseleaf or CD-ROM format to facilitate copying and customization of the material.

Pfeiffer also recognizes the remarkable power of new technologies in expanding the reach and effectiveness of training. While e-hype has often created whizbang solutions in search of a problem, we are dedicated to bringing convenience and enhancements to proven training solutions. All our e-tools comply with rigorous functionality standards. The most appropriate technology wrapped around essential content yields the perfect solution for today's on-the-go trainers and human resource professionals.

www.pfeiffer.com

Essential resources for training and HR professionals

*This book is dedicated to all of the practitioners in
the world who seek to help people improve the quality of human
relationships, no matter what their professional title or role. We believe
that developing the ability to consciously engage one's own
emotional energy with others' harmoniously will be the gift that
allows civilization to achieve sustainability.*

Handbook for Developing Emotional and Social Intelligence

Best Practices, Case Studies, and Strategies

MARCIA HUGHES,
HENRY L. THOMPSON, AND
JAMES BRADFORD TERRELL,
EDITORS

Foreword by JAMES M. KOUZES

Pfeiffer

A Wiley Imprint
www.pfeiffer.com

Published by Pfeiffer
An Imprint of Wiley
989 Market Street, San Francisco, CA 94103-1741
www.pfeiffer.com

For additional copies/bulk purchases of this book in the U.S. please contact 800-274-4434.

Pfeiffer books and products are available through most bookstores. To contact Pfeiffer directly call our Customer Care Department within the U.S. at 800-274-4434, outside the U.S. at 317-572-3985, fax 317-572-4002, or visit www.pfeiffer.com.

Pfeiffer also publishes its books in a variety of electronic formats. Some content that appears in print may not be available in electronic books.

Library of Congress Cataloging-in-Publication Data

Handbook for developing emotional and social intelligence : best practices, case studies, and strategies / Marcia Hughes, Henry L. Thompson, and James Bradford Terrell, editors.
    p.   cm.
Includes bibliographical references and index.
ISBN 978-0-470-19088-3 (cloth)
1. Emotional intelligence. 2. Social intelligence. 3. Leadership. 4. Executive coaching. I. Hughes, Marcia M. II. Thompson, Henry L. III. Terrell, James Bradford,
BF576.H35   2009
152.4—dc22
                                                                                        2008053152

Acquiring Editor: Holly Allen
Director of Development: Kathleen Dolan Davies
Developmental Editor: Susan Rachmeler
Production Editor: Dawn Kilgore

Editor: Rebecca Taff
Editorial Assistant: Michael Gilbart
Manufacturing Supervisor: Becky Morgan

Printed in the United States of America
Printing   10 9 8 7 6 5 4 3 2 1

Contents

Foreword

by James M. Kouzes

Three brief stories:

When I asked Don Bennett, the first amputee to climb Mt. Rainier, to tell me the most important lesson he learned from his historic ascent, he replied, "You can't do it alone." Here's a guy who just hopped 14,410 feet on one leg and two poles, who had done something no one else had ever done, and he attributes his success to teamwork.

When asked about why she was able to be so successful in her role as vice president of nursing at Beth Israel Hospital in Boston, Joyce Clifford, with a glorious laugh and a smile on her face, said, "I tell them they can do it. . . . I tell them I'm not smart enough to figure it out, but I know that they can. And, you know what? That's the truth. . . . Technically, I'm not the most competent person, but I know how to get people to think well about themselves." What a marvelous admission. And what an extraordinary skill. Knowing how to get people to think well about themselves is an ability that all of us could benefit from.

In speaking to our MBA students at Santa Clara University, Irwin Federman, a partner in U.S. Venture Partners and a former CFO and CEO, made this observation: "I contend, however, that all other things being equal, we will work harder and more effectively for people we like, and we will like them in direct proportion to how they make us feel." Like Don and Joyce, Irwin understands that leaders don't create excellence all by themselves. In the thousands of cases we've studied, we've yet to encounter a single example of extraordinary achievement that's occurred without the active involvement and support of many people. We've yet to find a single instance in which one talented person—leader or individual contributor—accounted for most, let alone 100 percent, of the success.

These are just a few examples of one fundamental point: Leadership is a relationship. It's a relationship between those who aspire to lead and those who choose to follow. Whether the relationship is with one or many, leadership requires engaging others. No matter how much formal power and authority our positions give us, we'll only leave a lasting legacy if others *want to* be in that relationship with us. Leadership requires a resonant connection with others over matters of the heart.

What is true for leadership is also true for exemplary teamwork, coaching, and teaching. It's all about the relationships. Successful human endeavors result from the effectiveness of the relationships among the people involved.

This is serious stuff. People can graduate at the top of the class from the best universities in the world, reason circles around their brightest peers, solve technical problems with wizard-like powers, have the relevant situational, functional, and industry experience, and *still* be more likely to fail than succeed—unless they can also work well with others.

Research over the last twenty-five years has helped us name and even measure those key behaviors that most contribute to developing human excellence. These best practices are what inspire us to risk and grow, whether as a team leader or as a new vice president. They help us imagine ourselves being better and performing more effectively than we currently do. They help us communicate the possibility and the rewards of improved performance to those whom we are charged with leading. They let us know in no uncertain terms what is valuable and should be pursued and what is to be avoided. This set of skills and learned abilities has come to be known as the field of emotional and social intelligence; research has proven it is our emotional energy that both communicates the vision and activates the common resonance necessary to achieve it.

Once they have learned and practiced these emotional skills, team members begin to inspire and challenge each other to higher levels of performance. Teachers can better discern the misunderstandings that limit their students' comprehension and transform them. Leaders are able to engage the discretionary efforts of the people they are leading and help them make their most passionate contributions. The mandate is very clear. You must build your personal abilities to recognize and manage your emotions and you must contribute to building others' abilities to work well together. How well you do this will have a direct impact on your personal and organizational success.

The book you hold in your hands, the *Handbook for Developing Emotional and Social Intelligence*, maps out effective ways for you to enable others to fully engage in their work, to develop a sense of belonging, and to contribute to creating a rewarding workplace. And it offers sound advice and counsel for a variety of settings: when coaching individuals and leaders; when working with systems, including teams, organizations, and cultures; when integrating different perspectives; and when working in the field of education.

Because different topics in this book will appeal more to you at different times than others, you need not read it straight through from cover to cover. Trust yourself to discover an order that will satisfy your desire to understand and communicate your own emotional energy even more effectively. With so many insightful contributions from leading experts in the field of emotional and social intelligence, you will find wisdom no matter where you begin your exploration. When you begin to put these powerful strategies to use in your work and life, you will be better able to make a lasting difference with clients, staff, colleagues, students, and family.

Acknowledgments

The editors wish to acknowledge and thank all of the following people:

The many coaches, coaching clients, teams, and organizations we have had the great honor to work with. You teach us daily.

Steven Stein, David Groth, Diana Durek, and all our brilliant colleagues at Multi-Health Systems who promote emotional intelligence daily. Reuven Bar-On, Peter Salovey, John Mayer, David Caruso, Daniel Goleman, Cary Cherniss, Richard Boyatzis, and Annie McKee for your pioneering emotional intelligence work.

Martin Delahoussaye, former senior acquisitions editor at Pfeiffer, for proposing this project and guiding and encouraging us with such good cheer; Lisa Shannon, our helpful executive editor; Holly J. Allen, senior acquisitions editor; Tolu Babalola, marketing manager; Susan Rachmeler, senior development editor, Dawn Kilgore, production editor; Marisa Kelley, assistant editor; and Rebecca Taff for all the professional effort and detail it takes to make a really good book! Michael Snell, our agent, for creating an excellent interface with our publisher and orchestrating a win-win process while continuing down the publishing path with us.

Robert Carkhuff, John Grinder, Richard Bandler, Leslie Lebeau, Judith DeLozier, Robert Dilts, Jean Houston, and Don Beck and all their teachers for the phenomenal contributions they have made to our understanding of human communication and how to improve it.

Marcia and James wish to thank our twenty-two-year-old daughter, Julie Linden Terrell (sometimes known as JT), who has endured a lot over the course of six books, but smiled, encouraged us, and demonstrated infinite patience with long hours and late dinners. Our brother, Don Hughes, for the many ways in which he has supported us; all of our parents, families, teachers, mentors, clients, and adversaries; and the grace and pluck that have gotten us each this far along the crazy paths we call our lives.

Dick wishes to thank his wife Grenae Thompson for her encouragement, brilliant insights, and exceptional editorial feedback and the outstanding High Performing Systems, Inc., project team—Debra Cannarella, Karen Schwind, Julie Gentry, Josh Billings, Farrell Bowdoin, Curt Cisrow, and Jennifer Brown—for insights and detailed reviews and feedback. He also wants to thank his numerous colleagues and clients who shared information and provided valuable feedback during the data collection, research, and writing process.

Introduction

The *Handbook for Developing Emotional and Social Intelligence* is a compendium of insights, strategies, and research that is designed to make the practitioner's work simpler and more effective. Whether you are a coach, a trainer, or an HR professional, some, if not all, of the contents of this book will capture your attention and engage you in exploring new ways to increase the emotional effectiveness of your own work. It is our hope that you will be able to see and understand what you do from a new perspective, a new vantage point. If you do, we are confident that you will even more effectively engage the great work of helping humans relate with each other with increased creativity and enthusiasm, and reduce the destructive competition and conflict.

Fortunately, we now have validated and reliable individual assessments, such as the EQ-i®, the MSCEIT®, and the ESCI, and team assessments such as the TESI® and the Team Diagnostic Assessment that give us the blueprint for measuring and developing the emotional and social intelligence (ESI) skills necessary to work through the full gamut of workplace challenges from team conflict, to developing high performers, to enhanced decision making within leadership environments. These skills are increasingly complex—*and they are not soft!* They're measurable, durable, and scalable, and it requires courage, strength, and persistence to apply them consistently and achieve truly sustainable success. ESI skills give us what it takes to manage the incredible stresses of not enough resources and not enough time; they are what help us balance our efforts appropriately between competition and compassion, and between the escalating demands of the workplace and the fundamental needs of our homes, families, and communities that commerce was invented to serve.

In high-tech economies in which measuring the quantifiable value of the bottom line has been so intensely promoted and enjoyed, the *qualitative* dynamics of emotional relationships have traditionally been easier to neglect. The result is that our faith in ourselves and our neighbors has been overtaken by our faith in the distant invisible systems of production and distribution that consistently deliver the flood of consumer goods upon which we now rely for our comfort, meaning, and life support. However, the costs of this reliance are similar to those of an organizational compensation system that rewards quarterly savings with big bonuses. It inevitably produces a deferred maintenance strategy that eventually leads to systemic failures and much greater costs and problems later on.

The most successful executive coaches help their clients develop the emotional and social effectiveness that enables the clients to expand their perspective and appreciate those they lead on the basis of the emotional connections that facilitate trust, synergy, and effective conflict resolution. Even in the most practical sense, research is now proving that this adds more value to the organization's bottom line than managing people as mere instruments of production.

Our intense focus on acquiring objective goals is due in part to the remarkable success of our technological gains since the Industrial Revolution, but these aptitudes can only achieve so much before the power of pursuing those values must swing back into the balance on a broader context. The mindset of acquisition generates a level of competition that eventually becomes so *dis*-integrative that, in order for life in the workplace to be tolerable, people must consciously learn to relate in ways that restore the value of human relationships to the business "equation."

In fact, the emphasis on the economic equation that seeks to set human value equal to objectively *quantified* measures *is* rebalancing with the social equation that values human participation according to subjectively *qualified* measures. The recent interest in emotional and social intelligence as a field of practice is the result of our desperate need to reintegrate our subjective communication skills that lag behind our skills in symbolic language and mathematical analysis.

Since Descartes we have been increasingly groomed to emphasize our quantitative analysis and expression of the objective world at the expense of our qualitative appreciation. This has left us increasingly cynical, knowing, as Oscar Wilde said, "the price of everything and the value of nothing." Now that this crucial aspect of human relations has also yielded to our relentless drive for metrics, we can *prove* that its omission has a huge cost to the bottom line in terms of conflict, mistakes, and delays. It is only the reintegration of these complementary functions that can generate a sufficiently comprehensive perspective and data set to accurately evaluate our real success and attend to the whole range of concerns that we must address if human life is to relate harmoniously once again within an intact global ecology. Without this integration, we will be unable to increase the effectiveness of our communication and the range of real productivity that has consistently delivered the progress we have traditionally called human civilization.

In order to assist you in finding the rich subjects and practical tips that will appeal to you most in this volume, a brief summary of each chapter follows.

PART ONE: COACHING: WORKING WITH LEADERS AND OTHER INDIVIDUALS

Chapter One, "Coaching with Emotional and Social Effectiveness," by Marcia Hughes and James Terrell, is addressed to the executive coach, life coach, mentor, and other professionals who seek to guide and grow the skills and life engagement of others. It is practical and provides experiential ideas for building emotional and social effectiveness (ESE) through work with clients, staff, and others. The chapter is built around the authors' core value of providing the client with tools to use to gain sustainable behavior change. Practical tips are provided to support the readers' clients in understanding and building emotional and social effectiveness. Clients seldom have challenges that neatly package into one specific emotional intelligence skills area. Rather, they have bigger challenges, such as how to believe in themselves and then make effective choices. Therefore, the authors construct their suggestions around five key areas of effectiveness—Valuing Self, Valuing Others, Responsive Awareness, Courage, and Authentic Success—all of which are supported by using skills in emotional and social intelligence.

Chapter Two, "Developing High Achievers Through Emotional Intelligence: More Intelligent Than Emotional," by Geetu Bharwaney, summarizes best practices in working with this unique group. High achievers in any organizational context have a very specific need and context for their work on emotional intelligence. Advice is provided on how to structure interventions that create impact. This will appeal to practitioners in a variety of contexts who are keen to work with star performers, the most critically important people in any professional work context. Case studies from three different projects are included to demonstrate emotional intelligence programs for high achievers in action.

Chapter Three, "Resonate Leadership for Results: An Emotional and Social Intelligence Program for Change in South Africa and Cambodia," by Annie McKee, Frances Johnston Eddy Mwelwa, and Suzanne Rotondo, details the results of the authors spending four years (2001–2004) conducting leadership development programs in South Africa and Cambodia in the fight to combat HIV and AIDS. They knew that they had to take a systems approach and that they had to focus on emotional intelligence, the heart of leadership development. They tell how they were able to use these skills to connect with a wide variety of leaders at different levels of emotional and cognitive development. They tell how they reached leaders on various levels in countries where the cultures are different from both the authors' and each others' cultures. In doing so, the authors include participants' stories and conclude with lessons they learned about working within non-western cultures. Although the narrative focuses on developing leadership in a global, non-profit setting, their findings will be useful to all practitioners as they explain the need for practitioners to demonstrate their own EI, to understand the culture in which they are working, and to use accessible language if they want to bring about large-scale, ongoing change.

Chapter Four, "When Enhanced EI Is Associated with Leadership Derailment," by Howard Book, finds that while emotionally intelligent leaders are better at motivating and developing employees than leaders with lower EI, leaders can be too high in some or all EI facets. Book concentrates on impulse control and optimism and points out that each requires a complementary facet that is equally or almost as high for the leader to have well-balanced skills. When a leader has adequate EI but is perceived as having low EI, then Book says that the problem lies elsewhere: organizational structure. Book finds that if the organization lacks formal structure—organizational charts, formal lines of communication, clear job descriptions, etc.—then employees often form a distorted view of the CEO's emotional intelligence. They either view the CEO as a savior, the only one in the organization who can provide any answers or solutions, or they view the CEO as a manipulative leader who wants to undermine his or her employees' work. Book advises coaches to examine both areas when working with EI.

Chapter Five, "Advanced EQ-i® Interpretation Techniques: The Concepts of Drag, Balance, and Leverage, by Rich Handley, provides concrete strategies for enhancing meaningful interpretation of the EQ-i® in a way that can easily be extrapolated to working with other EI measures as well. This chapter examines advanced EQ-i® interpretation techniques, specifically the concepts of *drag, balance*, and *leverage*. Handley guides the powerful use of the tool through tables and graphs that lead to practical applications by the practitioner.

Chapter Six, "Emotional Intelligence, Stress, and Catastrophic Leadership Failure™," by Henry L. Thompson, presents breakthrough research on the impact of stress on both cognitive ability and emotional and social intelligence (ESI). The data presented show two of the many ways that stress degrades the brain's ability to fully access cognitive and ESI potential. As the functions of the prefrontal cortex (the executive center of the brain) are degraded, effective decision making and appropriate emotional control and behavior are also degraded. Thompson suggests that there is a nonlinear relationship among stress, cognitive ability, and ESI such that, as stress increases, cognitive ability and ESI decrease gradually at first, but if the stress continues to rise, the person may experience a catastrophic drop in ability. Examples are cited of leaders experiencing what he labels Catastrophic Leadership Failure™.

PART TWO: TEAMS, ORGANIZATIONS, AND CULTURES: WORKING WITH SYSTEMS

Chapter Seven, "Building Your Team's Conflict-Resolution Skills with Emotional and Social Intelligence," by Marcia Hughes, provides research and practical tips for working with a critical organizational issue—effectively resolving team conflict. Measurement tools such as the Team Emotional and Social Intelligence Survey® (TESI®) and the Emotional Quotient Inventory (EQ-i®) are discussed, and the seven most influential skills in the EQ-i® for resolving conflict are highlighted. Teams taking the TESI® regularly report that conflict is their most difficult challenge. To address this, the author hypothesized that the capacity to use strong divergent thinking skills was central to conflict-resolution skills. Research on TESI® results is described showing that this team capability is influential. Analysis and tips are provided on guiding teams to work with typical challenges. Because emotions are contagious, teams need to be able to work with both the positive and negative emotions they experience. Tips on managing a team's difficult emotions are provided, including some of the biggest challenges leading to difficult emotions—conflict-adverse leaders and team members, passive-aggressive behavior, personality differences, difficult people or bullies, fear about scarcity of resources, and difficulty in exercising divergent thinking.

Chapter Eight, "From Individual to Organizational Emotional Intelligence," by Steven J. Stein, addresses organizational emotional intelligence, which the author defines as "an organization's ability to successfully and efficiently cope with change and accomplish its goals, while being responsible and sensitive to its people, customers, suppliers, networks, and society." A successful organization is one that is people-oriented, efficient, productive, and innovative. Through many examples of organizational and employee challenges, the author reviews the three foundations that underlie any truly great workplace today—the work itself, relationships at work, and work with purpose. The author created the Benchmark of Organizational Emotional Intelligence (BOEI) to provide an instrument that allows employees to express their feelings and thoughts about various aspects of the organization. The BOEI provides a snapshot of the organization's functioning from the perspective of employees—both line and management—and then discusses a summary of best practice options that the practitioner can use to work with the results once an organization has taken the BOEI.

Chapter Nine, "Zeroing in on Star Performance," by Diana Durek and Wendy Gordon, demonstrates that more than any other indices designed to predict performance, measures of emotional intelligence are showing real payoff power when it comes to workplace success. Over a decade of research has consistently demonstrated that those with higher emotional intelligence (EI), as measured by the Emotional Quotient Inventory (EQ-i®), are more likely to perform at high levels than their less emotionally intelligent co-workers. While IQ and technical skills are a requirement for many roles, once a person is in a given job, IQ no longer discriminates between those who succeed and those who do not. As you will see, factors such as empathy, assertiveness, optimism, and the ability to tolerate stress and control impulses are strong indicators of star performance. As top organizations replace less-effective selection and development activities with ones based on EI, they are beginning to document real bottom-line impact in the form of reduced turnover, increased customer satisfaction, higher productivity, better engagement, and improved leadership.

In Chapter Ten, "Emotional Intelligence: A View from South Africa," Jopie de Beer, Nicola Taylor, Renate Scherrer, and Christina van der Merwe write that the African philosophy of Ubuntu provides a unique understanding of the way indigenous people have survived with wisdom and dignity through thousands of years. This African worldview lays the foundation for the understanding and application of emotional and social intelligence (ESI) throughout Africa. This chapter describes the research in Africa with the EQ-i® and beginning research of the MSCEIT. The lives of Nelson Mandela, Desmond Tutu, and Steve Biko are tapped to demonstrate the living practice of ESI. The authors emphasize the importance of literacy training and note that this is a perfect ground for complementing the work with EI development "through song and dance, stories and poetry, role modeling of teachers, EI videos targeted at the youth, television programs, and community forums where Ubuntu principles are used as a vehicle to learn more about emotions and emotional management." The authors describe using EI to select the best candidates for reality shows, as the producers want to find candidates who have emotional resilience and fitting styles of coping with personal and interpersonal difficulties.

PART THREE: MULTIPLE PERSPECTIVES: COMBINING WISDOM

Chapter Eleven, "Personality Type and Emotional Intelligence: Pragmatic Tools for the Effective Practitioner," by Roger R. Pearman, examines the connection between the Myers-Briggs Type Indicator® (MBTI) and emotional intelligence, concentrating on the BarOn EQ-i®, and provides practitioners with practical suggestions to help clients enhance their overall leadership effectiveness as it relates to interpersonal skills. Pearman chose the MBTI and the BarOn EQ-i® because both instruments are self-assessments that "provide insight into behavior patterns and preferences . . . [and assume that] development is possible and desirable." Working with both models simultaneously gives practitioners several perspectives from which to work. Since the focus of this article is providing tools to help them coach clients, Pearman includes tables that list triggers for different preferences and types and that offer learning tactics for providing feedback and coaching.

Chapter Twelve, "Using the EQ-i® and MSCEIT® in Tandem," by Henry L. Thompson, provides a methodology for using the Mayer-Salovey-Caruso Emotional Intelligence Test (MSCEIT®), an ability-based ESI assessment, with the BarOn EQ-i®, a self-report ESI assessment, in tandem. The tandem approach provides a multiple-lens perspective on both ESI ability and actual applied behavior. The unique combination of these two instruments produces a robust view of ESI. Extensive comparisons of the two instruments and their relationship to each other and other popular assessments, such as personality (MBTI), interpersonal interaction styles (FIRO-B®), and cognitive ability (Wonderlic Personnel Test), are presented in a practitioner-friendly manner. Thompson also presents the perspective that everyone has "scores" on all instruments—and that the qualities that they measure are continuously interacting and influencing behavior. Often these influences don't become visible until the assessment has been completed and interpreted. An added feature of this chapter is the concept of ESI as situationally dependent. That is, ESI is not a single score, but rather a blending of ESI components that match a specific situation, such as a particular job. Examples of ESI success profiles and case studies are presented to explain the validity of this concept.

Chapter Thirteen, "Integrating Appreciative Inquiry and Emotional Intelligence for Optimal Coaching Results," by G. Lee Salmon and James Bradford Terrell, demonstrates how the intersection of emotional intelligence and appreciative inquiry is generating powerful new coaching techniques for clients who have traditionally been more difficult to serve. Appreciative inquiry is a "problem-solving" strategy that succeeds by overlooking the problem! A champion of the emotional skill called optimism, it begins its inquiry by directing attention to what is going right—What doesn't need fixing? What are the strengths of the individual, the team, or the organization seeking help? By identifying these, appreciative inquiry has located the sweet spot of motivation—what the people involved in a change process naturally enjoy being and doing and feeling the most. From here, it is not a long stretch to begin recovering the hopefulness and creativity that are often lost to the "predict and control" strategies of managing to the bottom line. New challenges call for new visions. Once these have been developed, emotional intelligence provides the playbook for guiding the behavioral changes that are necessary to achieve them.

Chapter Fourteen, "A Critical Perspective on the 'Social' Within Emotional Intelligence," by Carina Fiedeldey-Van Dijk, explores the results of separating social intelligence from emotional intelligence in the EQ-i®. She achieves this by using a composite data pool of over one thousand EQ-i® results. Combining two approaches, social intelligence can effectively be measured from the EQ-i® without the need for another assessment. She clears up two myths around social intelligence. Myth 1: Overall, people score lower in the interpersonal domain than in other domains making up total EQ. Her analysis shows that, on average, people score the same, indicating that they have what it takes to interact with others. Myth 2: Overall, people score higher in personal EQ than in social EQ. In fact, the opposite is found; people show more EQ when in the presence of others. This is further influenced by their gender, age category, job role/level, and emotional intelligence styles, leading to specific pointers for further developing people's social intelligence.

PART FOUR: EDUCATION: LEADERS AND STUDENTS

Chapter Fifteen, "A Sustainable, Skill-Based Approach to Building Emotionally Literate Schools," by Marc A. Brackett, Janet Patti, Robin Stern, Susan E. Rivers, Nicole A. Elbertson, Christian Crisholm, and Peter Salovey, argues for an increased understanding of social and emotional learning (SEL) in schools. The authors present their own program, called Emotionally Literate Schools, as an avenue for schools to increase their students' SEL and, therefore, their academic learning. The authors point out that students cannot learn social and emotional skills in a vacuum; as with academic skills, students learn what they see. For that reason, schools must integrate SEL throughout their curriculum and reinforce it in every class. To help them do this, the authors have developed a three-phase process schools can implement that involves training for all stakeholders: students, teachers, administrators, parents, and staff. Emotionally Literate Schools uses workshops, coaching, teaching techniques, parent workshops, and much more.

Chapter Sixteen, "Developing Emotional, Social, and Cognitive Intelligence Competencies in Managers and Leaders in Educational Settings," by Richard E. Boyatzis, looks at full- and part-time MBA students and shows that programs designed to help them see and use the benefits of their development at work, at home, and in their social lives enabled them to develop the *intention* to change. Intentional change is a process that begins with a person's ability to develop a personal vision of who he or she wants to be and ends with him or her participating in social and professional groups that allow him or her to achieve a new sense of identity, get feedback, and interpret the results. Although Boyatzis finds that few programs achieve the ultimate goal of helping leaders improve their competencies, his studies are, nevertheless, optimistic in that programs designed to focus on outcomes and to give participants the complex, inclusive view they need can have a profound and positive impact on leaders' social and emotional intelligence.

Chapter Seventeen, "Emotional Intelligence, Leadership, and the School Administrator," by James D.A. Parker, Howard Stone, and Laura M. Wood, highlights the growing body of research indicating that the type of social and emotional abilities linked with emotional intelligence are strongly related to one's ability to cope with life's demands and stressors. Trends in the recent literature on successful leadership suggest that EI appears to contribute to positive leadership behavior in several basic ways, and this is certainly true for school administrators. The authors review a study funded by the Ontario Ministry of Education and Training that was conducted to explore the relationship between emotional intelligence and school leadership. The study identified critical emotional and social skills required by school administrators (principals and vice-principals) necessary to successfully fulfill their roles and responsibilities. The results as well as future recommendations are reviewed.

We hope you will gain as much as we have from reading these articles and that your interest in emotional and social intelligence expands as you witness your clients gaining sustainable results through your use of EI strategies and concepts. We believe you will find that this is truly an idea and approach whose time has arrived.

Coaching: Working with Leaders and Other Individuals

CHAPTER 1

Coaching with Emotional and Social Effectiveness

Marcia Hughes and James Bradford Terrell

INTRODUCTION

Just as it takes a village to raise a child, it takes a village of types of intelligence to live a full and fulfilling life. There are many ways of being smart—IQ is one way. Another way of being smart, emotional and social intelligence, is at the forefront of much of today's leadership, team, and organization development around the world as this *Handbook* demonstrates. Others speak of cultural intelligence and spiritual intelligence. Howard Gardner (1999) is a leader in building awareness of multiple forms of intelligence. He has named at least eight different types of intelligence—logical, linguistic, spatial, musical, kinesthetic, naturalist, intrapersonal, and interpersonal—and then lists two others as possibilities: existential awareness and moral awareness.

This chapter is addressed to the executive coach, life coach, mentor, and other professionals who seek to guide and grow the skills and life engagement of others. It is practical and provides experiential ideas for building emotional and social effectiveness (ESE) through your work with your clients, staff, and others you influence. At Collaborative Growth, we have a core goal of providing the tools our clients need to gain sustainable behavior change. The goal of this chapter is to provide you with ideas and strategies that you can blend and include with your many other strategies, for assisting your clients to gain long-term benefits.

Working with your clients requires integrating many concepts and strategies as you fine-tune your approach. When focusing on what is usually termed emotional and social *intelligence*, we have found it is often best to reframe your discussion in terms they may find more inviting. Thus, we suggest you talk about understanding and building emotional and social *effectiveness*. Often the word "intelligence" causes people to feel cautious, if not defensive. Building effectiveness is common sense—it's why people are working with you as a coach.

Additionally, people seldom have challenges that neatly package into one specific emotional intelligence (EI) skill area. Rather, they have more global challenges, such as how to believe in themselves and then make effective choices. Therefore, for coaching purposes, we have identified five key areas of effectiveness: Valuing Self, Valuing Others, Responsive Awareness, Courage, and Authentic Success, which are supported by using skills in emotional and social intelligence. We refer to these as ESE strategies in our book, *A Coach's Guide to Emotional Intelligence* (Terrell & Hughes, 2008). All of these areas will be discussed in more detail later in this chapter.

SUSTAINABLE BEHAVIOR CHANGE THROUGH EFFECTIVE PRACTICES

Effective and lasting change can best be accomplished through a multi-tiered approach. Change is hard work—it's possible, yet it requires focused commitment and practice. In a true demonstration of collaborative leadership, Daniel Goleman and Cary Cherniss, with the assistance of Kim Cowan, Robert Emmerling, and Mitchel Adler, identified guidelines for best practices in developing emotional and social intelligence. The material is found on the website for the Consortium for Research on Emotional Intelligence in Organizations (www.eiconsortium.org/). (See also Cherniss & Adler, 2000.)

There are several chapters in this *Handbook* that can help you develop your ESE coaching practice. Lee Salmon and James Terrell discuss ways of integrating appreciative inquiry and emotional intelligence. The AI/ EI framework calls for a structured and positive approach focused on what works. It's a great tool to combine with the strategies suggested in this chapter. Similarly, Roger Pearman's chapter on combining the Myers-Briggs Type Indicator® tool and the EQ-i® demonstrates the importance of combining multiple forms of awareness in working with your clients. Understanding their personality preferences and combining that with your ESE approach is likely to greatly enhance your and your clients' effectiveness. Howard Book and Richard Handley both discuss the cost of having too high a score in particular emotional intelligence skills. Their chapters include tables connecting specific emotional intelligence skills with other skills that also need to be strong to complement strength in given competencies, as well as other strategies to consider if a skill is overused. For example, an overuse of impulse control can lead to rigid behavior. Someone with a great deal of assertiveness and much less impulse control may be perceived as more aggressive than assertive. Dick Thompson emphasizes the consequences of becoming over-stressed and the toll it takes on the ability to use ESE skills. The reader is guided to review these and the other chapters to further develop your coaching practice. Effective coaching requires integration of many forms of wisdom.

Coaching your client to change, grow, and act requires:

- Understanding (the cognitive part)
- Commitment (the inspirational part)
- Practice (the determined part)
- Feedback (the collaborative part)

The five ESE skills we are reviewing in this chapter (valuing self, valuing others, responsive awareness, courage, and authentic success) are built through tapping into all four parts of this change process.

ESE AND MEASURING EMOTIONAL INTELLIGENCE

While using an assessment to build your client's emotional and social effectiveness is not necessary, we recommend it. With the results from an assessment in hand, the coach and client can review the client's current capabilities as measured by the assessment and strategically engage in accurate coaching. An assessment also gives you data you may not be able to gain any other way, especially if a client is blind to some limitations or resists telling you about them. Different forms of assessments are available—some individually answered and others in a 360 multi-rater format.

Three EI assessment tools receive considerable attention in the literature and in practice: the EQ-i® (Emotional Quotient Inventory), the MSCEIT® (Mayer, Salovey, Caruso Emotional Intelligence Test), and the multi-rater assessment developed by Boyatzis and Goleman that includes both the ESCI (Emotional and Social Competency Inventory) and the ECI 2.0 (Emotional Competency Inventory). An article reprinted on the EI Consortium website by Reuven Bar-On (2006), creator of the Bar-On EQ-i®, describes the three major EI models:

> The *Encyclopedia of Applied Psychology* (Spielberger, 2004) recently suggested that there are currently three major conceptual models: (a) the Salovey-Mayer model (Mayer & Salovey, 1997) which defines this construct as the ability to perceive, understand, manage and use emotions to facilitate thinking, measured by an ability-based measure (Mayer et al., 2002); (b) the Goleman model (1998) which views this construct as a wide array of competencies and skills that drive managerial performance, measured by multi-rater assessment (Boyatzis et al., 2001); and (c) the Bar-On model (1997b, 2000), which describes a cross-section of interrelated emotional and social competencies, skills and facilitators that impact intelligent behavior, measured by self-report (1997a, 1997b) within a potentially expandable multi-modal approach including interview and multi-rater assessment (Bar-On & Handley, 2003a, 2003b). (www.eiconsortium.org/reprints/bar-on_model_of_emotional-social_intelligence.htm)

While each of the three EI assessments discussed above identify different scales, many of those scales overlap, and any of the three frameworks can be used well to support developing the five ESE skills we focus on in this chapter. To support your ability to develop the five ESE skills and use one of the three assessments, Table 1.1 lists each of the five skills, beginning with Valuing Self, and then lists the skills from the identified

Table 1.1. The Five Strategies and Related Skills from the Three EI Instruments

EQ-i®	MSCEIT®	ESCI
Valuing Self		
Self-Regard		
Emotional self-awareness	Perceiving	Emotional self-awareness
Empathy	Understanding	Accurate self-assessment
Flexibility		Self-confidence
Happiness		Emotional self-control
Optimism		Adaptability
		Optimism
Valuing Others		
Emotional self-awareness	Perceiving	Emotional self-awareness
Empathy	Understanding	Emotional self-control
Interpersonal Relations	Facilitating	Transparency
Flexibility	Managing	Adaptability
Optimism		Empathy
Social responsibility		Teamwork/collaboration
Reality testing		Optimism
Responsive Awareness		
Emotional self-awareness	Perceiving	Emotional self-awareness
Assertiveness		Accurate self-assessment
Empathy	Understanding	Emotional self-control
Flexibility		Adaptability
Impulse control		Empathy
Stress tolerance		Teamwork and collaboration
Reality testing		
Social responsibility		

(Continued)

Table 1.1. Continued

EQ-i®	MSCEIT®	ESCI
Courage		
Self-regard		
Emotional self-awareness	Perceiving	Emotional self-awareness
Self-actualization	Understanding	Emotional self-control
		Self-confidence
Stress tolerance	Facilitating	Adaptability
		Initiative
Assertiveness	Managing	Empathy
		Organizational awareness
Independence		Teamwork and collaboration
Reality testing		Change catalyst
Impulse control		Optimism
Optimism		
Authentic Success		
Self-regard	Perceiving	Emotional self-awareness
Emotional self-awareness	Understanding	Accurate self-assessment
Assertiveness	Facilitating	Self-confidence
Independence	Managing	Emotional self-control
Self-actualization		Transparency
Empathy		Adaptability
Social responsibility		Initiative
Interpersonal relationships		Optimism
Stress tolerance		Empathy
Impulse control		Organizational awareness
Reality testing		Service orientation
Flexibility		Developing others

EQ-i®	MSCEIT®	ESCI
Problem solving		Inspirational leadership
Optimism		Change catalyst
Happiness		Influence
		Conflict management
		Teamwork/collaboration

Source: James Bradford Terrell and Marcia Hughes, A Coach's Guide to Emotional Intelligence (Pfeiffer, 2008, pp. 11–13).

assessment—EQ-i®, MSCEIT®, and ESCI—that best support development of the identified skill. Additionally, when one EI scale is similar in other measures, they are aligned horizontally. Self-Regard from the EQ-i® scale supports the skill of Valuing Self. We didn't find similar scales in the other two measures. Emotional self-awareness is another EQ-i® scale that supports development of Valuing Self, which we find to have similarities with Perceiving under the MSCEIT® and to emotional self-awareness in the ESCI. By design, the ESE strategies are based on an integration of several emotional intelligence skills.

Use this table as a tool to help you select which EI capabilities you will focus on to help your clients develop, depending on which of the five ESE skills you select. For example, if your client is working to expand her skill in valuing herself, and she took one of these three assessments, you can evaluate her results and other aspects of her life circumstances to identify the capabilities you most want to work on together. If part of the goal is for her to become more aware of how she feels and why and to expand her ability to tell others, you will benefit from working on the EI scale of emotional self-awareness under the EQ-i® and the ESCI, and with understanding under the MSCEIT®. The scales in the three instruments are not exactly the same, but there are many similarities that support effective coaching. Depending on your clients' specific challenges, you may find that you are assisting them to develop some, but not all, of the skills listed for an ESE strategy. You may also incorporate other skills to meet the unique combination of your clients' assets and challenges. There is no cookie-cutter approach that works as well as your informed individual design.

STRATEGIES FOR BUILDING EMOTIONAL AND SOCIAL EFFECTIVENESS

This section provides you with one or two approaches for building each of the five ESE strategies. Consider the ideas with your clients' specific needs in mind and adjust as needed. In this discussion, the EQ-i® skills will be our primary point of reference; please feel free to adapt your application of the skills to any system you prefer in order to best utilize the assessments or processes that serve your practice. In the quest to assist your clients in gaining sustainable behavior change, we recommend that you consider a variety of approaches. Flexibility will help you adjust to each client's unique situation.

ESE Skill 1. Valuing Self

Your clients have a personal definition of who they are. It may be accurate or inaccurate, conscious or unconscious, but it's impossible for anyone with conscious awareness to avoid developing a personal sense of self. This sense of self is the nexus around which an individual builds relationships, selects goals, and makes individual choices about the quality and structure of one's life. The extent to which your client appropriately values him- or herself will determine the success of all of your work together.

A person's sense of self is built through childhood expectations and successes/failures and continues being influenced throughout adulthood. Building and maintaining a healthy sense of self grows out of applying skills in areas such as self regard and being emotionally aware while also valuing others. It's heavily influenced by the capacity to maintain a positive mood, embrace the moment and be happy with all that exists right now, as well to be optimistic about future opportunities.

Clients often enter coaching with a need for significantly adjusting the way and extent to which they value themselves. Many people are very hard on themselves, expecting behaviors and outcomes that are impossible. Others have an inflated sense of self-importance that guarantees others will be put off and strongly reflects weakness in their empathy and in the skill of effectively reading others and the environment.

The following strategies are sample approaches for guiding your clients to develop a strong sense of their own value while keeping in perspective the balance that is necessary by appropriately valuing others and the communities in which they are involved.

Healthy Self-Talk

Tibetan monks and other spiritual practitioners have developed the practice of quieting their minds during meditation. This is a powerful skill. Most people, however, experience their minds as a continuous chatter box, constantly evaluating thoughts, actions, and goals. Most people who walk by a mirror stop to tell themselves how they look and often it is not good enough—they are too fat, skinny, tall, or short.

You can guide your clients to enhance their skill in valuing themselves by improving their self-talk. Done well, this is not a simple or quick process, but it can be transformative. The process begins with investigating what they are telling themselves, and once this awareness is well established, beginning to alter the messages until the preferred messages occur that correspond with the preferred behavior as the habitual way of thinking.

There are three primary parts to this intervention:

1. *Fact Gathering.* Much of the value of this exercise is based in accurate and comprehensive fact gathering. That means paying attention to and accurately hearing those messages that are often so habitual they are virtually hidden. It also means finding out what triggers the message and how often it's likely to come up. Guide your client to become aware of *how* the message is communicated. Ask: "What is the tempo (or tonality or emotional texture) behind the words?"

    Say your client, Jeannette, is concerned that she's doing a poor job of presenting herself at work. She reports that she always berates herself whenever she leaves her boss's office because she didn't express herself well. Ask that every day for the next week she notice what she tells herself every time she leaves her boss's office. She should write quick notes about it as soon as possible and bring the notes to the next coaching session. Give her a note card to fill out such as:

    As I walked out the door I said to myself: _____
    My tonality was _____
    The energy I felt in the message was _____

I felt _____ emotionally.

Summary of event (why I was in my boss's office, the result, date)

Later thoughts: _____

Tell Jeannette not to take long notes unless she has time or wants to come back and add separate notes in the last section. The purpose behind the last rule is that if she thinks she has to be really comprehensive, there's a good shot she won't take the notes. It'll just be one more incomplete task.

When she comes in with a week's worth of data, you are likely to have some solid evidence to work with.

2. *Install the New Way.* Now work with her to:

- Identify the message she'd like to give herself. Coach her to develop a simple affirmative statement that supports her sense that she can appreciate herself now while also building her skills to do even better. The first step in doing a better job talking to her boss is believing she can.

- Help her practice how it sounds and feels when she changes her self message. Ask her what emotions come up when she says the new message. You're helping her build her emotional self-awareness as well as self-regard.

- Have her practice her new message, take notes again, and bring the notes in to the next session. Keep this up in detail for at least two or three weeks before going on to a new skill, such as expanding assertiveness. Have her expand her awareness of her self talk in other situations and continue the process of improving her messages to herself.

3. *Expand Resourcefulness, Then Add New EI Skills.* Begin building a resourceful state through improved self talk, and then one at a time add the strategies, such as assertiveness, impulse control, or problem solving, that she needs.

2% Solution

Life's 2% Solution (Hughes, 2006) provides a ten-step action plan your clients can follow to build their positive self regard. The 2% Solution calls for people investing 2 percent of their time, about thirty minutes a day, on something their hearts really call for them to do. The book is full of examples to guide them in finding their own calling if they don't already know. Some people write poetry, others expand their pottery practice, and some meditate. There's no end to a possible ways to spend the time. There are few key rules—the time must be spent on meeting their own heartfelt desires, not those of others, and it must be accompanied by conscious self-awareness. That means paying attention to what they are doing, why, and how it feels. Any awareness questions you want to build in that match your client can be helpful if you don't overdo it.

ESE Skill 2. Valuing Others

No one is an island; relationships with others govern our success and our perceived quality of life. Yet as important as this skill of valuing others is, it is a daily challenge for most. The expanding forms of communication—including voice mail, email, BlackBerries, iPod, podcasts, and personal Internet sites—present an undoubted challenge to effective relationships. Many people receive hundreds of emails a day, young folks send thousands of text messages a week, yet are we communicating better? Of course the answer is "It depends." But we must acknowledge that the quantity challenges quality. This is only one of the forms of cultural stressors that can impair relationships. It's possible that the consequences of expanding stress may take more of a toll on the ESE strategy of valuing others than on any other ESE strategy. When we're moving fast it can be difficult to effectively communicate value. One of our extended family members taught us a symbolic phrase—"Love ya. Mean it. Bye!" It's been fun when we heard it from Alan, but it also demonstrates that there's a lot of loose talk that may not be received as genuine communication.

Coaching your clients to build their skills in effectively valuing others requires that they have competence in many EI skills beginning with a healthy combination of emotional self-awareness (understanding themselves) and empathy (understanding and reading others). They need to invest in interpersonal relationships, be flexible and realistically optimistic. When you are coaching your clients to build their skills in valuing others, begin with assessing which part of this skill base represents their challenge.

Acknowledge Others

Practice acknowledging others. A few minutes a day of genuine recognition for the contributions of others can make a big difference in their day. To build the habit, ask your clients to commit to a given number of acknowledgements a day (probably three or four) and then to take five minutes toward the end of the day to write notes on whom they noticed, how it felt to your clients, and how those receiving the recognition responded. The positive results combined with increased awareness are likely to be highly reinforcing.

Enhance Awareness of Diversity in Personalities

Gaining information from a personality measure, such as MBTI®, Emergenetics®, or DISC® will promote awareness of differences and the ability to respond effectively. We find that when one of these instruments is presented to an individual, or even better to his or her team, the individual begins learning the possibilities of working with rather than against someone else's differences. Many people just aren't aware of the differences. One of the more obvious ones comes with the difference between introverts and extroverts. Coach your clients to understand their own preferences, preferably by taking one of these or a similar assessment, and then to apply their awareness by responding with empathy and understanding when someone responds differently than they do. For example, if your client, Carlos, is a considerable introvert, and thus very quiet, help him become aware of the impact his quietness has on colleagues, family, and his career. Then you can coach him to develop increased skills in speaking up when it is important. He also can learn to directly tell people that, while he may not speak often, he is listening very carefully and will speak up when he has something to contribute. As those around him gain this understanding, they will appreciate Carlos more. The next step for Carlos will be to expand his awareness of the importance of his own responses to those of others. Eventually, he may even want to practice increasing his understanding of people who have a lot of extroverted energy and seem to talk just to find out what they are thinking.

Roger Pearman's chapter (Chapter Eleven) offers excellent tips on bringing MBTI into your ESE development strategies.

ESE Skill 3. Responsive Awareness

Your clients will be more than doubly powerful when they are (1) aware of what is happening and (2) respond to the information they gain from their awareness. This ESE strategy is demonstrated supported by choosing responses from a broad-based and well-developed foundation of multi-dimensional awareness supported by paying attention to a whole spectrum of data—somatic (body), emotional, cultural, and systemic. To respond effectively, people can begin by drawing on the first two ESE strategies of valuing self and valuing others. In this way they will seek to understand the reasons for the emotions and other behaviors that may arise and then respond to them adroitly and compassionately.

Observing and Practicing Empathy

This exercise requires at least two people and is best if it's run with three people or groups of three people. One person, we'll refer to him or her as Person C, is an observer while Person A tells Person B about something in his or her life. Person A should speak for about three minutes and talk about something of moderate importance in his or her life. Person B listens and responds some, with the focus being kept on Person A. Person C watches Person A carefully, paying attention to the verbal as well as the non-verbal communication. After the three minutes, Persons A and C change chairs and Person C proceeds to retell the story as if he or she were Person A, seeking to match the qualities of the verbal and non-verbal communication that Person A just demonstrated as closely as possible. Now Person A observes, and Person B engages similarly to the first telling of the story. After three minutes, have them stop and discuss what happened, what they learned, and how they might want to apply what they understood to their future ability to understand to one another.

The three will rotate positions twice so each one plays each role.

As a coach, talk with the clients to help them debrief what they learned, and discuss how they can use this information and what interactions this can help them improve.

ESE Skill 4. Courage

In *A Coach's Guide to Emotional Intelligence,* we wrote that "Courage is the emotion that allows us to act on what matters to us, in the presence of danger, difficulty, uncertainty, or pain, accepting that there will be consequences without necessarily knowing what those will be but acting anyway, without being stopped by fear or being sidetracked from our chosen course of action" (Terrell & Hughes, 2008, p. 85). To exercise the ESE strategy of courage, we need many an EI skill, including feeling sufficiently good about ourselves that the required act of courage is worth the energy it takes. To exercise courage, we must have motivation, a sense of possibility, and a sense that we know how to go about the task at hand. It requires a healthy combination of optimism ("Yes, I can") with reality testing ("What are the pro's and con's?"). Responding with courage may require overcoming fear, inertia, or ignorance. It's a broad area, requiring good assessment on your part to assist your coaching client in understanding which EI skills and what data are needed for acting wisely.

One of the core presuppositions of neuro-linguistic programming (NLP) is that anything can be handled in small enough chunks. Breaking things into small, manageable pieces is one of the most critical strategies for effective courageous action. NLP was originated by Richard Bandler and John Grinder (1975a & b) for the purpose of making explicit models of human excellence, and particularly draws on the fields of neurology, linguistics, and computer science. Another central NLP presupposition is that "the map is not the territory." This provides a realistic guide to "reality," beginning with the recognition that as human beings, we can never know reality. Rather, we can only know our perceptions of reality. It is our maps of reality based on our neurology and our language systems that determine how we behave and that give those behaviors meaning, not reality itself. Thus, how effectively we behave in life is limited or enhanced by our maps of reality rather than by reality itself. Both of these presuppositions offer many opportunities to support effective coaching in building the ESE strategy of courage.

Chunk into Manageable Pieces

You probably know the telling question, "How do you eat an elephant?" The answer is: "One bite at a time." Suppose your client, let's call him Jeffrey, is overwhelmed, worried, and paralyzed in his current dysfunctional role at work, but he can't afford to quit. You can help him make progress by taking the issues and breaking them into smaller chunks. Find one small piece of the whole puzzle and develop a way to respond to that piece. Work with Jeffrey to guide his first response and to evaluate and celebrate the results. Then move to the next small step. This cumulative process whittles away at the big concern until Jeffrey eventually gets to resolution or peace with the process. Maybe it isn't realistic for Jeffrey to leave his position or organization, but he can reframe his attitude and add in one thing he does each day that feels positive and rewarding to him personally. There are a myriad of possible answers. A core benefit he should take from the experience is to learn the process so he can lead himself in breaking big concerns into manageable pieces.

Reality Check

Building on the concept that the map is not the territory, work with your clients to enhance their skills in implementing effective reality checks in their decision-making processes. When someone conducts a reality check, he or she pays close attention to what is happening in order to read subtle cues in the political, social, and emotional environments. It requires taking time to consider how you understand the process and then checking with other people on how well their understanding matches so you can make good decisions individually and collectively. This will support sustainable and collaborative decisions as it's a healthy way of building in respect for different points of view. This is the core of being capable and comfortable with divergent thinking, which is central to a team's skill in conflict resolution. (See our Chapter Five for more information.)

ESE Skill 5. Authentic Success

Does your client need a new boat to be successful? Will the boat make your client happier? The answer is very personal. Success is an individual decision. While many people spend considerable energy in a state of mild to moderate angst because they don't feel sufficiently successful, many haven't really thought through what success actually means to them. A knowledgeable personal definition of success calls for awareness of personal capacity, life circumstances, and their values and then bringing these elements together with realistic optimism. From the list of skills in the EQ-i®, self actualization is the closest to authentic success. However, it actually takes the ability to tap into each of the fifteen EQ-i® skills at different times to continually live a fulfilling life. A panoramic perspective of opportunities and conditions and a welcoming attitude toward an interesting mix of development opportunities is required to actually live with the satisfying feeling that one is enjoying authentic success.

The word "authentic" indicates that the success is genuine, not a fake or based on keeping up with others for the sake of appearances. Success means the achievement of something planned or that something turned out well. Authenticity is a significant qualifier to success because this is the link to reflective awareness; it requires taking the time to check out how well the result matches the expectation.

Connecting Values with Expectations

Work/life balance is getting a lot of attention these days. There's a deep longing for simplicity and for personal time as well as genuine interest in developing successful careers. It's very hard for many people to bring the two together. If you're coaching clients struggling with this balancing act, guide them in recognizing that they need to take responsibility for their choices. If they are about to apply for a promotion, it's a good time to list their values, notice how their time is divided across the different parts of their lives right now, and then decide whether they want the added responsibility. The answer may be yes. Hopefully, by going through this reflective process they can take responsibility for their decision to take on more and not feel like a victim or a failure when they have to make adjustments in their personal lives or when other changes occur. They may decide that work/life balance isn't a linear event, but rather a tapestry. At times one part of a person's life will gain more attention, at other times that can shift. However, working excessively can become a difficult habit to break. Thus, make sure your clients gain skills in reflective awareness, that is, taking time to honestly and fully assess how they feel and why, to notice the choices they are making, take responsibility for those choices and then consciously decide whether to keep things the same or make changes.

CONCLUSION

This chapter presents a review of the five strategies in emotional and social effectiveness that we have found most compelling for dynamic coaching. Each strategy calls upon a myriad of EI skills. Identifying the coaching practices needed to address every client's specific situation requires individual attention. We have presented one or two exercises to help your clients build skills in each of the five areas. Every situation is unique, so change and adjust the ideas we have presented as need be. However, we do encourage you to include these types of experiential learning as a fundamental part of your coaching practice.

REFERENCES

Bandler, R., & Grinder, J. (1975a). *The structure of magic I: A book about language and therapy*. Palo Alto, CA: Science & Behavior Books.

Bandler, R., & Grinder, J. (1975b). *The structure of magic II: A book about communication and change*. Palo Alto, CA: Science & Behavior Books.

Bar-On, R. (1997a). *The Emotional Quotient Inventory (EQ-i): A test of emotional intelligence*. Toronto, Canada: Multi-Health Systems, Inc.

Bar-On, R. (1997b). *The Emotional Quotient Inventory (EQ-i): Technical manual*. Toronto, Canada: Multi-Health Systems, Inc.

Bar-On, R. (2000). Emotional and social intelligence: Insights from the Emotional Quotient Inventory (EQ-i). In R. Bar-On and J. D. A. Parker (Eds.), *Handbook of emotional intelligence*. San Francisco: Jossey-Bass.

Bar-On, R. (2006). The Bar-On model of emotional-social intelligence (ESI). *Psicothema*, *18*, supl., 13–25.

Bar-On, R., & Handley, R. (2003a). *The Bar -On EQ-360*. Toronto, Canada: Multi-Health Systems.

Bar-On, R., & Handley, R. (2003b). *The Bar -On EQ-360: Technical manual*. Toronto, Canada: Multi-Health Systems.

Boyatzis, R. E., Goleman, D., & HayGroup (2001). *The Emotional Competence Inventory (ECI)*. Boston: HayGroup.

Cherniss, C., & Adler, M. (2000). *Promoting emotional intelligence in organizations*. Alexandria, VA: American Society of Training & Development.

Gardner, H. (1999). *Intelligences reframed: Multiple intelligences for the 21st century*. New York: Basic Books.

Goleman, D. (1998). *Working with emotional intelligence*. New York: Bantam Books.

Hughes, M. (2006). *Life's 2% solution*. Boston, MA: Nicholas Brealey.

Hughes, M., & Terrell, J.B. (2008). *Coaching for emotional intelligence*. San Francisco: Pfeiffer.

Mayer, J. D., Salovey, P., & Caruso, D. R. (2002). *Mayer-Salovey-Caruso Emotional Intelligence Test (MSCEIT)*. Toronto, Canada: Multi-Health Systems, Inc.

Speilberger, C. (Ed.). (2004). *Encyclopedia of applied psychology*. New York: Academic Press.

Marcia Hughes is president of Collaborative Growth® and serves as a strategic communications partner for teams and their leaders in organizations that value high performers. She weaves her expertise in emotional intelligence throughout her consulting, keynotes, facilitation, and team building. She is co-author of *A Coach's Guide for Emotional Intelligence* (2008), *The Emotionally Intelligent Team* (2007), *The TESI® Short Facilitator's Guide Set* (2009), *Emotional Intelligence in Action* (2005), and author of *Life's 2% Solution*. Hughes is co-creator of the Team Emotional and Social Intelligence Survey® (TESI®), which supports team growth world-wide. She is a certified trainer in the Bar-On EQ-i® and EQ-360®. She provides train-the-trainer training and coaching in powerful EQ delivery.

James Bradford Terrell is vice president of Collaborative Growth® where he applies his expertise in interpersonal communication to help a variety of public and private sector clients anticipate change and respond to it resiliently. Co-author of *A Coach's Guide for Emotional Intelligence* (2008), *The Emotionally Intelligent Team* (2007), *The TESI® Short Facilitator's Guide Set* (2009), and *Emotional Intelligence in Action (2005),* he coaches leaders, teams in transition, and senior management, using the Bar-On EQ-i®, the EQ-360®, and other assessments. Mr. Terrell is co-creator of the Team Emotional and Social Intelligence Survey® (TESI®), which supports team growth world-wide. He provides train-the-trainer workshops and educates coaches on how to develop the insightful interpretation and application of EQ results.

CHAPTER 2

Developing High Achievers Through Emotional Intelligence
More Intelligent Than Emotional

Geetu Bharwaney

High achievers in any organizational context have a very specific need and context for their work on emotional intelligence. This chapter summarizes best practices in working with this unique group. Advice is provided on how to structure interventions that create impact. This will appeal to practitioners in a variety of contexts who are keen to work with star performers, the most critically important people in any professional work context. Case studies from three different projects are included to demonstrate emotional intelligence programs for high achievers in action.

INTRODUCTION

This chapter is written for advanced practitioners in the field of emotional intelligence who already have the foundations for their success in place:

1. You know what you are doing and have specific expertise in leadership development based on emotional intelligence.
2. You are experienced with at least one major diagnostic tool. (All of the work with high achievers referred to in this chapter has involved the use of diagnostic tools for emotional intelligence including the Bar-On EQi®, the EQ360® and MSCEIT® (distributed by Multi-Health Systems, Inc., Toronto). The case studies cited all used a specific self-report tool for emotional intelligence, the Bar-On EQ-i®.)
3. There is a real business need that is being addressed through an emotional intelligence intervention and there is senior sponsorship for it (without this the intervention will not have impact).
4. You have already accessed knowledge and resources on the design aspects of emotional intelligence interventions.

Definitions

Throughout this chapter, emotional intelligence is defined as "the essential mix of emotional, personal, and social competencies that influences our ability to be personally effective and professionally productive" (Bharwaney, 2007b, p.184). These skills are needed more in today's society, and they distinguish high achievers in a variety of contexts.

People regarded as high achievers represent an important group in any context or organization. In some work contexts, the most senior person is considered the only high achiever, and in others it's appropriate to include in this select group the in-house technical experts who provide essential technical know-how to help the organization get results. I use three subgroups to describe the full set of people who might be considered as high achievers. They are the "Official Leaders" (for example, CEOs, senior executives, and experts), the "Potential Leaders" (those who have been earmarked within the succession plan as senior leaders who have some blockages to address before they are ready to step into a more senior role), and finally the "Unofficial Leaders" who would like to see themselves as Potential Leaders but are not yet considered to be. People in the last category of high achiever are often influential in the informal networks of the organization, and their participation in programs is necessary as part of a strategy to "keep the peace."

The term "high achiever" is used in this chapter to refer to people who are most relied upon to deliver results in an organizational context. They have usually reached or excelled beyond a level of "excellence" in their chosen professional arenas. Note that they may or may not be self-aware nor perfect role models for others; nonetheless they are regarded as high achievers in their particular context.

Context

The insights and conclusions relayed in this chapter are based on the author's work with high achievers in a variety of contexts. Some of the interventions with high achievers achieved dramatic results and others had only moderate success. The differences between the high- and lower-impact emotional intelligence interventions and the reasons why interventions have had different levels of success will be explored later.

Elsewhere writers have reported the links between emotional intelligence and leadership performance (Bharwaney, 2005; Langhorn, 2004; Ruderman & Bar-On, 2003; Slaski & Cartwright, 2002), so this chapter will not address the fundamental question, "Is emotional intelligence important for leadership success?" Instead, this chapter is designed to communicate best practices and tried-and-tested methodologies to effect change among high achievers as a unique "customer" for emotional intelligence interventions. It builds on three conference presentations made by Bharwaney (Bharwaney, 2007a, 2008; Bharwaney & MacKinlay, 2007a) and a chapter (Bharwaney, 2007b), which were all attempts to disseminate more widely the insights gained from working with high achievers around the globe.

Comparing High Achievers with Other Achievers

Where an emotional intelligence intervention is focused on high achievers alone, the territory of change is different fundamentally from that of other achievers. The well-prepared practitioner will be able to adapt his or her approach or offering to ensure the intervention has broad impact. Table 2.1 summarizes some of

Table 2.1. Comparison of the Characteristics of High Achievers with Other Achievers

	High Achievers	Other Achievers
People Skills	Generally of secondary importance to technical or intellectual ability	Generally higher importance attached to the role of people skills as a component of personal and professional success
Smarts (IQ)	Generally more focused on cognitive intelligence since early life rather than emotional and social intelligence	Generally more focused on the emotional/social aspects of intelligence rather than cognitive intelligence
Communication Abilities	Relatively weak communication ability, particularly listening skills	Generally strong communication ability
Ambition	Generally higher with the added pressure of high expectations from key stakeholders to achieve outstanding success without any formal development	Generally moderate ambition
Emotional Intelligence	Generally strong in the more practical and less emotional aspects of emotional intelligence, e.g., problem solving, reality testing, independence	More likely to be relatively stronger in the more social aspects of emotional intelligence— empathy, social responsibility, and interpersonal relationship— compared to high achievers

Source: Ei World Internal Briefing Note on Coaching High Achievers, 2006.

the key differences between high achievers and other achievers (defined here as "the people who have not yet broken through into the realms of 'excellence' in their particular context").

High achievers are often faced with stretched and sometimes impossible goals, unrealistic business plans, and lack of resources. Often extremely high standards are set by the individuals themselves (rather than being externally created). The author has found that there is a need to understand "the inner leader" as well as the leader who is projected on the outside in business interactions and personal relationships. Many existing leadership development processes overlook the importance of understanding the inner person as part of the desired change.

A number of research studies support the view that there is a palpable difference between high achievers and other achievers. Studies conducted by Feather (1989, 1991) report that attitudes among other achievers toward the failure of high achievers (whom he refers to as "tall poppies") were more negative than attitudes of other achievers toward the failure of an average achiever. He also found a relationship between low self-esteem on the part of the perceiver in relation to the extent of the negativity perceived. Sufficient evidence exists to suggest that there are differences between high achievers and other achievers, even though these differences have not been studied in the context of emotional intelligence interventions until now.

Yet these differences have a subtle influence on coaching outcomes, including what the high-achieving client will regard as a successful outcome of executive coaching and what style of coaching would be a mirror for his or her own aspirations. Some leadership interventions include follow-up coaching, which may be implemented as part of the fabric of a whole intervention or as an optional extra. In the author's experience, such coaching linked to leadership development programs is implemented most frequently as an optional extra, rather than as a key ingredient for success. This theme will be explored later.

The context of working with high achievers influences the context of emotional intelligence work in business settings, and there is increasing demand for practitioners (whether internal or external) who can work with high achievers in a highly focused way, with clear results and a well-thought-through plan.

Designing Interventions

Interventions with high achievers are usually based in coaching and may also be combined with group work (but rarely are constituted of group work alone). Interventions are often oriented toward helping someone or a team become more "personally effective or organizationally productive" (Bharwaney, 2007b, p. 184).

Jones (2006) highlights a number of coaching techniques particularly appropriate for high achievers. He also argues that the coach should have a good understanding of the world of high achievement and empathy for the total commitment required of a high achiever. What I explore here are the conditions for success when a whole group of high achievers is included in an emotional intelligence intervention, a subject that has not been explored in the wider literature on leadership development and emotional intelligence until now.

Design flaws usually become apparent later and not at the set-up phase of a project that is too often rushed and conducted at a business critical time without the luxury of reflection. My intention in writing this chapter is to shorten the learning curve for designers of emotional intelligence interventions so that practitioners who are knowledgeable and informed about the details have the opportunity to design interventions that both appeal to high achievers and also have significant impact for them. Both *appeal* and *impact* are important in the context of working with high achievers; you only have one opportunity to make a lasting impression.

STRUCTURING INTERVENTIONS FOR IMPACT

Three case studies are presented in the rest of the chapter—a successful intervention, a moderately successful one, and one that struggled to achieve impact. All three are described as indicative of the full range of possible outcomes from an emotional intelligence intervention with high achievers. Studying the case studies can shorten the learning curve for anyone designing an intervention for this particular group of people in an organizational setting. The contrasts among the three case studies illustrates the need for a robust design for such interventions.

Each case study relates to groups of leaders involved in a leadership development program based on emotional intelligence in the recent past. All are real client situations with tangible desired outcomes and business results. In the case of the second, and particularly the third, case study, certain design flaws at the start and in the middle of the interventions reduced the level of impact that was achieved.

Table 2.2 summarizes the key features of each intervention and will serve as a reference point for the rest of this chapter. All interventions were implemented with the purpose of effecting behavioral change, the assumed aim of emotional intelligence work with high achievers. The reader is referred to Skiffington and Zeus (2003) for a structured method for effecting organizational behavioral change, which they define as "the science and art of facilitating the performance, learning and development of the individual or team, which in turn assists the growth of the organization" (p. 6). Guidelines for designing and delivering interventions based on emotional intelligence can also be found on the website of the EI Consortium (www.eiconsortium.org), particularly in the technical paper on bringing emotional intelligence into the workplace by Cherniss, Goleman, Emmerling, Cowan, and Adler (1988).

Overview of Intervention, Particularly Participation

The choice of participating group is key here and whether or not a whole intact work group learns together or whether participants are drawn from multiple parts of a business or organization. Experience suggests that a mix of participants creates a healthy variety and is productive for emotional intelligence learning, although it is usual that some teams, particularly management or executive teams, may prefer to learn together as a whole intact work team. When working with high achievers who belong to an intact work team, who meet together on other occasions (for example, management meetings outside of emotional intelligence work as in the case of Group B), it is important for the meetings oriented toward learning new skills and tools to have a different look and feel compared to other meetings that participants engage in together. In the case of Group B, this was accomplished by changing the room layout, even when meetings took place in a similar location, and in bringing structures that were somewhat different to the usual meeting protocols.

The distinctions among high achievers offered earlier in this chapter—*official leaders, potential leaders or unofficial leaders*—is proposed as a simple framework for clearly defining the composition of the group. For instance, Group A was a group of mainly Potential Leaders, Group B contained Official Leaders, and Group C was a combination of Official Leaders and

Table 2.2. Summary of the Components of Three Different Emotional Intelligence Programs for High Achievers

	Case Study 1: Group A: High Impact	Case Study 2: Group B: Moderate Impact	Case Study 3: Group C: Low Impact
Overview of Intervention, particularly participation	Leadership development program for thirty-five high potential Individuals nominated within the company's succession plan who achieved top performance ratings in annual reviews. These participants took part in cohorts of twelve or thirteen participants and were considered to be potential leaders.	Leadership development program for senior executive team of six who were official leaders.	Leadership development program for ten senior managers who volunteered to take part in a high-profile pilot program, a combination of official and unofficial leaders.
Definition of high achiever	A person who had achieved followership and had progressed rapidly within the company with potential and an appetite for more progression in the future. Participants were drawn from a variety of business areas.	The most senior management group in the organization. This group of ten managers was part of a larger group of the most senior managers in the organization.	
The business imperative	Bottom-line growth of company not matched by investment in leadership development. Greater number of local managers desired on executive group (up until then the board consisted largely of expatriate managers). Better leadership in the company to support business growth aspirations.	Better team working. To address personal blind spots. Participants were all part of the same team in an organization that was just beyond its startup phase (four years).	Individual leadership development. Managers were from different functions across a large public sector organization.

Format of Program	Combination of one-to-one coaching (six hours in total) plus group work (four workshop days in total).	Combination of one-to-one coaching (six hours in total) plus group work (five half-days in total).	Primarily group work, with one-to-one sessions only at beginning and end. Six meetings in total, roughly half a day each.
Length of Program	Six months	Eight months	Twelve months
Learning Components	Launch of program with senior sponsor. Assessments of emotional intelligence, individually and collectively. Initial feedback on assessments. Creation of individual development plans, shared within the group. Initial one day workshop. Eight-week gap with learning materials for use with own team. Two day leadership workshop. Eight-week gap with further learning materials for use with own team. Final workshop. Repeat assessments and debrief at end of whole program. Communication of results back to key stakeholders and senior sponsors.	Consultative approach to creation of program. Assessments of emotional intelligence, individually and collectively. Initial feedback on assessments. Creation of individual development plans, where key themes (but not details) shared within the group. Five half-day workshops on collective themes. Repeat assessments and debrief at end of whole program. Communication of results back to key stakeholders.	No senior sponsor. Assessments of emotional intelligence, both individually and collectively. Initial feedback on assessments. No creation of individual development plans. Five half-day workshops on collective themes. Repeat assessments and debrief at end of whole program. Communication of results back to group.
Support Mechanisms	Strong internal advocate. Senior sponsors paired with each participant.	Limited support mechanisms, although external mentoring was suggested early in the program.	Limited buddying, but this was variable in its application.

(Continued)

Table 2.2. Continued

	Case Study 1: Group A: High Impact	Case Study 2: Group B: Moderate Impact	Case Study 3: Group C: Low Impact
Results achieved by the end of the intervention	Hard-hitting impact on P&L. Business results surpassed expectations. See Group Profile A (Figure 2.1) for increase on emotional intelligence—twenty of twenty-one scores increased in the group profile (all EQ components increased except impulse control where the change was not statistically significant). Fifty percent of participants took on roles of greater responsibility. Four participants joined the senior leadership team. Increased sense of collaboration across the business reflected in joint approaches to new business projects. Visible reduction in silo mentality. Personal development for high potential leaders with visible improvements in personal effectiveness in every participant.	Better team working. Personal blind spots addressed (one person left the team). Dramatic increase in emotional intelligence within the team. Better relationships within the team. Greater delegation to next line of managers below senior executives. See Group Profile B (Figure 2.2).	Some individual development of emotional intelligence. Two people accepted onto well-respected leadership development program for high achievers. See Group Profile C (Figure 2.3).

Design Flaws	None. The program continued to have impact even through a change in key senior sponsor. Initial time to secure senior sponsor commitment was lengthy (approximately twelve months). Executive team generated a number of competing commitments that almost affected participation on workshops.	Group chose to center their development on group work, rather than a mix of individual coaching and group work. Quantity of coaching and group development work inadequate for concrete changes to take root. External mentors were sought, but this feature was not properly embedded in the program.	Absence of individual coaching had a detrimental effect. There was no transparency of goals within the group, so peer support was restricted to what participants had disclosed about their development areas.

Sources: Reported in Bharwaney, Bar-On, and MacKinlay (2007).

Unpublished client report, Ei World, 2007a.

Unpublished client report, Ei World, 2007b.

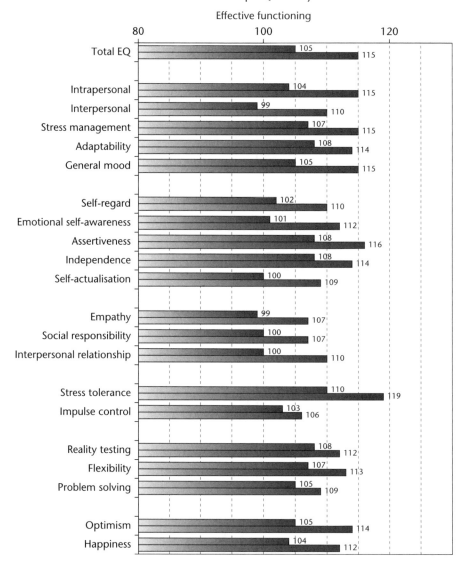

Before-After Group EQ-i unadjusted scores

Figure 2.1. Group Profile A

(n_{Before} = 35; n_{After} = 31)

Note: Within each set of two bars, top bar is "before" and lower bar is "after."

Source: Ei World internal document, 2007, using data from the BarOn EQ-i®. EQ-i scales. Copyright © 2002 Multi-Health Systems Inc. All rights reserved. 3770 Victoria Park Ave., Toronto, M2H 3M6.

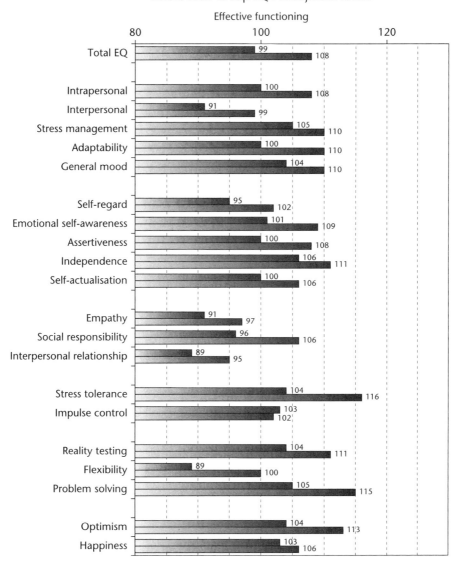

Before-After Group EQ-i unadjusted scores

Figure 2.2. Group Profile B

(n_{Before} = 6; n_{After} = 5)

Note: Within each set of two bars, top bar is "before" and lower bar is "after."

Source: Ei World internal document, 2007 using data from the BarOn EQ-i®. EQ-i scales. Copyright © 2002 Multi-Health Systems Inc. All rights reserved. 3770 Victoria Park Ave., Toronto, M2H 3M6.

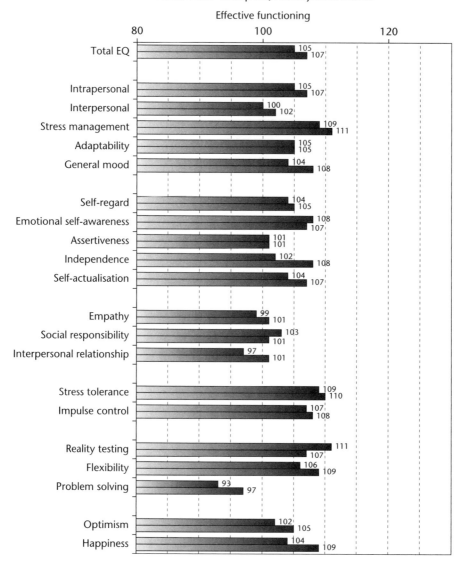

Before-After Group EQ-i unadjusted scores

Effective functioning

Scale	Before	After
Total EQ	105	107
Intrapersonal	105	107
Interpersonal	100	102
Stress management	109	111
Adaptability	105	105
General mood	104	108
Self-regard	104	105
Emotional self-awareness	108	107
Assertiveness	101	101
Independence	102	108
Self-actualisation	104	107
Empathy	99	101
Social responsibility	103	101
Interpersonal relationship	97	101
Stress tolerance	109	110
Impulse control	107	108
Reality testing	111	107
Flexibility	106	109
Problem solving	93	97
Optimism	102	105
Happiness	104	109

Figure 2.3. Group Profile C

($n_{Before} = 10$; $n_{After} = 9$)

Note: Within each set of two bars, top bar is "before" and lower bar is "after."

Source: Ei World internal document, 2007 using data from the BarOn EQ-i®. EQ-i scales. Copyright © 2002 Multi-Health Systems Inc. All rights reserved. 3770 Victoria Park Ave., Toronto, M2H 3M6.

Unofficial Leaders. It is perhaps useful to ask the question, "Is it appropriate for all these high achievers to learn together, or is it most effective for them to learn together with people from other functions?" Ultimately the goal of an emotional intelligence intervention is to create an increase in either personal effectiveness or organizational productivity, often both.

The Business Imperative

There is a range of possible outcomes that will result from embarking on an emotional intelligence intervention. It is important to prioritize these at the outset. This will include discussions with key stakeholders and usually involves eliciting goals that are meaningful to them and then reviewing progress against those stated goals mid-way through the intervention and at the end. A number of writers including Jones (2006) have indicated the importance of clear goals for interventions. The stated goals will also influence the content of mid-program and end of program evaluation. Of the three case studies mentioned here, Group A had by far the most significant business imperative for change. A key question to ask at the outset is: "What will be the external/visible evidence that this program has been successful?" Many interventions have rather immeasurable internal goals, e.g., to increase self awareness, to increase leadership development, or to increase team working. The emotional intelligence practitioner is encouraged to find the external visible business outcome that will create the energy and focus for a successful intervention. This will, of course, vary according to the context.

If you contrast Group A with Groups B and C, it is interesting to note that the goals for Group A were articulated both internally and externally. Announcing the business imperative elicits the deep motivation of high achievers to be effective. Without a clear business imperative, an intervention for high achievers may not have sufficient backbone to carry the needed drive and energy of a successful intervention. Groups B and C definitely lacked a clear and shared desire for change. Without this, it is hard to expect an emotional intelligence intervention to have high impact.

Format of Program

A famous Manchester Inc. study by McGovern, Lindemann, Vergara, Murphy, Barker, and Warrenfeltz (2001) concludes that an investment in executive coaching can yield results of up to six times the investment in coaching. In other words, for every dollar invested in coaching, a return of at least $6 is possible. Executive coaching has been found to be a useful adjunct to training, particularly for providing feedback and practice. In their study, Olivero, Bane, and Kopelman (1997) found that training alone increased productivity by 22 percent and training combined with coaching increased productivity by 88 percent. Rosti and Shipper (1998) point out the inherent difficulties in evaluating the impact of training alongside the impact of coaching. They conclude that, while it was difficult to attribute the changes in individual skills to a training program, they indicated that changes in overall profiles of the skills *can* be attributed to a training program. In other words, we might be able to see a broad shift in the emotional intelligence of a group and attribute that to a particular intervention, rather than being able to directly associate micro changes within individual components of emotional intelligence to the training intervention.

For emotional intelligence practitioners working with high achievers, the key learning points are these. First, it is valuable to include both training and coaching in the design of an intervention. Second, if you are keen to show results from your intervention, it is useful to include both individual and group assessments in your pre- and post-assessments. When using emotional intelligence measures, this is accomplished easily by generating group data on emotional intelligence profiles as well as individual data at the beginning of your intervention and repeating the use of these at the end of your intervention. In this way, the specific goals of your intervention are easier to locate at the outset within the context of a clear set of development needs (as assessed by diagnostic tools) and the impact of your intervention is more easily charted.

Table 2.3 summarizes the amount of coaching and training that each group received. Each group had a different quantity of coaching and group training. Group A received a total quantity of training and coaching that exceeded forty hours, compared with Groups B and C, who received fewer than thirty hours.

There is potentially a point at around thirty-two hours of combined coaching and training that tips into impact (perhaps the term "coachaining" or "trainoaching" would summarize this important marriage of learning methods). This would merit further research and exploration.

Table 2.3. Summary of the Split Between Coaching and Training for Three Different Emotional Intelligence Programs for High Achievers

	Case Study 1: Group A: Dramatic Success	Case Study 2: Group B: Moderate Success	Case Study 3: Group C: Potential of Program Not Fully Realized
Training (per person)	Four workshop days; approximately thirty-six hours in total	Five half-days = 2.5 workshop days; approximately 22.5 hours in total	Six half-days = three workshop days; approximately twenty-seven hours in total
Coaching time (per person)	**Eight** hours, including two hours at the beginning and two hours at the end focused on assessment, plus four hours of actual executive coaching.	Six hours, including two hours at the beginning and one hour at the end focused on assessment, plus three hours of actual executive coaching.	2.5 hours at beginning and end entirely focused on assessments.
Total Time	44 hours	28.5 hours	29.5 hours

Source: Ei World Client Project Documents, 2007.

Whilst more in-depth studies are needed in this area, initial research highlights the need for a minimum of thirty-two hours in total, including twenty-four hours of workshops combined with four hours of dedicated one-to-one coaching in addition to around four hours focused on assessments. This may provide a basic starting point for practitioners who design interventions for high achievers.

A further recommendation made by the author (Bharwaney, 2007b) was for a minimum twelve-hour executive coaching program to guarantee impact if carefully designed and implemented in situations where no group development is provided. A number of other conditions for success were highlighted: clear coaching goals, pre- and post-intervention assessments, a pre-defined structure and accountability, and involved stakeholders. The point here is that a twelve-hour coaching program does not sound too onerous for a high achiever, yet it is a duration of intervention that has proven to have a high return on investment from the author's own coaching work in this area. Stating that a commitment involves twelve very manageable hours is both appealing to high achievers whose time is often very pressured and it also communicates the notion of getting impact within a twelve-hour timescale. If a high achiever can accomplish a significant return on his or her time, it makes it much easier to show the impact of coaching.

Length of Program

A general guideline for the length of an emotional intelligence intervention with high achievers is four to twelve months (depending on the extent of the changes desired and the planned number of learning components). In my experience, I have found six-month programs to be the ideal—not too long to lose momentum and not too short to limit the potential for change. The key question here is: "How long will it take a high achiever to create the changes he/she desires and to sustain the changes?" Reflecting on the successes of the three programs described here, a six-month format in Group A seemed to work well. Groups B and C may have been too long; programs lose momentum if there is too long a period between the initial enrolment and the final evaluation.

Learning Components

For any emotional intelligence intervention for high achievers, clear deliverables should be defined at the outset. Usually a discussion with a group of key stakeholders will enable these to be defined with the business imperative in mind. The ideal is to map out the whole intervention with the key deliverables that relate to each activity. This will also include a discussion of the difference between deliverables that serve the notion of measurable behavioral change and others that are more about customer satisfaction, and keeping this clear distinction during the design phase of an intervention. The topic of accountability is important here. In other words, "Who is accountable for which aspects of the development goals and how will these be documented and shared?" In particular, it is important to separate out the responsibilities of the facilitators, the participants, and the senior sponsors.

It is good practice to set these out in a "Commitment Document" at the outset of the intervention.

It is important to have a range of learning components throughout all stages of the intervention from needs assessment through design, delivery, and evaluation. These four stages have been described in a previous series of papers by Bharwaney and Cannon (2000a&b, 2001a&b); the reader is referred there for best practices in articulating the deliverables of an emotional intelligence intervention. These are not different when working with high achievers. Jones (2006) indicated the importance of a coach providing a steady supply of relevant information that will stimulate thinking through continual improvement. In an emotional intelligence intervention, this can take the form of materials provided between workshops, tools to use within one's own team beyond the "classroom," and reading materials. All are useful components for emotional intelligence interventions.

Comparing the three case studies offered here, Group A had the largest number and widest range of delivery mechanisms. Less impact is achieved when the program has fewer learning components; thus, the practitioner is advised to incorporate as broad a range as possible.

Support Mechanisms

It is valuable to include the following four support mechanisms in the design of emotional intelligence interventions for high achievers: senior sponsors, development planning, buddying (a learning process wherein participants are randomly paired and asked to co-coach each other on certain aspects of their leadership development both during and after workshops), and focused coaching. These represent four pillars in support of an emotional intelligence intervention based on the group development needs identified in the collective profile computed at the outset (see Figure 2.4). All of these need to be aligned with the group's goals, rather than being used because they are favorite methods of the facilitator(s) or coach(es) involved.

In Table 2.4, each of the four support mechanisms is explained in relation to their appropriateness based on the three group profiles presented and their relative success.

Each of the four main support mechanisms is listed and considered in light of the high-, moderate-, and low-impact case studies.

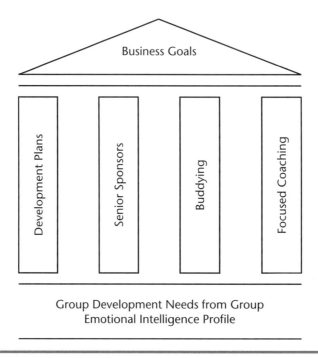

Business Goals

Development Plans

Senior Sponsors

Buddying

Focused Coaching

Group Development Needs from Group
Emotional Intelligence Profile

Figure 2.4. The Four Pillars of Support for Working with High Achievers

Senior Sponsors

The intervention for Group A relied heavily on a strong internal advocate. Such an advocate was not present in either Groups B or C. Within Group B, which consisted of the most senior group, it was recommended that the participants each seek an external mentor (in place of a senior sponsor, since they were already the most senior in their organization). From a glance at all three group EQ profiles (Figures 2.1, 2.2, and 2.3), it is evident that the Interpersonal dimension of emotional intelligence was low in all cases. This is one of the primary reasons why the inclusion of senior sponsors and buddying was a necessary ingredient in all three programs. With lower interpersonal functioning, the participants themselves are unlikely to communicate their successes to others so it is helpful to construct a framework for feedback on key learnings and for this to happen as a programmed part of the course. This usually enables the business outcomes to be more widely communicated. It can also go a long way to stopping a program going off the rails.

Table 2.4. Summary of the Main Support Mechanisms Implemented Within Three Emotional Intelligence Interventions

	Case Study 1: Group A: Dramatic Success	Case Study 2: Group B: Moderate Success	Case Study 3: Group C: Potential of Program Not Fully Realized
Main support mechanisms used	Senior Sponsor. Development Plans. Buddying. Some Coaching.	External mentors with varying degrees of commitment and skill. Development Plans. Buddying. Some coaching.	Absence of senior sponsors. Absence of Development Plans. Some buddying but variable in take-up within the group. Limited coaching.
Appropriateness to the group profile	The use of Development Plans was related to the need to increase impulse control. The other support mechanisms were conducive to developing interpersonal ability and self regard.	The use of Development Plans was related to the need to increase interpersonal functioning (as opposed to developing impulse control as with Group A). The other support mechanisms were also conducive to developing interpersonal ability. The use of buddying was most emphasized in order to assist with the development of interpersonal ability. The absence of senior sponsors other than the group itself and a reduced amount of coaching had an adverse impact on the overall results.	All support mechanisms were appropriate for the group development task. However, there was a lack of commitment to these both in terms of the financing of the project and in the personal motivations of the participants so these were not implemented to the extent that was originally envisaged.

Source: Ei World Client Project Documents, 2007a&b.

The projects involved in Case Studies 1 and 2 both had threats of budget cuts yet they survived. Case Study 3, which also faced budget cuts, was not repeated, as the early impact of the program was not clear. The lack of a senior sponsor can bring a certain amount of doom and gloom for an intervention with high achievers. It is a basic requirement and, in the face of no senior sponsor, it is probably not the right context in which to be working with high achievers.

Development Plans

In each of the case studies, there was a marked difference in how development plans were used. Members of Group A were asked to write their development plans, share them with their "buddies," and then, once all plans were firmed up, within each cohort of participants, the plans were collated and a full document was circulated to the participants. This ensured a degree of peer pressure in sharing plans and in implementing them fully. At the outset of the program, each participant was informed that in four months time they would be tasked with reporting successes and obstacles in the implementation of their plans. In other words, the plans were an explicit part of the learning.

In the case of Groups B and C, the story was very different. Group B used plans and shared the themes of their plans with colleagues, but there was no collective sharing of the full plan. Within Group C, there was a high degree of secrecy about individual development plans; most individuals were happy to share their plans with the facilitators of the program, but not with their fellow participants.

Development plans are perhaps one of the most visible indications of personal commitment to make a change happen. When this involves a public declaration of that commitment among high achievers, the plans seem to be accomplished to a higher level of completion. Perhaps where a more secret approach and a less-than-complete sharing of plans is built into the design of an intervention, the level of accomplishment is somewhat restricted. This would lead to a conclusion that the systematic structuring of development plans is one thing but the announcement of those plans by the owner of them is one of a number of important steps in the plan becoming real. It also perhaps adds some urgency to make an effort to carry out the plan once other people have heard about the plan from the owner of it. Practitioners are advised to build this key step into the implementation of development plans.

Buddying

The intervention for Group A relied heavily on buddying as a key learning method to ensure that there would be peer support for the actions that would be taken after each coaching session and each workshop. This created a strong bond within the group and also provided an opportunity for practicing coaching skills among peers. This was powerful. While buddying existed in both Groups B and C, its use was more sporadic and did not have the desired impact.

Focused Coaching

All interventions had some focused coaching. This style of coaching is highly oriented toward behavior change with clarity about what is desirable to change and robustness of process in helping to change. The author has documented elsewhere (Bharwaney, 2007b) the way in which such coaching is ideally introduced.

There is perhaps a "best fit" strategy for designing emotional intelligence interventions that create impact. Four key support mechanisms have been introduced that are likely to have a positive impact on the outcomes of the emotional intelligence intervention for high achievers. There is a need to be selective about the methods used and ideally to select the one method that is the lead method above the others. In Group A, the lead methods were Development Plans and Buddying. In Group B, it was Buddying. In Group C, there was no lead method. It is important also to keep the collective emotional intelligence profile in mind so that you are clear how the use of the support mechanism is going to enable your clients to develop their emotional intelligence. You are not looking for perfect alignment, but at least some connection between the development goals and the support mechanisms selected. It may not be possible to include all support mechanisms fully in any one intervention.

Results Achieved by the End of the Intervention

The graphs in Figures 2.1, 2.2, and 2.3 are representative of the results achieved. In Case Study 1, alongside a statistically significant increase in twenty of the twenty-one EQ scores, there was a positive impact on the P&L account (the specifics were not quantified at the time as the emphasis was on the original goals of increasing the number of local leaders in the executive team—it is clear that the results of an intervention with high achievers will flow directly from the business goals defined at the outset; it is not usual for an emotional intelligence practitioner to look for results in arenas that have not already been located as goal arenas). Half of the group took on positions of greater responsibility, and four people joined the executive team as a direct result of the actions they took on the leadership program. This was the most visible change in the business and was indicative of a successful intervention. There were numerous examples of joint work on projects that until then had been implemented with each divisional manager firmly sitting in his or her own silo. The intervention for high achievers created a high degree of collaborative working that was sustained beyond the end of the program.

The results in Case Study 2 were largely internal results, again flowing from the original objectives set. There was better team working and, once individuals had addressed their own blind spots, one person concluded that he was in the wrong role and decided to leave the organization. There was a considerable increase in emotional intelligence of the team; how much of that was due to the program or one particular individual leaving is hard to quantify. The visible changes included more delegation between senior team members and others in the level below the senior team and much better team working within the senior group, which was noticed by other more junior people in the organization.

The results of Case Study 3 leave much to be desired. Two people from the group were accepted onto a high-profile leadership development program within the civil service, which in itself can be claimed as a major triumph of the program. In both instances, the individuals were highly committed to their learning process and had almost full attendance in meetings. Unfortunately, these successes were not common across all participants. The design flaws already discussed presented a major obstacle to this program being more effective.

A central challenge is that the practitioner is often in uncharted waters—in other words, there is no accepted approach for creating the ideal mix of support mechanisms, one of the critical ingredients of leadership development as we have already seen. One way of pre-empting this is for practitioners to consider proactively the way in which each of four emotional intelligence support mechanisms mentioned here can be incorporated into the design of an intervention. This will go some way to building interventions that are effective and successful for the high achievers who are involved.

CONCLUSION

In this chapter, I reviewed three case studies, comparing the features of programs for high achievers that obtained high, moderate, and low impact, respectively. A key feature of such programs is the support mechanisms provided. Through case studies, it is clear that, while there are features that apply to all interventions, working with high achievers is a unique subset of emotional intelligence work.

To be effective in working with high achievers requires a high degree of structure, planning, and the qualities more associated with problem solving and cognitive intelligence. For this reason practitioners who embark on this work have to be able to step back and critically evaluate the impact of what they are doing. In the design of interventions with high achievers, there is a need to go about this in a highly intelligent way.

Working with high achievers is important for the future of the emotional intelligence field. This work provides access to key decision-makers and the people who are the lifeblood of an organization. An important starting point for anyone taking on board a project in this arena is to first identify the characteristics of high achievers in a particular setting through group emotional intelligence assessments and then to use this information to design support mechanisms that will enable the intervention to be effective. In other words, emotional intelligence work with high achievers needs the essential backdrop of key support mechanisms to ensure that the program is effective and that the changes stick. This task is definitely more intelligent than emotional in view of the need for analysis, structure, and rigor in design.

REFERENCES

Bharwaney, G. (2003). Emotional intelligence: The cutting edge of interventions in corporate and educational settings. Paper presented on the 29th of May 2003 at the Nexus EQ Conference, Halifax, Nova Scotia, Canada.

Bharwaney, G. (2005). Health, emotional intelligence and schools leadership: A study of Boarding Schools Association heads. Dissertation submitted for MSc Psychology of Health. Dept of Psychology, City University, London. Unpublished manuscript.

Bharwaney, G. (2007a). Developing high achievers through EQ. Presentation at the 2007 Nexus EQ Conference, September 2007, Sandton, South Africa.

Bharwaney, G. (2007b). Coaching executives to enhance emotional intelligence and increase productivity. In R. Bar-On, J.G. Maree, & M.J. Elias (Eds.), *Educating people to be emotionally intelligent*. Johannesburg, SA: Heinemann Educational Publishers.

Bharwaney, G (2007c). *Emotionally intelligent living*. Carmarthen: Crown House Publishing.

Bharwaney, G. (2008). Aiming high—Emotional intelligence development for high achievers. Presentation at the International Conference on Emotional Intelligence (ICEI). June 2008, MHS, Chicago.

Bharwaney, G., Bar-On, R., & MacKinlay, A. (2007). *EQ and the bottom line*. Ampthill, Bedfordshire, UK: Ei World.

Bharwaney, G., & Cannon, K. (2000a). Everything you wanted to know about implementing an EQ programme–1: Getting started. *Competency & Emotional Intelligence, 8*(1), 19–24. [Originally published as Orme and Cannon.]

Bharwaney, G. & Cannon, K. (2001a, Spring). Everything you wanted to know about implementing an EQ programme–3: Taking the show on the road. *Competency & Emotional Intelligence, 8*(3), 17–-24. [Originally published as Orme and Cannon.]

Bharwaney, G., & Cannon, K. (2001b). Everything you wanted to know about implementing an EQ programme–4: Assuring the highest standards. *Competency & Emotional Intelligence, 8*(4), 19–24. [Originally published as Orme and Cannon.]

Bharwaney, G., & Cannon, K. (2000b). Everything you wanted to know about implementing an EQ programme–2: Design. *Competency & Emotional Intelligence, 8*(2), 18–25. [Originally published as Orme and Cannon.]

Bharwaney, G., & MacKinlay, A. (2007a). Developing high achievers through EQ. Presentation at the International Conference on Emotional Intelligence (ICEI), June 2007, MHS, London, England (UK).

Bharwaney, G., & MacKinlay, A. (2007b). Coaching high achievers: A practical perspective. Presentation at the CIPD Forum meeting, May 2007, Chartered Institute of Personnel & Development (CIPD), London, England (UK).

Cherniss, C., Goleman, D., Emmerling, R., Cowan, K. & Adler, M. (1988). *Bringing emotional intelligence to the workplace: A technical report issued by the Consortium for Research on Emotional Intelligence in Organizations*, Rutgers University Graduate School of Applied and Professional Psychology (GSAPP). Available: www.eiconsortium.org.

Ei World. (2006). Internal briefing note on coaching high achievers.

Ei World. (2007). What is emotional intelligence? *EI World Overview*.

Ei World. (2007a). Client report: Senior executive team development.

Ei World. (2007b). Client report: Development of senior managers.

Feather, N.T. (1989). Attitudes toward the high achiever: The fall of the tall poppy. *Australian Journal of Psychology*, *41*(3), 239–267.

Feather, N.T. (1991). Attitudes towards the high achiever: Effects of perceiver's own level of competence. *Australian Journal of Psychology*, *43*(3), 121–124.

Jones, G. (2006). Coaching high achievers. *Human Resource Management International Digest*, *14*(7), 3–4(2).

Langhorn, S. (2004). How emotional intelligence can improve management performance. *International Journal of Contemporary Hospitality Management*, *6*(4), 220–230.

McGovern, J., Lindemann, M., Vergara, M., Murphy, S., Barker, L. & Warrenfeltz, R. (2001). Maximizing the impact of executive coaching: Behavioral change, organizational outcomes & return on investment. *The Manchester Review*, *6*(1).

Olivero, G., Bane, K.D., & Kopelman, R.E. (1997). Executive coaching as a transfer of training tool: effects on productivity in a public agency. *Public Personnel Management*, *26*.

Rosti, R.T., & Shipper, F. (1998). A study of the impact of training in a management development program based on 360 feedback. *Journal of Managerial Psychology*, *13*(½), 77–89.

Ruderman, M., & Bar-On, R. (2003). The impact of emotional intelligence on leadership. Unpublished manuscript.

Slaski, M., & Cartwright, S. (2002). Health, performance and emotional intelligence: An exploratory study of retail managers. *Stress and Health*, *18*, 63–68.

Skiffington, S., & Zeus, P. (2003). *Behavioral coaching: How to build sustainable personal and organizational strength*. Sydney: McGraw Hill Australia Pty Ltd.

Geetu Bharwaney is founder and managing director of Ei World Limited, a thought leader in the application of emotional intelligence in business. She has extensive experience of developing "high achievers," the critically important people in organizations who are responsible for accomplishing results. She has built emotional intelligence interventions and has proven measurable results from her work. She leads global projects involving leadership development, emotional intelligence, and coaching in a cross-cultural context. More information about her work can be found at www.eiworld.org.

CHAPTER 3

Resonant Leadership for Results

An Emotional and Social Intelligence Program for Change in South Africa and Cambodia

Annie Mckee, Frances Johnston, Eddy Mwelwa, and Suzanne Rotondo*

Between 2001 and 2005, the Teleos Leadership Institute conducted comprehensive leadership development programs in South Africa and Cambodia in the service

---

*This program was the result of so many wonderfully talented people, including Felice Tilin, Monica Sharma, Metsi Makhetha, Dominique AitOuyahia McAdams, and the groups of dedicated and innovative facilitators who continue to carry on this critical work.

of supporting leaders in the fight against HIV and AIDS. Men and women from all walks of life participated in these programs, including grassroots community leaders, civil service and non-governmental organization officials, members of Parliament, traditional healers, chiefs, religious leaders, and youth.

We conducted this basic Program twice in South Africa and Swaziland, three times in Cambodia, and a modified version in six Caribbean nations. For the purposes of this paper we focused primarily on our experiences in South Africa and Cambodia.

In this chapter, we will explain the theories and principles that guide our work. We will describe how we use a systems theory approach to foster and sustain learning and change in cross-cultural settings, and how emotional intelligence is at the heart of our approach to leadership development. We will describe the design process and the components of the Resonant Leadership for Results Program, referred to herein as "the Program."

Along the way, you'll hear stories directly from Program participants that capture the sensitivities and complexities of cross-cultural leadership development. We will conclude with a section on the lessons we have learned, with hope that these lessons will support our field in identifying best practices for supporting people as they develop the capacity for truly great leadership.

THE FOUNDATIONS: EMOTIONAL INTELLIGENCE (EI) AND SYSTEMS THEORY

We used emotional intelligence as a foundation for the Program, which allowed us to attend to both the objective and subjective realities of the people and communities in which we worked. The model of EI and resonant leadership allowed participants to see themselves and groups in new ways. It also enabled the leaders to focus on the power of hope and compassion for their countries and for the people infected and affected by HIV and AIDS.

We used action research to impact learning and behavior change that could then lead to wider social change, and we ensured that the Program utilized multiple levels of learning—individual, team, and community. The combination of EI and a systems approach resulted in profound change for people and led to the sustainability of the interventions over time.

Similarly, for us, the project was life transforming. We touched the essence of what it means to reach out, care for one another, and orient one's life toward helping people and their country grow and develop.

The Beginning

We stood rooted to the ground in the front of the group. We could not understand one word of what the elder was saying to us, loudly and with passion, from the back of the room. As she went on for what seemed like hours, not mere minutes, her speech was increasingly peppered with a few words we did understand … said with obvious sarcasm and challenge … "Philadelphia," "America," and "Emotional Intelligence." Standing there on the first day of our Resonant Leadership for Results Program in South Africa, over one hundred participants clearly enjoyed this leader's challenge to us. There was laughter, movement, and obvious curiosity about how we would handle the situation.

It was a difficult moment. We were excited to be in South Africa, ready to share our knowledge and practices that could help people lead more effectively. We had prepared: we had begun action research projects in the country and knew, to a certain extent, what the nature of the issues were, both cultural and with respect to the HIV and AIDS pandemic we were hoping to impact.

But despite our hope, commitment, and preparation, we were faced with a huge challenge. While we could not understand one word of Zulu, we did understand this leader's powerful objection. She was saying, with her words, her body, and her emotions, "Who do you think you are, and why do you think your Western, American management models have anything at all to do with what is going on in South Africa?" (adapted from McKee, Boyatzis, & Johnston, 2008)

She had a point.

As practitioners, we have been on a learning journey over the past ten years, finding ways to "translate" emotional and social intelligence and leadership development into languages and across cultural boundaries—and we have begun to have answers to the questions posed to us by the powerful Zulu woman on that memorable day.

As of 2008, we have conducted action research and leadership development programs in the public and private sectors in Cambodia, South Africa, Swaziland, Jamaica, Barbados, Trinidad and Tobago, Guyana, the Dominican Republic, Italy, the United Kingdom, Holland, Germany, Austria, and the United States. In several of these countries, we have also taught people to conduct action research and leadership development programs themselves, using our theories, techniques, program designs and materials. This chapter captures the learning we have found most useful to our practice.

The HIV and AIDS Leadership Challenge

Late in the year 2000, a senior leader from a prominent international development NGO (non-governmental organization) called and said, "The world has spent billions of dollars trying to arrest the spread of HIV and AIDS. As of today we have 33 million infected people and many millions more who are affected by the pandemic with no significant reversal of infection rate predicted. Entire countries' economies and developmental possibilities are being radically and negatively impacted by HIV and AIDS. We are convinced that the only path to transformational change is through improved leadership at all levels of the system. Can you help us build leadership capacity with the local leaders in the affected countries?"

We said yes. How could we do otherwise? Here was a chance to use our best practices in the service of humanity. But we weren't naïve. We knew this work would present huge challenges for us, personally and professionally.

The presenting problem was HIV and AIDS. Our sponsor believed that education and a medical response to this problem were not sufficient, and we agreed. While clinically a virus and syndrome, the spread of HIV and AIDS is deeply linked to issues of human behavior, including sexual behavior. Misperceptions, bias, stigmas, and tremendous sensitivity around how the virus spreads make it extremely difficult to address the effects of the virus on people and communities. Many of the unsafe practices that contribute to the spread of the virus are a result of longstanding habits and cultural practices, so even in the earliest stages of our work, we were aware that highly charged, systemic issues such as gender inequality, violence against women, and poverty were also at the heart of the issue.

We grappled with a variety of questions: Would emotional and social intelligence "translate" across the world? Would the experiential approach to adult learning we typically use be accepted and acceptable? How could we overcome our own lack of first-hand knowledge about specific cultures and people, while simultaneously engaging participants in a process of self-examination of their own deeply held beliefs and practices? How could we engage an entire social system in change, using leadership development as the vehicle for that change?

Our first decision was to ground our approach and work in what we know to be true about leadership development and human change:

1. *Emotional intelligence* is at the heart of effective leadership;
2. Any intervention, big or small, must begin with understanding the *objective and subjective reality* of the people who will ultimately benefit from the intervention; and
3. To bring about sustainable change, an intervention must touch multiple levels of system—in this case, the individual, families, institutions, and communities.

Emotional and Social Intelligence and Resonant Leadership

Research has shown that emotional and social intelligence is a better differentiator than technical expertise or IQ when leaders want to influence followers and create sustainable positive change in an organization's work culture, promote superior performance, and improve results (Cherniss & Goleman, 2001).

Much like modern corporations, countries faced with a national crisis need leaders who have resilience, hope, and the capacity to lead change. Whether a leadership program is aimed at the corporate environment or toward community mobilization, we believed that our stance, which focuses holistically and systemically on human emotions and behavior, would be relevant for leaders whose work was literally linked to life and death.

In working with leaders, we have always started with this basic premise: great leaders *move* people (Goleman, Boyatzis, & McKee, 2002). Resonant leaders, the best among them, engage people's hearts and minds, and they help people to direct their energy, individually and collectively, toward a desired end. As resonant leaders help people manage their energy, they also create a climate that is ripe with enthusiasm, hope, mutual support, and commitment. In other words, they lead with emotional intelligence to create resonant climates where people can thrive (Boyatzis & McKee, 2005).

Figure 3.1 presents a model of the elements of emotional intelligence.

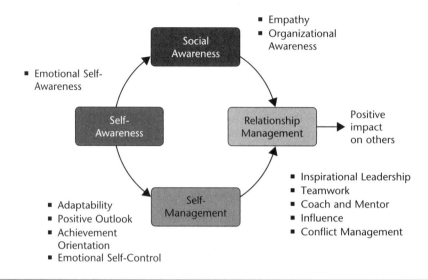

Figure 3.1. Emotional Intelligence Model*

*Adapted from Annie McKee, Richard Boyatzis, and Frances Johnston, *Becoming a Resonant Leader: Develop Your Emotional Intelligence, Renew Your Relationships, Sustain Your Effectiveness.* Boston, MA: Harvard Business Press, 2008.

The Human Brain and EI

The human brain has the same basic structures across cultures. All humans make use of the sensory and muscular-skeleton systems to orient and navigate themselves through their environments. Similarly, all humans use a combination of thoughts and feelings to understand and arrive at the meaning of the various experiences they encounter. And all humans work and live in social systems and need to understand how to more effectively lead, follow, and get things done together.

Notably, we feel before we think. When we sense a threat in our environment, when we are passionate, or when we are under a great deal of stress, it is the feelings that drive us into action.

And emotions are contagious. The human brain and our emotions function as an open system, meaning that we constantly send messages to one another about our emotional states. So humans are linked and influence each other, creating as we go an emotional reality in our groups, organizations, and communities (Fabbri-Destro & Rizzolatti, 2008; Kelly & Barsade, 2001).

Thus, being aware of, and able to manage, one's own emotions are core EI competencies and at the heart of effective leadership.

For example, we have seen that, when a leader expresses true empathy, he or she becomes more adept at enabling followers to engage proactively, creatively, and enthusiastically in the pursuit of collective goals. We saw this in action when we exposed leaders to the everyday suffering of AIDS patients. When our participants had experiences that triggered empathy, there was an increase in their capacity to relate emotionally to the people with HIV and AIDS, to each other, and to people in their own communities. In other words, empathy opened their minds to considering the problem in new and different ways, with less defensiveness and bias. They were then in a far better place to mobilize others and to foster change.

When coupled with the power dynamics between a leader and his or her followers, understanding this concept and consciously managing one's own emotions make a significant difference in a leader's ability to impact outcomes. A leader's whisper is a shout, and his behaviors serve as a model for others in the organization or community.

THE RESONANT LEADERSHIP FOR RESULTS PROGRAM

Overview

The overall Program involved three, five-day sessions, scheduled approximately eight weeks apart, with intersession work conducted in regional teams (see Figure 3.2). There were 80 to 140 participants and ten to twenty local facilitators in each Program in South Africa and in Cambodia.

The basic plan was straightforward: First, we would engage in diagnostic processes to identify key issues related to HIV and AIDS, leadership practices and cultural norms relevant to the issues, and to the design of a leadership program. Then, we would design a leadership development program, intending to deliver it to approximately one hundred people over a one-year period. And finally, we would develop a train-the-trainer program to certify a subset of local people to become faculty in the leadership program in subsequent years.

Figure 3.2. Program Overview

Identifying Diverse Participants

Finding participants who represented a cross-section of the community with the capacity to understand, engage with, and utilize the practices from the Program was essential. Hence, program participants were recruited and nominated from sectors as diverse as national and local government, non-government and communities, tribal chiefs, native healers, Buddhist monks, medical doctors, grassroots organizers, and, crucially, men and women living with HIV and AIDS. Participants' ages ranged from twenty to seventy, and they came from both sophisticated urban and remote rural communities.

Many of the participants were established, powerful local leaders. They were often quite aware of the national issues surrounding the spread of HIV and AIDS from a medical or macroeconomic perspective. In many cases, though, they either did not acknowledge the impact of the virus on them or actually had no personal, emotional exposure to the issues surrounding HIV and AIDS.

Discovering the Emotional Reality: The Dynamic Inquiry Process

Our first steps included conducting a Dynamic Inquiry, which is a methodology designed by us to get at the emotional reality of the organization or community (McKee & McMillen, 1992). To begin, we held dozens of conversations with local leaders, as well as a disciplined investigative process. We spent considerable time with the local representatives of our sponsor, a non-governmental organization (NGO) that has an international presence and local offices. These meetings were both formal and social, and we got to know people *as* people, quite well.

The goal of the Dynamic Inquiry process and analysis was to identify the underlying root causes of the spread of HIV and AIDS and the role of leadership. We were also interested in identifying inherent strengths of each country that could play an important part in reversing the trend.

We conducted twenty-five one-on-one confidential interviews in South Africa and fifty-five in Cambodia. After compiling our verbatim interview notes, we conducted a thematic analysis, following qualitative research protocol (Boyatzis, 1998).

We then checked out our initial themes with focus groups, including people who had not participated in the interview process, to confirm and help us to adjust our analysis. The focus groups helped us to ensure that the thematic analysis had a realistic and cultural "fit" and was not influenced by our assumptions.

What the Dynamic Inquiries Revealed

The Dynamic Inquiry helped us uncover several root causes and systemic issues involved in the spread of HIV and AIDS and to understand the cultural interpretation of concepts such as leadership, power, poverty, and change. We were exposed to local and national perceptions, perceived collective strengths and weaknesses, and readiness for change. We also got a "feel" for the participants, including how they interacted with us. And we met, for the first time, many of the amazing people who would participate in the Program.

The Dynamic Inquiry studies directed us to focus our Program designs on issues of gender equity in both countries, but with different emphases. In Cambodia, the study showed how important and how elusive women's leadership was in the country. Therefore, we designed into the Program a learning community and experiences that were empowering to the female participants, and that encouraged them (and the men) to speak openly about their life experiences and how gender affected their decisions and behavior. In South Africa, the study revealed the prevalence of non-monogamous sexual practices in both women and men and the link between these behaviors and the spread of HIV and AIDS. Thus, we needed to make room for and elicit frank discussions of sexuality between the men and women in our learning community.

We also learned that power dynamics were extremely complex in both countries. We found that there was a clear and honored social stratification in Cambodia that we needed to design for. During the Program, we paid particular attention to examples of successful cross-social class interaction and collaboration that would support a multi-sector response to issues related to HIV and AIDS. In South Africa, we came to understand that the interaction effects of gender, tribal origin, and political affiliation would clearly drive communication patterns in large and small groups—again, an important design consideration.

One man's story summarizes the impact dealing with some of the underlying issues—such as power and gender equity—had on him.

The man in the olive drab clothes of a past Communist era is a leader. You can feel it when in his presence; you can see it in how the other participants sit up and take notice when he speaks. Once deeply aligned with the goals of the Khmer Rouge regime, in the past he had committed unspeakable acts of brutality and cruelty.

Today he is a senior government official in democratic Cambodia. Twenty years after the war, he carried deep shame about his actions during the war years. No manner of rationalizing ("I had no choice") had fully exorcised his guilt. While generally a nice fellow in his everyday life, on the weekends, this leader joined his fellow veterans in heavy drinking, avoiding any discussion of past behavior. As a government official, he had great power and was instrumental in allocating resources and prioritization for many programs.

On the final day of the Program, the room hushed as he rose to speak. He recounted losing his parents in the war and the behavior of his youth. He linked that past with his more recent self-destructive behavior and abuse of his wife. He shared that, as a result of the insights about emotional intelligence he had had during the Program, he was changing his behaviors. He had curtailed the partying and had even confronted his fellow war veterans about their persistent use of prostitutes. He was more compassionate with himself and with his wife.

His Regional Change Group had visited families orphaned by HIV and AIDS and had built a house for two families. In his personal life, he knew his behavior put him at risk for infection, and that if infected, he would in turn infect his wife, potentially leaving his children orphans. He did not want that fate for his children, and now understood the link between his past and his recent unhealthy behavior. Most importantly, he now had a deeper belief in his capacity to change his own behavior.

If that was all, we would be grateful for his personal transformation, and that one more orphaned family had been avoided. But institutional change hadn't yet happened. With the support, challenge, and resources of the Leadership

Program, this leader decided to change the way staff in the provincial government worked with the other divisions and with the NGOs in the area. He understood that change needed to happen in his team and in how his institution interacted with the community.

"We need to add more women in our staff," he declared. He told us how he had brought a few of the people he had met in the Program who worked for international aid agencies, and those from other key governmental departments, together to meet so they could find a better way to address HIV and AIDS and provide support to poor families.

They were invited to call on him directly; a coalition was formed that ended up building wells for water and health centers faster and closer to families orphaned by HIV and AIDS.

This man is an example of how utilizing emotional and social intelligence can positively impact very difficult social situations by bringing hope, compassion, and the practice of resonant leadership to bear. We firmly believe that, had we not done significant rigorous research prior to Program implementation, we would never have understood our participants' objective and subjective realities. In a word, we would not have been able to reach them.

The DI (Dynamic Inquiry) process enabled us to learn *how* to use our concepts, theories, and tried-and-true leadership development practices in cross-cultural, highly complex social systems. We gained insight and knowledge about the countries, the people, the issues, and the cultures. This allowed us to deliver the Program *for the people, rather than to the people.*

Program Enrollment Meetings and Customization

After the DI and Program design phases, we held a number of *enrollment meetings* to share initial results of the Dynamic Inquiry research, to engage participants in a few experiential sessions, and to gain commitment to the leadership development process. Through these meetings, participants and other local leaders had an opportunity to try out our experiential methodology and have a brief introduction to the core concepts embedded in the leadership development process. These meetings enabled us to see how our approach and concepts were received and allowed us to adjust our methods and processes in final customization for each country.

Launching the Resonant Leadership for Results Program

We designed the Program to include three five-day workshop-like sessions with large groups from 80 to 140 participants. These sessions focused on resonant leadership, emotional intelligence, and personal as well as collective explorations of issues related to HIV and AIDS. Learning was largely experiential, and included activities, mini-lectures, small- and large-group dialogue, and reflection. We designed the Program in such a way as to build trust and front loaded it with exercises that were conducive to sharing emotions, supporting each other, and exploring power dynamics.

Large group community conversations were extraordinarily powerful. We knew that there would be a few "essential conversations" that would need to happen, and that if the conditions were right, these conversations could lead to significant transformation. As trust grew, we introduced the "hot" issues: bias, stigma, poverty, gender relations, and sexuality.

In addition to the large-group sessions, participants met regularly in two small facilitated groups of ten to fifteen people. The first group was called an "EI Practice Group" and met only during the Program sessions. The goal of these groups was akin to personal growth groups and had as their primary task the emotional and relational growth of each individual. These EI Practice Groups met three to four times within each session to build upon, deepen, and apply learning that had begun in the large-group sessions. Facilitators engaged these EI Practice Groups in exercises, led discussions about personal experiences and feelings, and gave and received both supportive and challenging feedback.

The second small-group structure was a "Regional Change Group." The Regional Change Groups engaged in action learning projects between sessions (see Dotlich & Noel, 1998). For example, between sessions one and two, participants used the DI methodology to interview community members. Group members worked with their facilitators to look for and understand the root causes of the spread of HIV and AIDS. The Change Groups then articulated preliminary ideas for change projects and brought those ideas back to the larger community in session two.

During session two, the Program focused on key issues identified in the Dynamic Inquiry, especially the "hot" issues such as gender and power dynamics. During these powerful sessions, the Change Groups revisited their ideas for their transformational change projects. They presented their ideas to the entire cadre of participants, received challenging feedback, and selected a change project to implement. Between sessions two and three, the Change Groups conducted the change projects. Then in session three, they brought their stories of what happened back to the community.

Program Facilitators

Facilitators were integral to Program success. We were attempting to deliver leadership development "at scale"—meaning very large participant groups, engaging in very complex and emotional learning experiences. We needed facilitators. Moreover, we needed facilitators who were part of the culture, who could help us to bridge the distance between us and our participants. An equally important goal of the Program was capacity development: we wanted to develop a core group of people to facilitate aspects of the Program itself *and* learn to become faculty and change agents, fully trained in our methodologies. Because capacity development was an explicit goal, not a nice-to-have, we set out to find, train, and certify people to use our materials, design, and so forth. We were ultimately able to leave behind a well-trained, emotionally intelligent group of faculty who could lead the Program without Western-Northern support.

In both South Africa and Cambodia, our sponsor had helped us to identify twelve to twenty individuals who were likely to succeed in this challenging role. A few of these people had some background in teaching, training, or organization development. Fewer still had extensive experience in these areas. All were deeply committed to supporting the Program's goals and to their own learning and development.

Just as in any organizational engagement, providing sufficient support to the facilitators was essential for the group to be able to take ownership of the work and to continue it beyond our engagement. Therefore, we provided daily tutorial sessions on leadership, emotional intelligence, adult learning, group dynamics, process consultation, change theory and practices, and the facts around HIV and AIDS in their country and around the world. These sessions took place morning, noon, and night, around and between the Program modules. In addition, we supported the facilitators in their work with their EI and Change Groups. This was particularly challenging between sessions: time zone differences and facilitators' access to computers and phones were just two of the many obstacles we all encountered.

MAKING CHANGE SUSTAINABLE: A SYSTEMS APPROACH

In our experience with both corporate clients and in communities, we have found that truly sustainable change happens when leaders inquire, focus, and intervene simultaneously on more than one system level. Therefore, we designed the Program to include *individual* leadership development, collaborative learning and work in *groups*, and action learning projects that were conducted in the larger *communities*.

The use of action learning and Regional Change Groups facilitated the real-world application of the emotional intelligence and resonant leadership models. The participants learned to use action research to investigate and then design social interventions. The results of the projects astounded the sponsoring agency, and often, the participants themselves. They had never had the experience of systematically looking at how their leadership, with a team, could result in action felt by thousands of people.

Through action research and then action learning projects, people realized their own capacity to make a difference at more than one level of system. They learned to see and take action at the individual, team and organization, and community/culture levels. Change Projects included:

- Creation and dissemination of truly resonant radio programs and public service messages on HIV and AIDS
- Design and execution of "an underground railroad" system of transportation of HIV positive, poor people who did not have access to appropriate healthcare in their geographic region to areas where they could and did receive care
- Design and delivery of numerous experiential and inspiring workshops in workplaces, governmental agencies, and communities on HIV and AIDS and how to prevent the spread
- Creation of a nationally broadcast radio call-in show on sex and sexuality
- Church-based parent and teen forums to discuss sexuality

- Interagency co-sponsoring of HIV and AIDS policies
- A forum for government leaders and their wives on HIV and AIDS
- Creation of a system for sponsoring families orphaned by HIV and AIDS

More than sixty self-funded, locally designed and executed change projects targeted either the spread of HIV or the isolation and deprivation of infected people and their families. These projects had significant, systemic impact on the countries and were very often extremely creative and emotionally engaging. Many have been assimilated into society and continue to this day.

LESSONS LEARNED

Taking our practices into these new contexts revealed a number of critical lessons for EI and leadership development in a global setting:

1. Faculty practitioners must demonstrate and maintain emotional intelligence individually and as a group;
2. Global work requires culturally-specific understandings of the I-We continuum;
3. The facilitator group must find practices for developing and sustaining emotional intelligence in themselves;
4. Faculty practitioners are responsible for using language that is accessible: no jargon allowed. And conducting complex emotional and theoretical programs through simultaneous translation is possible, but it demands careful consideration as an important aspect of design and program delivery.

Lesson One: You Must Develop EI in Yourself If You Hope to Teach It

We simply cannot teach emotional intelligence if we don't develop it in ourselves first. To do so, practitioners must hold ourselves to high standards when it comes to personal and professional development by continually developing self-awareness, our capacity for self-management, social awareness and our ability to build strong, healthy relationships, and our skill at intervening in conscious ways that build capacity and offer hope.

Some of the most important learning occurred when the concepts of emotional intelligence, and emotional contagion, came to life in the classroom. For example, in the second year of conducting the Program in South Africa, a large number of participants were chiefs and traditional healers. They were asked to deeply examine the traditional beliefs and practices that may have been contributing to the spread of the HIV virus. At one point, a discussion began in the large group about which of these beliefs and practices still served them well, and which, if any, did not serve them individually or collectively as well as they had in the past.

Some of the participants, including one powerful chief and several other strong men, took this dialogue to be a criticism of the local polygamy system. They were angry, and clearly stated that the conversation was inappropriate and that our Western ideas were an attempt to undermine long-held cultural practices. The tone of the conversation was dissonant: negativity, conflict, and fear spread like wildfire. In a very short period of time, hardly anyone was talking.

One of us—our male, Zambian faculty—decided to take on the dissonance in the room. He stepped directly into the conflict, speaking clearly and powerfully—self-aware, self-managing, *and* empathetic. His stance alone woke the room up and enabled people to move, emotionally, far enough away from the fear and the anxiety that they could begin to engage once again. He led a courageous discussion, beginning with his own experience as an African man, and the importance of his culture, sexual expression, and family.

A note on using one's self as a model of emotionally intelligent leadership, as our faculty did: it could be argued that only our male, African faculty could have led this particular discussion. His status—male, older, African—had a profound effect on the group, and he had license to speak out about practices in a way that the rest of us (female, Western) could not. Once he began the discussion, however, we could, and did, join—modeling our own leadership, emotional and social intelligence in handling the discussion and our collective willingness as a faculty team to share leadership of the Program and to let each of us create resonance in the group when and how we could.

As he spoke openly about beliefs that may have served his ancestors well but that did not serve him personally, today, the conversation took a very different turn. People spoke up. One woman stood and countered the stance that managing sexuality was a threat to the culture, and that HIV was spread largely by prostitutes. She said, "I am HIV positive." Few people in the room knew this. "And I did not get this virus from a prostitute, I am not a prostitute. I got this virus from my *husband.*"

Her courage opened the door for a much deeper, collective conversation about the issues. People began to talk about the spread of HIV and AIDS being exacerbated by people not respecting the *traditional* polygamy system. Specifically, in a closed polygamous group, all people remain faithful to the arrangement and no one engages in sexual activity outside the group. This conversation resulted in people reexamining root causes and unconscious behavior that exacerbated the spread of HIV and AIDS.

To sustain our own effective leadership of these Programs, we learned that we had to *live emotional intelligence* and develop practices of mindfulness, hope, and compassion to support us in creating resonance in the face of the intensity of the entire process (Boyatzis & McKee, 2005).

The Programs were intense, challenging, exciting, and stressful. We sometimes found ourselves losing our edge and our emotional intelligence, and we realized we needed to learn how to manage the stress and pressures of the situations and our roles as leaders of the Program.

We found that staying focused on the passion for the work we were doing, attending carefully to ourselves individually and as a group, and attuning to our participants' needs and desires helped us to stay grounded in the face of hard work and challenge. Finally, the love, warmth, and compassion we felt toward each other and the countries and people we worked with helped sustain us through the difficult times.

We had discussions among ourselves about how we reacted to various encounters; acknowledged and talked through our own prejudices; and involved facilitators in supporting us to work through some of the issues. We also created a structure—end-of-day reflection sessions—during which we met with facilitators to debrief, support one another, and consider our experiences of the day. We built in these meetings at the end of very long days because we know that people (including ourselves) are best able to sustain resonance when they are emotionally grounded, fully engaged, and they have adequate support to work through difficulties.

Lesson Two: The "I-We" Continuum

One of our most challenging experiences was in transitioning the approach we used in individualist societies to societies that operate within a communal or collective cultural framework. All of us on the faculty, even our African colleague, had learned and worked primarily within the context of norms associated with a focus on the individual.

In cultures focused on the individual, such as the United States and the UK, the collective "we" seems to exist to serve the individual and, therefore, an individual tends to have expectations of entitlement from the collective. In more communal cultures, it is the collective that sets the norms and expectations of an individual, who is expected to predominantly act in the service of the collective. In other words, individuals are subordinated to the collective.

In South Africa and Cambodia, it seems that the "I" exists in the service of "we." Therefore, we needed to find ways to work and teach from the perspective of the "we" while legitimizing some discussion of the "I." This latter perspective, while often difficult to raise in the context of Cambodia and South Africa, offered a different focus and strategies for tackling issues of HIV and AIDS in the communities. Notably, balancing the "I" and the "we" enabled conversations about community responsibility, *and* individual responsibility and accountability.

For many participants, the collective realization that even one person could make a difference and affect the spread of HIV and AIDS was an awakening. As they moved toward the "I," our faculty group moved toward the "we." Somehow, we met in the middle and collectively developed a much more sophisticated dialogue about HIV and AIDS, poverty, and leadership.

Lesson Three: Creating a Resonant Facilitator Group Is Essential and Challenging

In both countries, our expectation that the facilitator group learn to work well together proved more challenging than we had originally predicted. The facilitator groups were a microcosm of the wider society (by design) and therefore came into the Program with longstanding differences, stereotypes of each other, competitive feelings, and other dynamics that needed to be dealt with. Given that the entire Program focused on conscious, emotionally intelligent leadership, we could not simply allow these groups to muddle through and learn the hard way—it would have taken too long, and by the time they realized some level of team effectiveness, they would likely have created dissonance in the Program. So we attended to these groups in productive, resonant ways, not only for their health, but because of their impact on the wider system as a leadership team. We met with them regularly; we surfaced issues; we helped them manage internal team conflict and called on them to find the higher purpose together when conflicts were difficult to resolve.

While we found this challenging (and exhausting), we realized early on that this group was a bellwether for the total group—if they were resonant, so was the larger group. If they were experiencing dissonance, it was something we had to pay attention to, and quickly. And, of course, they held a very important and influential role in the Program—they managed the Emotional Intelligence Practice Groups, where much of the learning was digested and expanded. They also managed the Regional Change Groups, where the learning from the Program was expanded to impact local and national institutions and the wider communities.

As we write this chapter in 2008, the Cambodian facilitators have built strong relationships with one another and in the process have become a significant cross-political party, multi-sector male and female leadership development group in the country. With our help, they have worked through significant intra-group conflict and have bonded in their common love for their country and desire to make a positive difference. They are now running the Program at the regional level. In South Africa the facilitators and participants have been utilizing the concepts and Program elements in numerous arenas in the country. They have partnered together and worked to integrate emotional intelligence into leadership and capacity building initiatives in systems as varied as local governments, major industry, national planning, and regional traditional leadership.

Lesson Four: Eliminate Jargon and Manage Translation

As organization development consultants, we are on guard against using language that is familiar in our field but experienced as jargon by everyone else in the world. This was and continues to be challenging. As in many professions, we are so used to our borrowed phrases and redefined words we don't even notice when we are using them. And yet, this use (or misuse) of language results in confusion, misunderstanding, and even mistrust. When people believe you are either "talking above them" or using language that only people in the "club" understand, they become defensive and tune out. During Program sessions we tried to avoid *all* confusing language, terminology, and jargon. And in cases when we wanted to deliberately introduce new concepts (e.g., emotional intelligence) we deliberately provided significant and rigorous explanations and research. We also consciously led discussions about how the concepts "translated" in the local cultures.

Translations of concepts were just the first step in our learning. We had a fundamental language issue as well: in both countries, it was impossible to conduct all aspects of the Program in English. In Cambodia, it was impossible to conduct *any* of the Program in English, including facilitator meetings, so we had to conduct all Program activities using simultaneous translation.

A team of translators would take turns translating our lectures, instructions, comments, and participant interactions. We realized that the translation process itself can interrupt other forms of communicating—focusing intensely on the spoken word can take attention away from non-verbal behavior, shifts in the group's mood, etc. This, of course, caused us to have to redesign aspects of the Program as we went along—yet another challenge.

We also discovered that delivering Programs in Cambodia took longer than in the other countries partly because of the need to work though translation, and partly because of the difficulties people had understanding the translated theoretical concepts. Teaching through faculty demonstration such as role plays and fishbowl discussions worked well for some of the difficult to translate and/or understand concepts. We found ourselves relying heavily on experiential and process learning versus didactic instruction followed by exercises.

In South Africa, English could be used, but participants did not share a common language (there are eleven official languages in the country). We learned that paying attention to language differences was often a proxy for calling attention to regional and tribal differences that are much more difficult to talk about. We found that we had to deliberately focus on which language was being used, by whom and for what—this gave us clues about what was going on in the group.

Since our trial-by-fire in Cambodia and South Africa, we have continued to conduct emotional intelligence and leadership development programs through translation—and it works. The keys to success are, first and foremost, patience and good humor on all sides. Beyond that stance, it is essential to work closely with the translators. They must become deeply steeped in the concepts and research, and they must exude emotional and social intelligence and resonance themselves. This means that faculty must spend significant time with the translators, teaching, mentoring, and building good relationships. It is worth the effort: they have a tremendous impact on the group's ability to grasp concepts, and they also impact the group's mood.

EMOTIONAL INTELLIGENCE AS PART OF THE GLOBAL SOLUTION

Over four years, more than five hundred leaders in South Africa and Cambodia learned to apply resonant leadership, emotional and social intelligence, and systems dynamics in the service of personal development and large-scale change. The year-long, multi-faceted learning experiences enabled participants and facilitators to assess, change, and develop new and more effective leadership practices and to combat HIV and AIDS and poverty in new and powerful ways.

Despite the magnitude of the leadership challenge of reversing the spread of HIV and AIDS in vulnerable populations, emotional intelligence touched the passion, unleashed inherent inspiration, stimulated core leadership skills, and provided tools for change for the leaders involved. As consultants, emotional and social intelligence carried us through stressful, but stimulating and novel teaching situations and enabled us to find the doors to emotional communications across wide cultural differences.

In Cambodia, participants renamed resonance to be an experience of "open loop, open heart" between leaders and followers. For them, this was a profound reframing of the leader-follower relationship.

In both countries, group structures were used to reinforce and deepen individual learning and to create new neural pathways between leadership and compassion. Beyond the experience of the Program itself, processes were designed that would challenge the participants to take their learning to the broader community. Participants were practicing new leadership behavior while forming and working in multi-sector groups whose task was to engage the larger community in projects to address issues related to HIV and AIDS.

This project was life-transforming for each of us. And, as expressed in Program evaluations, reports, and ongoing personal correspondence, our participants were transformed as well. Together we discovered shared humanity and common desires for health, happiness, and interconnection in each of the countries where we worked. Together, we built bridges from the West to the East, South to North, and watched as warring factions within our participant groups forgave past transgressions and looked toward the future together.

REFERENCES

Boyatzis, R. (1998). *Transforming qualitative information: Thematic analysis and code development.* Thousand Oaks, CA: Sage.

Boyatzis, R., & McKee, A. (2005). *Resonant leadership: Renewing yourself and connecting with others through mindfulness, hope and compassion.* Boston, MA: Harvard Business School Press.

Cherniss, C., & Goleman, D. (2001). EI competencies of outstanding leaders. In C. Cherniss & D. Goleman (Eds.), *Emotional intelligence: A theory of performance in the emotionally intelligent workplace.* San Francisco: Jossey-Bass.

Dotlich, D.J., & Noel, J.L. (1998). *Action learning: How the world's top companies are re-creating their leaders and themselves.* San Francisco: Jossey-Bass.

Fabbri-Destro, M., & Rizzolatti, G. (2008, June). Mirror neurons and mirror systems in monkeys and humans. *Physiology, 23*(3), 171–179.

Goleman, D., Boyatzis, R., & McKee, A. (2002). *Primal leadership: Realizing the power of emotional intelligence.* Boston, MA: Harvard Business School Press.

Kelly, J.R., & Barsade, S. (2001). Groups have moods: Moods and emotions in small groups and work teams [working paper]. Yale School of Management, New Haven, Connecticut.

McKee, A., Boyatzis, R., & Johnston, F. (2008). *Becoming a resonant leader: Develop your emotional intelligence, renew your relationships, sustain your effectiveness.* Boston, MA: Harvard Business School Press.

McKee, A., & Johnston, F. (2006). The impact and opportunity of emotions in organizations. In B.B. Jones & M. Brazzel (Eds.), *The NTL handbook of organizational development and change* (pp. 407–423). San Francisco: Pfeiffer.

McKee, A., & McMillen, C. (1992). Discovering social issues: Organizational development in a multicultural community. *Journal of Applied Behavioral Sciences, 28*(3), 445–460.

Annie McKee, Ph.D., is a founder of the Teleos Leadership Institute, where she advises leaders of some of the largest organizations in the world. A scholar on the cutting edge of leadership, organizational culture, and change, she is dedicated to making good leaders better and world-class corporations even more successful. Annie recently co-authored the book, *Becoming a Resonant Leader: Develop Your Emotional Intelligence, Renew Your Relationships, Sustain Your Effectiveness* with Richard Boyatzis and Frances Johnston. She is also the co-author of *The New York Times* best-seller *Primal Leadership* (with Goleman and Boyatzis), and *Resonant Leadership* with Richard Boyatzis. Annie serves on the faculty of the Graduate School of Education at the University of Pennsylvania and teaches at the Wharton School's Aresty Institute of Executive Education.

Frances Johnston is a founder of Teleos Leadership Institute, where she consults and coaches some of the world's greatest business minds. Widely considered one of the leading experts in a systems approach to transformational change, Fran has worked closely with a wide variety of leaders ranging from former Khmer Rouge generals in Cambodia to CEOs of Fortune 100 companies. She is the author of a number of chapters and articles on leadership, group dynamics, and organizational culture transformation. Fran teaches at Wharton Business School's Aresty Institute of Executive Education and is on the faculty of the Gestalt Institute of Cleveland.

Eddy Mwelwa, Ph.D., is managing director and senior consultant with Teleos Leadership Institute. Eddy has extensive experience consulting in different cultures in private and not-for-profit organizations. He has interest in the interplay between I/WE and how leaders and managers utilize these in organizations for effective communication and influence.

Suzanne Rotondo, MPA, is the executive director of Teleos Leadership Institute. Suzanne's expertise is in strategic planning, executive coaching, and communications, which she uses in the service of creating cultures that unlock potential and allow individuals to thrive. Suzanne worked for a number of years as a business book editor for Harvard Business School Press and was founding publisher of a weekly newspaper in northern California.

CHAPTER 4

When Enhanced EI is Associated with Leadership Derailment

Howard Book

Emotional intelligence (EI) is not a new concept, and its beginnings can be traced back as far as Marcus Aurelius' second-century text, *Meditations*. If we fast-forward to the last half of the 19th century, what we currently view as EI was the mainstream of numerous writings such as Emerson's *Self Reliance* (1841), Thoreau's *Walden* (1854), and Smiles' *Self Help* (1859), all of which continue to sell briskly even today. If we limit our view to books written between 1900 and 1964, we witness the publication of immensely successful books that, without using the term EI, also deal with this concept: Shinn's, the still popular, *The Game of Life and How to Play It* (1925), the groundbreaking, *How to Win Friends and Influence People* (1936) by Dale Carnegie, Norman Vincent Peale's acclaimed, *The Power of Positive Thinking* (1952), Maxwell Maltz's best-seller *Psycho Cybernetics* (1960), and Joseph Murphy's *The Power of Your Subconscious Mind* (1963). These are only a few of the highly popular and widely read books that champion what is currently labeled emotional intelligence in that, thematically, all emphasize how success in life depends on positive self-regard, optimism, impulse control, social responsibility, independence, accountability, sensitivity to the needs of others, and the acknowledgement that our thoughts impact our feelings, and how thoughts and feelings drive our actions.

The last two decades have witnessed a radical shift in our conceptualization and approach to emotional intelligence, and a linking of EI to leadership success. Two factors have driven this change: The first has to do with the scientificization of EI. Over the past twenty-five years or so, social scientists began to study what factors, other than cognitive intelligence (IQ), might be important in order to be successful in life (Mayer, 2001). They were able to identify a number of skills that they re-conceptualized under the term emotional intelligence, and brought a research-oriented, evidence-based approach to behaviorally defining these skills, measuring them, benchmarking them, and enhancing them. With this scientificization came evidence-based findings that demonstrated how specific skills of emotional intelligence are crucial for leadership success (Cherniss, 1995; Cherniss & Goleman, 2001; Luskin, Aberman, & DeLorenzo Jr., 2001; Stone, Parker, & Wood, 2005) and how these skills can be enhanced in those leaders in whom they exist in only moderate strengths. Enhancing these skills leads to an enhanced higher level of functioning in a leadership role.

The second factor responsible for the emergence of EI as pivotal to workplace success was the publication of Daniel Goleman's 1995 groundbreaking book, *Emotional Intelligence.* In this book, Goleman made EI and its relevance in the workplace more accessible to general readers. As a result, business schools and CEOs were exposed to the scientifically backed, evidence-based relevance of EI for success in leadership roles.

This chapter, however, focuses on two obverse—and less recognized—scenarios: those circumstances in which the presence of enhanced EI skills may lead to, or nonetheless be associated with, leadership derailment and subsequent organizational mediocrity. It also offers a methodology to identify these emerging two scenarios before they occur, assess the risk of their occurring, and presents interventions to reduce the risk of leadership derailment.

WHEN STRENGTHS BECOME WEAKNESSES: WHEN TOO MUCH EI CAN DERAIL LEADERS

This scenario focuses on situations in which an enhanced EI skill may become a disability, that is, where the benefits of enhanced emotional intelligence are outweighed by their hidden costs. This chapter will rely on the BarOn EQ-i® instrument and the skills it measures because it is the instrument with which the author is most familiar—using, teaching, and training consultants in its applications.

A brief outline of the BarOn (1997) EQ-i® follows: developed and refined over twenty years ago by Dr. Reuven Bar-On, an American-born Israeli, the EQ-i is a valid and reliable self-reporting questionnaire, consisting of 125 to 133 questions, the answers to which are arranged in a five-point Likert scale. It takes approximately ten to twenty-five minutes to complete online. The BarOn model of emotional intelligence is conceptualized around five components: an intrapersonal component reflecting how one deals with and understands one's self; an interpersonal component speaking to how one understands and deals with others; an adaptive component measuring how one deals with a changing environment; a stress management component linking to how one manages stress; and a mood competency reflecting one's sense of pleasure and optimism.

Each of these five composite scales is made up of two to five skills. There are a total of fifteen basic skills that constitute Emotional Intelligence, as illustrated in Figure 4.1.

Although all fifteen skills are important for success, the skill set or mix of skills differs for different roles. For example, the skill set of a successful leader is different from the skill set of a successful parent. Rather than deal with each of the fifteen skills, I will list those skills that, based on my professional experience of working in this field for over twenty years, as well as anecdotal published reports (Christman, Chua, & Sharma, 1998; Charon & Colvin, 1999; Goffee & Jones, 2000; Kotter, 2001), seem to be a prerequisite for

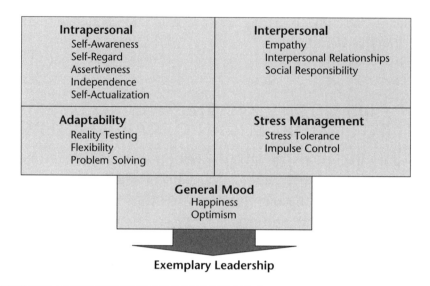

Intrapersonal	Interpersonal
Self-Awareness	Empathy
Self-Regard	Interpersonal Relationships
Assertiveness	Social Responsibility
Independence	
Self-Actualization	
Adaptability	**Stress Management**
Reality Testing	Stress Tolerance
Flexibility	Impulse Control
Problem Solving	

General Mood
Happiness
Optimism

Exemplary Leadership

Figure 4.1. Bar-On Model of Emotional Intelligence

leadership success: impulse control, self-awareness, empathy, assertiveness, flexibility, reality-testing, and optimism. I will go on to deal with two pivotal skills—impulse control and optimism—in detail. The methodology offered can be applied to all other EI skills.

Impulse Control

As defined generally, impulse control is the skill to rein in the pressure to take action or to execute. Specifically, it is the capacity to hold onto, rein in, and not act on angry impulses. Leaders who lack this skill are described as tempestuous, hot-headed, short-tempered, or volatile. Their aggressive behavior intimidates others, undermines relationships, and often turns what were collaborative relationships into adversarial stances.

Although less blatant, but equally destructive, such leaders often leap before they look, act before they think, and consequently suffer from flaws in decision making. They are leaders who have a "Ready, Fire, Aim" mentality. Leaders with impulse control difficulties as evidenced by a low EQ-i score have trouble delaying gratification. They cannot wait and, as a result, offer themselves little time to ponder, reflect, weigh options, or plan. They execute immediately. They are characterized by the seemingly meaningful adage that, "When the going gets tough, the tough get going." However, this can be problematic because, often, the tough get going without knowing where it is they are going or how it is they will get there. As a result, their lack of impulse control puts them at risk for executing arbitrarily and irresponsibly. The impact of poorly thought-out plans has an unsettling affect on those around them, resulting in a domino effect of top-down faulty decision making and a sense of franticness, both of which quickly spread throughout the organization.

On the other hand, leaders with strong impulse control are described as being cool under pressure, unflappable, reliable, bringing a reassuring sense of calm dependability to turbulent situations. Obviously, impulse control is a relevant EI skill for those in leadership positions. Calmness under pressure enhances the ability to make thoughtful decisions in adverse situations and has a calming, reassuring affect on those around them.

Impulse control is thus a primary skill upon which all other cognitive and emotional skills depend. With poor impulse control, decisions are made in a haphazard way, and faulty decision making results in unsuccessful outcomes. Unsuccessful haphazard outcomes trigger anxiety and uncertainty, and both begin to escalate and spread through the organization. The emergence of this widespread anxiety not only interferes with decision making company-wide, but also amplifies previously hidden fault lines in all EI skills, rendering them less effective. As EI skills across the organization become strained, there is a growing risk of leadership failure throughout the organization.

The following two vignettes illustrate impulse control in action. Please note that, although the dynamics illustrated in all vignettes used throughout this chapter are taken from real-world situations, the names, roles, and businesses have been fictionalized for the purposes of confidentiality. The first vignette, with Andrea, a CEO, is a fine example of the importance of impulse control for leadership success. The second vignette, focusing on Neil, a VP of acquisitions, demonstrates a situation in which enhanced impulse control is truly a weakness, because it conceals a significant deficit in the complementary skill of implementation.

When Andrea Phillips, the CEO of eCarental, an online car rental service with a niche market for those who need an automobile for less than twenty-four hours, found out that the company's first quarter earnings were 50 percent less than expected, she immediately thought that Dave Bowlby—the VP of advertising, with whom she had a contentious relationship—was the root of this calamity: "That SOB wants to sink me and the company just as revenge for my disagreeing with him!" she thought.

"He always has been contrary," she continued, "and now his behavior is going to put the whole organization at risk. Well, let him be the fall guy! I'm going to call him in and fire him!"

Andrea then took a few deep breaths, and thought, "Well, maybe I should explore this more, get more info before I fire him. I'll speak to the VP of accounting to see how our competitors are doing. This will also give me an opportunity to cool off. I'm upset, and it's not really right to fire anyone when I'm in this state."

Andrea's ability to rein in her impulse to fire Dave gave her an opportunity to step back, ponder, and wonder about the poor sales. It also gave her a chance to gather more information about the situation. This process of reflecting and of gathering more information garnered some important facts: all rental agencies experienced a 15 percent drop in sales during the first quarter, and there was an accounting transposition that made eCarental's results look worse than they were. In fact, their actual diminished sales were less than the industry average of 15 percent.

Consider what would have occurred had Andrea called in Dave and fired him on the spot. She would have overlooked the real factors and would have fired a committed, although somewhat contrarian, senior executive. In addition, she would have risked being viewed by the senior executive team as a hot-headed, vindictive leader, who loses her cool under pressure. Ultimately, she would be at risk for being seen as a leader who shoots first and asks questions later. This perception might create a culture of fear and opaqueness that could undermine the current spirit of transparency and collaboration, resulting in a less motivated and less effective workforce.

Impulse control is important. However, when a leader has enhanced impulse control, there is a risk that this heightened impulse control may actually cover deficits in a complementary EI skill, as the following vignette illustrates.

> Neil Venture, the senior VP of acquisitions at CondoCorp, had an enhanced score on his impulse control. And indeed, he was viewed as an unflappable senior executive who was cool under pressure, seldom angry, and one who thought before he acted.
>
> However, there were frequent instances when his close associates believed that the due diligence he carried out before implementing an acquisition seemed to take too much time. The result was that a number of potential acquisitions were picked up by other companies who were quicker off the mark. Neil's behavior came to be characterized by his never seeming satisfied with the information he was given, always wanting more statistics or history of current acquisition costs. Over time, his CEO noticed that, since he had been hired, the actual acquisition of condominiums had begun to drop. When confronted with this, Neil's response was usually the same: "We don't have enough information; it's too risky to execute without having all our ducks in a row." As time passed, it became clear that he never had sufficient ducks, and that the row was never straight enough.

With Neil, what seemed like enhanced impulse control came at a great cost. His behavior masked a significant difficulty with executing. Through coaching, Neil was able to recognize that at the root of his difficulties was a powerful but unrecognized fear of making a mistake. Neil was highly risk-aversive, and unless every deal was 100 percent guaranteed to be successful, his irrational fear of impending failure paralyzed his ability to implement the purchase.

Through coaching, he began to recognize that much of his fear was related to his upbringing, where obtaining 95 percent on examinations was met with his parents' response of, "What happened to the other 5 percent?" rather than their genuine pleasure over his ability to achieve such a superb mark. Through coaching, Neil was able to become more comfortable with the idea that not achieving 100 percent did not mean that he was a complete failure.

Optimism

Optimism is the capacity to maintain a realistically positive attitude in adverse situations. Optimistic leaders are described as confident, enthusiastic, and assured and as people who embolden others with a sense of confidence, hope, enthusiasm, creativity, and heightened motivation.

To illustrate, consider the following scenarios:

Arnold Blank is a 32-year-old CEO of a one-year-old, small, start-up online life insurance company. At 7 p.m. Monday he arrives home from the office and greets his wife with a large sigh: "No activity. I don't know what the problem is. I hate when Monday starts this way. Very little going on in the way of sales. And it's only Monday; it just makes me feel that the rest of the week is going to be downhill. I don't know how I can take this. It's not a good sign. I should be getting more hits. I gave hell to the guy who is supposed to be fine-tuning our search engine optimization program, but I'm not sure that program will help either."

Think for a moment of what Arnold's attitude or mood will be like when he arises to face Tuesday. How will his sense of pessimism impact his ability to inspire the senior vice presidents of his firm with whom he will be meeting that day? What effect will his pessimism have on colleagues, and how will it upset those below him who look to and expect a sense of reassurance and security from him?

Pessimism hurts. It demoralizes and demotivates those with whom Arnold comes in contact, and it unrealistically amplifies his own sense of worry.

Let's look at how this may play out with David Downer—a two-year veteran of the online insurance business, who, speaking with his wife, states: "I know the number of hits we've had is going down. I figure it's just a blip and it'll change. And don't tell me I've been saying this for the past six months; I know it. And that kind of talk is only a reflection of your negativity and pessimism. A year ago, we were doing fine; sure, sure, I know that was before the field got flooded with other online guys. And if they're doing better, chalk it up to beginner's luck. We were here first, so we have the edge. And the fact that some think our territory has shrunk doesn't mean a thing to me. It's just negative thinking. I don't want to hear about it! Things will work out."

At first glance, David might seem to be showing enhanced optimism: a persistent positive attitude, strong upbeat tempo, and a tenacious certainty that the situation will improve.

However, what David is doing is seeing the world the way he wants it to be and avoiding the difficult but accurate reality that his business is in a downward spiral. His positive attitude is not rooted in, or confirmed by, evidence. Closely examined, his attitude does not reflect enhanced optimism, but rather a deficiency in his skill of reality-testing, another EQ-i® skill. This is not optimism; it is denial masquerading as optimism. Ultimately, this masquerade will undermine David's capacity for success.

Let's compare both of these situations to Annie Poss, also a CEO of a young online life insurance business, as she speaks to her husband, Ken, about her day:

"It's been another difficult day. It certainly doesn't help to start the week off this way, but we've had very little activity on our website. However, I'm not disillusioned—this is about par for the course with insurance start-ups. In speaking with our three VPs, I think we can differentiate ourselves from the other guys out there and try tweaking our OSE program to highlight our presence. Despite lower activity, I'm feeling OK—it's early, we've got a good business plan, and a specific focus that differentiates us from our competition. I expected the first nine to ten months would be iffy anyway. I haven't seen any unexpected red flags, and I've certainly been looking out for them. I think I am just going to have to tough this out, at least for another six to ten months. We've got a good and a different product, and our needs assessment shows that there is a need for it that no one else is filling. I think we'll get someplace. Numerically, our activity is small, but as a percentage it's up 30 percent over last month. I like the challenge; it tends to motivate me more.

Think a moment about Annie's optimistic attitude: she realistically acknowledges the difficulties she faces, yet remains upbeat. The important difference between her and David is that her positive attitude acknowledges the difficulties—does not turn her away from them—and is based on a realistic assessment of these problems, their underlying causes, the steps she is taking to address them, a definite timeline to do so, and a reality-based backup plan. It is "grounded optimism" compared to David's "blind" optimism, and contrasted to Arnold's pessimism.

However, because optimism *does* pay, we consultants and our clients are at risk of overvaluing levels of enhanced optimism. We may be tempted to think that if a good dose of optimism facilitates success, a great dose of optimism will guarantee it. However, as the vignette about David illustrates, when any EI skill is enhanced beyond a certain level–two standard deviations or 30 points above the mean on the EQ-i®–there is a risk that this enhancement may more accurately reflect a hidden deficiency in another, complementary EI skill. That is, what looks like robust optimism may really signal a hidden weakness in reality testing.

HOW TO IDENTIFY WHETHER STRENGTHS ARE BECOMING WEAKNESSES

In the real world, any time our assessment, be it instrument-driven or clinically informed, shows a significantly enhanced skill, we consultants should also search to see whether its complementary skill is effectively and robustly present. The presence of a complementary skill reduces the risk that the enhanced competency is actually a hidden weakness.

Think about Neil, the VP of condo acquisitions, whose enhanced impulse control really reflected his inability to execute. His high score on impulse control was checked against the complementary skills of problem solving and assertiveness. When this was done, both problem solving and assertiveness were found to be low, pointing to deficits in his ability to implement. Coaching him on these skills, along with exploring the family's basic assumption that if you're not 100 percent certain of success, then you must be 100 percent destined to fail, helped him become better at executing plans.

With David, who was so certain the situation would improve despite objective evidence that his company was in a downward spiral, checking the complementary skill of reality testing revealed it was only modestly present. This finding supported the hypothesis that what appeared to be an enhanced level of optimism more accurately spoke to an inadequacy in his reality-testing.

Table 4.1. Complementary Skills

Enhanced EI Skill Set	Risk/Weakness	Effective Complementary Skill Set
Intrapersonal Skills		
Self-Awareness, Assertiveness, Empathy	"Analysis Paralysis," Aggressiveness, Difficulty Setting Limits	Problem Solving, Empathy, Assertiveness
Adaptability		
Reality Testing, Flexibility	Lack of Creativity, Indecisiveness	Optimism, Assertiveness, Independence
Stress Tolerance		
Impulse Control	Procrastination, Passivity, Risk Aversion, Lack of Spontaneity	Assertiveness, Problem-Solving
Mood		
Optimism	Denial of Problems; Head in the Sand	Reality Testing

Although this chapter has detailed how enhanced levels of impulse control more accurately can reflect concealed deficits in assertively executing, and that enhanced levels of optimism can signal hidden weaknesses in reality testing, all enhanced EI skills may carry with them cloaked deficits in another complementary skill. From an EQ-i® standpoint, Table 4.1 illustrates the complementary skills that must be present to ensure that the enhanced skill is a true strength and not a Trojan weakness, concealing a hidden deficiency in one or more complementary skills.

HOW TO EXPLORE STRENGTHS AS WEAKNESSES

As consultants, when we are faced with an enhanced skill—such as enhanced optimism—we should check to see if a complementary skill is effectively present. We should then also explore with our client whether this strength brings with it a weakness by asking the costs of that skill. That is, when a client scores very high on Optimism, we first explore the presence of this strength by asking for real-world examples: "This instrument says that you have an abundance of optimism. Is this accurate?" If the client agrees, then we should not take this answer at face value, but rather ask for real-world examples, where he or she used optimism with a successful outcome.

Then we might ask, "Tell me about the costs you pay for being optimistic. Give me some examples of when your optimism got you into trouble." If the client is unable to come up with examples, we might offer some ourselves: "Sometimes people who are overly optimistic tend to dismiss or overlook very real warning signs when these do exist. Tell me about a situation like this." Or we might offer the person a hypothetical scenario in which optimism may be useful, but may come with a cost, such as: "How would your optimism show itself in a situation when your last three quarters were poor, and your senior guys are beginning to wonder about the seriousness this may represent? How might you use optimism here?"

We might use their answer to probe more deeply by asking, "What could be the costs that you are going to incur if you took that optimistic perspective?" Or "I realize that I am asking you that question now, but would you bear that question in mind in situations in which there is no one around to explore that with you as I am doing here?"

This approach of checking for the presence of complementary skills on the instrument, asking for real-world examples of when optimism was helpful, and then inquiring about real-world examples of when optimism may have been a hindrance should help determine whether enhanced optimism is a true strength or whether it comes with a significant cost. Although it is prudent to ask the potential costs of any enhanced skill that is relevant to the role, it is particularly important to do so if the complementary skill is sub-optimal or only adequately present.

HOW TO REPAIR WEAKENED STRENGTHS

Enhanced strengths that really reflect an ineffective complementary skill are addressed by enhancing that complementary skill through coaching. This results in a more robust primary skill; in the case of Optimism, leading to what has been called "grounded optimism," which is based on evidence rather than reflecting "blind unrealism."

With Neil, whose enhanced impulse control was really a reflection of a weakness in problem solving and implementation, coaching focused on his underlying fear that unless he could guarantee 100 percent success, then he was 100 percent doomed to failure. In Neil's early coaching sessions, the focus was not so much on the enhanced impulse control, but on the underlying fears of failure that were translated into his procrastinating instead of executing. During this coaching, Neil became aware of how his parents' subtle criticism for any marks less than 100 percent filled him with a faulty assumption that, in his work, anything less than 100 percent guaranteed success was viewed by him as being 100 percent doomed to failure. As he became aware of the faultiness of this assumption, Neil became more comfortable with taking even small risks and, as a result, his propensity to procrastinate, put off, and not execute diminished.

With David, whose optimism was really a reflection of a weakness in his complementary skill of reality-testing, coaching focused on the unsoundness in his reality-testing, specifically his underlying propensity to see the world as he wanted it to be, rather than in the way it really was. In David's early coaching sessions, what became quite quickly evident was his unarticulated assumption that failing was better than giving up. "Going down fighting" or "never abandoning the ship" were unarticulated, unquestioned, and unquestionable beliefs that had their roots in the unspoken rules of the family in which he was raised. That one should move focus, decide that what one was doing wasn't working, or question how one was pursuing one's goals was anathema. Self-questioning was viewed as self-doubt. And self-doubt or self-uncertainty was the worst possible state in David's family. It was much better to be certain and fail, to not give up, but give things "the old college try" rather than change one's direction.

These unspoken, but powerful assumptions had an enormous impact on David's capacity to confront problems directly and recognize that there was always an option of not continuing on that path. As a result of discovering and discussing these assumptions, he was able to see more realistically that there are situations in which one should cut one's losses and move on.

As consultants, when faced with an enhanced skill on the measuring instrument we are using, we should always check to ensure the complementary skill is present and at least adequate, and also explore with the client whether he or she pays a cost for having that enhanced skill. If so, coaching the client around the problem with the complementary skill will diminish this cost.

INFRASTRUCTURE DEFICITS

Like the previous section, this section also explores situations in which a leader with enhanced EI flounders. Although it is tempting to hold this up as another example of where strengths become weaknesses, in this situation, there is a different explanation. The real cause is the absence of requisite organizational structures. That is, in companies where there are no clearly defined, well-communicated structures, such as formal lines of communication to and from the leader, mission, organizational chart, and job descriptions; or where there exists an absence of clarity around reporting, authority and accountability; and where formal objective performance reviews and the criteria on which these reviews are based are lacking, the CEO is at risk of being viewed in a distorted way by his or her direct reports, regardless of how robust his or her EI might be. How does lack of infrastructure result in this faulty perception that the leader's EI is suboptimal?

Without clear, firm, supportive infrastructures, a sense of ambiguity emerges among the leader's direct reports. Situations in which it is unclear who reports to whom, what one's goals are, or how one is being evaluated result in ambiguity, and ambiguity triggers widespread anxiety among the direct reports. When people experience anxiety, a peculiar psychological phenomenon is set in motion: subordinates develop a distorted view of even an emotionally intelligent leader. Simultaneously, they develop a complementary distorted view of themselves and their EI. This phenomenon puts the leader at risk of having his or her behavior misinterpreted and his or her motives misconstrued. This distorting process usually results in one of two scenarios. In this first situation, which social scientists have labeled "the dependency assumption" scenario, the leader is unrealistically viewed as having the answer to all organizational problems, while simultaneously, the direct reports view themselves as helpless and inept (Bion, 1961; Kernberg, 1998).

In the second situation, called "the fight-flight assumption" scenario, even an impeccable and guileless leader is distortedly viewed as vengeful and untrustworthy, while senior executives reporting to him or her experience themselves as persecuted by him or her (Bion, 1961; de Board, 1978; Kernberg, 1998). These two scenarios are illustrated below.

For all of us consultants, when faced with concerns from the organization that the leader seems deficient in particular EI skills, our first task should always be to check and ensure that necessary organizational structures are in place. If our organizational scan shows they are not, we should then try to understand with the CEO why these structures are absent and then facilitate a process by which structures can be put in place. After this has happened, we should evaluate over time whether the view of the leader has changed, and whether the skills that he or she has are now being recognized.

The Dependency Assumption

In this scenario, ambiguities in, or lack of, organizational structure stir up anxieties among direct reports. Under the impact of this anxiety, workers commonly start to turn more and more to their leader, with the misperception that only he or she can solve this ambiguity and cure all their workplace issues. Simultaneously, they begin to behave as if they are helpless in bringing about any solutions. As this spiral continues, they abdicate more and more responsibility for solving any of their work issues to the leader and increasingly come to believe company salvation rests entirely with him or her—while increasingly viewing themselves as inept and helpless.

This is a version of groupthink: a phenomenon wherein a group comes under the sway of faulty decision making because of group pressures—often unspoken—that lead to a deterioration in logical, realistic, and moral judgment (Janis, 1972). Ultimately, this uncritical acceptance of illogical beliefs and decision making spreads among and impacts employees throughout the company. Held by this groupthink, the whole workforce behaves as if their leader is the savior to all their difficulties—regardless of how emotionally intelligent he or she may be or how he or she may value delegation and decision sharing. As a result, passivity takes the place of assertiveness among the workforce, and an accurate view of the leader's role gives way to unrealistic rescue fantasies wherein all difficulties rest on the shoulder of the leader.

Obviously, such a situation results in ineffective organization-wide functioning, as the next vignette shows:

> Rita Stirling, the CEO of NowGreetings, a brick-and-mortar and eline card purveyor, describes her increasing dissatisfaction with her senior executive team: "They're grown-ups! I don't understand why they can't carry out and manage the process we all agreed on. What happens, though, is that they continually turn to me, asking more and more questions, wanting more and more support, and seeking more and more directions. They behave as if they are far more junior than they are. I can't understand why they can't implement these actions themselves, without needing to be reassured by me. I end up feeling that I am simply the target of their reverse delegation!"

> At the same time, one of her VPs, Helen, voiced a quite different perspective and experience of this situation: "It's hard to get a hold of Rita. She doesn't have any formal meetings with us, and there are no channels of communication to let us know what she wants. As a result, I've become somewhat tentative about what I'm doing, and find myself checking with her more than I want to, just to ensure that I am on the right track. This checking erodes my self-confidence, and that makes me seek her out even more and more! It really is an undermining process."

This scenario speaks to a spiraling process that spread throughout the organization: subordinates increasingly turning to their supervisors for solutions that, in fact, they are capable of making; they do so out of a sense of confusion that reflects the lack of infrastructures that facilitates their faulty belief that they cannot do it right.

This process ultimately erodes the subordinates' self-confidence, resulting in their feeling less capable of making decisions on their own, and causing them to turn even more frequently to their supervisors to solve issues that they have the ability and skills to resolve.

The root of this difficulty lies not in the leader's EI skills, or with the subordinates' skills, but rather reflects an organization-wide reaction to the lack of formal two-way communication channels and formal weekly meetings.

The Fight-Flight Assumption

An even more malignant form of groupthink is triggered by the anxiety stirred up by infrastructure absences, when direct reports develop a distorted view of even an impeccable leader with enhanced EI as being instead, duplicitous, deceptive, and vengeful. Under the power of their distorted view, ultimately workers at all levels simultaneously experience themselves as unfairly treated and in danger of the leader's vengefulness. This groupthink is so pervasive that others in the workplace—perhaps those who have been seen as being friendly to the leader—become distortedly viewed as being "on his or her side" and, thus, "one of the enemy." The following vignette demonstrates such an occurrence.

Ron Friendly, the laid-back and friendly CEO of Construct Clothing, a manufacturer of wearables for the construction industry, was a true believer that creating a level playing field with employees motivated them to work better. From his perspective, hierarchical structures and a wide separation between superiors and subordinates undermine creativity and foster rigidity. To ensure a healthy experience of spontaneity and to offset bureaucratization, Ron flattened the organizational chart, implemented self- and peer supervision, and embraced multitask training so that every employee had one major function, but could also fill in and carry out two other roles.

Although this idea seemed very democratic in principle, in practice the loss of clarity inherent in the role ambiguity, diffuse supervision, and lack of formal channels of communication only resulted in confusion. Confusion was reflected in the increasing number of errors and spiraling inefficiencies, all of which were reacted to by mutual finger-pointing and further disorganization. This blaming-process further eroded efficiencies and ultimately played a major role in the collapse of Construct Clothing.

Linda, VP of Sales, noted sadly: "We had a great product, but there was so little communication, I never knew whether products we lined up for sale got produced, let alone delivered. Customers reacted by dumping on us for over-promising and under-delivering. All I heard was how poorly we were doing. Next I found out that a third of our salespeople had been cross-trained to market the product, and the marketing VP thought she was the only one with authority over them. When I discovered that, I became furious with her, told her to stop stealing my staff, and demanded of my staff that they cease having anything to do with her."

Without clarity over who did what, and who was accountable to whom, and with the absence of formalized communication, one division had no information on what was occurring in other divisions on which it depended. Additionally, workers did not know for what and to whom they were responsible. The multi-tasking resulted in managers fighting with each other over which subordinates were accountable for what and to whom. This confusion led to a spiraling sense of anxiety, which triggered angry accusations and irresponsible blaming. At one point, the situation reached such levels that some senior managers began to think that Ron had purposely set this situation up to demoralize and then fire "unfavored" managers so that he could promote certain other "favored" managers.

This lack of collaboration and the suspiciousness that went on between departments, along with the view senior managers had of Ron behaving in a manipulative fashion, resulted in burdensome inefficiencies and, ultimately, to the significant loss of market share of Construct Clothing.

Linda illustrates this lack of collaboration and suspiciousness when she accused the marketing VP of stealing her people, then demanded that her staff have nothing to do with her whatsoever. With these words, she demonstrates the emergence of a strong but distorted view of the marketing vice president as a secretive, devious individual, purposefully out to steal her workers. In fact, this was not an accurate perspective. The marketing VP was neither secretive nor devious. She was simply embroiled in the same confusion and anxiety that emerged from the lack of requisite infrastructure as was Linda herself.

In both these vignettes, the issue is not with the leader's EI; the problem is in the lack of organizational structures that results in confusion and anxiety for his or her subordinates. This confusion sets in motion a regressive pull that clouds how this group of subordinates perceives their leader and themselves. In the first situation the leader—regardless of her EI—is idealized and misviewed as their savior; while in the second, he is scapegoated and misperceived as untrustworthy or even malevolent!

How to Identify When Infrastructure-Absence Undermines the Leader's EI

When there is a question whether the leader has sufficient strengths in EI skills necessary for him or her to function at an exemplary level, our first undertaking as consultants should be to scan for the presence of these requisite organizational structures. Why? Because without these infrastructures, even a leader blessed with extraordinary EI skills is at risk of being experienced as lacking these very skills. The prior section outlined the scenarios of confusion, anxiety, and resultant groupthink.

Scanning for the presence of organizational structures is carried out through the following approach. We should ask for and study the organization's written mission, senior executives' job descriptions and performance reviews, lines of formal authority and accountability, formal meetings for information-giving, the existence of formal lines of communication up and down the organizational chart, formal meetings of executives to discuss concerns and questions they have about their roles, the leader's role, and the direction of the organization. It is also helpful to do a 360-degree evaluation of the leader, carry out a formal EI evaluation of the leader, and carry out a formal or informal evaluation of the organization's culture.

This approach allows us to compare the leader's EI based on an objective assessment tool to how he or she is experienced by senior executives. If the requisite infrastructure is absent, we should expect that the 360-degree evaluation of the leader by his peers is lower than the objective EI evaluation. This paints a picture of a leader with healthy EI skills who is being perceived by those around him as lacking in these skills. If this is so, then through our infrastructure scan we should find many of the necessary infrastructures to be missing. The absence of these infrastructures stirs anxiety, which ultimately puts into motion either a "dependency assumption" or a "fight-flight assumption." Both of these assumptions result in the subordinates developing a distorted view of the leader. This distorted view is a reflection of infrastructure deficits, rather than an accurate view of the leader's EI skills.

However, what makes this situation even more dangerous to the organization is that, under the impact of being misperceived as lacking such skills in EI, a leader is at risk for having these very skills deteriorate. Ironically, this may lead to a situation in which even a competent leader who embraces delegating, under the sway of being turned to time and time again by his staff who may be seeing him as their savior, ultimately may think, "It's just easier doing this myself than being hounded by them." As a result, he or she may give up delegating and increasingly take over responsibilities that are his or her subordinates, paradoxically beginning to fill the distorted role they have about him or her in their minds. Or, a rather open and trustworthy leader, under the barrage of being treated as if he or she is Machiavellian, begins to retreat more and more from interacting with his or her subordinates, reinforcing their distorted view of him or her as being secretive and non-trustworthy (Bion, 1961; de Board, 1978; Kernberg, 1998).

The remedy for this situation is to diagnose why these necessary infrastructures are lacking, what occurs as a result of their lacking, and attempt to help the senior team develop and implement these necessary structures with input from the rest of the organization.

The result should be less confusion, less anxiety, a more accurate view of the leader by those around him or her, and a lessening of cultures of inappropriate dependency or malignant suspicion.

SUMMARY

This chapter, while embracing the concept that emotionally intelligent leaders are better equipped to fulfill their role and better able to develop a highly motivated and high-functioning organization, focuses on those situations in which enhanced EI may lead to, or be associated with, leadership derailment and organizational inefficiencies. I have focused on two situations in which there is a risk of this occurring. In the first, the enhanced EI skill conceals a deficit complementary skill set. For example, a leader who at first appears to be highly flexible may on closer examination be understood more accurately as having a deficit in assertiveness. As a result, what may at first glance appear to be flexibility is really an arbitrariness, an inability to stand his or her ground or take an unpopular stance.

In this situation, when we consultants note enhanced flexibility scores on the EQ-i®, we should seek out the score on the concordance skill of, in this case, assertiveness. If this ranking is low, then what presents as flexibility more authentically speaks to a limitation in assertiveness—a limitation that can be addressed through coaching.

In the second situation, when the leader in fact has adequate EI, but is experienced as having a deficit of EI, the culprit may be the lack of essential organizational structures. Without requisite structures in place, a particular psychological phenomenon emerges: lack of structures leads to ambiguity, which stirs up anxiety in subordinates, and under the sway of this anxiety, the subordinates begin to view the leader in one of two distorted ways. Commonly, they begin to view the leader who actually delegates well and treats his or her subordinates as highly capable as a savior who will rescue them from all their challenges and difficulties, while simultaneously, experiencing themselves as inept. Or, in the second scenario, a leader who is in truth transparent and imminently trustworthy will be viewed as having a hidden agenda and behaving in manipulative ways, while subordinates will experience themselves as unfairly treated and under attack. In both of these scenarios, the difficulty is not with the EI skills of the leader, but rather in the lack of structure, which promotes a distorted view of the leader in the eyes of the subordinates.

In these situations, the issue is not the leader's emotional intelligence, but the lack of organizational structures—an absence that promotes anxiety, confusion, regression, and ultimately a distorted perception of the leader by his or her subordinates. What makes this situation so additionally risky is that, under the impact of such misperceptions, the leader is prone to ultimately behave in the way that he or she is being misperceived. As a rule of thumb, we consultants should ensure the presence of these structures before assessing the EI of leaders. Otherwise, our ability to accurately assess a leader's EI is compromised by the downward spiral fueled by both the followers' misperceptions and the impact that has on the leader's emotional intelligence.

Much literature exists on how high-functioning leaders have strong intrapersonal and interpersonal skill sets and how good leaders become better leaders through enhancement of these skills. This chapter outlined two situations in which leaders with high EI skills may, paradoxically, be nonetheless at risk for derailment. I outlined an approach for identifying and addressing these two situations in order to maintain a positive connection between enhanced emotional intelligence and leadership success.

REFERENCES

Aurelius, M. (1997). *Meditations*. Mineola, NY: Dover Publications.

Bar-On, R. (1997). *BarOn emotional quotient inventory technical manual*. Toronto ON: Multi-Health Systems.

Bion, W.R. (1961). *Experiences in groups*. New York: Basic Books.

Book, H. (2003). How leadership and organizational structure can create a winning corporate culture. In J. Kahn & A. Langlieb (Eds.), *Mental health and productivity in the workplace*. San Francisco CA: Jossey-Bass.

Carnegie, D. (2007). *How to win friends and influence people*. UK: Vermilion, a division of The Random House Group. (Original work published 1936).

Charon, R., & Colvin, G. (1999, June 21). Why CEOs fail. *Fortune*, pp. 68–71.

Cherniss, C. (1995). *The business case for emotional intelligence*. Available: www.eiconsortium.org.

Cherniss, C., & Goleman, D. (2001). The economic value of emotional intelligence competencies and EIC-based HR programs. In *The emotionally intelligent workplace: How to select for, measure, and improve emotional intelligence in individuals, groups, and organizations*. San Francisco, CA: Jossey-Bass.

Christman, J.J., Chua, J.H., & Sharma, P. (1998). Important attributes of successors in family businesses: an exploratory study. *Family Business Review*, *11*(1), 19–34.

de Board, R. (1978). *Psychoanalysis in organizations*. New York: Routledge.

Emerson, R. (1993). *Self-reliance*. Mineola, NY: Dover Publications. (Original work published 1841).

Goffee, R., & Jones, G. (2000, September/October). Why should anyone be led by you? *Harvard Business Review*, *78*, 63–70.

Goleman, D. (1995). *Emotional intelligence: Why it can matter more than IQ*. New York: Bantam.

Janis, I. (1972). *Victims of groupthink*. New York: Houghton Mifflin.

Kernberg, O.F. (1998). *Ideology, conflict, and leadership in groups and organizations*. New Haven, CT: Yale University Press.

Kotter, J.P. (2001). *John P. Kotter on what leaders really do*. New York: Perseus.

Luskin, F., Aberman, R., & DeLorenzo. A., Jr. (2001). *The training of emotional competence in financial services advisors*. Available: www.eiconsortium.org.

Maltz, M. (1989). *Psycho cybernetics*. New York: Pocket Books. (Original work published 1960).

Mayer, J.D. (2001). A field guide to emotional intelligence. In J. Ciarrochi, J.P. Forgass, & J.D. Mayer (Eds.), *Emotional intelligence in everyday life: A scientific enquiry*. Philadelphia, PA: Psychology Press.

Murphy, J. (1988). *The power of your subconscious mind*. Englewood Cliffs, NJ: Reward Books. (Original work published 1963).

Peale, N. (2007). *The power of positive thinking*. Wichita, KS: Fireside. (Original work published 1952).

Shinn, F. (2007). *The game of life and how to play it*. Chicago, IL: BN Publishing. (Original work published 1925).

Smiles, S. (2006). *Self help*. Bel Air, CA: Waking Lion Press. (Original work published 1859).

Stein, S., & Book, H. (2006). *The EQ edge*. Hoboken, NJ: John Wiley & Sons.

Stone, H., Parker, J., & Wood, L. (2005). *Report on the Ontario principals' council leadership study.* Available: www.eiconsortium.org.

Thoreau, J. (2006). *Walden.* New York: Alfred A. Knopf. (Original work published 1854).

Howard Book, M.D., holds the rank of associate professor in the Department of Psychiatry and in the Department of Health Policy, Management, and Evaluation, both with the Faculty of Medicine at the University of Toronto. He is a guest faculty member at the INSEAD School of Management in Fontainebleau, France, where he teaches emotional intelligence to consultants, senior executives, and CEOs worldwide. Dr. Book is also an organizational consultant and psychoanalytic psychiatrist who for the past fifteen years has worked with mid- to large-sized multinational corporations. Dr. Book coauthored *The EQ Edge: Emotional Intelligence and Your Success,* cited by *The Globe and Mail* as the third best business book available in Canada in 2000. Dr. Book is an invited member of both the Boston-based Consortium for Research on Emotional Intelligence in Organizations and the European-based International Clinical Coaching Organization. He is a past board member of the International Society for the Psychoanalytic Study of Organizations.

CHAPTER 5

Advanced EQ-i® Interpretation Techniques

The Concepts of Drag, Balance, and Leverage

Rich Handley

In this chapter I will examine advanced EQ-i® interpretation techniques, specifically the concepts of *Drag*, *Balance*, and *Leverage*. The EQ-i® (BarOn Emotional Quotient Inventory) was written by Dr. Reuven Bar-On, and was published by Multi-Health Systems (MHS) in 1997. It is a widely used self-report assessment and is an excellent tool to provide a snapshot of an individual's emotional and social intelligence.

Many professionals use the EQ-i®, but may not be familiar with some variations in interpretation of results that can significantly improve the effectiveness of feedback and give the client a more coherent understanding of his/her results. This chapter will provide a review of these techniques and explain how they may be applied.

DRAG

Let's begin by examining the concept of *Drag*. In the hands of a skilled practitioner, the EQ-i® can help individuals recognize areas of performance drag currently limiting their top-end potential. Drag comes from the world of aerodynamics and is a force that opposes the forward motion of an object. To locate drag and determine the aerodynamic profile of an object, the object is typically placed in a wind tunnel, where these areas of drag can be profiled and examined so that they might be modified to reduce drag and improve performance and efficiency. This yields a drag coefficient: the lower the number, the more efficient the design and the less *drag* the object has. The focus is generally on the overall *shape* of the object. Typically, the areas that are sticking out too much create the most drag. So, often the designers try to even out the shape to make it smoother to lessen drag. For example, the windshields on today's cars are more at an angle (laid back more) versus the more upright designs of the 1950s to decrease drag.

The quest to reduce drag and thereby boost performance and efficiency is more widespread than you might think. As mentioned, one can see it in the shape and design of cars today versus the cars of the 1950s, and everywhere from the winter Olympic bobsled designs, speed skating suits, and downhill skiing gear to the summer Olympic swimmer's "skins" patterned after shark skins to the exotic bikes and riders' gear used in the time trials of the Tour de France. The key to improving performance is to first locate the areas of drag in an existing design. Following this line of reasoning, drag as applied to the EQ-i® is about the *shape* of the scores as represented by the bar graphs in the EQ-i® Report. The EQ-i® can be viewed as a wind tunnel test of sorts, which helps locate skill set drag that *limits human potential*. The EQ-i® Report produces a profile of an individual's social and emotional skill set in the form of bar graphs depicting scores among fifteen dimensions (subscales) of social and emotional intelligence. Viewed in this manner, areas that are deficient can be seen as areas of skill set drag, which impact performance and efficiency and can be targets for intervention.

One of the clear facts from the laws of aerodynamics is that you can't cheat drag. There is always a price to be paid in terms of performance and efficiency for having a high drag profile. To illustrate this fact, most predators in nature who have to depend on speed to eat have very efficient drag profiles (sharks, killer whales, cheetahs, raptors, etc.) Conversely, elephants and hippos that have very inefficient drag profiles are largely vegetarians. Since their food typically isn't trying to run away from them, they don't have to worry that much about their drag profile. The same applies to the EQ-i®, except most of us want to be like (or think we actually are) cheetahs in terms of our EQ drag profile, when in actuality we more resemble the hippo. We are trying to be efficient—fast so to speak—but are carrying around an EQ drag profile that ensures we won't be.

An illustration to help drive home this point is in order. Runners and elite athletes often purposely try to create drag by running with a small parachute attached to their waists. The purpose is to create resistance (drag) as they run, which increases their stamina and strength. As long as they try to run with this parachute attached, they will never reach the level of performance and efficiency they could have without it. In fact, many of the designs allow the runner to release the chute as he or she is running to get the effect of acceleration, which is dramatic once the parachute (drag) is gone. Think of emotional and social skill set deficits as a parachute behind the individual, creating resistance and holding him or her back. The EQ-i® tells him or her what specifically is creating the drag, in a sense, what is in their parachute, such as poor Impulse Control, or low Self-Regard, and so on. The idea is that, whether an individual chooses to work on his or her skill set deficits or not, there will always be a price to pay for the drag that is created by those skill set deficits because drag can't be cheated. No runner will ever break an Olympic record running with a parachute attached. It's about *wasted human potential.*

No person can ever be as effective as he or she could be, or reach the potential he or she could have, while carrying around a drag parachute comprised of significant social and emotional skill set deficits. Remember: you can't cheat drag. Following this logic, the object of effective functioning on the EQ-i® is to have equally balanced subscale scores (represented by equally distributed subscale bar graphs on the EQ-i® Report), because bar graphs that are all about the same length represent even skill set development and, as the shape suggests, have less drag (because no bar is too high or too low). An optimal profile in terms of drag will have no more than a 10-point range between the highest score and the lowest score. The more tightly ordered all the bar graphs are to the individual's mean, the less drag he or she has in his or her profile. Personally, this author believes that the focus of the EQ-i® should be on obtaining even skill set development (less drag), versus focusing on achieving high scores. In theory, *if* the scores are first evenly distributed, *then* higher scores would indicate advanced functioning. But it could be argued that an individual that had all their scores range from 100 to 107 on all fifteen subscales of the EQ-i® with a total EQ score of 105 (even skill set development with less than a 10-point distribution in range) could be more effective overall than an individual whose scores ranged from 85 to 130 (three standard deviation scatter), even though the latter may have a higher total EQ score of 120.

Let's first look at the high drag profile of a senior executive shown in Figure 5.1. Visually, pay attention to how the patterns of bars are arranged. Imagine if this were an object placed in a wind tunnel, and air was flowing across the tops of all the bars, from the top, Total EQ, down to Happiness.

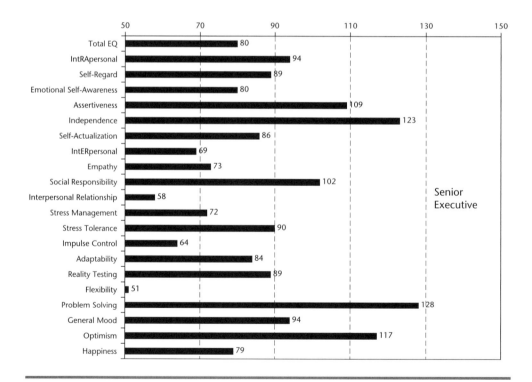

Figure 5.1 High Drag Profile

The flow would be interrupted significantly because of the irregular shape of the bars and would meet particular resistance when hitting the longest bars (because they are sticking up too much). Obviously, if this profile were more tightly ordered around the individual mean (no more than 10 points from the highest to the lowest score), it would be more smooth, hence would create less drag, and would represent more even skill set balance.

There are many things we can take away from viewing this profile. First, notice the range. This individual's scores ranged from a high in Problem Solving of 128 to a low in Flexibility of 51. This represents a 77-point spread between the lowest score and the highest score. This is greater than five standard deviations. This represents significantly uneven skill set development, which behaviorally plays out most everyday in this leader's interactions with others. Next, we mentioned previously that, for optimal performance, the range between the highest score to the lowest score needs to be no greater than 10 points, which indicates even skill set development. In other words, all the bar graphs are tightly ordered around the mean. Another helpful technique to illustrate this concept is to draw a line down their results at their own personal mean, not the mean of the assessment, and compare the distribution of scores to their own personal mean, as illustrated in Figure 5.2.

This technique works well in several situations. First, it makes the illustration as shown here of drag, or uneven skill set development. It can also be helpful with individuals who have lower scores all the way down, such as someone whose mean is 90, and most of whose scores are at that point. This indicates that generally the person is very conservative in how they rated themselves, perhaps seldom giving themselves a "1" or "5" answer on the assessment. You can confirm this by examining the Pie Chart in the Counselor's Section of the EQ-i®. This displays how often the individual chose the 1 through 5 answers. If individuals primarily marked the "2, 3, 4" answers, their scores will move toward the middle range. Thus, to take their mind off their not seeing high numbers in their scores, draw a line down the subscale scores that represents their mean, and help them examine how tightly their scores are ordered along their own mean, and look for areas that are more than 10 points above or below their own mean as representing areas of drag. Ideally, there should be no greater than a 10 point spread between the lowest to the highest subscale score. The same technique works for individuals with all their scores above the mean (high scores).

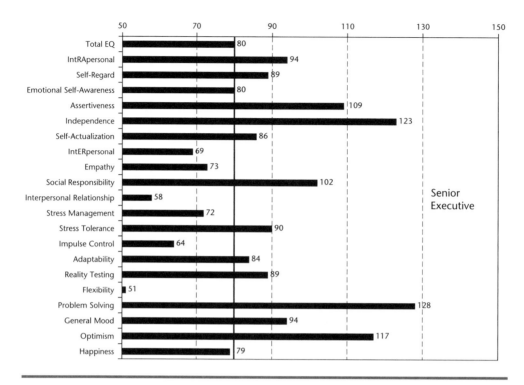

Figure 5.2. High Drag Profile with Personal Mean

Next, let's look at a profile that represents low drag, Figure 5.3. First, notice the shape of the bar graphs. You can clearly see that they are much more tightly ordered along the line drawn to illustrate their mean, which is 110. The lowest subscale scores are Empathy, Social Responsibility, and Interpersonal Relationship, which are all 103. The highest subscale score is Flexibility, which is 111 (the major component score – Adaptability – is 112). The range then is 8 points from the lowest subscale scores (103) to the highest (111). Additionally, it can be seen that this individual predominantly has subscales that fall on the lower side of the individual mean rather than the higher side. So, this individual's drag is minimal, but is slightly skewed on the lower side of the mean to represent slight skill set drag relative to their personal mean in the Interpersonal component area, though it is very slight (7 points beneath their mean). Again, just looking at how the bar graphs are graphically depicted falling along the line drawn clearly illustrates low drag and tight order along the line. When we

Handbook for Developing Emotional and Social Intelligence

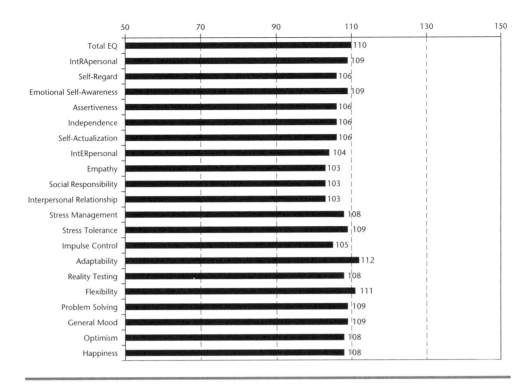

Figure 5.3. Low Drag Profile with Personal Mean

compare it to the previous illustration, Figure 5.2, of high drag, we can see that the differences are stark.

BALANCE

Now that we have discussed the concept of drag, let's examine the concept of *Balance*.

Traditionally, feedback on the EQ-i® is given by discussing an individual's areas of strength and weakness. This can be effective, but it misses the idea that at times the strength can be the weakness. This suggests that a more effective way to view EQ-i® results and to give feedback is to understand the concept of balance. Taking this view, any area that is in the low range (89 and below) or the high range (110 and higher) needs to be evaluated in terms of the subscales that offset or balance them. All of these can be obtained from the subscale correlation chart (Table 6.10) found in the EQ-i® Technical Manual (Bar-On, 2004). Let's illustrate by examining the subscales that offset high scores so as to balance or temper them, using Assertiveness as our example. Let's suppose an individual has an Assertiveness score of 130, which is very high (two standard deviations above the mean). With this score, this individual would typically have no difficulty taking a stand on issues, speaking up, stating his or her case, telling people what he or she thinks, and so on.

But could this be exercised to a fault? Could the person be viewed as being too assertive at times? To gauge this, we can examine the correlations for Assertiveness in the EQ-i® Technical Manual and locate the subscales that are least correlated with Assertiveness, hence would be somewhat opposite of Assertiveness, and could be viewed as acting to restrain or temper high Assertiveness. The subscale that is least correlated with Assertiveness is Impulse Control at .18. Thus, having an equally strong Impulse Control score helps temper being overly Assertive (a driving force) by an equal amount of restraint. Simply put, Impulse Control acts as a restraint to Assertiveness. An assertive person may feel like speaking up and telling someone what he or she really thinks, but with the restraint of good Impulse Control, he or she chooses to temper it a bit. The model that depicts this relationship would be:

Impulse → Consideration (Impulse Control) → Speech/Action (Assertiveness)

Without this balance between Assertiveness and Impulse Control, the person would not have the restraint necessary to temper the Assertiveness and could say and do things that he or she later might regret. For example, if your Assertiveness score is 130 and your Impulse Control score is 85, you'd be lacking restraint. The model that depicts this is: Impulse → Speech/Action (Assertiveness).

The idea is that, whatever the high score is (e.g., Assertiveness = 130), the balancing subscale needs to be of nearly equal strength to balance, temper, or restrain that high score. To gain restraint, this score should be no lower than 10 points beneath the high score. Thus, if Assertiveness is 130, Impulse Control would need to be 120 or higher to be strong enough to balance or temper the high Assertiveness. In our example of Assertiveness = 130 and Impulse Control = 85, we can see that the Impulse Control score is three standard deviations lower than the

Assertiveness score, thus it is far too weak to balance it or restrain it. In this case, this person would have unrestrained Assertiveness, and would typically be a loose cannon.

If you were to examine the subscale correlations of the EQ-i® found in the Technical Manual, you would notice that the next two subscales that are least correlated with Assertiveness and tend to act as a balance to it are Empathy and Social Responsibility. Again, following our previous logic, to adequately restrain high Assertiveness, one needs an adequate degree of Impulse Control. Second, one needs Empathy. Empathy helps one be aware of and consider the other person's feelings and helps keep Assertiveness from being so strong that it hurts the other person. Empathy is a social radar of sorts that reads social and interpersonal situations, helping guide one's actions. Empathy can help guide Assertiveness by helping one gauge the other's current emotional state, read the situation at hand, and determine what degree of Assertiveness might be helpful in the situation without being so much that it harms or hurts the other person. Without an adequate amount of Empathy to restrain and guide high Assertiveness, it is left unchecked and can be high to a fault, hurting others.

The third area that helps offset high Assertiveness from the EQ-i® subscale correlations is Social Responsibility. Good Social Responsibility helps temper high Assertiveness in that good Social Responsibility represents a concern for the interests of others, a desire to act in the best interests of others in a socially responsible way, and to be a good team player. Thus, if an individual is highly Assertive, he or she may feel like telling the team or the group what he or she really thinks, but with the restraint of high Social Responsibility, he or she chooses to temper statements because he or she realizes it might not be in the best interest of others, or the team, or to group cohesiveness to say what is felt without restraint or filtering.

Let's look at a real-world example of an individual, we'll call him Pete, who didn't have this balance to his high degree of Assertiveness. Pete was assessed with the EQ-i® as part of routine leadership development training. Shortly after being assessed, Pete was under senior management scrutiny because of some complaints by his subordinates related to his lack of anger management skills and his perceived overly aggressive behavior toward others. Once Pete learned that he was under management scrutiny because some of his employees had reported his behavior, he began threatening them, which led to his being removed from his position.

Pete's scores with regards to Assertiveness and its balancing subscales were:

Assertiveness 109   Empathy 100
Impulse Control 47   Social Responsibility 107

In this example, this individual's highest subscale score was Assertiveness, which could be considered his most dominant area. True enough, this was the area that behaviorally he was known for. But when we look at the balancing subscales, we see the problem.

Pete's Assertiveness score (109) is overpowering his low Impulse Control (47). In fact, the difference is 62 points, which is greater than four standard deviations. Remember, we said that, to temper a high score, the balancing subscale should be no lower than 10 points from the high score. Thus, with an Assertiveness score of 109, Pete's Impulse Control score would need to be 99 or higher to be strong enough to counter the Assertiveness. Pete not only had no restraint to his Assertiveness, but he also had an explosive temper. If we examine the other two balancing subscales (Empathy 100 and Social Responsibility 107), we can see that they were adequate, but couldn't compensate for the imbalance between the relatively high Assertiveness (109, Pete's most dominant subscale) and the chronically low Impulse Control (47, Pete's weakest subscale). Even though it would be correct to have provided feedback on his EQ-i® results noting his strength in Assertiveness and his weakness in Impulse Control, it is not until we connected the dots by examining the interaction between the strengths and weaknesses (the concept of balance) that we could fully see the problem. The concept of balance is somewhat the concept of the yin and the yang, of propelling and restraining forces. In this case, the propelling force, Assertiveness, is not adequately balanced by the corollary restraining force (Impulse Control).

If we were to use the EQ-i® subscale correlation chart in the EQ-i® Technical Manual to determine the primary subscale that balances a high score for each of the fifteen subscales, we would see that Impulse Control balances six areas, and Empathy balances five areas. Following this logic, it could be said that Impulse Control and Empathy are the most important subscales on the EQ-i® because they are primary balancers of more areas than any others. This very fact leads to the final concept that we want to illustrate, the concept of *Leverage.*

LEVERAGE

Generally, at the end of most EQ-i® feedback sessions, the practitioner should help the client focus on one or two areas that he or she can work on for improvement. Too often, practitioners just tell the person to work on the area that is the lowest. The concept of leverage indicates that the person should work on the subscale that will provide the most leverage in impacting his or her EQ-i® scores, not necessarily the lowest score. For example, an individual, we'll call her Marissa, who took the EQ-i® scored lowest in Stress Tolerance (77), Flexibility (80), Empathy (82), and Impulse Control (85). Her highest scores were in Assertiveness (127), Self-Regard (125), Independence (122), and Reality Testing (121).

Following the traditional feedback method, Marissa might have been told to focus on improving her Stress Tolerance score because it was the lowest (77). The concept of leverage would suggest she should focus on improving the Empathy score (82), even though it's not the lowest, since it provides the greatest leverage in impacting other areas, as shown in Table 5.1. Besides the need to improve Empathy in and of itself, improving Empathy will help balance or restrain the high Self-Regard score (125), the Independence score (122), and the Reality Testing (121) score. Also note that the Impulse Control score (85) is too weak to balance Assertiveness (127). This could be a valuable second leverage point.

Table 5.1 illustrates the *primary* balancers for *high* scores in each of the fifteen subscales of the EQ-i® taken from Table 6.10 in the EQ-i® Technical Manual.

To restate: locate the individual's strengths (typically represented by any subscale score over 110). Next, look at the strength of the balancing subscale (refer to Table 6.10 in the EQ-i® Technical Manual or Table 5.1 in this chapter). The balancing subscale score has to be within 10 points or less of the high score to be strong enough to keep it in check, or balance it. Once all the strengths are plotted with their balancing subscale, the leverage subscale

Table 5.1.   Primary Balancers for High Scores

EQ-i® Subscale	Primary Balancing Subscale
Self-Regard	Empathy
Emotional Self-Awareness	Impulse Control
Assertiveness	Impulse Control
Independence	Empathy
Self-Actualization	Impulse Control
Empathy	Independence
Social Responsibility	Assertiveness
Interpersonal Relationship	Impulse Control
Reality Testing	Empathy
Flexibility	Empathy
Problem Solving	Interpersonal Relationship
Stress Tolerance	Empathy
Impulse Control	Assertiveness
Happiness	Impulse Control
Optimism	Impulse Control

would be the one that occurs the most number of times as being *too weak* to balance the strong score (greater than 10 points lower). Suffice it to say that if either the Impulse Control or the Empathy score is weak, they should be of primary focus because together they are the primary balancers of *high scores* in a total of eleven of fifteen subscales. If the individual doesn't have any scores in the high range (so strong that they can become a weakness if they aren't balanced), then it could be appropriate to just focus on the balancers for the weaker subscales (refer to Table 6.10 in the EQ-i® Technical Manual).

One additional important point that needs to be made is that, when looking at EQ-i® results for balance, begin with checking Self-Actualization first. If one doesn't feel a great sense of meaning, direction, fulfillment, enjoyment, engagement, and purpose in his or her life, it impacts several other areas. Most strongly impacted are Optimism, Happiness, and Self-Regard. This makes sense. If an individual does feel this way, he or she typically isn't that happy or optimistic, and this also impacts his or her Self-Regard. Correlations help you avoid focusing the coaching or intervention on symptoms (low Optimism, Happiness, and Self-Regard), and instead focus on the root cause (low Self-Actualization), which will provide the greatest leverage for change. This is an essential concept of leverage: finding the subscale that leverages or has the most impact for change, instead of focusing on individual subscales that often are symptoms and not the root cause. Self-Actualization is the most important of these to always check first.

One more area that supports this idea is that when looking at the Counselor or Coach Section of the EQ-i®, an elevated Positive Impression score is common. Positive Impression is one of the validity results presented in the Counselor Section. Elevated Positive Impression indicates that the individual marked the positively worded questions that make up the Positive Impression scale in a very positive fashion. It indicates the need to check with the client to determine whether he or she answered with an unusually positive style because of a perceived need to look good or whether there are other reasons for the results. This often alarms practitioners, who often don't know what to do or how they might address this.

To put this result in perspective, first check the Optimism score. If this is also strong, this indicates that the person generally does have a very positive outlook, but, is the person realistic? Next, check the Reality Testing score. If it is strong also, it indicates that the person probably is very Optimistic/positive (hence could have elevated Positive Impression), but is realistic as well. If the person doesn't have a strong Reality Testing score, it does support the idea that he or she has an overly strong Positive Impression, which has colored the results.

CONCLUSION

In conclusion, we have discussed several concepts that can be useful in providing a framework for advanced EQ-i® Interpretation Techniques. First, we discussed the concept of *Drag*. We noted that it is helpful to portray the EQ-i® as a wind tunnel test of sorts, designed to present a snapshot in time of an individual's drag profile. The areas of potential *drag* are those areas that are low, but we next discussed the concept of *Balance*. In the case of balance, we noted that drag can occur from those subscales that aren't balanced properly in the case of high scores. In this case, the strength can be the weakness because it is to a fault, without the proper balance. Finally, we discussed the ultimate quest in helping an individual gain the most total impact to his or her EQ-i® profile is to help him or her locate the areas that will provide the most *Leverage*. As we mentioned, helping individuals target their improvement efforts isn't so simple as just locating the person's lowest score (although in some cases it could be). It is a matter of doing an analysis of the balance of the EQ-i® results, locating the areas of imbalance, and identifying the subscale that overall will balance the most other subscales. This will then give the person the most leverage for change. It is hoped that this information will be helpful to EQ-i® practitioners in providing advanced interpretation techniques so that they provide more helpful feedback so that ultimately the client is impacted more positively for the good.

REFERENCES

Bar-On, R. (1997). BarOn emotional quotient inventory (EQ-i®). Toronto, Ontario: Multi-Health Systems, Inc.

Bar-On, R. (2004). *BarOn emotional quotient inventory (EQ-i®) technical manual.* Toronto, Ontario: Multi-Health Systems, Inc.

Dr. Rich Handley is president/founder of EQ University (www.equniversity.com). He is a pioneer in bringing emotional intelligence to the workplace and in corporate applications of emotional intelligence. He has worked with Fortune 500 firms in areas such as employee selection, organization and leadership development, employee development, and sales training. Rich coauthored the book *Optimizing People,* the EQ360® Assessment, the EQ Interview, a book chapter on emotional intelligence, and fifteen web courses on EQ University with Dr. Reuven BarOn, the author of the BarOn EQ-i®. Rich also co-authored the Behavioral Health Survey and was senior consultant for the Benchmark for Organizational Emotional Intelligence. His work has been featured in *Fast Company* Magazine, *Harvard Business Update, Training, HRMagazine, CFO* magazine, *Selling Power, Working Woman,* the *Dallas Morning News,* MSN, ABC, and Fox News. Dr. Handley is also an instructor in leadership and emotional intelligence with the University of Texas Professional Development Center.

CHAPTER 6

Emotional Intelligence, Stress, and Catastrophic Leadership Failure™

Henry L. Thompson

Why do smart leaders with proven track records sometimes suddenly begin making really bad decisions—or no decisions? Numerous well-known public examples, such as Enron, WorldCom, Tyco, FannieMae®, FreddieMac®, AIG®, and Hurricane Katrina, illustrate poor leadership decisions, and thousands of lesser-known examples happen every day. CEOs are being replaced at a record high rate of 7.6 per business day in the United States. Over 28 percent of these CEOs were in position less than three years, and 13 percent less than one year (Challenger, Gray, & Christmas, 2005). Research (Thompson, 2005) shows that stress and its impact on cognitive and emotional abilities may provide at least a partial explanation of what I call *Catastrophic Leadership Failure™* (CLF).

Cognitive intelligence (IQ) and emotional intelligence (EI) abilities are required for successful leader performance—at all levels. My experience and research on leadership, stress, IQ, and EI over the last twenty-five years indicate that when a leader's stress level is sufficiently elevated—whether on the front line of a manufacturing process, in the emergency room, the boardroom, or on the battlefield—his or her ability to fully and effectively use IQ and EI in *tandem* to make timely and effective decisions is significantly impaired. This impairment often leads to catastrophic results.

A war for talent is underway. Hiring, developing, and retaining talented leaders with high IQ and EI are the three major battles of the war. The war will be won or lost by leaders who are able to control stress at the leader, team, and organizational levels. In this chapter I will show that EI does not *manage* stress. Stress negates talent, IQ, and EI.

Practitioners will learn the systemic relationship of the three key factors for bolstering resistance to CLF: Stress Management Capacity (SMC), Cognitive Resilience (CR), and Stress Resilient EI™ (SREI™). Practitioners will also learn the seven best practices for building capacity in these areas: Awareness, Rest, Support, Exercise, Nutrition, Attitude and Learning (ARSENAL™). When resistance to CLF is enhanced using the best practices described in this chapter, not only is there a decreased probability of experiencing a CLF, but there tends to be an increase in a leader's access to his or her cognitive and emotional ability, increased job performance, improved health, and more effective interpersonal relationships and a lowering of stress.

To adequately explore a concept as complex and important as CLF requires a common starting point and framework. This chapter creates a trajectory that will piece together a mosaic leading to a plausible understanding of why and how a CLF occurs and a reasonable set of best practice interventions that reduce a leader's probability of experiencing a CLF. This journey begins with an exploration of stress and its correlates, followed by an overview of the cognitive ability and emotional intelligence landscapes, their intersection with each other, and best practices.

THE STRESS OF LEADING

Some leaders describe life on the leadership landscape as being similar to living every day in a blender, waiting for someone to push the *puree* button.

Leadership is stressful and all leaders do not seem to have the same ability to make effective decisions under high levels of stress. From the 17th century until the middle of the 1900s, stress was defined as what happened when you put a load on a bridge (Lazarus, 1999). Then, Hans Selye (1978) redefined stress, and in so doing, created what some have called the "20th century disease."

Selye defined stress as *the body's non-specific response to any demand made on it*—whether you win a million dollars or lose a million dollars, you will experience stress. The appropriateness of how you react to stress influences your success and health.

It has been estimated that stress in the workplace costs industry in the United States over $300 billion a year (Tangri, 2003). It is the key factor in absenteeism, lost productivity, accidents, and medical insurance, a cause of 75 to 85 percent of all industrial accidents, and is linked to the six leading causes of death in the United States. Similar effects have been reported in Canada and the United Kingdom. Stress is costly.

The appropriateness of the action a leader takes in response to a stressor will have an impact on his or her health. Leaders are continually being bombarded by stimuli requiring them to perceive, appraise, become motivated, and take appropriate action to handle difficult situations.

When a leader encounters a stressor, a cascade of neurotransmitters and hormones (including catecholamines—epinephrine, norepinephrine, dopamine—and the stress hormones cortisol and glucocorticords) are released into his or her system, resulting in an initial increase in the ability to concentrate, strength and a decrease in reaction time. In the short term, these changes may be helpful in effectively responding to the stressful event.

If the stress level becomes too elevated, or chronic, deleterious effects follow. The initial release of neurotransmitters and hormones also results in additional physiological responses. For example, heart rate and blood pressure increase; more blood sugar is released into the blood for additional energy; blood concentrates in the major muscle groups to provide additional oxygen and energy; capillaries in the skin constrict; coagulation factors are released into the blood to reduce bleeding from injuries. Pupils dilate, perspiration increases, saliva is reduced, and digestion is inhibited, as well as many other changes.

If stress is prolonged or initiated on a regular basis, these physiological responses can result in negative health consequences. For example, the increase in cortisol leads to fat deposits on the abdomen, insulin resistance, fat cravings, and increased appetite. Cortisol can reduce the body's ability to heal itself by causing immune system dysfunction and insomnia (the body needs rest, especially sleep, to heal itself).

Most leaders are aware that, when they encounter a stressor, there is an immediate jump in their stress level. What they do not realize is that if nothing else stressful happens the rest of the day, it may take three to five hours to reach their original excitation (stress) level before the stressor was experienced. The probability of a leader going the rest of the day without another stressor is almost zero.

When the leader encounters the next stressor, the new stress is added to the residual on the current decay gradient (Figure 6.1). Psychologically, the total level of stress the leader is now experiencing tends to be attributed to that last stressor (Thompson & Richardson, 1983; Zillman, 1978). Each time the leader encounters an additional stressor, his or her total stress level climbs higher. If the leader's stress level is not abated, that leader will eventually cross the "crazy threshold" and his or her "evil twin Skippy" will emerge.

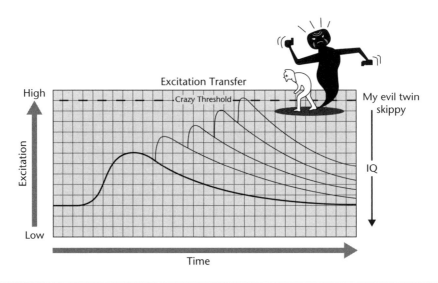

Figure 6.1.   The Excitation Transfer Model

©1988 Henry L. Thompson, Ph.D. Reproduced with permission.

As a leader's stress level increases, he or she not only incurs a significant change in blood chemistry, but also experiences a significant performance degradation of the prefrontal cortex (PFC), the part of the brain that controls decision making, logic, and reasoning, among other cognitive functions. As stress increases, or continues at an elevated level, behavioral changes such as risk taking, slow decision making, nervousness, apathy, aggressiveness, one-track thinking, impulsive behavior, forgetfulness, negativism, and so on will begin to impair cognitive performance.

Stress arouses the reticular activating system and parts of the PFC, resulting in motivation, attention, and other factors required to perform successfully. Yerkes and Dodson (1908) found a relationship between stress levels and cognitive performance (Figure 6.2). If a leader's stress level pushes him or her beyond the optimal performance level, cognitive performance will decrease. In a sense, as the leader's stress increases beyond the optimal level, his or her IQ goes down. Stress level up, IQ down because the leader cannot adequately access the functions of the PFC. Stress is actually turning the PFC "off." Cognitive performance degradation experienced by leaders under high levels of stress emanates from the same process that causes performance degradation resulting from test anxiety in students and performance anxiety in athletes—the PFC is shutting down. Amy Arnsten (1998) refers to this inability to perform well under stress as "the biology of being frazzled."

I found a similar "frazzled" response during research on performance degradation as a result of sleep deprivation. Leaders were kept awake for

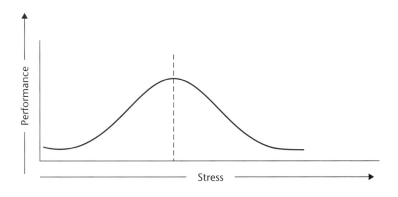

Figure 6.2. The Optimal Performance Curve

©2008 Henry L. Thompson, Ph.D. Reproduced with permission.

long periods of time (days) while a series of cognitive and emotional evaluations were made of them every four hours (Thompson, 1983). One finding was that after twenty-four hours of sleep deprivation, leaders showed a decline of 25 percent in their ability to perform simple cognitive tasks like adding and subtracting numbers. There was a significant amount of change in cognitive ability after being awake for twenty-four hours—and it continued to decline over the next two days.

Perhaps the more alarming finding was that the leaders were not aware of any performance drop. When asked, "How do you think your performance is now compared to yesterday when you started?" they all said, "I did just as well this time as I did yesterday." No one recognized that his cognitive ability had dropped. And it continued to decline each day. By day three, everyone was aware that his performance had declined dramatically. The participants' moods also declined (became more negative) across time, and this was related to perceived leader and team member effectiveness.

Stress is dynamic. Within a twenty-four-hour period, stress shows a sigmoid curve of ups and downs. Additionally, leaders are experiencing stress in their personal lives, which impacts their stress level at work—stress is cumulative! Good stress-coping techniques for both personal and work stress are necessary to keep stress under control.

THE COGNITIVE INTELLIGENCE LANDSCAPE

Cognitive intelligence as used in this chapter refers to IQ. Recent and extensive research that IQ directly impacts leader performance has been firmly established in the leadership performance literature (Schmidt, 2002; Schmidt & Hunter, 1998). There is, however, some debate about the contribution and role of IQ to leader success. Zagorsky (2007) reports finding no relationship between IQ and wealth, although those with higher IQ do tend to be paid higher salaries than people with lower IQs. Lynn and Vanhanen (2002) found that the mean IQ of 185 nations strongly correlated with the macroeconomic performance of the nations and explained half the variance in gross domestic product per capita.

Schmidt and Hunter (1998) reviewed eighty-five years of leadership research and found that general mental ability (IQ) was a strong predictor of leadership success (r = .51) and concluded that IQ should be the primary personnel measure for hiring decisions, using the other eighteen measures evaluated as supplements to IQ. They found this to be even more valid for complex jobs, such as higher-level leader roles.

My research and observations of the relationship of IQ to leader performance over the last twenty-five years lead me to believe that IQ tends to be predictive of learning ability and speed of information processing, which contribute to leadership performance, particularly at the higher leader role levels. For example, I found a steady increase in the average leader IQ from the front-line leader (mean = 105) to the CEO (mean = 125), especially in larger organizations (Thompson, 2007a).

IQ appears to be the price of admission for executive level leadership positions. It is very difficult to rise to the top of the corporate ladder without an IQ in the 125 range. The higher rungs on the corporate ladder are just too far apart to reach without sufficient IQ. Thus, IQ "levels" the cognitive landscape, with high IQ being the new average at the upper levels of leadership.

There is a direct link between a leader's IQ and the functioning of his or her PFC. Goldberg (2001) describes the PFC as the CEO of the brain where executive decisions are made and emotions are controlled. PFC processing/control characteristics include the following: voluntary control, conscious intent, emotional control, rational thought, understanding, thinking, and decision making. The PFC is controlling IQ.

Full access to and use of IQ is a dynamic process and varies across time scales as short as nanoseconds. For example, a leader would not want to take an IQ test, give an important presentation, or make a complex decision under high stress or without adequate rest. Not getting enough sleep, or other forms of stress, results in PFC performance degradation, which then lowers access to one's full IQ ability. IQ is a dynamic ability that is constantly vacillating based on the PFC performance.

THE EMOTIONAL AND SOCIAL INTELLIGENCE LANDSCAPE

What follows is a brief introduction to the field of emotional intelligence (EI). It is a young field with the usual controversies of a new theory (see Murphy, 2006), for example, lack of a standard definition of EI. For the purpose of this paper EI is defined as:

> A person's innate ability to perceive and manage his/her own emotions in a manner that results in successful interactions with the environment and, if others are present, to also perceive and manage their emotions in a manner that results in successful interpersonal interactions. (Thompson, 2006, p. 14)

My experience in studying human abilities, physical or mental, shows that very few people are operating at their full ability level all of the time. As shown above, IQ is dynamic. So is EI!

The most "common" view of emotional intelligence can be described as a two-by-two model (Table 6.1) of *Awareness* (self and others) and *Management* (self and others). The four quadrants of the model contain *Self-Awareness*, *Other-Awareness*, *Self-Management*, and *Relationship-Management* (Other-Management).

A more sophisticated approach to modeling EI than the two-by-two model involves a nonlinear dynamical systems appraisal-based model (Figure 6.3). In this model, a *stimulus* is *Perceived*, and an *Appraisal* of the stimulus is made using both *cognitive* and *emotional* information and processes that result in a *Motivational Complex* which moves the leader to initiate an *Action Pattern*. All sub-processes are part of a nonlinear dynamical system, and, therefore, are recursive. That is, each component feeds back on the others, creating a dynamic, constantly changing system. Many of the processes, decisions, et cetera, in the model are outside of the individual's consciousness, making it more difficult to intentionally determine the "correct" Action Pattern (Gillett, 1987).

Table 6.1. A Two-by-Two Emotional Intelligence Model

	Self	Others
Awareness	Self-Awareness	Other-Awareness
Management	Self-Management	Relationship Management

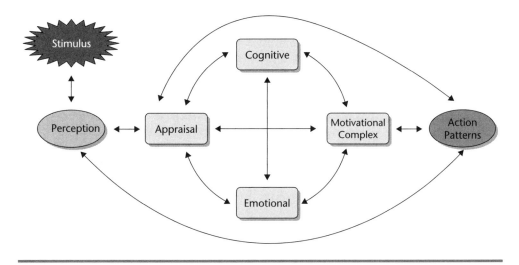

Figure 6.3. The Perception-Appraisal-Motivation-Action Model of Behavior™

©2005 Henry L. Thompson, Ph.D. Reproduced with permission.

When I see you, I see a multifaceted, dynamic stimulus. Typically, one type of information I'm trying to Appraise is emotional cues from your face. As I begin to Appraise "you," you're constantly changing, which changes what I Perceive, which changes my Motivational Complex, and that changes my behavior (Action Pattern) toward you. If Paul Ekman (2003) is correct and what I Perceive is a stream of micro-emotions lasting a half-second or less, then I must make many rapid Appraisals of what's going on and be constantly adjusting my Motivational Complex and Action Pattern toward you. It's like driving a car in heavy rush-hour traffic where you are constantly adjusting to all the vehicles around you as they adjust to you.

Perceiving a stimulus and making an Appraisal (using a blend of cognitive and an emotional components) in the model in Figure 6.3 is similar to Awareness in the two-by-two model mentioned previously. Cognitive and emotional components of the Appraisal process, when grouped with the Motivational Complex, are similar to the Self-Managing quadrant. If I am aware of my emotions and your emotions, then I can begin to manage myself by using cognitive and emotional processes to manage my Motivational Complex. Action Patterns are similar to Relationship-Management, that is, managing both your actions and mine as we interact.

The time from Perception to Action can be so fast that one executes an Action Pattern before one is conscious of why. For example, you are walking along a sidewalk and a car backfires nearby. You duck before you realize it was just a car. Many of our emotions and follow-on actions are designed for survival and take place so fast that we act before we are conscious of the Motivational Complex. The Motivational Complex and Action Pattern can happen automatically and before the PFC has finished processing the information!

To be considered emotionally intelligent, one's behavior (Action Pattern) must be "emotionally intelligent." On the inside, I might Perceive my emotions, the other person's emotions, know how to use that information, but yet initiate an Action Pattern that is not emotionally intelligent. The Perception-Appraisal-Motivation-Action Model of Behavior™ helps explain how an accurate Appraisal can become derailed and lead to inappropriate cognitive and/or emotional behaviors.

EI-STRESS EFFECT™

When a stimulus is Perceived, the brain's thalamus acts like an air traffic controller, sending information to various parts of the brain, particularly "up" to the PFC and "down" to the amygdala, part of the emotion center of the brain (see Figure 6.4). If we have the right blend of thinking and control from the PFC with the right amount of emotion from the amygdala, an appropriate Motivational Complex forms, moving the person to execute an appropriate Action Pattern to respond successfully to a particular event (stimulus). If the process is working "correctly," then one is said to have acted intelligently, both emotionally and cognitively.

Research (Damasio, 1994, 2000; Goldberg, 2001, 2005; LeDoux, 1996, 2002) has shown that the PFC is relatively slow in making decisions (100 milliseconds) compared to the amygdala (15 milliseconds). The amygdala tends to respond so quickly to information that in some cases it overrides the PFC. When the thalamus sends information directly to the amygdala, and little input is allowed from the PFC, the amygdala produces uncontrolled, automatic responses. These responses are based on prior experience (historical data) with the pattern recognition analogues of the stimulus stored by the

Handbook for Developing Emotional and Social Intelligence

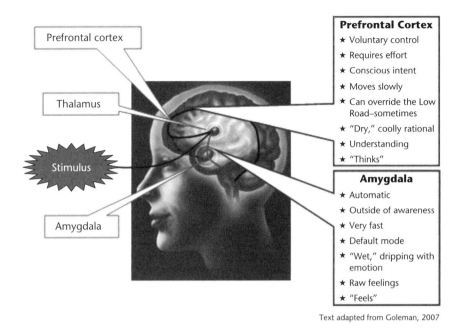

Prefontal Cortex
★ Voluntary control
★ Requires effort
★ Conscious intent
★ Moves slowly
★ Can override the Low Road–sometimes
★ "Dry," coolly rational
★ Understanding
★ "Thinks"

Amygdala
★ Automatic
★ Outside of awareness
★ Very fast
★ Default mode
★ "Wet," dripping with emotion
★ Raw feelings
★ "Feels"

Prefrontal cortex

Thalamus

Stimulus

Amygdala

Text adapted from Goleman, 2007

Figure 6.4. Thalamus, PFC, and Amygdala Functions

©2005 Henry L. Thompson, Ph.D. Reproduced with permission.

amygdala, and tend to be instinctual with raw feelings, very fast and automatic. Inappropriate words may come out of people's mouths before they realize what they are saying—and might not know what they have said after they have said it. This emotional (amygdala) hijacking (Goleman, 1995) is sometimes known as "foot-in-the-mouth disease."

Too much stress not only "turns off" the PFC, but also "turns on" the amygdala. This turning "off" and "on" action exacerbates the effect of the amygdala, creating an oversensitive, heightened emotional state. The person becomes very emotional—don't hear intelligent. Just the opposite in most cases. When leaders interact using the right blend of high road (PFC) and low road (amygdala), they respond appropriately. If the high road is blocked, then everything takes the low road and the interaction may become overly emotional and unintelligent.

In a study looking at the *Rooster Effect* (Thompson & Richardson, 1983), two men and a woman (all allegedly strangers) met together briefly; then the woman (a confederate) chose one of the men (another confederate) over the other man (the real participant) to form a two-person team to compete against the real research participant. They were notified that the losing team for each round of the competition would receive an electrical shock administered to their wrists by the winning team. Having the woman choose the other man created a significant level of stress in the research participant (non-selectee). All variables measured, including the electrical shock levels delivered to the two-person confederate team by the research participant, and the interaction that followed were significantly impacted by the induced stress and resulted in aggressive and emotionally unintelligent behavior on the part of the research participant.

A similar change in emotions and aggressive behavior was found with participants listening to a baby crying (Thompson, 1981). Stress level was manipulated by varying the decibel level of the crying. The higher the stress, the less emotionally intelligent the participants behaved. Successful interpersonal interactions require a certain amount of conscious intention using both the PFC and the amygdala to create a blended response. When something interferes with the functioning of the PFC, the probability of making an inappropriate interpersonal decision, and subsequent behavior, increases.

Over a number of years, I have studied the impact of stress on people taking self-report instruments (Thompson, 2002, 2003, 2006, 2007b, 2008; Thompson & Walsh, 2000). I'm going to limit the discussion here to the EQ-i® (an EI self-report instrument) and the MSCEIT® (an EI abilities test). How do responses to these EI instruments change under stress? To explore this question with the EQ-i®, I had sixty-two participants complete the EQ-i® under normal and simulated "stressed out" mindset conditions. The "normal" Total EQ-i® (TEI) score averaged 101. (The EQ-i® has a mean of 100 and a standard deviation of 15.) The "stressed out" mindset had a TEI average score of 80—more than a standard deviation lower than the "normal" average. Figure 6.5 shows that all fifteen EQ-i® subscales experienced significant degradation under the "stressed out" condition (Thompson, 2005). The results of this study support the data presented above that suggest that stress may reduce the leader's access to his or her full EI ability.

It could be argued that the EQ-i® is a self-report instrument and, as such, is sensitive to moods. A second study was conducted using the

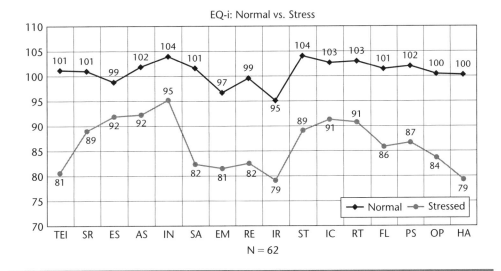

Figure 6.5. EQ-i® Normal vs. Stressed Scores

© 2005 Henry L. Thompson, Ph.D. Reproduced with permission.

MSCEIT®, an EI abilities *test*. In this case, it would be reasonable to assume that if the participants know the answers in the non-stressed mindset, they should know them in the stressed mindset. To explore this question, I had sixty-five participants complete the MSCEIT® under both normal and simulated "stressed out" mindset conditions. The "normal" MSCEIT® Total (Total) score averaged 97. (The MSCEIT® has a mean of 100 and a standard deviation of 15.) The "stressed out" mindset had an average Total score of 84—almost a standard deviation lower than the "normal" average. Figure 6.6 shows that the four Branch and eight Task scales all experienced degradation under the "stressed" mindset (Thompson, 2008).

What is interesting in this study compared to the EQ-i® study is that Branch and Task scales show a differential response to stress, that is, some Branches (Management) and Tasks (SMA, EMA, SEN, BLE and USE) dropped significantly, while others seemed to be more resistant to the stressed out condition. Overall, this study also supports the EI-Stress Effect™.

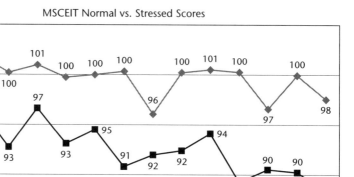

Figure 6.6. MSCEIT® Normal vs. Stressed Scores

©2008 Henry L. Thompson, Ph.D. Reproduced with permission.

EI AND LEADERSHIP

What does EI have to do with leadership? There are a number of studies that suggest a relationship between emotional intelligence and leader performance. My own experience working with supervisors, managers, executives, and CEOs in a variety of different types of organizations leads me to believe there is a relationship between leader effectiveness and certain components of EI.

Dries and Pepermans (2007) conducted a study of 102 managers and found that high-potential managers had higher EQ-i® scores than "regular" managers. This was especially true for the EQ-i® sub-scales of Assertiveness, Independence, Optimism, Flexibility, and Social Responsibility. The authors suggest that these five sub-scales might be "covert" high-potential criteria.

In a study of seventy-six CEOs, Stein (2002) found that CEOs had higher EQ-i® scores on Independence (105), Assertiveness (109), Optimism (112), Self-Regard (107), and Self-Actualization (108) than the average person (100). A regression analysis revealed that Empathy, Self-Regard, and Assertiveness predicted the CEOs with the best financial performance.

CATASTROPHIC LEADERSHIP FAILURE

Serving in a leadership capacity can be very stressful—especially as one climbs higher in the organization. Organizational stress appears to be increasing, which increases stress on leaders. An important aspect of a leader's job is to manage his or her stress, workplace stress, and the stress of direct reports. A leader's failure to adequately manage stress can have severe negative consequences on the leader, the organization, and its members.

As discussed above, as a leader's stress level increases, not only does his or her IQ decrease, but so does EI. Catastrophic Leadership Failure occurs when a leader's stress level rises to the point at which there is a sudden, dramatic loss in his or her ability to access and use the executive functions of the PFC (cognitive decision-making abilities, including IQ) combined with a heightened, uncontrollable emotional state in the amygdala. With the PFC turned "off" and the amygdala turned "on," a leader becomes incapable of making well-thought-out, "IQ-EQ-blended," or cognitive-emotional decisions that are appropriate for the situation. The result is a sudden, *catastrophic* drop in leader performance.

All leaders are human and make occasional "bad" decisions that they later change or wish they could change. Making a poor decision because of faulty information, lack of experience, or the Peter Principle (Peter, 1969) is not necessarily CLF.

When a CLF occurs, it is sudden and causes a catastrophic change in the leader's ability to perform successfully. The leader will exhibit some or all of a characteristic set of behaviors, such as becoming mentally paralyzed and unable to make appropriate decisions. In a scene from the movie *Pirates of the Caribbean 3*, a leader (commander) needs to make a critical and immediate decision. He stands there, staring blankly ahead, experiencing a CLF while his people are asking, "What do we do? Make a decision! What do you want us to do?" He just continues to stand there. Cognitively and emotionally, he is temporarily paralyzed and unable to function as a leader. He is in the hold of a CLF.

Sometimes, CLF results in selfish decisions that meet short-term needs. The leader takes care of him- or herself. The chief financial officer says, "We can set up several shell companies in Bermuda and flow a few million dollars into them, make millions of dollars, and not pay tax." During CLF, this might sound like a good idea because the PFC has been significantly degraded and IQ and EI have dropped dramatically. The following list shows examples of CLF symptoms.

CLF Decision-Making Characteristics

Not listening	Over-analyzing
Stops making decisions	Makes "low-quality" decisions
Makes "emotional" decisions	"Flip-flops"
Very short-term decisions/focus	Reactive decisions
Defensive	Rationalizing
Self-satisficing	Hedonistic
Denial	Attentional blindness
Fear-based decisions	Anger-facilitated decisions
Automatic decision making	

Reexamining Stein's (2002) CEO study in light of Thompson's (2005) "stressed" study reveals an interesting possibility. If Stein's CEOs encountered a high stress situation and the assumption is made that their EQ-i® scores, and presumably their EI, would show a degradation similar to what the average participant in the Thompson study experienced, the CEOs' scores would fall into a range that would predict a high probability of CLF.

The evidence above suggests that a high stress environment would be expected to restrict leaders' access to their full EI (and IQ) potential. A reasonable prediction based on current research would be that the lower the leader's starting EI, the faster he or she will fail under high stress. A corollary is that the lower the leader's starting EI, the less stress it will take to produce a CLF. There are mathematical models that allow for examining nonlinear, multivariable scenarios, such as CLF. One such model is Thom's (1975) catastrophe model. (See Thompson, 2005, for an explanation of how catastrophe theory explains CLF.)

BEST PRACTICES FOR AVOIDING CATASTROPHIC LEADERSHIP FAILURE™

This section focuses on best practices for avoiding catastrophic leadership failure™, which include building capacity in the three key interdependent CLF factors: Stress Management Capacity™ (SMC), Cognitive Resiliency™

(CR), and Stress Resilient EI™ (SREI™). These factors and their justification as key to CLF have been discussed in detail above. CLF is not a single event or instant, but is a system of interdependent components operating within a larger system. The CLF factors should be addressed across at least three layers of system complexity: leader, team, and organization.

Figure 6.7 shows the systemic relationship of CLF, its three key factors, and the seven best practices for building capacity in these areas. When used together, the ARSENAL™ best practices increase Stress Management Capacity, Cognitive Resiliency, and Stress Resilient EI™. When the three CLF factors are enhanced, not only does the probability of experiencing a CLF decrease, but there also tends to be an increase in cognitive and emotional ability and improvements in job performance, health, and interpersonal relationships and a lowering of stress.

General techniques for building the three key CLF factors include the following:

- Assess employees', leaders', teams', and organizations' stress capacity, EI, and cognitive ability.
- Provide education on stress, EI, and cognitive ability.

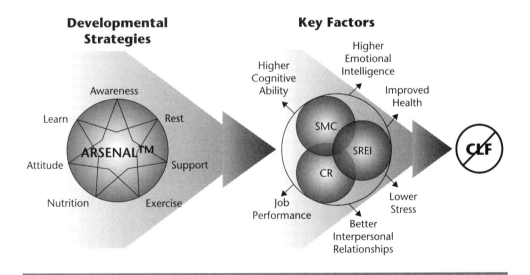

Figure 6.7. ARSENAL™ Best Practices Model

©2008 Henry L. Thompson, Ph.D. Reproduced with permission.

- Build strategies and skills for managing leader, team, and organizational stress, EI, and cognitive ability.
- Make systemic changes to remove unintelligent stress, EI, and cognitive ability behaviors across the organization.
- Make stress, EI, and cognitive ability a leadership responsibility.
- Monitor leader, team, and organizational stress, EI, and cognitive ability performance on a frequent basis.
- Use stress, EI, and cognitive ability coaches and mentors.
- Implement stress, EI, and cognitive ability training.
- Create a culture that encourages behavior that increases Stress Management Capacity, Cognitive Resiliency, and Stress Resilient EI™.
- Build strong stress, EI, and cognitive ability teams around leaders.
- Assess EI and practice the behaviors that strengthen both individual and team strengths and weaknesses.

Each CLF factor will be introduced to the practitioner and discussed separately beginning with Stress Management Capacity.

Stress Management Capacity

SMC refers to the capacity of the leader, team, or organization to manage stress. For example, everyone has an ability to handle a certain amount of stress. The "current ability" is the leader's current stress capacity. If the leader's stress load exceeds this capacity, there will be a deleterious affect on the leader's cognitive and emotional performance and, perhaps, health. Fortunately, the capacity to manage stress can be significantly improved for most leaders, teams, and organizations.

Some general characteristics of SMC are

- Minimization of the dynamic fluctuation of stress.
- Individualized coping strategies.
- Stress preventive measures are in use.
- Fine-tuned awareness.
- Strategies for minimizing EI degradation are used at each level of the organization.
- Stress assessments are made on a frequent basis.

- Support networks are in place.
- Stress management is monitored and appropriate training is conducted.

Building Stress Management Capacity is crucial to building the other key CLF factors of Cognitive Resiliency and Stress Resilient EI™.

Cognitive Resiliency

Cognitive Resilience is the ability of the prefrontal cortex to resist stress, adapt to demanding situations, and bounce back from performance degradation resulting from stress. The ability to maintain and use working memory effectively is critical to both cognitive and emotional intelligence. Some general characteristics of a person who exemplifies this skill are

- Stress containment strategies are in place.
- Protective and preventive measures against stress have been implemented.
- Cognitive competence "under pressure" has been achieved.
- Cognitive degradation recovery techniques have been learned.
- Only minor drops in the use of the PFC, IQ, control, decision making, logic, and so forth are evident under stress.

Stress Resilient EI™

Resilience refers to the propensity to rebound quickly, resist stress, and exhibit a psychological "hardiness." Thus, SREI™ refers to EI that has been developed in the leader, team, and organization to the point that there is a strong resistance to stress and ability to rebound quickly from stress-induced performance degradation. In general, leaders, teams, and organizations show a wide variation in this type of resilience. Some general characteristics of SREI™ are

- Responds positively to stress.
- Containment strategies for minimizing EI loss are in place.
- Habits are developed for appropriate responses under stress.
- Support mechanisms are active.
- Training and monitoring are ongoing.

- Self-awareness and impulse control are maximized.
- Defensiveness is minimized by increasing divergent thinking, such as the ability to expect and accept paradox and tolerate it.

SREI™ assists leaders, teams, and organizations in maintaining emotionally intelligent behavior, even when situations become stressful.

Each of the CLF factors above share a common interdependent relationship with the seven ARSENAL™ best practices. The basic process for bolstering CLF resistance around the key CLF factors involves focusing on these seven best practice areas.

ARSENAL™ Best Practices: The Seven Best Practices for Bolstering CLF Resistance

A common set of seven interdependent best practices for Awareness, Rest, Support, Exercise, Nutrition, Attitude, and Learning (ARSENAL™) may be used to significantly enhance the three key CLF factors (see Figure 6.7).

Table 6.2 gives examples of how the ARSENAL™ best practices might be applied across the leader, team, and organizational levels.

Considerable evidence in the stress, cognitive ability, and EI literature, some of which has been presented, supports that the seven ARSENAL™ best practices will enhance the three key CLF factors and that they are also linked to each other in an interdependent manner. Thus, a synergy toward CLF reduction may be achieved by working on all seven ARSENAL™ areas. The ARSENAL™ best practices are described below.

Awareness

Best practices for Awareness include assessments, feedback, metrics, and any type of information that helps make and keep leaders, teams, and organizations aware of what is going on in the SMC, SREI™, and CR areas. Techniques for raising and keeping awareness high include:

- Administer EI assessments such as those mentioned in this chapter.
- Build trust and open communications.
- Monitor and provide feedback on cognitive performance.
- Monitor and provide feedback on stress levels.
- Monitor and provide feedback on physiological conditions such as blood pressure, physical condition, fatigue, anxiety, caffeine level, and others.

Table 6.2. CLF Bolstering Factors by Level

	Awareness	Rest	Support	Exercise	Nutrition	Attitude	Learning
Leader	EQ-i®, MSCEIT®, ESC-2, stress assessments, coaching	Sleep, relaxation, meditation, music	Significant other, family, best friend(s), associations, coach	Walk, run, swim, gym	Food, water, vitamins, supplements	Motivated, like my work, feel significant & competent, drive for results, mindset	Reading, webinars, classes, puzzles, brain software
Team	Group Report, team surveys, team stress assessments	Breaks, project downtime	Friends on the team, team leader, team social activities	Team sports	Meals, snacks, coffee, water, education	Like my team, put team before myself, pride in my team, have fun with my team	Team problem solving, stretch assignments
Organization	BOEI, employee surveys, interviews, town hall meetings	Vacations, retreats, company outings	Friends in company, EAP, coach	Company gym, exercise, breaks	Healthy cafeteria, vending products/ selections, water coolers, nutritionist	Socially responsible, have confidence in the company	Simulations, conferences, training

Awareness is the building block for developing all ARSENAL™ best practices, which lead to the development of SCM, CR, and SREI™.

Rest

All high-performing systems need rest—and sleep is the most critical. Do not lose sleep if at all possible. Keep in mind that sleep loss is cumulative. If you lose an hour tonight and an hour tomorrow night, you have lost two hours in terms of what your body needs. As mentioned earlier, cognitive and emotional abilities begin to degrade quickly as you enter into sleep deprivation, and you probably will not be aware of it until it is too late (Thompson, 1981). The body needs rest to recuperate from the day's activity. General techniques include:

- Sleep
- Play, have fun, relax
- Meditate
- Listen to music
- Use biofeedback
- Hobbies
- Vacations
- Power naps in the early afternoon

Resting, especially sleep at night, allows the brain to process the day's activities, transfer information into long-term memory, and repair itself. Rest prepares you to function at your cognitive and emotional peak.

Support

Research suggests that the more relationships you have, the longer you may live. Family, friends, coaches, and work relationships provide the needed support to make you feel connected, included, secure, and more self-worthy. Techniques to keep support high include:

- Keep in touch with friends.
- Spend time with your family and significant other.
- Nurture relationships at work.
- Use all resources available including the employee assistance program.
- Belong to support groups.

Having a support network helps keep security high and stress low.

Exercise

Exercise has been shown to have a significant affect on stress management and cognitive and emotional ability by increasing blood flow and, thus, oxygen to the brain. Exercise regimes also increase attunement to physiological conditions (Thompson, 1981) and the ability to maintain a healthy functioning PFC. Exercise regimes should include:

- A blend of cardiovascular and anaerobic activities
- Activities that work on agility, such as balancing and jumping
- Stretching
- Endurance training

Exercise has the added effect of stimulating brain development. Exercise pumps the blood through the system and helps flush out some of the stress hormones that are in the system.

Nutrition

The food you put into your body influences your stress level and, consequently, cognitive and emotional performance. General guidelines include:

- Avoid foods with high fructose, trans-fat, and with little nutritional value.
- Monitor your caffeine intake. Caffeine has been shown to increase physical performance, but at the same time, it releases a cascade of stress hormones into your system—know your "buzz" level.
- Increase your intake of "brain foods," such as omega-3.
- Stay hydrated—drink plenty of water.
- Limit or eliminate smoking. The brain needs a certain level of oxygen to function effectively (Moss & Scholey, 1996). Nicotine significantly reduces the amount of oxygen carried to the brain. One cigarette reduces the amount of oxygen carried to the brain as much as breathing air at an altitude of 5,000 feet, thus reducing PFC performance.

Everything entering your system, for example, air, water, food, and chemicals (caffeine, vitamins, and prescription drugs) has an affect on your stress level, IQ, and EI. What you put into your system affects your mental, emotional, and physical performance.

Attitude

Attitude is critical in establishing a person's motivation and determination toward managing stress and building resilience. Your attitude, how you think, influences which hormones are released, their quantity, and their duration. These hormones, in turn, influence all of the body's systems in a positive or negative manner. Techniques for raising and sustaining your attitude include:

- Participate in activities you enjoy.
- Always strive to do your best in whatever activities you undertake.
- Don't give up.
- Engage in activities that build your self-confidence and self-esteem.
- Be socially responsible.

Learning

Continuous learning keeps the brain stimulated and growing. Solving problems and puzzles are great brain exercises. Novelty and whole brain workouts are critical for developing and maintaining high capacity and resilient cognitive and emotional capacity. Samples of learning activities for the brain are shown in Table 6.3.

Table 6.3. Learning Exercises by Level

Exercises	Individual	Team	Organization
Puzzles	Sudoku, cross-word	Scrabble®, team exercises, ARSENAL™ initiatives	Restructuring initiatives, strategic planning
Problem Solving	International assignments	Process improvement teams, Six Sigma, cross-functional teams, matrix teams, virtual teams, product development teams	Organizational change initiatives, mergers and acquisitions
Software	Brain Age®, BrainFit®	Microworlds, simulations	Capability exercises

©2008 Henry L. Thompson, Ph.D. Reproduced with permission.

Novelty and whole brain learning are key factors in keeping the brain sharp. Just doing one kind of puzzle solving, such as Sudoku, does not give your brain a complete workout. You must also work your memory, eye-hand coordination, audio skills, and more.

CONCLUSION

The purpose of this chapter has been to provide the practitioner with knowledge about the systemic affect of stress on the human body in general and the brain's PFC in particular. The PFC is the executive center and chief executive officer of the brain. Anything that degrades the performance of the PFC affects all brain functions, including both cognitive and emotional intelligences.

To assist in understanding the nonlinear dynamic interaction of the PFC, stress, and cognitive and emotional intelligences, an overview of the Perception-Appraisal-Motivation-Action Model of Behavior™ was presented. This model elucidates the complex interaction of the processes involved in what happens from the time a stimulus is first perceived through the appraisal processes involving both cognitive and emotional components to the formation of a motivational complex that eventually leads to the initiation of an action pattern. All of these processes are recursive and, as such, constantly feed back on one another.

The three keys for bolstering resistance to CLF—Stress Management Capacity, Cognitive Resilience, and Stress Resilient EI™—were discussed in detail. The three factors form an interdependent triad with the capability of significantly reducing the probability of experiencing a CLF.

Seven best practices were identified that systemically affect the three key bolstering factors. These are Awareness, Rest, Support, Exercise, Nutrition, Attitude, and Learning. These seven best practices not only decrease the probability of experiencing a CLF, but increase cognitive and emotional ability and improve job performance, health, and interpersonal relationships while lowering stress.

This chapter has covered the tip of the CLF iceberg. The other 80 percent of the iceberg remains to be explored. Evidence for the impact of stress on cognitive and emotional intelligences and the overall affect on leader performance is continuing to mount. Out of new research will come additional best practices.

REFERENCES

Arnsten, A. (1998). The biology of being frazzled. *Science, 280*, 1711–1713.

Bar-On, R. (2002). *BarOn emotional quotient inventory: A measure of emotional intelligence.* (Technical Manual). Toronto, Canada: Multi-Health Systems, Inc.

Challenger, J.A., Gray, T.M., & Christmas, A. (2005). Biggest CEO turnover year on record. METRICS 2.0. www.metrics2.com.

Damasio, A. (1994). *Descartes' error: Emotion, reason, and the human brain.* New York: Avon Books.

Damasio, A. (2000). *The feeling of what happens: Body and emotion in the making of consciousness.* New York: Harvest Books.

Dries, N., & Pepermans, R. (2007). Using emotional intelligence to identify high potential: A meta competency perspective. *Leadership & Organization Development Journal, 28*(8), 749–770.

Ekman, P. (2003). *Emotions revealed: Recognizing faces and feelings to improve communication and emotional life.* New York: Owl Books.

Gillett, E. (1987). The relationship of repression to the unconscious. *International Journal of Psycho-analysis, 68*, 535–546.

Goldberg, E. (2001). *The executive brain: Frontal lobes and the civilized mind.* New York: Oxford University Press.

Goldberg, E. (2005). *The wisdom of paradox: How your mind can grow stronger as your brain grows older.* New York: Gotham Books.

Goleman, D. (1995). *Emotional intelligence: Why it can matter more than IQ.* New York: Bantam Books.

Goleman, D. (2007). *Social intelligence: The new science of human relationships.* New York: Bantam Books.

Lazarus, R. (1999). *Stress and emotions: A new synthesis.* New York: Springer Publishing.

LeDoux, J.E. (1996). *The emotional brain.* New York: Simon & Schuster.

LeDoux, J.E. (2002). *Synaptic Self: How our brains become who we are.* New York: Penguin Books.

Lynn, R., & Vanhanen, T. (2002). *IQ and wealth of nations.* Westport, CT: Praeger Publishers.

Moss, M.C., & Scholey, A.B. (1996). Oxygen administration enhances memory formation in healthy young adults. *Psychopharmacology, 124*(3), 255–260.

Murphy, K. (Ed.). (2006). *Critique of emotional intelligence: What are the problems and how can they be fixed?* Mahwah, NJ: Lawrence Erlbaum Associates.

Peter, L. (1969). *The Peter principle: Why things always go wrong.* New York: William Morrow & Company.

Schmidt, F.L. (2002). The role of general cognitive ability and job performance: Why there cannot be a debate. *Human Performance, 15*, 187–210.

Schmidt, F.L., & Hunter, J.E. (1998). The validity and utility of selection methods in personnel psychology: Practical and theoretical implications for 85 years of research findings. *Psychological Bulletin, 124,* 262–274.

Selye, H. (1978). *The stress of life.* New York: McGraw-Hill.

Slaski, M., & Cartwright, S. (2002). Health, performance and emotional intelligence: An exploratory study of retail managers. *Stress and Health, 18,* 63–68.

Stein, S. (2002, November 25). The EQ factor: Does emotional intelligence make you a better CEO? Special Report: Innovator's Alliance, Ontario, Canada.

Tangri, R. (2003). *Stress costs, stress cures* [online book]. Available: www.Stress-Cures .com.

Thom, R. (1975). *Structural stability and morphogenesis.* New York: Benjamin-Addison-Wesley.

Thompson, H. (1981). Baby crying as an antecedent of child abuse. Unpublished doctoral dissertation, Department of Psychology, The University of Georgia, Athens, Georgia.

Thompson, H. (1983). Physical fitness as a moderator of cognitive degradation during sleep deprivation. Unpublished master's thesis, U.S. Army Command and General Staff College, Fort Leavenworth, Kansas.

Thompson, H. (2005). The impact of stress on the BarOn EQ-i® reported scores and a proposed model of inquiry. Watkinsville, GA: High Performing Systems, Inc., Technical Report 15-5.

Thompson, H. (2006). Exploring the interface of the type and emotional intelligence landscapes. *Bulletin of Psychological Type, 29*(3) 14–19.

Thompson, H. (2007a). A summary analysis of IQ and EQ by leader level. Watkinsville, GA: High Performing Systems, Inc., Research Report 5-07.

Thompson, H. (2007b). The impact of stress on the sequential use of Jung's function-attitudes in MBTI Types. Watkinsville, GA: High Performing Systems, Inc., Research Report 1-08.

Thompson, H. (2008). How stress impacts the Mayer-Salovey-Caruso emotional intelligence test scores. Watkinsville, GA: High Performing Systems, Inc., Research Report 2-08.

Thompson, H., & Richardson, D. (1983). The rooster effect. *Journal of Personality and Social Psychology, 9*(3), 415–425.

Thompson, H., & Walsh, P. (2000, Winter). Is there a difference between job type and home type? *Bulletin of Psychological Type, 23*(1), 14, 16, 18.

Thompson, H.L. (2002). The influence of a "job" versus "home" mindset on Element B scores. Watkinsville, GA: High Performing Systems, Inc., Technical Paper 5-02.

Thompson, H.L. (2003). The influence of a "normal" versus "stressed" mindset on reported Element B scores. Watkinsville, GA: High Performing Systems, Inc., Technical Paper 3-02.

Yerkes, R.M., & Dodson, J.D. (1908). The relationship of strengths of stimulus to rapidity of habit formation. *Journal of Comparative Neurology and Psychology, 18,* 459–482.

Zagorsky, R. (2007). Do you have to be smart to be rich? The impact of IQ on wealth, income and financial distress. *Intelligence.*

Zillman, D. (1978). Attribution and misattributions of excitatory reactions. In J.H. Harvey, W.J. Ickes, & R. F. Kidd (Eds.), *New directions in attribution research* (Vol. 2, pp. 335–368). Mahwah, NJ: Lawrence Erlbaum Associates.

Henry L. (Dick) Thompson, Ph.D., is president and CEO of High Performing Systems Inc., an international management consulting and training firm he founded in 1984. Over the last thirty years, he has gained valuable experience developing and leading teams—from the battlefield to the boardroom. He is an internationally recognized consultant, researcher, speaker, and author. His areas of expertise and research include leadership, emotional intelligence, FIRO®, stress, psychological type theory, chaos and complexity, and teams.

PART TWO

Teams, Organizations, and Cultures: Working with Systems

Building Your Team's Conflict-Resolution Skills with Emotional and Social Intelligence

Marcia Hughes

OVERVIEW

A classic issue faced by organizations world-wide is how to effectively promote their teams' abilities to resolve conflict. Conflict just is—it's not good or bad on its own; it's just something that happens. What makes it useful or destructive comes from the attitude and capabilities of those charged with responding to the conflict. Emotional and social intelligence (ESI) skills are at the forefront of what it takes to respond effectively. Depending on the conflict, a mix of technical competence, organization resources, and individual and team ESI skills is required to address any challenging scenario. Because these skills frequently show up as behaviors, we'll refer to the terms ESI skills and ESI behaviors interchangeably.

Seven behaviors required for team success are identified in the book I co-authored with James Terrell, *The Emotionally Intelligent Team* (2007). These skills are assessed by the team survey associated with the book, the *Team Emotional and Social Intelligence Survey®* (TESI®). (Hughes, Thompson, & Terrell, 2008) and are the focus of *The TESI® Short Facilitator's Guide Set* (2009). Conflict resolution is one of the seven skills, and it's the one that teams most often struggle with. In this chapter I will discuss why that is so and what teams can do about it. This chapter is addressed to you as a consultant/coach, team leader, or team member with the goal of providing you with ideas and strategies to enhance your practice in building team effectiveness through heightened capability in resolving conflict.

After reviewing key concepts and definitions, I will discuss the convergence between divergent thinking and conflict resolution skills as measured by the TESI® survey. A study evaluating TESI® results of team skills, especially related to conflict resolution, was conducted to consider the relationship of conflict resolution to skills in divergent thinking and in relationship to the other six skills assessed by the TESI®. The research reported here finds that there is a strong relationship between a team's ability to appreciate and use divergent thinking and its effectiveness in solving conflicts.

There are several good EI tools available for assessing individual skills. One of the measures, the BarOn EQ-i®, is briefly reviewed with a focus on how to use it to diagnose individual team members' conflict resolution capabilities and to strategically expand that capacity.

Finally, I will demonstrate ways that teams can work with both positive and negative emotions to expand their conflict resolution skills. Strategic combinations of team skills will be offered as well as tips for working with teams.

TEAM AND EMOTIONAL AND SOCIAL INTELLIGENCE

Ever-increasing challenges, including the complexity of globalization, 24/7 service expectations, constantly changing hardware and software, and economic pressures at every level—whether organizational, national, or global—are putting heightened demands on teams resulting in an increased experience of conflict. Teams that have the capability to handle conflict well have a decided edge in meeting their own as well as their organization's needs. This chapter seeks to help you support your team or those you consult with by increasing their skills in handling conflict. Let's begin by clarifying key terms.

Team: We define a team as a group of two or more people who interdependently seek to meet a common purpose, often through solving problem(s), in order to meet goals established by their organization as well as their own goals. At a minimum, a team should be a cooperative unit and, at its best, a team functions collaboratively. Teams may exist for a short-term, specific function, for the long term, or be an embedded part of an organization such that it's expected that if the organization exists the team does as well. A good example of the latter is a senior executive team. Many people serve on multiple teams and have different roles and responsibilities according to each team. This can require that the people be able to vary their approach to effectively engage with conflict based on the function and personalities of the team. It often helps to think of each team as being associated with some metaphor, such as a different color hat, so when team members go to the red hat team they distinguish what's needed from them there as compared to their functions on the blue, yellow, or purple hat teams.

Team emotional and social intelligence (ESI): Emotional and social intelligence at the team level is an expression of the collective capabilities of a team in exercising core skills such as emotional awareness, conflict resolution, and positive mood. Team ESI reflects the ability to recognize and manage individual emotions by team members and to recognize and respond effectively to those of others. It includes understanding their organizational and interpersonal relationships and engagement with others from the "big picture" point of view as well as the ability to direct and adapt to change. Whether working with just one other individual on the team, a large group, or a community, this process of adding in the complexity of understanding and responding to someone else requires social intelligence. This need to work with others is often referred to as the capacity to be other-oriented.

Team Emotional and Social Intelligence Survey® (TESI®): The TESI provides a way for team members to conduct a survey of their team in order to discover how team members believe the team is performing on the seven skills most important for team functioning: team identity, motivation, emotional awareness, communication, stress tolerance, conflict resolution, and positive mood. A team average is reported from all the individual responses and a range is shown for each scale to depict how much variation there is in the ratings by the various team members. Demographic break-outs and individual reports are also provided.

Focusing on Conflict Resolution

As Figure 7.1 highlights, this chapter focuses on one piece of the team pie. It's a big piece, as it is the skill teams frequently find to be the most challenging. This skill can never be used in isolation; each one of these seven skills influences one another, which is why they are pictured in a circle rather than linearly or on a continuum. We'll review research on TESI® results related to conflict resolution later in this chapter.

Team conflict is a challenge occurring where there is disagreement based on different perspectives, values, or priorities, and which rises to some level of disturbing an effective team system. Conflict resolution is the process followed by the individuals and teams faced with the challenge to resolve the matter. Many styles of resolution can be engaged including

Figure 7.1. Conflict Resolution—One of the Seven Team Skills

Handbook for Developing Emotional and Social Intelligence

avoidance, compromise, cooperation, confrontation, competition, and the most sophisticated—collaboration.

In *The Emotionally Intelligent Team*, we discuss nine ingredients that compose a team's skill in handling conflict. These include skills exercised by team members in the patience and willingness to work problems through, the ability to use the ESI skills of empathy and assertiveness, recognizing and working with differences in personality among team members, and the ability to choose different strategies for resolving conflict according to the specific circumstances of an individual event. For example, a team has to avoid some problems—it's called choosing their battles. And there are times it pays to be competitive rather than cooperative or collaborative—although competitive benefits may be limited to a stimulating challenge such as the first one to solve a complex problem gets a free lunch.

Using Individual EI Measures

There are several individual emotional intelligence measures available; the one we find to be the most valuable is the BarOn EQ-i® for the self-rating and the EQ-360® for multi-rater feedback, which combines the individual's results with the ratings on the same skills from those of others such as direct reports, their manager, and family and friends. The EQ-i® identifies fifteen capabilities or skills that Bar-On (1997) found to be most critical to support success in meeting the demands and pressures from our complex environments. Working with conflict is key to achieving that success.

Teams are successful partly because of the individual ESI capabilities of their members and partly due to their collective engagement. Research shows that team members with higher ESI are likely to elevate a team's capabilities (Elfeinbein, 2006). Thus, the individual capability of team members is important. The EQ-i® is a useful tool for promoting individual assessment and highlighting development areas to support an individual in working well with conflict.

While all fifteen EQi competencies are potentially related to success in resolving conflict, the seven we have found to be most influential in our conflict resolution work at Collaborative Growth are

- Self-regard—each individual team member has to believe in him- or herself sufficiently to have the courage to engage in the conflict and to raise issues. The stronger the appropriate self-regard, the more likely the individual can listen to concerns and respond in a healthy fashion without being defensive.

- Emotional self-awareness—team members need to be aware of one another's emotions. This is virtually impossible to do accurately unless they have developed the individual skill to understand and express their own emotions.
- Assertiveness—requires being able to speak up for oneself while also providing space for others to contribute to the dialogue. Assertiveness requires cultural sensitivity to know, for example, how thoroughly to engage in a dialogue and what tempo of speaking and raising issues is acceptable and persuasive.
- Empathy—to move people involved in a conflict from no to yes requires empathy—the expression of genuinely caring about the others involved. Suggestions from an advice-giver who provides feedback with empathy are perceived as much more valuable than advice from someone who seems not to care.
- Impulse control—the capacity to have patience and to manage impulsivity, frustration, and anger. Skills in handling every one of these emotions heavily impact the success in resolving a conflict.
- Reality testing—helps the individual accurately assess the situation and realistically define a response.
- Optimism—the can-do, hopeful sense that, with appropriate work and resources, the challenge can be solved.

The more individuals bring these skills to the team table, the more capable the team is likely to be as a whole in finding effective responses to the opportunity that conflict brings them.

Divergent Thinking

Divergent thinking is a thought process or method that is essential to effective team work because it's at the heart of the ability to generate ideas and to listen to highly different perspectives. It is an essential skill when teams seek to be creative or solve problems. The goal of divergent thinking, as discussed here, has several applications, with the primary benefit being the capacity within the team to think along different lines and to feel safe and supported in discussing the differences. It includes generating numerous ideas about a topic in a short period of time and may involve breaking a topic down into component parts to gain insight about different aspects of the matter. In the best of circumstances, divergent thinking occurs in a spontaneous, free-flowing manner, such that the ideas are often generated in a random, unorganized fashion. During conflict, divergent thinking requires strength at the individual and team level to consider alternative scenarios even when there may be a strong temptation to protect the original way of assessing a problem. Working in an environment safe for divergent thinking leads to Collaborative Intelligence™, the pinnacle of team emotional and social intelligence as reflected by the Collaborative Growth team model, which is fully described in *The Emotionally Intelligent Team* (Hughes & Terrell, 2007) and at www.EITeams.com.

In the best cases, divergent thinking by team members or the team as a whole is followed by the ideas and information being organized using convergent thinking, that is, putting the various ideas back together in a new organized and structured way. Without divergent thinking, teams cannot reach the payoff of in-depth consideration before arriving at convergent thinking, because they haven't fully considered the problem they are seeking to address. Yet, diverse thinking can be difficult at a team level because of a process known as groupthink. Janis (1972) demonstrated the effects of groupthink by describing that even after groups become aware of the risks of an unfavorable process, they'll go along with it because of the pressure for achieving group consensus. ESI is a big help in preventing groupthink as being aware of emotions around the team, and having effective response strategies, will support the courage to get beyond the compulsion to agree with one another. Reus and Liu noted that "a group's ability to promote divergent thinking and cooperative behaviors is at least partially determined by an ability to recognize and regulate its members' emotions" (2004, pp. 246–247). Their article addresses emotional capability as a significant construct to explain performance of knowledge-intensive work groups. Team ESI can be used to counter groupthink, mitigate stress, and tighten the bonds of commitment to one another. Reus and Liu state that "this research indicates that groupthink originates from extreme uncertainty about appropriate responses and the need to maintain good relationships with other group members" (p. 249).

Social intelligence is a critical component to counteracting groupthink. It is exercised by the team having sufficient awareness and trust that members can recognize what is happening and feel free to speak up, even if the message won't be popular at the time. The intention to collaborate isn't accidental; rather, it involves an explicit intention to articulate and address divergent messages, and to take time to listen to different approaches in order to tap into collective wisdom and the full capacity of the team. When this is achieved, we say the team is operating with Collaborative Intelligence™.

TESI® RESEARCH ON CONFLICT RESOLUTION SKILLS AND DIVERGENT THINKING

Divergent thinking is so important to a team's ability to perform at a high level of effectiveness that we analyzed the TESI® to determine how much divergent thinking is called for within the seven different scales and how that skill affects overall team capacity. We hypothesized that there is a strong connection between the fact that many people rate their team lowest in conflict resolution skills and the team's ability to apply divergent thinking. The research did find a strong connection between the ability to engage in divergent thinking and the perception of a team's ability to resolve conflict well.

The results described here are based on a composite sample of 229 employees, most of whom were leaders or managers, who each rated their work team through the TESI® assessment, which is comprised of fifty-six items that cluster into seven distinct scales as highlighted earlier. In addition, participants also provided an overall rating of the effectiveness of their team prior to responding to the scale items. Our thanks to Carina Fiedeldey-Van Dijk, Ph.D., president of ePsy Consultancy, for her assistance in this research.

Demographics of Research Participants

A segment of data from our early research was analyzed to explore how individuals in leadership and emotional intelligence trainings rated their teams. The participants were drawn from seven groups residing in the United States and Canada. The participants represented three different industries from the broad areas of education and governing. They were dominantly in their forties and fifties. Male and female participants were fairly equally spread between the different age groups.

The ages of the participants ranged between twenty-seven and sixty-one years, with an average age of forty-six years and nine months. Participants varied with respect to the number of years they were with their team at the time of the assessment, and reported an average time of three years and six months. The demographic descriptions add credibility to the accuracy with which they rated the emotional and social intelligence of their team because their composite nature helps minimize the potential for response skews in the TESI® assessment.

Teams performed similarly on the TESI® scales and in their global rating of overall team effectiveness and in their use of divergent thinking, whether rated by males or females.

Levels of divergent thinking are statistically significantly impacted by age category ($p < 0.05$). The older the participants, the higher they rated their teams on divergent thinking.

Results

One hundred seventy-four participants gave an overall rating of their team in addition to responding to the fifty-six items in the survey. On average their overall team effectiveness rating was 3.97 out of 5, or 73 percent. This percentage gives us an overall feel of where the emotional and social intelligence of the team lays according to the perspective of the individual rating his or her team.

The seven components of TESI® are in alignment with this overall team rating. However, a distinction is that there is a somewhat lower rating in conflict resolution, which is further evaluated here. Figure 7.2 shows the results in comparison to the overall team effectiveness rating, which is indicated by the line above the bars.

Note that only Motivation and Positive mood are on par with the participants' ratings of overall team effectiveness. On average the line reflecting the overall team effectiveness is higher than the individual bars, which can be attributed to several factors including the likely factor that more than just ESI is considered when rating team effectiveness

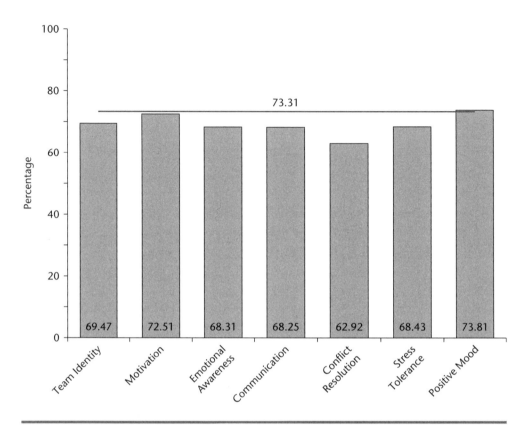

Figure 7.2. Individual Scale Results in Comparison to Overall
Team Effectiveness Rating

overall. It is therefore significant that the TESI® scales are generally lower than the line as it indicates there is room for development on the ESI front.

Through regression analysis, we further found that the three scales that together best explain the variation in overall team effectiveness ratings with, as much as 58.25 percent, are positive mood, emotional awareness, and motivation. Conflict resolution made it into the model in fourth place, followed by communication. More details on the regression analysis can be found by viewing the research article at www:EITeams.com.

TESI® and Divergent Thinking

Apart from the seven scales measuring team emotional and social intelligence, it is also possible to categorize the TESI® items into three groups to measure divergent thinking (DT). This was done by assigning each of the fifty-six questions of the TESI® to one of the following three categories:

- No or limited divergent thinking (twenty-five items)
- Moderate divergent thinking (twelve items)
- Strong divergent thinking (nineteen items)

The measurement of divergent thinking through the TESI® is an overlay on the seven TESI® scales. The greatest number of strong divergent items was in conflict resolution and communication. In contrast, stress tolerance and positive mood only had a few moderate divergent items, with no strong divergent items.

To check how much divergent thinking seems to impact a team's results, Figure 7.3 was created to contrast the results on which divergent thinking was required against the results for which no or limited diversity of thinking was required and to research its association with conflict resolution.

The moderate and strong divergent thinking items were grouped together to form an overall divergent thinking measure, using a weighted ratio of 1:2, that is, 1 point for a moderate divergent thinking question and 2 points for a strong divergent thinking question. Specifically, they were drawn from the TESI® scales as shown in Table 7.1.

The participants scored about two percentage points higher in the no/limited divergent thinking items than in the moderate and strong divergent thinking items combined. This difference was found to be statistically significant ($p < 0.01$). This means that participants observe their team to have slightly higher team emotional and social intelligence when no/limited divergent thinking is called for than when moderate or strong divergent thinking is called for. However, we need to remember that is with regard to all scales considered together, without breaking out the seven scale results. It also reflects what we would expect: teams are perceived as being more skilled in areas for which the demands are not as challenging.

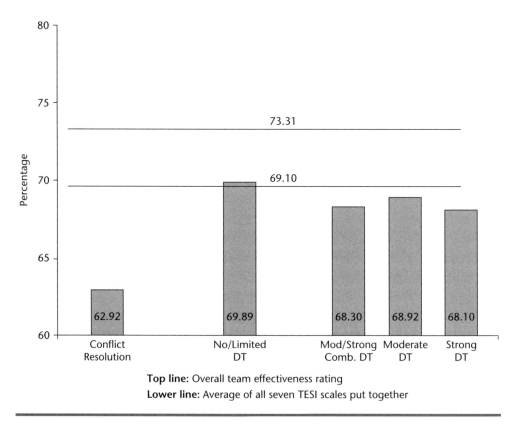

Top line: Overall team effectiveness rating
Lower line: Average of all seven TESI scales put together

Figure 7.3. Level of Divergent Thinking Required

The participants scored lowest in the strong divergent thinking items. However, again we need to remember that this data is with regard to all scales as if they are one score, without breaking out the seven scale results.

To consider where most of the three levels of DT items lie with regard to the seven TESI® scales, we considered the three different DT scores in a regression model to investigate the impact of divergent thinking on the overall effectiveness of teams. We found that both moderate and strong DT together explains 61.08 percent of the variation in overall team effectiveness ratings. Note that moderate DT alone explains 60.69 percent of the variation in overall team effectiveness. Moderate DT items were dominantly drawn from motivation and positive mood, the two TESI® scales in which teams performed the highest.

Table 7.1. Amount of Moderate and Strong Divergent Thinking Required

Scale	Amount of Moderate and Strong Divergent Thinking Required
Team Identity	3 strong and one moderate = 7
Motivation	2 strong and 3 moderate = 7
Emotional Awareness	1 strong and 2 moderate = 4
Communication	7 strong = 14
Conflict Resolution	6 strong and 1 moderate = 13
Stress Tolerance	2 moderate = 2
Positive Mood	3 moderate = 3

The regression model suggests that teams will rate themselves as being more effective if they believe they are competent in exercising moderate divergent thinking. This is a helpful recognition for the practitioner and the team, as it reflects a strengthening capacity in divergent thinking for the team, although there is still room to grow. It also helps explain the challenge that team members have in working with skills requiring more complex divergent thinking, such as conflict resolution. It comes as no surprise then that teams displaying underdeveloped divergent thinking will likely struggle with conflict resolution.

In summary so far, important learning from the TESI® is that:

1. The emotional and social intelligence of teams, as measured by the seven TESI® scales, are somewhat lower than the global effectiveness that team members report.
2. Teams' emotional and social intelligence are rated higher when no or limited divergent thinking is required.
3. Divergent thinking capability is important to teams' overall effectiveness rating.
4. Divergent thinking is tied to conflict resolution, a scale in which teams are particularly challenged.

We wanted to know whether teams' emotional and social intelligence as measured by the seven TESI® scales looked different depending on the level of divergent thinking in each skill. From Figure 7.3 we know that at the most basic level, all teams have two DT scores: one for limited/no DT, and one for moderate/strong DT combined. The difference between these two scores will reveal whether team ratings displayed comparatively restricted, typical, or prominent divergent thinking. The teams were conservatively divided into three distinct groups of approximately equal size based on their DT rating:

- Restricted DT—difference ratings lying above 1.00 (meaning that these teams had no/limited DT scores of at least one percentage point higher than all DT scores)—36.2 percent of all teams
- Typical DT—difference ratings lying between −0.40 and +1.00 (meaning that the no/limited DT and moderate/strong DT scores were very similar)—34.1 percent of all teams
- Prominent DT—difference ratings lying at or below −0.40 (meaning that these teams had higher moderate/strong DT scores than no/limited DT scores)—29.7 percent of all teams.

Figure 7.4 shows how teams' emotional and social intelligence differ depending on the level of divergent thinking capability they reported.

Looking at the TESI® scale scores for teams within different categories of DT is telling: Figure 7.4 clearly shows the extent to which teams with perceived restricted divergent thinking capability have visibly lower competence in conflict resolution than teams with perceived higher divergent thinking capabilities. Note that communication follows a similar pattern, albeit less prominently, while stress tolerance and positive mood follow a different pattern that is non-linear in nature (a cup shape). It is possible to work efficiently in building the conflict resolution skills of teams by having an in-depth understanding of the relationship between conflict resolution and the other six TESI® scales as well as understanding the importance of developing divergent thinking capabilities.

Through regression analyses, we investigated next how teams' conflict resolution ratings were impacted by the other TESI® scales. We found that the TESI® scales that best explain the variation in conflict resolution scores

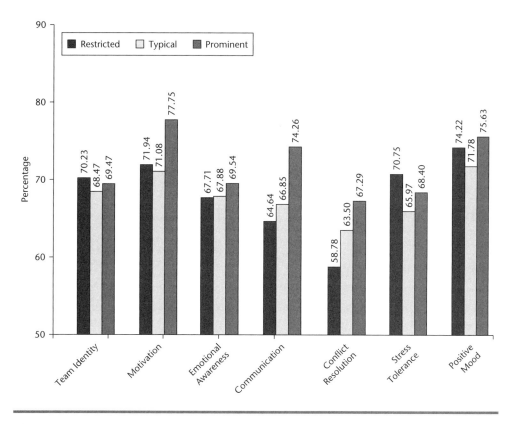

Figure 7.4. TESI® Scales and Levels of Divergent Thinking

are communication, emotional awareness, and positive mood. These are also the three scales that correlated highest with conflict resolution. This is good news, as it means that working with any one of these scales in training and coaching is likely to also positively influence the other two scales that are important in their own right.

It makes sense that these three are correlated with conflict resolution, as the mastery a team has—or lacks—in communication skills will deeply affect its members ability to speak with empathy, listen effectively, and reason cogently both internally and with others. Being emotionally aware provides the team members with the ability to respond effectively as a team to internal and outside challenges, as they are more likely to understand what is actually at the root of the conflict. When a team is in a positive mood, members have more resilience and flexibility to find creative and workable answers to challenges. You can build on these three areas as you work with your team(s) to heighten their conflict resolution skills. The next part of this chapter supports you in working with teams to build their capacity to effectively use their ESI in solving conflict through divergent thinking and other strategies. The more the effective use of positive emotions is employed and the capacity is developed to respond to difficult emotions, the greater the capacity will be for the team to use divergent thinking.

EMOTIONS AROUND THE TEAM TABLE

One of the first steps in enhancing conflict resolution skills at the team level is to assess and improve a team's awareness of and comfort with emotions. Team members need to become aware of their emotions individually and collectively, and they need to know how to capitalize on useful emotions and manage those that are creating a drag on their success. If you ever need to debunk a team's assertion that emotions are fluff, ask questions such as: "What happens to a team when . . .

- They get word they are selected as one of the finalists in their organization's contest for the best-designed widget?
- They learn a long-time team leader was just diagnosed with a terminal disease?
- They hear the organization may merge with a big competitor?
- They're told they've done such a great job that they get next Friday off with pay?"

What do your team members express in these types of circumstances? Do they talk with one another about both positive and negative feelings and events? What do they do with information about another's feelings? Do some converse while others are left out? How does that affect team functioning? Noticing these types of engagement will tell you a great deal about your team and how you can support team members in expanding their conflict-resolution skills. Beginning with building positive mood and emotional awareness may be your best strategic point of the seven skills when working with a team struggling with its conflict-resolution skills.

Teams and individuals do have emotions, and they use them constantly. The question is whether they are making conscious and effective choices with that data or whether they are on auto-pilot. This is heavily related to the bottom line because it is fundamental to strategic decision making. A big part of your job is to coach team members to become increasingly aware of how they are choosing to engage with their own and others' emotions. Are they open and flexible with one another, trusting and ready to back up one another when the going gets tough? If so, they are accurately working with the emotional data, whether they know it or not. If the contrary scenario holds true, they're probably making many decisions with partial data and are not very resilient.

What emotions are your team members catching from one another? Emotions are contagious. Sigal Barsade (2002, p. 670) found that "group members experience moods at work; these moods ripple out and, in the process, influence not only other group members' emotions but their group dynamics and individual cognitions, attitudes, and behaviors as well." She emphasizes that "people are walking mood inductors." Team members sub-consciously mimic one another through facial expressions, tonality, and in other ways, usually non-verbally. Additionally, they share social information with one another. For example, if one team member is really angry that his boss passed him up for a promotion, his close colleagues may be angry as well, both on his behalf and because it raises feelings of their own vulnerability. Teams need to be able to work with both the positive and negative emotions they experience.

Positive Emotions

Considerable discussion exists on team engagement with negative or difficult emotions, and that is a very real part of a team's challenge. However, teams that excel understand how to work with all types of emotions—both positive and negative. They use positive emotions deliberately and expertly. Positive emotions range from agreeable to enjoyment to laughter to joy to elation. They are less likely to arise when a team is faced with conflict; however, these positive emotions help on both sides of conflict. Paying attention to positive emotions leads a team to focus on what works and can support a team in creating a trajectory that bypasses unnecessary conflict. On the other hand, when a conflict is successfully resolved, the team that takes time to share positive, hopeful feelings and to celebrate is much more likely to anchor the results so that the resolution will be owned by individual members of the team and will be long-lasting. It provides the fodder for hope that they can also find the energy and commitment to resolve the next conflict that comes their way.

Our team survey research found through regression analysis that the most influential scale of the seven on team effectiveness is positive mood. Thus, if you're focusing on helping a team grow its conflict-resolution skills, developing positive mood can be one of the most strategic places to begin. Positive mood is often associated with a "can-do" attitude. It provides the energy and zest to tackle difficult issues. It also supports creative problem solving, which is directly tied to the capacity for divergent thinking. It's no surprise that the closest scale of the seven connected with conflict resolution is communication as demonstrated by the regression analysis and Table 7.1, which highlights the amount of moderate and strong divergent thinking required in each of the scales.

It seems that members on every team we work with indicate they need to improve their communication skills, and that's probably true, as it's such a large and complex skill. A great start to communicating well is to be in a positive mood. It's just easier to be respectful, gracious, and open to divergent thinking if it seems like things are going right.

While there is a lot of power to positive mood in a team, there can be times when a team is too positive and needs to recalibrate that emotion as well. They may be looking through rose-colored glasses, missing essential details, and be naïve about the way others will accept their information or what data others will share. In this case you might help them build critical thinking skills. Build in some key questions team members should ask themselves before rushing in, such as:

- Assume someone won't give us what we need to implement our decision successfully. What might we end up missing? What's our plan B?
- Assume it is six months down the road since we've solved the problem. What's happened? Is it all unfolding as we hoped? What challenges have come up?

You don't want to overdo challenging their hopefulness, yet a healthy dose of reality testing can actually strengthen their can-do sense of team strength.

Tips on growing your team's positive mood:

- Ask them what will work to solve a particular problem and then create space for some free discussion. It's amazing how much most teams know about their own circumstances and capabilities. Ask and you might receive a gold mine.
- Start meetings with acknowledging what works. Find every way you can to acknowledge success and legitimately honor those successes. Be authentic, not trite, with acknowledging the positive.

Difficult Emotions

Difficult emotions have a broad range, from annoyance to frustration to anger to rage. It's highly likely that when most of these emotions are surfacing, the team is confronted with conflict. The type of difficult emotion surfacing should guide the team's response. For example, the level of intensity needed for a response, how immediately it's needed, whether extra resources are needed, be it money or a mediator, all depend on the nature of the challenging emotions. Working with challenging emotions is considered equivalent in this chapter to dealing with conflict. When a team is caught in difficult emotions, its capacity for divergent thinking is compromised. Thus, the strategies suggested for working with the following difficult emotions may well result in improving the team's willingness and capacity to exercise divergent thinking.

Some of the biggest challenges leading to difficult emotions are

- Conflict-averse leaders and team members
- Passive aggressive behavior
- Personality differences
- Difficult people or bullies
- Fear about scarcity of resources

I will review each of these and provide strategies for response.

Conflict-Averse Leaders

One of the biggest challenges teams face occurs when their leader avoids conflict. We call it the bumpy carpet syndrome because every difficult conversation is pushed under the carpet. Dysfunctional behavior is guaranteed if conflict isn't dealt with early. The conflict-averse leader leaves others on the team or in the organization to deal with problems. This leadership behavior needs to be addressed for the team to be able to work effectively, as it can cause severe limitations on productivity and considerable repercussions, such as unnecessary conflict among team members and inadequate decision-making. This challenge can be diagnosed by observing team behavior, interviews with the team leader and members, and through EI assessments such as the TESI® or the EQ-360®.

Possible responses once this concern is identified other than replacing the leader include:

- Intervene with the leader to help him or her recognize the issue and develop his or her skills. The intervention can come from a superior or may surface during coaching. It usually takes coaching and some real motivation from the leader for this change to be made effectively. When someone is afraid of conflict, there are usually fairly deep seated reasons. Understanding those reasons and practicing the new behaviors can work to change the behavior, but it takes time, commitment, and practice. Thus, a reality check on whether these elements are available is worthwhile.
- As a partial solution, a member on the team who has implicit authority can sometimes help address conflict. It's not the best scenario, but it's much better than leaving the team to falter. We have also seen teams that evolved to becoming a self-managing system and handled conflict on their own. This requires fairly high skills and commitment. It is impressive when it does occur.

Passive Aggressive Behavior

Teams encounter passive aggressive behavior when an individual, be it a leader or team member, responds passively to all sorts of challenging events while indicating he or she doesn't care. Being passive means not expressing one's opinion, not influencing the outcomes, and not contributing one's expertise. On its own this can limit a team's success. However, seldom is a person truly passive; he or she has thoughts, opinions, and concerns, but they aren't being expressed. Often this will reach a critical mass—you could say that a molehill has grown to an emotional mountain—and then the individual erupts in anger or takes some other aggressive action. The mixed message is disconcerting and could even derail a team, especially when it comes from the team leader.

This is a complex challenge to remedy. It can entail moving the individual to another position where the behavior doesn't sabotage the success of others. Or it can entail helping the individual recognize his or her behaviors, their consequences, and how to change. Change is possible; however, the first prerequisite is the individual must want to change. If the desire is there, a trained professional, such as a coach, can help the individual make choices that support his or her success and the team's success. Absent qualified intervention and the desire to change, this pattern of behavior is unlikely to shift.

Personality Differences

Our world is much more interesting because people are different, but it certainly adds complexity to team life. When the differences are recognized, the team can take advantage of the diversity and use those different perspectives in responding more effectively to clients, in analyzing problems, and in meeting organizational demands. The differences become strengths. Before the differences are understood, they are likely to be a team weakness and contribute to conflict. For example, when some members can't understand why others are so deliberate, they may become impatient with the cautious, deliberate style. Those cautious folks may be irritated by the fast-moving, reckless style of the first group. One of the best ways to help a team understand the differences in preferences for thinking and behaving can be for each to take a personality measure such as the Myers-Briggs Type Indicator® (MBTI), Emergenetics®, or the DISC® Profile. Each of these popular measures offers information that allows individuals to understand their own preferences better and then to understand the team interaction. By working with a well-trained facilitator, team members can learn to celebrate their diversity. Building awareness and the ability to embrace differences promotes divergent thinking and, therefore, the ability to resolve conflict.

Difficult People or Bullies

When we're discussing working with difficult people we generally start out by asking people to raise their hands if they have *never* been considered a difficult person. We have yet to have anyone raise his or her hand. Taking some personal ownership that this can happen to any of us often helps team members be less judgmental of one another. However, this challenge runs in a continuum, from a somewhat challenging person to a seriously difficult person who is quite disruptive. Encountering the latter types of people means that challenging emotions will be rising. Other team members may feel annoyed, frustrated, hopeless, or angry. As a consultant or team leader helping the team work with this situation, several interventions are possible. In making your decision on what to choose, be guided by how much power or influence you have, by your resources and skills, and by the willingness of the individuals involved. It may be that the individual is open to coaching or communication training. The whole team may benefit from some team building that supports team members' understanding of one another and honest evaluation of how they are working together and what changes they can agree to in order to improve team functioning.

If the person is a bully, a different response is required. The first step is to be certain everyone feels safe, so call in extra resources if necessary. This is the type of situation that demands a response if you are committed to team effectiveness.

Fear of Scarcity of Resources

Difficult emotions rise up for many reasons for a team. In addition to challenges with one another, fear of inadequate resources can affect a team's productivity and lead to turf battles between team members. The first step in developing an effective team response is to clarify the reason for the upset. Perhaps it's that the team doesn't have the funding to buy the necessary supplies to do the project or doesn't have enough time or the technical capacity to perform the work. Finding that it's a resource rather than a personality issue helps the team respond much more effectively. Too often the deep concern team members have about resources is unrecognized or is treated dismissively. If left undiscovered, it's all too likely to be projected onto someone else and become a personality issue. Once the concern is identified, the response must relate to the current circumstances. For example, if the resource just isn't available, it will still help a team feel more respected if their concern is acknowledged. If changes can be made, finding out the nature of the concern is the necessary first step to providing those resources.

Tips on Managing Your Team's Difficult Emotions

Several tips already have been identified to support a team in working with difficult emotions. Some additional broad-based steps include:

- Assess the team to find out what's going on and what types of emotions are being experienced—look for both the positive and the difficult emotions. Use personality and EQ measures such as the EQ-i® and the TESI®.
- Acknowledge their feelings and respond as fully as time and resources allow. If you promise a response—do it. Don't make promises you won't keep; it will only make matters worse.
- Build awareness and willingness to be emotionally aware of the members of the team and the collective team emotions.
- Build communications capacities.
- Build positive mood.

SUMMARY

In summary, we applied TESI® data accumulated so far on individual ratings on their teams from leadership and emotional intelligence training groups to conduct an in-depth analysis of conflict resolution and its relationship to divergent thinking. This analysis was triggered by individuals rating their teams as least capable in exercising skills in conflict resolution and our hypothesis that this was due in part to the increased requirement for using divergent thinking to be accomplished in this skill. We found in looking at the TESI® scale scores that teams with perceived restricted divergent thinking are rated as having visibly lower competence in conflict resolution than teams with perceived higher divergent thinking capabilities. Further, communication follows a similar pattern, albeit less prominently and it, too, requires a higher level of divergent of thinking than do the other scales. This supports the hypothesis that divergent thinking is a skill that will support teams in meeting a key challenge. It is an area team leaders and consultants will do well to work on with their teams. It is hoped that the insights gained with this report will provide valuable food for thought for publication and client applications.

The chapter highlighted the importance of working with both positive and negative emotions for a team to excel at conflict resolution and offered some recommendations on how to manage situations that arise from several different types of difficult emotions.

REFERENCES

Bar-On, R. (1997). *The emotional quotient inventory (EQ-i®): Technical manual.* Toronto, Canada: Multi-Health Systems, Inc.

Barsade, S. (2002). The ripple effect: Emotional contagion and its influence on group behavior. *Administrative Science Quarterly, 47,* 644–675.

Elfenbein, H.A. (2006). Team emotional intelligence: What it can mean and how it can affect performance. In V.U. Druskat, F. Sala, & G. Mount (Eds.), *Linking emotional intelligence and performance at work.* Mahwah, NJ: Lawrence Erlbaum Associates.

Hughes, M., & Terrell, J. (2007). *The emotionally intelligent team.* San Francisco: Jossey-Bass.

Hughes, M., Thompson, H., & Terrell, J. (2008). *TESI technical manual.* Golden, CO: Collaborative Growth.

Janis, I.L. (1972). *Victims of groupthink.* Boston, MA: Houghton Mifflin.

Reus, T.H., & Liu, Y. (2004). Rhyme and reason: Emotional capability and the performance of knowledge-intensive work groups. *Human Performance, 17*(2), 245–266.

Marcia Hughes is president of Collaborative Growth and serves as a strategic communications partner for teams and their leaders in organizations that value high performers. She weaves her expertise in emotional intelligence throughout her consulting, keynotes, facilitation, and team building. She is co-author of *The TESI® Short Facilitator's Guide Set* (2009), *A Coach's Guide for Emotional Intelligence* (2008), *The Emotionally Intelligent Team* (2007), *Emotional Intelligence in Action (2005),* and author of *Life's 2% Solution.* Hughes is co-creator of the Team Emotional and Social Intelligence Survey® (TESI®), which supports team growth world-wide. She is a certified trainer in the Bar-On EQ-i® and EQ-360®. Marcia provides train-the-trainer training and coaching in powerful EQ delivery.

CHAPTER 8

From Individual to Organizational Emotional Intelligence

Steven J. Stein

Carlos woke up bright and early. It was Monday morning and he was already excited about his day. His mind was racing, trying to solve a complex puzzle at work. He was developing a new system for his company's website. He had thought of a novel way to track visitors to the site and customize information packets specific to their indicated interests. The website had a history of poor ratings on its effectiveness, and Carlos and his team had been turning it around with huge increases in customer ratings for responsiveness. He couldn't wait to present his new ideas to his supervisor and his team.

A few blocks away, Nicole, after hearing her alarm clock go on for the third time, knocked it over while trying to shut it off. She'd give anything to stay in bed. She dreaded the thought of going to work. She had never been so bored at a job before and she had nothing in common with her co-workers. She felt her supervisor only spoke to her when she was doing something wrong. The very thought of going to the office made her stomach ache.

Nicole and Carlos are both very talented individuals with a lot to offer an organization. They're close in age, have similar academic qualifications and, until recently, similar work backgrounds. How did they end up at such different places in their careers? Was Carlos smarter than Nicole? Or was he just luckier? Did he make wiser career choices along the way?

There's probably no simple answer to the question of why some people find the job they love and contribute so much to the success of their organizations. Or, on the other hand, why some talented individuals end up miserable in their careers and, rather than contribute, become a drain on their organization's resources.

In fact, one of the most frequent questions I hear from other CEOs goes something like, "How do I motivate my people?" There seems to be this perception out there that, if only we could turn on the right switch, find the precise carrots, or the best sticks, we could turn our workforce into the champion race horses we thought we hired. After all, how often have we heard the catchphrase, "Our people are our most important asset"? One acerbic (and fairly unpopular) boss once told me that if they're so valuable maybe he should sell them.

WHAT'S EMOTIONAL INTELLIGENCE GOT TO DO WITH IT?

While the concepts of emotional and social intelligence have been alluded to for over fifty years, psychologists Peter Salovey of Yale University and John (Jack) Mayer of the University of New Hampshire were the first to publish a scientific article outlining the currently accepted notion of the topic (Salovey & Mayer, 1990). The case for the importance of individual emotional intelligence in our work, life, and family was further elaborated by Dan Goleman (1995). The first published test measuring social and emotional intelligence was developed by Reuven Bar-On (1997).

Together with co-author Howard Book, I have provided more detail on the case for emotional intelligence at work in our book, *The EQ Edge: Emotional Intelligence and Your Success* (Stein & Book, 2006). As well, we have provided examples and step-by-step exercises that can help you increase your emotional and social intelligence. Our book also cites numerous scientific studies supporting the benefits of emotional and social intelligence.

I've had the privilege of observing many organizations derive the benefits that accrue from focusing on emotional and social intelligence skills in their people. These gains have occurred through applications in employee selection, development, teams, and leadership. However, even with significant gains being made, it soon became apparent to me that there were even greater achievements that could be made through focusing on the organization as a whole. Highly emotionally and socially intelligent employees, managers, teams, and leaders are necessary but not sufficient to become a really great organization.

WHAT'S AN EMOTIONALLY INTELLIGENT ORGANIZATION?

Imagine an orchestra filled with virtuoso musicians. Each musician is well-trained and accomplished. Each individual or small group of instruments (e.g., woodwinds or brass) can produce wonderful music. It would only seem obvious then that a room full of highly accomplished musicians could do nothing but produce the best music. However, great musicians, even when they work well in teams or sections, do not guarantee an orchestra's success.

As in any organization, having the best people is only one step toward a highly successful enterprise. Making sure the right person is in the right place, or in the right seat on the bus as Jim Collins (2001) would say, is the next step. However, in order for the organization to be truly world-class, you need to pay attention to other factors that include leadership skills, shared purpose, teamwork, mutual respect, and a responsive management.

Most work in today's world involves dealing with other people. Even those who work remotely encounter others they must communicate with either virtually (using text only), face-to-face, or virtually face-to-face (using video). Your ability to navigate these relationships helps determine your success at work. But again, there are factors outside any one individual that help determine organizational success. This chapter focuses on those factors.

An organization is clearly more than the sum of its parts. We need to look even beyond the satisfaction, motivation, and goals of each individual for determining organizational success. The ability to measure and understand the organizational emotional and social intelligence is the first step toward helping an organization reach its full potential.

However, before we can measure a concept such as organizational emotional intelligence, we need to define it first. Organizational emotional intelligence involves people's feelings and thoughts about the work they do, their co-workers, supervisors, top leadership, the organization itself, and their impact on the world around them.

My definition of organizational emotional intelligence is

> An organization's ability to successfully and efficiently cope with change and accomplish its goals, while being responsible and sensitive to its people, customers, suppliers, networks, and society. (Stein, 2007, p. 89)

I also look at the organization through two functionally different aspects—the *tactical* and the *strategic*. The tactical level involves the daily transactions that go on in almost any workplace. These include such things as the way managers manage their people—the rewards and punishments used to get compliance with written and unwritten rules. Also included are people's individual needs and values, job-skills match, motivation, and teamwork.

The strategic component involves a more transformational level. This includes the organization's mission and strategy, its leadership, and the overall organizational culture. Strategic change, unlike some tactical changes, requires major commitment and initiatives involving senior people of the organization.

WHAT MAKES A TRULY GREAT WORKPLACE?

After having studied a variety of workplaces that ranged from poor to great, I have identified seven key factors that every organization needs to pay attention to if they want to excel (Stein & MHS Staff, 2005; Stein, 2007).

My definition of a successful organization is one that is people-oriented, efficient, productive, and innovative. It's the kind of organization where talented people want to work. Leaders of these organizations tend to ask me how to select from among the dozens of great applicants that come to their doors. In contrast, I meet other leaders who tell me that there seems to be a serious shortage of talent to choose from.

But before getting to the seven keys, I want to outline the three foundations that I believe underlie any truly great workplace today. These are the work itself, relationships at work, and work with purpose. Let's look at these factors through the eyes of Carlos and Nicole.

The Work

Carlos loves his work. He even problem solves work situations during some of his free time on weekends. In his job, he is able to take control over a project and determine the best way to get it done. He works with a team and each person has clear roles and responsibilities. Communication is open and decisions are made based on what is in everyone's best interest. He chooses how to go about designing and fixing.

For Nicole the work is quite different. While she has the same training in information technology as Carlos, her role is well defined as a small piece of a larger puzzle. Because she doesn't receive information about the "big picture," she works away at small tasks. Sometimes the tasks have to be redone because she eventually learns that the protocol she was using doesn't fit with the bigger picture. Nicole is often micro-managed; her supervisor may check on her progress several times a day. She is basically told how she is to program each part of the project she works on.

While Carlos and Nicole both became information technology specialists because they liked the creative aspect of putting together computer code in order to bring applications to life, only Carlos has experienced the excitement of the process. Nicole describes her work as tedious, frustrating, and uninspiring. Carlos sees his as challenging, innovative, and creative.

How people feel about their work is a critical aspect of work success. While the workplace environment has a lot to do with how people feel about their work, another critical aspect involves the match between the person and the job. Much of the time and effort put into selection has to do with getting the right person into the right job at the right organization. Too often companies tend to hire the best warm body they can find for a job that is open. But how do you determine who the best candidate is?

Unfortunately, resumes are often padded and rarely checked carefully for inaccuracies. The most widely used criteria for selection has been the job interview. Interviews provide an opportunity for candidates to show their best performance. The two biggest problems with interviews are their low reliability and low predictive validity.

Low reliability in this case means that the chance of two people agreeing on a candidate's performance during an interview, using an objective scale, is low. Predictive validity is the ability of the interview presentation and content to determine how well someone will actually do on the job. So while a candidate for a sales position may wax eloquently about his or her past successes and brilliant sales strategies, we know all too well from both experience and research that a great interview does not necessarily mean that a candidate will be a star, or even a good sales person in the new organization.

Psychometric testing is the fairest, most objective, and scientific way to determine the likelihood of a candidate's success. While interviews, resumes, and references may be useful checks in the process, validated assessment procedures give you the most educated guesses on future performance. Although many kinds of tests have been used in selection—cognitive (IQ), aptitude, interest, personality—there has been much promise in the use of validated emotional intelligence testing such as with the Emotional Quotient Inventory® (EQ-i®) and Mayer-Salovey-Caruso Emotional Intelligence Test (MSCEIT®) (Stein, 2007).

One of the first steps in developing high-performance organizations involves placing the right people in the right positions. By looking at a person's emotional and social skills and strengths as well as his or her technical skills and abilities, you maximize the chances of success. Selecting people who are high in empathy, for example, has been associated with success in jobs that include relationship sales or business development. On the other hand, if scores in emotional self-awareness are too high, it may predict lower performance in jobs that involve excessive negative customer interaction such as making sales cold calls or high-intensity customer service.

Finding people who love the work they do is one of the keys to building a successful organization. It's important to make the right match between a person's strengths and the requirements of the job. For example, someone having a passion for working with numbers should explore working in a position that maximizes that passion. Likewise, someone who loves meeting with people and building relationships should look for a job that emphasizes those skills.

Relationships

One of the things about his job that Carlos gets excited about is his team. As a group they really click. Not only do they work well together but they have a number of shared interests. They follow the same sports teams, regale in stories about their kids' activities, and enjoy talking about politics.

On the other hand, Nicole feels she's on a different planet from her co-workers. They share very little in common. Some of them will share stories about the previous night's TV shows. Another colleague talks constantly about her problems with childcare for her three-year-old. Other than specific work tasks, Nicole has little to talk about with her associates. Once her work for the day is done, she is happy to leave the office as quickly and quietly as she can. She even avoids company-organized social activities.

Organizations have only recently begun to pay attention to the importance of social interactions at work. Ten years ago employers were fearful of promoting work relationships. The temptation of the office romance was seen as dangerous to the work environment. However, there is now more discussion and acceptance of the idea of having a best friend at work. Studies by Gallup (Rath, 2006) have found that people with a best friend at work were as much as seven times more productive than those who did not socialize with co-workers.

Purpose

Nicole's view of her job is to get her work done as best she can and collect a paycheck. She has little real interest in the bigger picture of the project she's working on, the customer's perspective of the program, or even how the project may help her company get bigger and better projects as a result of the experience gained. Carrying out her duties is seen by her as a way to pass the time. While she is quite conscientious about her work and tries to perform well, she sees no greater purpose in her work than getting one job done and moving on to the next one. The reality is that the project she's working on could be helpful to and make a difference in the lives of thousands of people worldwide suffering from a serious medical condition.

By contrast, Carlos sees himself as making a significant contribution to society. While his group is just one piece of a much larger project, he sees the importance of his work in the overall success of the project. Even more importantly, he sees the overall project as having a noticeable effect in the world. The program his company is developing can impact hundreds of thousands of people who are in need of government services.

We all know people who come to work each day for a paycheck. They have little interest in their work or the workplace in general. On the other hand, there are others who come to work because they feel that their work helps make the world a better place in some way. Whatever it is you do for a living, the chances are high that some aspect of your work has a positive impact on other people somewhere or in your community at large. Whether it's your fellow employees, customers, students, the environment, or the community, somewhere down the line there is most likely a beneficiary to the work you do.

MEASURING ORGANIZATIONAL EMOTIONAL INTELLIGENCE

How does one go about understanding an organization's culture and level of emotional intelligence? One way might be to spend a year or so living in the organization, getting to know the people, the different teams, the leadership, and so on. Another more efficient and objective way is to survey as many people as possible from that organization.

The Benchmark of Organizational Emotional Intelligence (BOEI) (Stein & MHS Staff, 2005) was designed to do that. An anonymous survey, taken on paper or online, allows employees to express their feelings and thoughts about various aspects of the organization. Based on normative data from dozens of organizations in a number of countries, the BOEI provides a snapshot of the organization's functioning from the perspective of employees—both line and management.

The BOEI assessment is comprised of factors that range from workplace necessities to company ideals. These areas were developed based on our

Table 8.1. BOEI Factor Structure

Scales	Subscales
Job Happiness	
Compensation	Pay/Benefits
Work/Life Stress Management	Stability/Stress Management/Work/Life Balance
Organizational Cohesiveness	Co-Worker Relationships/Teamwork
Supervisory Leadership	
Diversity and Anger Management	Diversity Climate/Gender/Racial Acceptance/ Anger Management
Organizational Responsiveness	Training and Innovation
Optimism and Integrity	Courage and Adaptability/Top Management Leadership
Positive Impression	Negative Impression
Total BOEI	

From Stein and MHS Staff (2005). Reprinted with permission of Multi-Health Systems. www.mhs.com

definition of organizational emotional intelligence, reviews of the research literature on organizational surveys, pilot study data collection with earlier versions of the BOEI, and ongoing statistical analysis to ensure the BOEI is a valid and reliable measure. The factors measured and their subscales can be found in Table 8.1.

COMPARISON OF WORK SETTINGS

Both Carlos' and Nicole's workplaces have participated in a BOEI survey. Carlos works for a company that we'll call Acme Systems. Their survey results appear in Figure 8.1.

Contrast those results to Nicole's organization, which we'll call Bounty Systems, seen in Figure 8.2. As can be seen, there are distinct differences

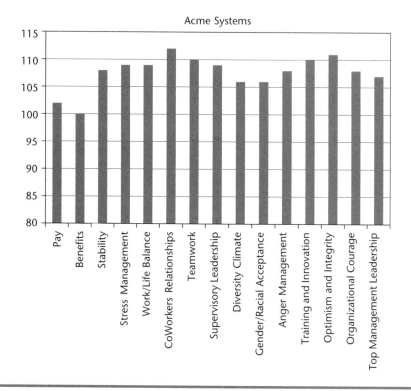

Figure 8.1. BOEI Results for Acme Systems

Used with permission of Multi-Health Systems Inc.

between how these employees feel about their workplaces. I will highlight a few of the areas where the differences are striking.

Does Pay Really Matter?

One surprise in the BOEI results of these companies was the finding related to how employees felt about their pay. In our surveys of organizations in general, pay and benefits are usually the most challenging of the ratings made. Interestingly, the salaries paid at Bounty Systems are roughly the same as those at Acme Systems. However, as seen in the graphs, Acme employees report feeling better about their pay than Bounty employees do. At Bounty, the top leaders believe their employee pay scales are high in comparison to the industry standard. Managers at Bounty feel they are entitled to make unreasonable demands on employees because of the high amounts

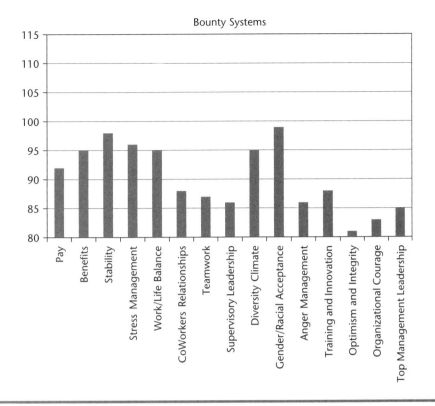

Figure 8.2. BOEI Results for Bounty Systems

Used with permission of Multi-Health Systems Inc.

they are paid. The overriding sentiment is that if people are not happy with heavy workloads and unpredictable work schedules, then they are free to leave Bounty. For many years it has been relatively easy to find new employees willing to accept these conditions. However, according to their human resource manager, good candidates have been much harder to find lately.

Acme, on the other hand, looks at pay systems as a strategic aspect of their employee engagement program. Unlike Bounty, they are not generally regarded as among the highest-paying companies in the industry. Their reputation is one of a more exciting place to work with great opportunities to learn and develop. Acme has a carefully constructed earnings system in which every employee is rewarded based on performance. Performance, however, is not just a measure of each individual's effort. Each person, from senior executive to mail room staff, has three levels of goals. These include individual, team, and company goals. In order to realize any pay incentives, an employee must first reach 90 percent of his or her individual goals. To receive an additional pay incentive, that person's team must reach its group goals. To become fully incentivized, the entire company must reach its projected targets and goals.

People working at Acme feel they are part of an integrated system. They get excited whenever any part of the organization is successful, because they know that it ultimately affects them directly. When a major new contract is acquired or when a customer writes in praising outstanding customer service, everyone from the accounting staff to the programmers feel a part of the success.

Employees at Bounty Systems are pretty detached from each other. Business development people only worry about their commission and bonus and pay little attention to after-service issues. Tech-support people go to any length to prevent calls from escalating to their supervisors, who usually deal with complaints by reprimanding the support staff for not keeping the customer quiet. People at Bounty have little awareness about what goes on in other departments, nor do they seem to care.

The pay structure at Acme brings strong benefits to other areas of the company, as seen on the BOEI. As previously mentioned, the nature of the compensation system affects co-worker relationships. Not only do co-workers at Acme see their colleagues as important to their financial success, but they try hard to attract people they like to the organization. Acme goes out of its way to promote positive social relationships in the workplace.

It's About the People

There are many examples of people-friendly policies and initiatives at Acme. For example, every Friday the company sponsors a breakfast for all its employees. The breakfast is seen as a way to get people from across the organization to get to know each other better. After all, you never know when Sue in marketing needs some extra detailed information from Ali in accounting or help in getting a package out quickly from Brad in shipping.

At Bounty, the departments function more as silos and the marketing people would have a hard time trying to figure out who to contact in accounting for some specific sales information. The first step would be to go to a supervisor, who would then contact her manager, who would then get to the senior accounting manager, who would eventually assign the task down to one of the junior accounting people. Chances are the specific request has changed somewhat from its original shape and form and the timeliness of the information has been lost by then.

Several initiatives were eventually implemented at Bounty resulting in their being more responsive to employees. A major effort was made to improve communications throughout the company. Teams were set up with representation from different departments and were tasked with making the organization a more integrated, people-friendly place.

Managing to Manage

Unfortunately, Bounty Systems has a history of arbitrarily promoting its best technical people to manage others. While it's important to reward your best technical and professional people, making them managers is not always the best way to recognize their good work and loyalty. Managers need specific sets of skills in order to be effective. In today's world they need to be good at coaching others.

As part of the intervention that followed up the BOEI, all managers at Bounty Systems were offered an opportunity to participate in a management development program. First, they were introduced to the skills required to be good managers. Then they were offered opportunities to practice the skills and be evaluated in their implementation. As a result, some managers discovered they were better off in more technical positions and were relieved that they could forgo their "people management" responsibilities without being penalized by the company. For others, it opened up a whole new vista of what management was really about. It allowed them to develop and use skills they had barely flexed before.

WHAT'S THE ORGANIZATION'S UNDERLYING MOOD?

One interesting measure of an organization's health or functioning is the score on the Anger Management Scale of the BOEI. Often consultants will look at this scale to get an idea of the underlying mood in the organization.

In some organizations, people seem relatively happy at a surface level, but underlying what you see can be a degree of anger that works toward slowly sabotaging the workplace. Interestingly, when you interview employees, even as an outside consultant, people often do not admit to these feelings or to the negative behaviors. Apart from a lack of trust, there remains a fear of negative repercussions, no matter how confidential the discussion. However, when people respond anonymously to a survey that captures these issues, it's amazing how often feelings of anger around the organization are willingly reported.

In our examples, we see that Bounty has a fairly low score in this area, especially when compared to Acme. It seems that employees at Bounty have expressed anger to others while at work. The scores indicate that an intervention as soon as possible would be advised. With topics as sensitive as this, an outside consultant is usually the best one to explore the issues raised.

One of the advantages of the BOEI is that there is an option for each individual who completes the survey to receive an individual report comparing his or her results to others in the organization. This often serves as a useful counseling tool. For example, any person who scores significantly lower than the rest of the group may discover that he or she is currently misplaced either in his or her job or in the organization as a whole. This is often a good opportunity for coaching. Many organizations make available the option for employees to seek an external coach. This provides the benefit of an objective sounding board for the individual to get a better understanding of her or his needs and the degree to which they are being met. Some organizations are fearful that they may be paying to "coach" an individual out of his or her job (which is not always the outcome). However, it's better to have someone in the job who wants to be there and is committed to the work, rather than someone who is just passing the time (referred to as presenteeism) until something better comes along.

While going over the results with an individual, team, or department, a consultant can get people to discuss the issues that may have led to particular scores. At Bounty, the consultant discovered that people felt a lot of resentment toward the leaders and the organization. Many of the employees felt that they were taken for granted and that their efforts weren't appreciated. From reviewing the BOEI results, the consultant knew about these feelings before she even met with the staff and managers. The Anger scale tipped her off, as it reflected people losing their tempers with fellow employees as well as some acting out against the company. Because she knew about this going in, she was able to ask sensitive questions and quickly zero in on this area and get people talking about what made them angry. Ordinarily, this level of feeling about the organization might not be uncovered until much later in the process, if at all.

Leading the Organization

Feelings about top management of the company was another area that differentiated Acme from Bounty. At Bounty the leaders were invisible. Occasional emails were sent out regarding one policy or another. Employees rarely saw top leaders. Many employees could not even name the members of the executive team directing the company.

At Acme there are quarterly town hall meetings where the top leaders meet in a large room with all the employees at the head office. The meeting is video-conferenced live to all employees around the world where they participate via their computers. Questions about the company and its policies are anonymously sent to the executive team from employees. They are answered at the town hall meeting (or at least initially addressed and any further action required is outlined). There is a sense among people at Acme that issues are dealt with. Not every request is accepted, but there is a good understanding about what is behind the decisions and how they are made.

From Information to Action

While there may be many areas of concern that are identified in surveys like the BOEI, the ability to select two or three key areas and begin intervening is important for success. Although many interventions are suggested in the BOEI reports, the consultant can creatively adapt suggestions to meet the specific needs of the client. At Bounty, for example, it was important to set up a communication avenue that worked from the bottom up. Employees felt that they had no decision-making input in the company. Being heard was one of the ways of defusing increasing employee anger and resentment. It also led the way to many other improvements throughout the organization.

Because many of the problems at Bounty were transformational and not merely transactional, major changes were required. In order for there to be any success in a situation such as this, all of the senior managers had to be fully engaged in a strategic process. The BOEI results were a major component of a senior executive retreat for planning purposes. Dramatic changes were proposed with specific goals, targets, timelines, and responsibilities. Each of the senior executive managers committed time to implement the changes, which involved them being more involved with line managers and employees. Communication processes were completely overhauled to ensure that leaders were accessible.

As part of employee involvement in the process of change, specific taskforces were set up to deal with issues of concern. Employees volunteered to participate based on their specific interests. There were groups set up that were empowered to work on compensation systems, work/life balance, communications, organizational social responsibility, employee social activities, and other areas.

Initiatives were set up to get employees such as Nicole engaged at work. It was never her intention to withdraw from the workplace. She was bright, energetic, and always saw herself as hard-working and wanting to contribute. She joined a committee at work that focused on ways in which the company could improve the local community. She got to know other people in the company who shared her interests and values. The project she worked on involved helping children of low-income families in need of mental health services. This work helped lead to a dramatic change in Nicole's attitude to work and in her relationships with some of her fellow employees.

CONCLUSION

Engaging people at work is not the end result of any single initiative. It usually involves a comprehensive set of activities that, when well coordinated, gets people caring and involved. Understanding emotional intelligence and how emotion permeates the workplace at both an individual and group level is the first step in employee engagement. It is not a one-time activity, but rather a concerted ongoing effort that requires an investment in time and energy. This is definitely one investment that can lead an organization to some major payback. After all, what can be more important for any organization than investing in its people?

Summary of Best Practice Options

1. Introduce an assessment, such as the BOEI, as a way to specifically measure strengths and weakness in the organization.
2. Before staff is asked to take the assessment, lay the foundation for the importance of their feedback, confidentiality, and how they'll receive feedback.
3. Follow through on results, for example:
   - Meet with the executive team to review the whole set of results and help them set a few strategic goals to begin with.
   - Present a summary of organization-wide results to all staff in person (town hall, video-conference) if possible. Let people know that this is the beginning of a process and thank everyone for their participation.
   - Meet with each team, department, or group leader individually and go over their results and compare their group to the organization. Get feedback on their perception of results, how it was perceived by staff at the town hall meeting, and suggest next steps.
   - Meet personally with each department (group, team, or division), preferably without the leader present, and review results of their group in comparison to the organization as a whole. Get group feedback on the results and discuss possible next steps and solutions.
   - Send a summary of results to all staff identifying the major strengths and weaknesses. Identify the first steps that will be taken. Above all, thank them for their very useful feedback.

REFERENCES

Bar-On, R. (1997). *BarOn emotional quotient inventory (EQ-i®) technical manual.* Toronto: Multi-Health Systems Inc.

Collins, J. (2001). *Good to great: Why some companies make the leap and others don't.* New York: HarperCollins.

Goleman, D. (1995). *Emotional intelligence.* New York: Bantam Books.

Rath, T. (2006). *Vital friends: The people you can't afford to live without.* New York: Gallup Press.

Salovey, P., & Mayer, J.D. (1990). Emotional intelligence. *Imagination, Cognition and Personality, 9,* 185–211.

Stein, S.J. (2007). *Make your workplace great: The 7 keys to an emotionally intelligent organization.* San Francisco: Jossey-Bass.

Stein, S.J., & Book, H.E. (2006). *The EQ edge: Emotional intelligence and your success.* San Francisco: Jossey-Bass.

Stein, S.J., & MHS Staff. (2005). *The benchmark of organizational emotional intelligence technical manual.* Toronto: Multi-Health Systems Inc.

Dr. Steven J. Stein is a clinical psychologist and CEO of Multi-Health Systems (MHS), an internationally known psychological test publishing company. Dr. Stein co-authored (with Dr. Howard Book) the international best-selling book *The EQ Edge: Emotional Intelligence and Your Success* and is the author of the more recent book *Make Your Workplace Great: The 7 Keys to an Emotionally Intelligent Organization.* A leading expert on psychological assessment and emotional intelligence, he has consulted to military and government agencies, including the Canadian Forces, U.S. Air Force, Army, Navy, special units of the Pentagon, FBI Academy, as well as corporate organizations, including American Express, Air Canada, Canyon Ranch, Coca-Cola (Mexico), and professional sports teams. Dr. Stein is the past chairperson of the Psychology Foundation of Canada. He is a former assistant professor in the psychiatry department at the University of Toronto and former adjunct professor of psychology at York University in Toronto. He has appeared on over one hundred TV and radio shows throughout Canada and the United States. He has also been quoted in numerous newspapers and magazines. Dr. Stein often appears as a keynote speaker and has shared information on emotional intelligence with audiences throughout Canada, the United States, Mexico, Europe, Australia, and Asia.

CHAPTER 9

Zeroing in on Star Performance

Diana Durek and Wendy Gordon

More than any other indices designed to predict performance, measures of emotional intelligence (EI) are showing real payoff power when it comes to workplace success. Over a decade of research has consistently demonstrated that those with higher EI, as measured by the Emotional Quotient Inventory (known as the EQ-i®), are more likely to perform at high levels than their less emotionally intelligent co-workers (e.g., Bachman, Stein, Campbell, & Sitarenios, 2000; Jae, 1997; Sitarenios & Stein, 1998). While IQ and technical skills are a requirement for many roles, once a person is in a given job, IQ no longer discriminates between those who succeed and those who do not (Cherniss, 2000). As you will see, factors such as empathy, assertiveness, optimism, and the ability to tolerate stress and control impulses are strong indicators of star performance. As top organizations replace less-effective selection and development activities with ones based on EI, they are beginning to document real bottom-line impact in the form of reduced turnover, increased customer satisfaction, higher productivity, better engagement, and improved leadership.

Emotional intelligence can be improved through training and thus provides an excellent means of identifying strengths and potential growth edges, as well as measuring the effectiveness of individual and organizational development initiatives. Since studies (see Stein & Book, 2006) show that emotional intelligence accounts for 15 to 45 percent of work success, even the most intelligent or highly technically qualified person may not have the emotional makeup to handle the demands of the job environment effectively. Research studies have demonstrated that emotional intelligence predicts effective transformational leadership skills and leadership performance (Barling, Slater, & Kelloway, 2000) and that the absence of emotional intelligence is related to career derailment (Ruderman, Hannum, Leslie, & Steed, 2001). With companies pouring huge amounts of money into selecting and retaining human capital, it's no wonder these studies are revolutionizing how we hire and train talent.

Some of the most dramatic changes are happening in organizations that recognize that certain emotional and social skills are critical in specific roles and embed these skills into their human capital strategy through selection, goal setting, and development. These are the organizations that hone in on their star performers and figure out what makes them stand out. They then actively seek and train individuals to match these skill sets. For some organizations, this process can seem daunting, but there are principles and best practices that apply—no matter the size, budget, sector, or culture—to help ensure that your organization determines the key aspects of emotional functioning to its best advantage.

At MHS, the international publisher of the EQ-i®, our specialists and partners have worked with thousands of organizations—including a significant number of Fortune 500 companies—to help build EQ-i®-based selection and development programs tailored to their needs. The best practices and real-life cases presented in this chapter highlight some of the premiere work examining the role of emotional intelligence and top performance in today's work world. Probably one of the most defining features of the EQ-i® model is the framework it provides for coaching and development. Unlike cognitive skills, a person's emotional intelligence is not fixed at a young age and can therefore be taught and enhanced with practice. It is this opportunity for

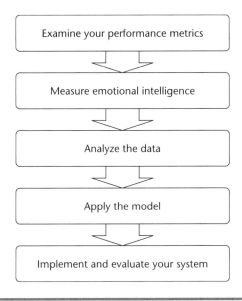

Figure 9.1. The Star Performer Five-Step Process

growth upon which top organizations are building development programs that focus on the unique set of EI skills that predict success within a given job in a given organizational culture. But how do you know which skills are critical for success?

The five-step process presented in this chapter and summarized in Figure 9.1 represents the best practices for building star performer programs used by leading organizations throughout the world. The data are real and often so compelling that many well-known organizations with major international profiles are reluctant to identify themselves as EQ-i® users precisely because they wish to protect the competitive advantage conferred on them by using EI-based star performer systems. What these organizations share is a winning formula for hiring and developing top performers in the workplace.

STEP 1. EXAMINE YOUR PERFORMANCE METRICS

Meet Telplus (a pseudonym used here to protect the company's privacy). Telplus is a large, international telecommunications firm employing more than 8,500 employees. The company provides a full range of Internet, data, voice, mobile, and fixed line calling services, with revenue over $3.5 billion in fiscal year 2005. That same year, Telplus contracted an experienced EI consultant to help them improve leadership within the company. To fully understand what's important to the organization, the consultant gathered performance data for over seventy senior leaders across client services, sales, finance, marketing, HR, and IT, and a statistician divided the leaders into performance groups. As in many organizations, three criteria were used to measure performance at Telplus:

1. *Engagement:* Expressed as a percentage of the individual's direct reports who are engaged based on a series of questions answered by the direct reports themselves. The questions were based on one of the major engagement models and were customized for Telplus. The senior managers who scored in the top one-third were assigned to a "high" group; those who scored in the bottom one-third were assigned to a "low" group.

2. *Leader Competency Model:* Measured by self- and 360-degree ratings collected from managers, peers, and direct reports, this metric is a reflection of the degree on a five-point scale to which the individual effectively:
   - Thinks strategically
   - Makes effective decisions
   - Manages time
   - Encourages innovation
   - Sets goals
   - Motivates and develops others
   - Fosters communication
   - Meets customers' needs

   The overall competency score is expressed as a number from one to five. The score is calculated by averaging all raters' scores in each of the eight areas, then averaging the eight scores for each leader to yield a total competency score. Those who scored in the top one-third were assigned to "high" group; those who scored in the bottom one-third were assigned to a "low" group.

3. Goal Attainment: Three performance groups were created based on the percentage of goals achieved. Each individual was ranked between one and three, with three being the highest performing group, and one

Table 9.1. Goal Attainment Criteria at Telplus

Performance Group	Goals Attained
1	Not Met (Less than 95 percent)
2	Met (95 to 100 percent)
3	Exceed (More than 100 percent)

being the lowest. Table 9.1 highlights how individuals in the top performance group fared on goal attainment compared to low performers.

These groupings identified those workers who really excelled at Telplus compared to those who were falling short so that differentiating features of each group could be compared. Next, the consultant prepared to measure the emotional intelligence variables of all the leaders. The results of this step are used in Step 3, and therefore this process can be conducted simultaneously with Step 2, or perhaps after EI is measured. However, it is first advisable to determine whether sufficient performance data are available to conduct such a study.

STEP 2. MEASURE EMOTIONAL INTELLIGENCE

Any organization can benefit from engaging the principles of EI; however, applying an instrument such as the EQ-i® is more effective because it was developed from a theoretical model, has been used by over one million respondents, and, as this chapter will later demonstrate, has proven itself to be one of the singular most predictive assessments in measuring workplace success. Part of the EQ-i's primacy lies in its intuitive model, which breaks down the concept of EI into five composites, and further into fifteen subscales. These fifteen factors, often dubbed "the building blocks of emotional intelligence," have been shown to predict a person's effectiveness in work and home life, influencing both cognitive and non-cognitive abilities such as conflict resolution, problem solving, coping, memory, and critical thinking. Consider the next time you have to make a decision under an immense amount of pressure. If you take a moment to suspend your impulses, consider how your mood is influencing your perception, and then choose how to respond, you'll realize just what a difference emotional intelligence makes. Instead of reacting in a state of panic, you will be better able to examine all the relevant information and make a successful decision. The fifteen EQ-i® factors are shown in Table 9.2.

The EQ-i® was the first scientifically validated instrument produced for the purpose of assessing emotionally intelligent behavior. It was developed from the comprehensive integration of theoretical knowledge and empirical sophistication guided by state-of-the-art psychometric methodology. Age- and gender-specific norms are available based on a normative sample that exceeds 3,800. Development of this instrument, following scientific methodology, ensures that it assesses emotional and social functioning in a dependable and consistent manner. Without this careful attention to development, obtained scores could not be compared to a yardstick, and would thus be irrelevant. Without norms, scores would be merely numbers and could provide no useful information. Researched and developed in accordance with the highest test development standards, including ongoing analyses to examine the relationships between EQ-i® scores and gender, age, culture, race, and occupation, the EQ-i® is a reliable choice for star performer studies.

The EQ-i® consists of 125 first-person (or self-rated) statements, each with five (Likert scale) response options ranging from "Seldom or never true of me" to "Often or always true of me." Respondents can complete the inventory online or on paper in about fifteen minutes. To ensure conventional levels of statistical significance in star performer studies, it is recommended that a minimum of seventy individuals be tested for emotional intelligence. This threshold poses a challenge for smaller organizations or those wishing to develop a star performer model for unique positions in which only a handful of individuals are employed. In situations such as these, the principles of EI can be used in selection and development without a predictive model that has been empirically derived (see Step 4 later in this chapter). Telplus' goal was to understand the relationship between their performance criteria and emotional intelligence. With the target group established, the senior leaders completed the 125-item EQ-i® online, responding to questions related to the fifteen building blocks of emotional intelligence.

Table 9.2. Skills Assessed by the EQ-i®

EQ-i® Scales	The EI Skills Assessed by Each Scale
Intrapersonal	**Self-awareness and self-expression:**
Self-Regard	To accurately perceive, understand and accept oneself
Emotional Self-Awareness	To be aware of and understand one's emotions
Assertiveness	To effectively and constructively express one's emotions and oneself
Independence	To be self-reliant and free of emotional dependency on others
Self-Actualization	To strive to achieve personal goals and actualize one's potential
Interpersonal	**Social awareness and interpersonal relationship:**
Empathy	To be aware of and understand how others feel
Social Responsibility	To identify with one's social group and cooperate with others
Interpersonal Relationship	To establish mutually satisfying relationships and relate well with others
Stress Management	**Emotional management and regulation:**
Stress Tolerance	To effectively and constructively manage emotions
Impulse Control	To effectively and constructively control emotions
Adaptability	**Change management:**
Reality-Testing	To objectively validate one's feelings and thinking with external reality
Flexibility	To adapt and adjust one's feelings and thinking to new situations
Problem-Solving	To effectively solve problems of a personal and interpersonal nature
General Mood	**Self-motivation:**
Optimism	To be positive and look at the brighter side of life
Happiness	To feel content with oneself and life in general

STEP 3. ANALYZE THE DATA

The first step in analyzing your EI data is to ensure that the data are valid or, in other words, that they provide an accurate reflection of an individual's self-reported emotional and social functioning. If an average inventory takes fifteen minutes to complete, you might consider removing protocols that were completed in eight minutes or less, or ones in which respondents used a recognizable response pattern (such as 1, 2, 3, 4, 1, 2, 3, 4). These results are labeled "invalid" by the EQ-i® due to the likelihood that they do not represent a person's actual responses. Another advantage of the EQ-i® is its ability to flag respondents who present an unusually positive view of themselves; those with elevated scores on Positive Impression (PI) can be removed from the sample so as not to skew the results. The PI score is considered elevated if the score exceeds two standard deviations above the mean (30 points). Once invalid test protocols have been removed, a valid set of data remains that can be analyzed by a statistician or similarly trained professional. Often, this step is best performed by an outside consultant, since connecting individual performance ratings with EQ-i® scores is generally a highly confidential activity. Prior to completing the inventory, the administrator is responsible for informing respondents of who will have access to their results.

Calculation of the contrasting EI skill levels involves comparing each performance group's scores across the fifteen EQ-i® factors. By averaging the Total EQ scores of the individuals in each "high" group, we can see the emotional and social functioning of the top performers in the organization. Repeat the calculation for those in the "low" groups, and you have the average EQ of the low performers. Since Telplus identified three performance criteria, resulting scores compared high versus low scorers in engagement, leader competency, and goal attainment. Like many IQ tests, a score of 100 on the EQ-i® represents an individual with average emotional and social functioning. Figure 9.2 shows the Total EQ of high versus low performers with respect to leader competency. As you can see, those with high leader competency had significantly ($p < .05$) higher EQ-i® scores than those with low competency, suggesting that emotional intelligence is related to workplace success.

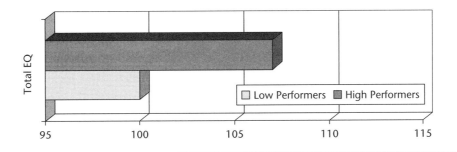

Figure 9.2. Total EQ of Telplus Leaders by Leader Competency Rating

The relationship of emotional and social functioning to performance is a persuasive statistic when aiming to reframe an organization's selection and development strategies, but it is not the star performer model itself. Powerful predictive models zero in at the micro level, thin slicing the specific skills that make a person successful in a given role in a given organization. What makes a successful customer service representative in a call centre that values speed and accuracy may be different than at another that values a friendly and pleasant customer experience. Predictive models using the EQ-i® have higher potency (statistical significance) and are much easier to train toward when framed in terms of the fifteen building blocks of emotional intelligence. Figure 9.3 illustrates the emotional and social functioning of the Telplus leaders, this time broken down by subscale. Once again, the trend is that higher scorers in leader competency have higher EQ-i scores than lower ones, but here we can begin to see specific differences that set the two groups apart.

The next step is to perform statistical analyses that examine the two scores (high Leader Competency group versus low Leader Competency group) for each EQ-i factor, evaluating whether these differences are statistically significant. Table 9.3 shows the results of *t*-tests comparing the high and low Leader Competency groups.

We are now armed with the EQ-i® factors that are statistically different between performance groups. Next, a statistical technique such as discriminant function determines how much of a factor emotional and social

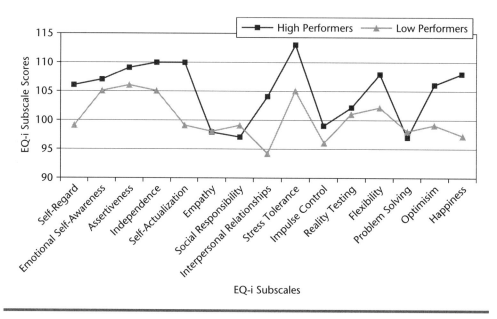

Figure 9.3. EQ-i® Scores of Telplus Leaders by Leader Competency Rating

functioning plays in the performance of a given role and which EQ-i® scales contribute to success. At Telplus, EQ-i® scores accounted for 48 percent of the variance in leadership competency scores between high and low performers. In other words, one half of the skill set required for successful execution of this organization's leader competencies is comprised of emotional and social skills. Specifically, top performance was best predicted by higher scores in Happiness (24 percent), Self-Regard (12 percent), Self-Actualization (9 percent), Interpersonal Relationship (2 percent), and Optimism (1 percent). These factors form the crux of the star performer model at Telplus. To examine the ability of the EQ-i® to predict each aspect of performance important to the organization, the statistician repeats this process for all the other performance metrics. In the case of Telplus, this process was repeated for the engagement and goal attainment metrics. Emotional intelligence was found to play an important role in all three of the performance metrics used by Telplus.

Table 9.3. EQ-i® Scores for Low vs. High Performing Groups in Leader Competency at Telplus

Scale	Low Leader Competency		High Leader Competency		Statistically Significant?
	Mean	Standard Deviation	Mean	Standard Deviation	
Total EQ-i®	100.05	9.52	106.94	9.25	Yes*
INTRAPERSONAL	103.10	11.30	110.11	10.31	Yes*
Self-Regard	98.80	9.44	105.89	9.57	Yes*
Emotional Self-Awareness	105.00	12.24	107.39	14.35	No
Assertiveness	105.75	12.32	109.44	12.19	No
Independence	105.35	13.16	110.22	7.79	No
Self-Actualization	99.15	11.83	109.61	10.00	Yes**
INTERPERSONAL	95.15	10.09	100.67	11.69	No
Empathy	97.60	11.45	98.11	13.72	No
Social Responsibility	98.60	9.45	97.44	10.65	No
Interpersonal Relationship	93.80	11.99	103.61	13.79	Yes*
STRESS MANAGEMENT	100.85	9.89	107.17	8.83	Yes*
Stress Tolerance	105.20	10.13	113.11	10.57	Yes*
Impulse Control	96.45	12.22	99.00	10.87	No
ADAPTABILITY	101.05	10.23	103.00	11.36	No
Reality Testing	102.20	13.17	102.17	13.18	No
Flexibility	102.25	11.93	107.83	8.49	No
Problem Solving	98.05	7.54	97.22	13.04	No
GENERAL MOOD	97.95	11.18	107.56	7.98	Yes**
Optimism	99.40	8.15	106.39	11.11	Yes*
Happiness	97.40	15.27	108.11	7.87	Yes**

* $p < .05$, ** $p < .01$.

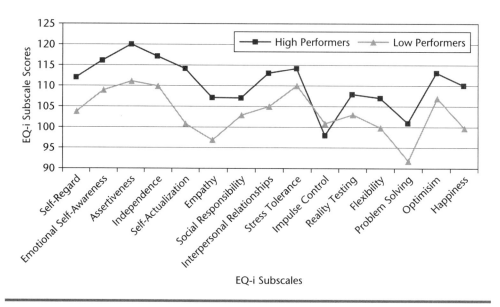

Figure 9.4. EQ-i® Scores of Sales Directors at a Fortune 100 Company by Executive Performance Rating

Studies in other organizations demonstrate that star performer models are not transferable. In one Fortune 100 financial services provider, the EQ-i® formed the basis of a star performer model used for selection. Here, a subjective rating was used to determine performance level. A group of sales directors took the EQ-i® and were rated by executives as high or low performers. Statistical analyses later confirmed that the high-rated directors actually did out-perform the others in terms of sales. The four-year compound annual growth rate (CAGR) for the high performing group was 15 percent—much higher than that of the lower performers (–1 percent). Figure 9.4 shows that those managers rated as "excellent" by the executives had higher EQ-i® scores across fourteen of the fifteen subscales than those rated at a lower performance level.

For the sales directors, scores were highest in the Intrapersonal skill set (Emotional Self-Awareness, Assertiveness, and Independence). Interestingly, when we compare the profiles of these leaders to those at Telplus (Figure 9.3), we can see that the patterns are quite dissimilar, suggesting that factors such as industry, organizational culture, the company's life cycle stage, and competitive strategy affect which EI factors will be most relevant to performance at a particular point in time. You may recall from Table 9.3 that the subscales scores that were statistically different between Leadership Competency performance groups at Telplus were Self-Regard, Self-Actualization, Interpersonal Relationship, Stress Tolerance, Optimism, and Happiness. For the Fortune 100 sales directors, however, the factors that were statistically different between the two groups were Independence, Empathy, and Assertiveness. Just as was done at Telplus, we conducted further analyses to identify the subscales that predict performance for the Fortune 100 sales directors. Recalling the 16 percent span in CAGRs between top and bottom sales groups, it was extremely exciting to see that the directors' EQ-i® scores accounted for 24 percent of the team's overall sales. The two studies suggest that, although it might be temping to borrow star performer models for comparable roles, it is important to use your organization's own performance metrics to identify the key EI skills important to a particular job function, and thus, to ascertain the value of emotional intelligence.

STEP 4. APPLY THE MODEL

The predictive model starts with an optimal profile of emotional and social functioning gleaned from comparing the EQ-i® results of high and low performers in the same role. The model can be comprised of any number of EQ-i® factors, depending on the combination that accounts for the differences in performance. In selection applications, when a candidate completes the EQ-i®, a value is generated to express the strength of a candidates' match against known high performers in the position. For example, a candidate's EQ-i® results may indicate that she has a 72 percent chance of becoming a star performer. Accurate in predicting star performers nine times out of ten, Telplus' star performer model lends empirical support for embedding EI into human capital initiatives.

At Telplus, the factors Happiness, Self-Regard, Self-Actualization, Interpersonal Relationship, and Optimism were incorporated into the leadership programs to increase training efficacy. In this case, the high amount of leadership competency accounted for by EQ-i® scales demonstrated the powerful impact of EI on leadership at Telplus. The ratio of EI skills to non-EI skills (Figure 9.5) shows how important emotional intelligence is in Telplus leader success.

Telplus implemented an EI-based coaching and training program for senior managers that, at the time of this writing, has continued to drive performance for over two years. The star performer model supported the business case to use emotional intelligence as the foundation of their learning and development strategy. Like several other organizations, Telplus found that high scores on the EQ-i® are not always the best predictors of all aspects of high performance. For example, results also revealed that leaders with average scores in assertiveness and problem solving had employees with higher levels of engagement. Given that most people want to solve their own problems and are empowered by the opportunity, this relationship is not surprising. When a subordinate approaches his manager with a problem and the manager solves it rather than supporting the employee to find the solution, the subordinate does not have the opportunity to learn and, over time, may become frustrated and ultimately less engaged. Understanding how emotional and social functioning directly affects engagement enables Telplus to pinpoint leaders who routinely overshadow

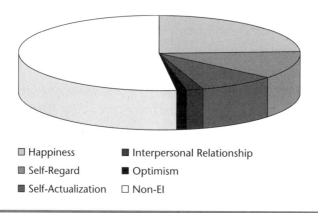

Figure 9.5. Leader Competency Predictors for Telplus Leaders

their subordinates' problem-solving opportunities and to help these leaders learn how to involve direct reports in daily decisions.

How do you decide whether the star performer model is best used in selection or development? The short answer is to identify the organization's pain points and align the star performer model with required organizational outcomes. If the company is experiencing costly dropouts, as was the case with Air Canada, a selection system that incorporates emotional intelligence is the place to start. In the past two years, Air Canada has used the EQ-i® as part of the process in the selection of over 650 new pilots. "Incorporating the EQ-i® into Air Canada's pilot selection process has enabled our company to identify candidates who possess not only the advanced technical skills but also the necessary emotional and social competencies predictive of long-term success as an Air Canada pilot," says Capt. David Legge, vice president of flight operations.

"An airline captain is, if you want to look at it in a certain way, a team leader. He's overseeing the cockpit crew, the flight deck crew as well as the cabin crew. And he's not only interacting with the other crew members but also with other departments within the airline," Legge reports. "Obviously, if you have to interact well with other people, these are instruments that we can use during the selection process to identify people who have these enhanced skills," he says. "At the end of the day, we want to have a better idea of who we're hiring." Air Canada's original pain point was the high cost of training dropouts, so by aligning emotional intelligence to the goal of increasing pilot trainee retention, the company was able to address the issue and see quick outcomes.

Rather than focusing on one process in isolation, some business challenges require a more integrated, systemic approach. In a study evaluating the development of an EI training program at American Express, Cary Cherniss suggests infusing emotional intelligence into the organization in a variety of ways. "Multiple infusion helps to normalize and generalize the concept," Cherniss reports. "It also creates a culture in which people are repeatedly reminded of what they have learned and thus are more likely to apply it on the job" (Cherniss, n.d.). A systemic approach means considering not only the organization's selection system, but also how it develops and rewards its employees. Together, these three systems combine to create the organization's human capital strategy shown in Figure 9.6. Here, emotional

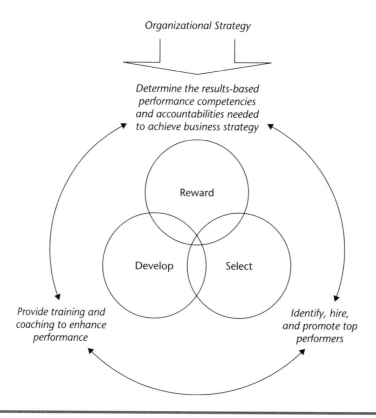

Figure 9.6. Human Capital Strategy

intelligence can be worked into a multi-system solution so that initiatives such as succession planning, hiring, coaching, and leadership development are aligned with business goals.

In fact, the more emotional intelligence can be worked into each of the three areas strategically, the more likely the organization will have enhanced outcomes throughout its system. Further, this multi-dimensional approach has synergistic effects as the successes complement one another. This strategy demonstrates that EI is important to the organization and its success at all levels. When performance metrics, selection criteria, development plans, and organizational goals are complementary, employees get a consistent message that the organization will support them in achieving its goals.

For example, when interpersonal skills are important to success within your organization, it is critical for you to hire for these skills, as well as foster and reinforce desired behaviors. To integrate emotional intelligence skills into individual performance management, create descriptions of relevant interpersonal behaviors. These behaviors can then be rated and appropriate actions taken to leverage your employees' overall performance.

STEP 5. IMPLEMENT AND EVALUATE YOUR SYSTEM

Telplus recognized the advantages of integrating EI training into its learning and development strategy and used the outcomes of the star performer analysis to build a business case for creating a training and coaching program. Now, leaders at Telplus participate in programs designed to build virtually every aspect of their emotional intelligence, supporting the development of happiness, self-regard, self-actualization, interpersonal relationships, and optimism.

To date, one of the most well-known studies undertaken that examined the role of emotional intelligence and success was with the U.S. Air Force in 1996. The head of the recruitment project, Lieutenant Colonel Rich Handley, initiated the testing of 1,500 Air Force recruiters and found that EQ-i® scores accounted for 45 percent of success. Five EQ-i® subscales were identified that differentiated those who achieved 100 percent of their quota versus those who achieved less than 80 percent. MHS created a star performer model for hiring new recruiters, and the EQ-i® responses of all potential recruiters are captured and compared with this model. To this day, prospective candidates also take part in a structured EQ-i® interview developed to confirm the areas of strength or weakness pinpointed by the self-report instrument. Among the initial 250 to 300 recruiters the Air Force hired using this formula, the retention rate increased by 92 percent. Factoring in the costs of hiring, training, and settling a new recruit into a position, this translated into a $2.7 million savings (Stein & Book, 2006).

The differences in the ways Telplus and the U.S. Air Force applied the star performer results illustrate the two major decisions organizations need to make to determine the scope of EQ-i® integration. The first decision involves the strategic areas in which the model is implemented (see Figure 9.6), while the second decision concerns which skills will be developed and reevaluated (see Figure 9.7). Whereas the Air Force hired and trained recruiters based on the five discrete scales identified (Assertiveness, Empathy, Happiness, Emotional Self-Awareness, and Problem Solving), Telplus implemented a holistic approach to creating their development program, embracing emotional intelligence as a marriage of many complex and interdependent skills. The Air Force's targeted approach included using specific interview questions to explore for empathy, for example, and then reinforcing this particular skill by training. At Telplus, participants review their results on all fifteen EQ-i® scales and work with a coach to determine the areas of development most pertinent to their roles. In both cases, the organizations were able to boost the emotional and social skills necessary for high performance because they chose the scope that was right for their organization and its aims.

Like the U.S. Air Force, organizations such as the Canadian Imperial Bank of Commerce (CIBC) are finding EQ-i® star performer models to be immensely impactful in selection and development. Brian Twohey, head of CIBC's Global Private Banking and Trust, firmly believes that emotional intelligence is key to his team's performance. When the EQ-i® scores of the global sales force were compared to their sales, CIBC found that EQ-i factors accounted for 32 percent of sales and 71 percent of sales "in the hopper." Like Telplus, CIBC's sales force performance was largely accountable to each member's interpersonal relationships skills and level of self-actualization. But at CIBC, other factors predictive of higher sales were empathy, flexibility,

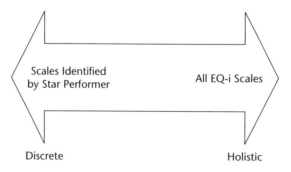

Figure 9.7. Potential Scope of EQ-i® Scale Integration

Handbook for Developing Emotional and Social Intelligence

and the ability to tolerate stress. When these factors were combined together in a star performer formula, Twohey found he had a powerful tool to use both in the selection of new personnel and in his efforts to improve the already superior skills of his current staff.

A similar star performer study was conducted by the Ontario Principals' Council (OPC) by James Parker, Howard Stone, and Laura Wood. Their research (related in Chapter 17 of this book) identifies seven key emotional and social skills required by school administrators and offers an excellent illustration of how a star performer model can be used to establish emotional intelligence training. In organizations such as OPC, Telplus, and Deloitte, development programs based on the EQ-i® model of emotional and social functioning are proving to have a positive effect on key competencies and the bottom line.

Another study involving American Express Financial Advisors aimed to improve sales by helping advisors manage the emotional conflicts that they sometimes encountered when working with clients around life insurance matters. An Emotional Competence Program for Financial Advisors was implemented as part of the learning and development strategy to great success. The sales of the Financial Advisors who attended the program were 16 percent greater than the company as a whole (Consortium for Research on Emotional Intelligence in Organizations, n.d.).

SUMMARY

As you can see, these results have powerful implications for selection and development initiatives in organizations. A thoughtfully planned and implemented EI-based star performer system is an empirical method of improving hiring and training across a variety of positions. When preparing your initiative, remember these best practices:

1. For each position in question, collect a separate set of performance data and develop a unique star performer profile. Profiles are not transferable among positions or organizations.
2. Ensure the sample is comprised of at least seventy employees performing a similar role upon which to draw your data.

3. Find out what criteria the organization uses to determine its top performers. Based on these performance metrics, divide the sample into high, middle, and low performance groups.

4. Measure the emotional intelligence of the sample using a scientifically validated instrument. Do not include any invalid protocols in the analyses.

5. Through statistical analyses, determine the EI factors that differentiate the high and low performance groups. Use a statistical technique such as discriminant function to determine how much of a factor EI plays in the sample's performance.

6. Determine the scope of implementing the resulting profile. Will it be used solely for the selection of a single position or integrated into development initiatives in an overall human capital strategy? Will the organization concentrate on only the most predictive factors or use a more holistic approach and provide training on all areas of EI?

7. Evaluate your system by determining cost savings and improved performance, or whatever other metrics are meaningful to the organization. Effective communication of outcomes can be the most persuasive means of boosting the visibility of your initiative.

By following the best practices in this chapter, any organization can use a scientifically validated test of emotional intelligence to gauge the importance of emotional and social skills in the organization. Like the leading organizations we've highlighted, consider the impact of developing an empirically based predictive model in order to enhance the selection and development of human capital in your organization.

REFERENCES

Bachman, J., Stein, S. J., Campbell, K., & Sitarenios, G. (2000). Emotional intelligence in the collection of debt. *International Journal of Selection and Assessment, 8,* 176–182.

Barling, J., Slater, F., & Kelloway, E.K. (2000). Transformational leadership and emotional intelligence: An exploratory study. *Leadership & Organization Development Journal, 21*(3), 157–161.

Cherniss, C. (n.d.). *Guidelines for securing organizational support for emotional intelligence efforts.* Retrieved July 1, 2008, from www.eiconsortium.org/reports/guidelines_for_securing_org_support.html.

Cherniss, C. (2000, April). *Emotional intelligence: What it is and why it matters.* Paper presented at the Annual Meeting of the Society for Industrial and Organizational Psychology, New Orleans.

Consortium for Research on Emotional Intelligence in Organizations. (n.d.). *Emotional competence training—American Express financial advisors.* Retrieved July 1, 2008, from www.eiconsortium.org/model_programs/emotional_competence_training.html.

Jae, J. H. (1997). *Emotional intelligence and cognitive ability as predictors of job performance in the banking sector.* Unpublished master's thesis. Ateneo de Manila University, Manila, Philippines.

Ruderman, M.N., Hannum, K., Leslie, J.B., & Steed, J.L. (2001). *Leadership skills and emotional intelligence.* Greensboro, NC: Center for Creative Leadership.

Sitarenios, G., & Stein, S. J. (1998). *Emotional intelligence in the prediction of sales success in the finance industry.* Toronto, Multi-Health Systems.

Stein, S. J. & Book. H. (2006). *The EQ edge: Emotional intelligence and your success.* Toronto: Stoddart.

Diana Durek is an expert in the area of emotional intelligence and its bottom-line impact on selection, development, and leadership initiatives in organizations. During her nine years with MHS, a leading global psychological test publisher, she has worked closely with Fortune 500 organizations to develop star performer systems powered by an emotional intelligence framework. Through integration with human capital strategy, Diana has helped organizations such as American Express and Air Canada increase revenue and save money by predicting and improving individual and organizational performance. The scientific rigor of her models and their alignment to business outcomes allows Diana to provide best practices to capitalize on employee potential.

Wendy Gordon, a writer, has held leadership and instructional design roles in the field of technical communication for more than ten years. During her eight years with MHS, she has contributed to the development of emotional intelligence tools and supporting materials—most recently the BOEI™ and Dr. Steven Stein's book *Make Your Workplace Great: The 7 Keys to an Emotionally Intelligent Workplace*, which highlights how emotional intelligence interventions can transform organizations. Wendy's writing focuses predominantly on the world-renowned EQ-i® model, including the manuals and certification curricula for the EQ-i® and EQ-360®.

CHAPTER 10

Emotional Intelligence
A View from South Africa

*Jopie de Beer, Nicola Taylor,
Renate Scherrer, and Christina
van der Merwe*

INTRODUCTION

In order to understand the emotional and social skills of the African people, one has to understand the context of the people, their cultures, and the continent. Slightly more than 150 years ago, the African continent was largely an unexplored, unknown, mystical, and mysterious place to the Western world. Explorers such as David Livingston courageously explored parts of the continent, sharing information with the rest of the world on the beauty and wonder of the land, the nature of the people, and in particular the horrors of the slave trade (Pakenham, 1991). After Livingston's death in 1873, between 1880 and 1902 the continent once ruled by Africans became a continent ruled by rivaling European countries. Germany, France, Britain, Portugal and Italy, as well as

Spain and Belgium, had divided Africa into thirty new colonies and protectorates, thus acquiring millions of square miles of new territory and millions of new subjects. Colonialization may have been inspired by Livingston's dream of "Commerce, Christianity and Civilization" for the African continent, but it also at times included the conquering and exploitation of natural resources and of the people (Pakenham, 1991, p. xv). It was about fifty years later, when the African countries started reclaiming their independence, that Europe's conquest of Africa began disintegrating (Pakenham, 1991).

The African continent is more than three times the size of the United States. It is the planet's largest continent after Asia and is home to more than 900 million people living in fifty-four different countries. Africa accounts for about 14 percent of the world's human population (American Friends Service Committee, n.d.). The vast majority of the people on the continent are indigenous and their various histories go back millions of years to the development of Hominidae or the later development of Homo Habilis and Homo Erectus (Broodryk, 2007). Scientists widely believe that humans originated in Africa.

The San and Khoikhoi populations form part of the richness of people on the African continent. It is generally accepted that they may be descendants of the late Stone Age people, having inhabited Southern Africa thousands of years before the other indigenous groups such as the Nguni (Zulu, Xhosa, Ndebele, or Swazi) or the Sotho, Tsonga, and Venda groups arrived (Broodryk, 2007). Descendants of European nations such as Germany, Holland, England, France, and Portugal have also settled in Africa and today regard Africa as home.

Africa is an oil, natural gas, and mineral rich continent, which has ensured continued business interest over many years from countries such as the United States, the United Kingdom, Brazil, China, Japan, India, Malaysia, and South Korea. China is doing progressively more business in Africa (Daniel, Lutchman, & Comninos, 2007). Other Asian states such as India, Japan, and Korea are all expanding their interests and involvement in Africa, as boosting trade between Asia and Africa is seen as a top priority (Coetzee, Large & Smith, 2008). Recent investment in Africa has contributed to a continental growth rate of between 5 and 7 percent, which is higher than the world average (Daniel, Lutchman, & Comninos, 2007). The African economic environment is becoming progressively more user- friendly and efficient and South Africa plays a very important part in this process. It is estimated that in excess of three hundred South African companies have established formal business in other African countries and that hundreds of thousands of people in the various countries are being offered employment (Daniel, Lutchman, & Comninos, 2007).

It is expected that South Africa, in the years to come, will continue to trade with other African countries with regard to banking and investment, telecommunications, mining, energy (oil, gas, and electricity), technology (turning oil and gas into liquid fuels), and the retail sector providing consumer goods. South Africa's involvement is also diplomatic and military in nature (Daniel, Lutchman, & Comninos, 2007). Given the abundance of natural wonders and wildlife in Africa, tourism is particularly important and is expected to continually grow. It is a continent that can represent the best of what rural and indigenous lifestyle can offer as well as being able to compete in terms of first world practices.

The most valuable and unique resource in Africa is its people. It is a resource that has endured much over the ages with wars, colonialism, apartheid, the scourge of HIV and AIDS, poverty, crime, corruption, and poor leadership. African wisdom has much to teach those of us passionate about understanding how emotional and social endurance and resilience help people survive hardships and become successful in life. The African philosophy of Ubuntu, practiced throughout Africa, provides a unique understanding of the way in which the indigenous people have survived with wisdom and dignity through thousands of years.

The African Philosophy of Ubuntu

Ubuntu provides a framework that guides and defines effective and successful individual and group behavior. All the African languages on the continent have a word or a term for Ubuntu, and it has been taught to children by the elders over many generations. The belief system is based on a value of relationships, respect, and human dignity. The most well-known and respected example of a person living according to Ubuntu principles is Nelson Mandela.

Ubuntu literally says "umuntu ngumuntu ngabantu" and means "I am a person through other persons" (Broodryk, 2007, p. 1), referring to the fact that you cannot be human alone, that you find meaning and fulfillment in community with others, and that you are who you are because of others. This belief translates into a respect and acceptance of people as they are, respecting their human dignity, accepting the important role of emotions and feelings as drivers of behavior, and believing that every person has potential to become the best of what he or she can be. They believe that one should in all circumstances respect others and appreciate their humanness and accept that people have a major impact on the happiness and hope of others. African people believe that their fellow human should always be put first (Mbigi, 2005).

To listen to people or to have "indaba" (meetings or discussions) with people takes time, and the African people prefer to deal with human relations in a relaxed way. They do not generally appreciate the strong Western pressure and focus on time (Broodryk, 2005, 2007).

People in Africa would not eat alone when they know someone else is hungry. They take care of those in need and they share what they have without expecting anything in return. Everybody is regarded as a member of an extended family, and sometimes members of a community will refrain from eating until strangers and visitors have had something to eat (Broodryk, 2005, 2007; Mbigi & Maree, 2005).

The African person shares in the heartache of others with a similar emotional intensity. Being compassionate generally discourages people from achieving at the cost of others. Greeting others is done with warmth and courtesy, as they socialize very easily. They hug often, laugh heartily, and deal informally with each other, trying to keep the interpersonal atmosphere light. Fun is usually not to be had at the expense of others, and the humiliation of others is unacceptable. Life according to Ubuntu is based on values of caring, respect, compassion, negotiation, peace, humanity, sharing, and a spirit of community. The African people tend to be tolerant, preferring to live in harmony with others rather than having to face conflict (Broodryk, 2005, 2007; Mbigi & Maree, 2005).

African societies have a clear social order in which every member knows his or her place. The individual's position in society is linked to the historical position of the family. Generally, those leaders who abide by the Ubuntu principles distinguish themselves as dignified and able to win the trust and confidence of followers. Rules, respect, obedience to authority, and discipline are taught to all. Dignity and respect are shown to all people, from those who are illiterate to those highly qualified.

In Africa, Ubuntu is seen as the art of being human, a lifestyle to strive toward and a way to counter inhumanity (Broodryk, 2007). African people explore, acknowledge, and manage emotional events through dance, storytelling, music, and poetry. African cultures treat music and dance as foundations of their social lifestyles (Mbigi, 2005). Folk tales have been handed down over many generations and usually illustrate emotionally laden events being managed by way of a moral lesson.

African people often use group songs to sing the praises of a leader or at times to communicate suffering, protest, or happiness. They derive emotional sustenance from togetherness, as when spontaneous song and dance erupts when groups decide to communicate solidarity to emotionally laden situations. The African Shona Proverb puts it in perspective by saying, "Chara chemise ha chit swana inda" or "a thumb working on its own is useless. It has to work with the other fingers to get strength and be able to do anything" (Mbigi & Maree, 2005, p. 103).

They are also very spiritual people, with a strong belief in God and ancestor spirits playing a role in their everyday life. Sangomas (African medicine people) are consulted to advise on messages from ancestors, love triangles, illness, or business issues, and their authority is respected (Broodryk, 2005, 2007; Mbigi & Maree, 2005).

Children are regarded as family wealth and the names given to children often describe the parents' expectation or the emotional significance of their birth. Names such as Happiness, Lucky, Perseverance, Patience, Courage, Intelligence, Grace, and Sorrow are all found in African culture.

Core to being African is the importance attached to people. Steve Biko said "One of the most fundamental aspects of our culture is the importance we attach to man," and he further stated, "We believe in the inherent goodness of man. We enjoy man for himself. We regard living together not as an unfortunate mishap warranting endless competition among us but as a deliberate act of God to make us a community of brothers and sisters jointly involved in the quest for a composite answer to the varied problems of life" (Biko, 1978, pp. 45–46). The African worldview is about being a good community member, about living and enjoying life, about accepting one's destiny rather than trying to control life (Mbigi & Maree, 2005).

The person adhering to and living the Ubuntu values exercises self-control and shows perseverance, keeps calm, and acts in a dignified manner. Such a person is friendly, warm, showing an interest in both friends and family. Many could wonder why, on a continent that has ascribed to Ubuntu for hundreds of years, the emotional and social behaviors of some are directly contrary. Not all people adhere to the Ubuntu philosophy. Stealing, corruption, greediness, crime, and other misdeeds are contrary to the cooperation and peaceful co-existence that the ordinary African person ascribes to. Questions are asked about the possible effects of colonialism, Westernization, the destruction of families through HIV and AIDS, and prolonged and desperate poverty, to mention a few possible or contributing factors to the moral and emotional ills in Africa today.

African Role Models

Emotional and social capabilities are core to the behavior of role models such as Nelson Mandela, Desmond Tutu, Kofi Annan, Mahatma Gandhi, and Steve Biko. In Africa and the rest of the world, these people are revered for their unique leadership style and the human and emotional qualities they represent. It is generally believed that they demonstrate well-developed emotional and social intelligence.

Steve Biko's life and work serve to illustrate his ability to live an Ubuntu lifestyle, reflecting a deep understanding of and reasoning on emotional experiences in his life and the lives of others.

During the apartheid years, Steve Biko (1946–1977) was a prominent figure in the development of the Black Consciousness movement in South Africa. Some of his insights on the role, impact, and management of emotions can be summarized as follows (Biko, 1978):

- The more African people developed a sense of self-awareness, self-confidence, and independence in their thinking, the more they believed in their own potential power to change apartheid as an unacceptable social system. The Black Consciousness movement provided a vehicle whereby the identity and self-regard of the African people could be reinforced. Their confidence and sense of identity brought hope to many Black people in South Africa, helping them believe that there was "a way out" of an unacceptable and very difficult social context.

- People with a pride and a sense of history can more easily channel and control their emotional energy in acceptable and recognizable directions.
- Living close to nature provides an emotional richness and a depth in the empathy of people as they have time to listen, reflect, and experience life in a natural form.
- There are limits to how much emotional strain people can manage, as indicated by the following statement: "Grounds for a revolution is always fertile in the presence of absolute destitution" (Biko, 1978, p. 33).
- During the apartheid years, black people too easily accepted the leadership of others, given their preference for harmony and acceptance of perceived authority. Their acceptance, however, evolved into a form of learned helplessness, which lowered their self-confidence and caused them to perceive themselves as victims.
- The problem-solving style of the Westerners, being systematic, scientific, and logical, driving toward an end result, is very different from the style of African problem solving, which allows for the natural evolution of a situation. For the African person, the focus is less on analysis and more on allowing an understanding of the needs and responses of people to evolve over time.
- After years of colonialism, Westerners expected the African people to conform to their ways and be evaluated by Western standards. Biko noted that "It leaves behind a bastardized culture that can only thrive at the rate and pace allowed by the dominant culture. This is what happened to the African culture" (Biko, 1978, p. 50).
- Africa would in the future be able to make a special contribution to the world in terms of human relationships. Biko noted that "The great powers of the world may have done wonders in giving the world an industrial and military look, but the great gift still has to come from Africa—giving the world a more human face" (Biko, 1978, p. 51).

Steve Biko will be remembered by many for his passion, his deep sense of social responsibility and empathy, and his ability to bring optimism and hope to many. In his life he illustrated a deep understanding that the self-regard of people is critical to being able to assert their views and demand their rights. He showed strong leadership, humility, and dignity, while managing his own stress during periods of extreme hardship. His self-knowledge and self-management ensured and supported a keen and sensitive awareness of the needs of others whilst seeking to solve their emotional needs. Similar to Desmond Tutu and Nelson Mandela, Steve Biko is an example of African emotional capacity, strongly influenced by the age-old Ubuntu philosophy.

In a number of African countries, wars and tribal conflict have been rife, and many villages and communities have lost their men and elders. This trend has continued with the loss of lives through HIV/AIDS and further wars, leaving a younger generation to grow up without the guidance and direction of their elders. This lack of leadership, coupled with the introduction of vices such as alcohol, drugs, and weapons, seems to have created a generation with a disregard for their parents' values and the philosophy of Ubuntu. The focus appears to have shifted from "identifying myself through my relationship to others" to a more self-centered materialism. It could be argued that the need for emotionally intelligent leaders of the caliber of Steve Biko and Nelson Mandela to promote the values of Ubuntu is crucial, and fundamental to the development and prosperity of the nations in Africa.

Emotional Intelligence in South Africa Today

In South Africa, there is a national pride in the ability of the country to have transitioned peacefully from the apartheid regime to a democratic dispensation and much of the reason for this transition can be ascribed to the quality of leadership of Nelson Mandela. His understanding, dignity, integrity, congruence, tolerance, empathy, hope, calmness, pride, and passion persuaded all South Africans to respect and appreciate him as leader.

South Africa has also developed and changed significantly since the democratic elections of 1994. The country is striving to retain the best of both the indigenous cultures and the opportunities offered by the Western world. Mbigi and Maree (2005, p. 3) refer to "a celebration of global citizenship where people can be both tribal and cosmopolitan." In South Africa, as elsewhere in Africa, the interface between African and Western values provides a unique opportunity for using the best of both worlds. Emotional and social competencies are generally recognized as important and often critical for living a successful life. This is further illustrated by a strong African contingent having attended various conferences on emotional intelligence (hereafter referred to as EI) hosted in South Africa, and a number of books have been written by South Africans on the subject (Bar-On, Maree, & Elias, 2006; van Jaarsveld, 2003; Vermeulen, 1999).

Nowadays in South Africa, individuals who embrace the traditional values of Ubuntu often work and live together with individuals who focus on self-enrichment. While this is ideal for creating diversity in the workplace, the potential for conflict is high, and diversity management through EI development can be seen to be essential.

RESEARCH

The EI assessments most commonly used in South Africa for individuals are the various forms of BarOn Emotional Quotient Inventory (EQ-i®) (Bar-On, 1997) and the Mayer-Salovey-Caruso Emotional Intelligence Test (MSCEIT®) (Mayer, Salovey, & Caruso, 2002). For organizations, the Benchmark of Organizational Emotional Intelligence (BOEI™) (Stein & MHS Staff, 2005) is often used.

BarOn Emotional Quotient Inventory (EQ-i®)

Emotional intelligence can be described as "an array of personal, emotional, and social competencies and skills that influence one's ability to succeed in coping with environmental demands and pressures" (Bar-On, 1997, p. 3). The EQ-i® is a self-report inventory that measures these skills and competencies on the basis of five composite scales, namely Intrapersonal EQ, Interpersonal EQ, Adaptability EQ, Stress Management EQ, and General Mood EQ. Dr. Reuven Bar-On did much of the work developing the EQ-i® in South Africa and as such much research has been done on the validity of the assessment in the South African context.

South African norms were published for the EQ-i in 2006 (Gallant, 2005a). The South African normative sample consisted of 9892 respondents of which 36.4 percent were women and 63.6 percent were men, between the ages of nineteen and sixty years. Gender as well as age differences found in the South African data suggested a need for separate age and gender norms. However, the suitability of using the EQ-i® in South Africa was confirmed.

The results of the research showed that South Africans scored somewhat higher than North Americans on nearly all aspects of emotional intelligence as measured by the EQ-i® instrument. This is good news for South Africans, although there may be a number of factors that created this distinction. It could be argued that the North American data were collected before emotional intelligence became recognized as an important construct, and that nowadays there is more of a focus on developing an awareness of one's emotions and using them to effectively make decisions than there was at that time. Also, the EQ-i® is a self-report inventory, which means that people's self-perceptions will have an impact on their overall scores. These higher scores at least show self-confidence, adaptability, and optimism, which are positive indications for the diversity found in the South African context.

The research has also indicated that South African men and women report different strengths when it comes to emotional intelligence. These differences are very similar to those found in previous North American research (Bar-On, 1997), although there were no differences between men and women on the Adaptability EQ and General Mood EQ scales in the South African normative group. South African women report being more aware of their own emotions, showing more empathy, acting more socially responsibly, and relating better interpersonally than men do. On the other hand, South African men report being more assertive, having a better self-regard, being more independent, and being able to tolerate more stress than women do. These differences give a unique flavor to how people cope in different situations. The results provide some insight into how men and women could differ in terms of their interpersonal styles and help identify areas of development for individuals within the different gender groups. Table 10.1 shows the direction of differences for men and women in both South African and North American normative samples.

In terms of ethnicity, it was found that there is little or no difference in emotional intelligence across South African ethnic groups. This is extremely encouraging, as many psychological assessments are criticized on the basis that they discriminate against certain groups in one way or another, and this particular assessment does not appear to do so. The three

Table 10.1. Gender Effects for the South African and North American Normative Samples

EQ-i® Scale	South Africa*	North America**
Total EQ		
Intrapersonal EQ		
Emotional Self-Awareness	F > M	F > M
Assertiveness	M > F	M > F
Self-Regard	M > F	M > F
Self-Actualization		
Independence	M > F	M > F
Interpersonal EQ	F > M	
Empathy	F > M	F > M
Interpersonal Relationships	F > M	F > M
Social Responsibility	F > M	F > M
Adaptability EQ		
Problem Solving		M > F
Reality Testing		
Flexibility		M > F
Stress Management EQ	M > F	
Stress Tolerance	M > F	M > F
Impulse Control		
General Mood EQ		
Happiness		
Optimism		M > F

Note: From *Gallant (2005a) and **Bar-On (1997)

scales where significant effects were found are Assertiveness, Impulse Control, and Self-Regard, but the mean score difference between the highest and lowest scoring groups on these scales did not exceed 0.50 raw score points.

Although international research shows a trend of an increase in emotional intelligence with age, the South African data show that younger South Africans rated themselves higher on emotional intelligence than older South Africans did. This is a very positive result, indicating that the younger generation (ages twenty to thirty) are equipping themselves with the necessary skills to cope with the many demands placed upon them in the present South African context. One interesting difference, however, was that the younger group indicated that they were less independent than the older groups. One could hypothesize that this could be a factor of the life stage: starting a career or a family and having to consult others in making decisions would certainly impact on levels of independence. Table 10.2 shows the pattern of EQ-i® scale differences across age groups in South African and North American samples.

Mayer-Salovey-Caruso Emotional Intelligence Test (MSCEIT®)

Emotional intelligence as measured by the MSCEIT® (Mayer, Salovey, & Caruso, 2002) is conceptualized as an ability to perform tasks and solve emotional problems that is not affected by issues such as personality, self-concept or response style (Mayer, Salovey, & Caruso, 2002). The MSCEIT® is based on a Four-Branch model of emotional intelligence, where an individual is said to be able to perceive emotions, use them to facilitate thought, understand those emotions, and thereby manage them. The MSCEIT® consists of Total EI, two Areas (Experiential and Strategic), four Branches (Perceiving Emotions, Facilitating Thought, Understanding Emotions, and Managing Emotions), and eight Tasks (Faces, Sensation, Changes, Emotion Management, Pictures, Facilitation, Blends, and Emotional Relations). Two types of scoring are available for the MSCEIT®, namely General Consensus and Expert Consensus scoring.

An initial study of the MSCEIT's performance in South Africa (Gallant, 2005b), consisting a sample of 310 South African MSCEIT® respondents, revealed acceptable internal consistency reliability coefficients using General Consensus scoring for the Total EI scale ($\alpha = 0.91$) and Area scales (Experiential $\alpha = 0.90$, Strategic $\alpha = 0.81$). The internal consistency reliability coefficients for the Branches ranged between 0.66 (Understanding Emotions)

Table 10.2. Age Effects for South African and North American Normative Samples

EQ-i® Scale	South Africa	North America
Total EQ	1,2 > 3 > 4 > 5	4,3,5 > 2,1
Intrapersonal EQ		
Emotional Self-Awareness		4,3,5 > 2,1
Assertiveness	1,2 > 4 > 3 > 5	
Self-Regard	1,2 > 4 > 3 > 5	4,3,5 > 2,1
Self-Actualization	1,2 > 3 > 4 > 5	4,5,3 > 2,1
Independence	3 > 4 > 5 > 1,2	4,3 > 5 > 2,1
Interpersonal EQ	1,2 > 3 > 4 > 5	
Empathy		5,4 > 3 > 2,1
Interpersonal Relationships	1,2 > 3 > 4>5	
Social Responsibility		5,4 > 3 > 2,1
Adaptability EQ		
Problem Solving		4 > 3,5 > 2,1
Reality Testing		3,4 > 5,2 > 1
Flexibility	1,2,3 > 4 > 5	3,4 > 5,2 > 1
Stress Management EQ		
Stress Tolerance	3 > 4 > 1,2 > 5	4 > 3,5 > 2,1
Impulse Control	1,2 > 3 > 4 > 5	4,5 > 3 > 2,1
General Mood EQ		
Happiness	1,2 > 3 > 4 > 5	
Optimism	1,2 > 3 > 4 > 5	4,5,3 > 2,1

Age groups: 1 = Less than 20 years, 2 = 20 to 29 years, 3 = 30 to 39 years, 4 = 40 to 49 years, 5 = 50 years or over.
Note: From Gallant (2005a) and Bar-On (1997).

and 0.93 (Perceiving Emotions), and for the Tasks ranged between 0.35 (Blends) and 0.90 (Pictures). The pattern of lower reliability for the task scales was also found in the North American normative sample (Mayer, Salovey, & Caruso, 2002), indicating that caution should be exercised when interpreting results at subscale level. Similar results were obtained for the Expert Consensus scoring method.

Confirmatory factor analysis showed good fit for 1-factor, 2-factor, and 4-factor models of the MSCEIT®, as determined by the theory. The factor structure of the MSCEIT was therefore supported in the South African context. Upon comparison of the South African average scale score to the North American mean of 100; however, it appears that the South Africans in the sample tended to score significantly lower than the North American normative group on all of the MSCEIT® scales for both scoring options, with the exception of the Facilitation task scale. This is a clear indication of the need to develop separate norms for South Africans on the MSCEIT®.

The sample in Gallant's study was not representative of the South African population, and there were not enough respondents in each of the age groups to attempt to create norm groups. The majority of the sample consisted of men (63 percent). Once the South African database of MSCEIT® respondents reaches an acceptable level of representativeness, further consideration will be given to the development of a South African norm group.

Benchmark of Organizational Emotional Intelligence (BOEI™)

The BOEI is an organization development assessment tool designed to measure the level of emotional intelligence in an organization. Organizational EI is conceptualized as the organization's ability to effectively cope with change and reach its goals, while remaining responsible and sensitive to all its stakeholders, and developing its most important commodity, namely people (Stein & MHS Staff, 2005). The BOEI™ evaluates an organization's ability to manage aspects such as job happiness, compensation, work/life balance, organizational cohesiveness, supervisory leadership, diversity and anger management, and organizational responsiveness. While it is still a fairly new assessment tool, the BOEI™ is being used on an increasing basis in South Africa to help organizations to create better working environments for their employees and thereby increase their own performance.

APPLICATION

There are a number of contexts in which EI is utilized in South Africa. The most common areas of application tend to be the following:

- Educational
- Organizational (including selection, reality shows, leadership development, workshops, group or team development, and organization development)
- Individual development
- Sport

Educational

Most of the work in this field is focused on the development and enhancement of human potential. Emotional intelligence as a set of survival skills is critical for the youth who will be the leaders of South Africa in the future. It is impossible to work with the youth without acknowledging the importance of parents and teachers who reinforce and model emotionally intelligent behavior.

It is essential to note that poverty, crime, and poor schooling still exist in some regions and that low literacy levels have a debilitating effect on the individual's effectiveness in dealing with the demands of life. EI cannot be regarded as the only reason why intelligent and potentially talented children could "fall by the wayside." Low literacy also cast doubt on the reliability of typical EI assessments used to determine the existing level of EI competencies and skill. In such instances, literacy training should be given priority, but it can be linked to EI development, through song and dance, stories and poetry, role modeling of teachers, EI videos targeted at the youth, television programs, and community forums wherein Ubuntu principles are used as a vehicle to learn more about emotions and emotional management.

An excellent example of a home-grown and culturally appropriate system of personal and interpersonal development is in work done by

Life College in South Africa. Life College's operating principles are based on the work, life, and teachings of Steve Biko and his philosophy of Black Consciousness. Life College works among the previously disadvantaged youth and families in South Africa to lead them to self-pride, self-confidence, self-reliance, resilience, and freedom from "slavery of the mind." This College strives to fulfill Nelson Mandela's call to action that South Africa needs to become a "Nation of Champions." Enhancing emotional and social competencies and skills is a core component of the Life College Programme. Life College is seen as the cradle of future Champions in South Africa, and supporting this venture are prominent South African businesses and business people as well as an international network of business, sports, and entertainment celebrities who offer mentorship and leadership coaching to Life College students. By their ten-year anniversary (2007), more than 2,500 students had benefited, and by 2020 they will have reached more than 100,000 students. The purpose of Life College is not to replace the existing school system but to support academic institutions to empower the youth, their families, and their communities to excel in those EI competencies and skills not usually attended to in schools. Life College starts its students off with character education, teaching its students core EI competencies, and entrenching principles and values, which are then tested in real-life projects and supported by mentorship and leadership coaching. For more information, visit www.lifecollege.org.za.

The EQ-i® youth version is in the process of being translated into Afrikaans, Sesotho, Setswana, isiZulu, and Sepedi. Being able to ascertain the emotional and social capacity of the youth will make it possible to devise appropriate and group-specific workshops for EI development. One particular study focusing on the development of resilience of children with HIV-infected mothers is currently underway in South Africa. The EQ-i® youth version will be used to determine the effectiveness of a theory-based support intervention, which would help HIV-infected mothers promote resilience in very young (age three years) and school-aged (ages six to ten years) children.

At government and private schools as well as universities, awareness has been created about the urgent need for EI training at schools (Klaasen, 2004). Attention is being given to developing culturally appropriate methods of enhancing the emotional and social competencies and skills of both teachers and students. Emotional and social self-awareness and self-management is being included in the curricula of some schools while teachers are becoming progressively focused on how they model EI to children. Research has been done on the nature of first-year students who are at risk of not being academically successful (Swart, 1996), as this allows for interventions directed at these risk factors.

A recent study involving twenty-five schoolchildren between the ages of nine and thirteen years was conducted in order to determine the effectiveness of twelve modular workshops focusing on resilience-building. These workshops were conducted after hours over a period of one month, and were based on a program developed in South Africa. The children completed the EQ-i® youth version before the workshops commenced, and then one week after the workshops ended. Some interesting changes in terms of EI emerged from the results. On average, all aspects of EI had increased, but the most notable increases were in intrapersonal skills and overall EI. Although there was very little change in the development of interpersonal competencies, this indicates to some degree that the intervention was successful in its goal of developing a child's inner resources, with less focus on relationship-building (Jopie van Rooyen & Partners, 2006).

At a number of South African private schools, EI awareness is relatively easily integrated with life skills training and the general curriculum. Both teachers and students are provided with opportunities to assess and develop their EI skills. It is difficult to offer the same benefits to children and teachers in poverty-stricken and rural areas where arguably the need for EI development is of particular importance. Community-based teacher and student EI training programs that acknowledge the cultural and social context of these communities are currently being developed. Teachers from eight South African schools have volunteered to participate in a program of EI awareness and development. The program is designed to have a cascade effect and it is envisaged that "thousands of learners will have benefited . . . most of them will have benefited from developing EI for the first time" (BarOn, Maree, & Elias, 2006, p. 157).

Organizational

Many South African workers are people who have experienced apartheid, were part of the protest movements, and have been victims of poor education.

The average age of people in South Africa is twenty-four years, which makes the South African workforce very different from that of the developed world, where the graying workforce is an issue to contend with. Important workforce trends in South Africa since the change of government in 1994 have been, among others, the effect of HIV and AIDS, which is particularly prevalent amongst the younger age groups; emigration of skilled workers; the legal requirements on industry of affirmative action seeking to ensure the speedy integration of previously disadvantaged people; and globalization. Consulting on EI to South African industry takes cognizance of the context with full understanding of the emotional and social skills required to successfully survive the turbulence and demands of the new world of work in South Africa.

Selection

The use of EI assessments for the selection of employees has been on the increase in South Africa over the last decade. Used as part of a comprehensive selection battery that may include measures of ability, personality, and organizational fit, instruments such as the EQ-i® can add important information to help predict the success of an individual within an organization. Scientific practices such as ideal candidate profiling and creating selection equations can help organizations identify their ideal candidates, although this should be undertaken with the knowledge that the results from psychological assessments should never be taken in isolation from the context of the individual or the needs of the organization.

In South Africa the use of psychological tests, specifically within the selection context, is highly regulated. The South African Employment Equity Act 55 of 1998 (*Government Gazette*, 1998) clearly stipulates that only valid and reliable assessments may be used and that assessments should be used in a manner that is considered fair and free from bias. Legally, only psychologists and psychometrists may purchase, score, interpret, and give feedback on psychological assessments in South Africa, Using EI assessment scores in any selection context by default implies that the assessment should have been thoroughly researched and applied and interpreted by an appropriately trained psychologist or psychometrist.

Reality Shows

Another form of selection using EI assessment has been done in South Africa for some reality shows. The international trend of reality shows in entertainment has also crept into South Africa and exploded in a series of "franchised" local versions of most of the international reality shows. While some shows illicit voyeuristic tendencies from audiences, the lure appears to be being able to watch the unedited reactions of "normal" people to stressful or unique situations. The use of a variety of psychological tests, including assessments on EI, in selecting participants in reality shows tends to run opposite to the selection of effective employees. In some cases, you would select participants on the basis of whether they would create "good viewing," and not necessarily react in an emotionally intelligent way to conflict (while ensuring that the response will not cause harm to fellow participants). The EI scores used in selecting the best candidates for the reality shows are of particular importance given that the shows primarily seek to elicit ways in which candidates cope with personal and interpersonal difficulties as well as the emotional resilience that they show. Evidence for face validity has been obtained by being able to relate EI scores with actual behavior on screen.

Leadership Development

At a number of South African universities, the master of business administration (MBA) or master of business leadership (MBL) courses routinely include coursework on EI, applying it to areas such as leadership, managing knowledge workers, succession planning, organizational climate, or selection. Students are also provided the opportunity to have their EI assessed and to use the results for personal development.

Many South African leaders undergo executive coaching, which often includes some time spent on self-knowledge gained through the results of the EQ-i® or the MSCEIT® or sometimes a combination of both. The purpose of using such assessment tools is for clients to be able to translate these results to optimal self-management, including having an understanding on how they may be perceived by others and how to constructively and congruently deal with such perceptions. Leadership requires emotional and social insight, resilience, and an ability to be committed to the welfare of employees while ensuring the viability and profitability of the organization they work for. Results from a study done by Stuart and Paquet (2001) confirmed that those with leadership potential report higher scores on the EQ-i®, specifically in terms of optimism and self-actualization, than those with little leadership potential. Evidence for the link between the principles of transformational leadership theory and EI was therefore established.

Emotional exhaustion for leaders in Southern Africa is a real risk, and working emotionally wise is critical to their own and their companies' survival. Working with an assessment such as the EQ-i® provides a useful way of understanding the level of a leader's emotional energy and resilience. Interventions such as coaching or attending modular workshops on EI are often done, after which a re-assessment of the EQ-i® could indicate the effectiveness of the intervention.

It is particularly useful to use both the EQ-i®, as a self-report measurement of EI, and the MSCEIT®, indicating EI ability, in combination. The similarity or discrepancy between these scores makes for very useful information to be dealt with in leadership development interventions. For optimal value, it is useful to add the EQ360® to such a developmental process. Emotional intelligence is an aspect of female leadership development that is of particular value. By understanding, for instance, the effect of life stage on the emotional resilience of women or how emotional labor results from having to fulfill multiple roles allows for personal emotional insight and optimizes self-management.

Preliminary research results indicate that some facets of EI as measured by the MSCEIT® make a significant contribution to facets of leadership effectiveness (Herbst, Maree, & Sibanda, 2006). Herbst and his colleagues (2006) included five indicators of leadership from the Leadership Practices Inventory (Kouzes & Posner, 2001) in measuring leadership effectiveness, namely Challenging the Process, Inspiring a Shared Vision, Enabling Others to Act, Modeling the Way, and Encouraging the Heart. Modest correlations were found between the Managing Emotions branch of the MSCEIT® and two of the leadership abilities, Challenging the Process and Inspiring a Shared Vision. The results from a multiple regression analysis indicated that leaders' ability to understand and manage their emotions best predicts their ability to inspire a shared vision in their followers and, along with experience, predicts their overall effectiveness as leaders (Herbst, Maree, & Sibanda, 2006)

Workshops

In South Africa and the other African countries, EI workshops vary in their nature, intensity, and duration, depending largely on the knowledge and judgment of the facilitator. There is, however, no doubt that the most effective workshops should:

- Be visibly supported by the leadership of the team, department, or corporation
- Acknowledge the culture and environment within which each individual lives and works
- Acknowledge the value system, such as Ubuntu, that an individual and a culture adhere to. This could provide a very valuable basis on which further EI development can be done
- Require individuals to voluntarily attend and fully understand the nature and purpose of the workshops
- Be developed and offered with full acknowledgement of adult and experiential learning principles
- Be based on soundly formulated scientific theory and reliable and valid assessment tools
- Be modular in nature and span over several months
- Be quality controlled by having regular checks built into the process, including follow-up with the individual and his or her organization some time after the last module attended

It is generally accepted that workshops with a duration of an hour or a day are information sessions only, and that real behavioral change should and cannot be expected in such a short time frame. However, there is still a certain amount of value to be gained from this information. Change starts with awareness. Many people in Southern Africa get their first exposure to EI through attending workshops on the topic.

Group or Team Development

Research done in South Africa confirms that EI, as measured by the EQ-i®, predicted approximately 40 percent of the variance in team effectiveness (Sipsma, 2000). Work done with groups and teams that include using an EI assessment could provide a benchmark set of information in terms of the functioning of the team or group. Interventions with groups depend on their specific needs and on the assessment results. Team-building interventions usually start with the team self-awareness, and this information should be worked with in terms of the team dynamics. One way in which EI work in teams is done in South Africa is to take the team to a wilderness area where the team is required to work as a team to "survive." Much is learned about the importance of emotional and interpersonal dynamics of a team to ensure such survival. Another team intervention has been developed by a South African company using the analogy of the emotional and interpersonal behavior of various animals such as lions, African wild dogs, zebras, or cheetahs to explore, practice, illustrate, and develop effective teamwork. More information is available from www.peopledynamic.co.za.

Organization Development

By using assessments such as the BOEI™, it is possible to assess the emotional capacity of a department or organization. The premise that "what is known can be managed" will enable a skilled OD practitioner and facilitator to identify both the strengths and potential dilemmas within an organization. Interventions can be devised to manage the emotional fallout of a company.

The BOEI™ has been used in South Africa to help the management team of a large commercial bank identify specific areas of concern for employees regarding the working environment and the opportunities available to them. As a tool in a wider change management process, the BOEI® was effective as a gauge of the company climate and led to focus groups that would look at implementing initiatives such as flexible working hours, changes to reporting and team structures, and addressing gender/diversity issues.

Individual Development

There is enormous human potential in Africa. The potential of the people has not generally been acknowledged, given the political, social, economic, and emotional realities that have plagued the continent. Much needs to be done to provide opportunities for the potential of people to be identified, recognized, and developed.

Emotional intelligence has in the last years become very valuable in processes of individual career coaching. In addition to other relevant information such as interests, skills, values, personality orientation, and career anchors, knowledge and understanding of clients' emotional competencies and skills provides very valuable additional information to be used for enhancing their self-awareness and in helping them to optimize their self-management. A significant relationship between EI and self-actualization supports the importance of taking cognizance of EI in career development and career planning (Barnard & Herbst, 2005).

Some clients request an assessment and feedback process that includes the measurement of EI, personality, values, possible derailers, and 360-degree feedback to provide a holistic and comprehensive plan for their personal development process. The EQ-i® is also often used by psychologists as part of a therapeutic intervention related possibly to marital problems, burnout, stress, and anxiety disorders or interpersonal dysfunctions. The therapist would encourage development of EI skills and competencies to strengthen emotional resilience.

Sport

Within the sporting context, EI can add valuable insight at all levels of accomplishment. In South Africa, assessments of EI are occasionally used in the selection of individuals for management positions, administrative positions, and even sports coaches. On a larger scale, research is being done in South Africa on which aspects of EI contribute to the success of athletes and team sports players in a number of different sports. Other research would look at the impact of EI coaching and workshops on team performance, as well as the development of EI in young players as part of a South African sports development initiative.

CONCLUSION

In this chapter, the assessment, development, and research of EI in individuals, teams, groups, and organizations was discussed. Research is currently being done in South Africa on the role of EI in various contexts, such as determining levels of EI in individuals applying to participate in reality shows or developing EI in sports teams. This chapter also explored the value of developing EI in individuals who are illiterate through the use of song, dance, and poetry.

The philosophy of Ubuntu provides a unique way of understanding elements in the South African culture and emphasizes how important interpersonal relations are in the everyday life of the South African people. South Africa and Africa are examples of how national cultures can be impacted on by the level of EI of the leadership. There are a number of examples of how the creation of a negative cultural context by leaders could lower personal resilience through the subsequent hardship of the people.

Schein makes the point that, when investigating corporate culture, "culture matters" (1999, p. 3). The same has to be said about national cultures and the role played by leaders in creating such a culture. Schein further elaborates that "Culture matters because it is a powerful, latent, and often unconscious set of forces that determine both our individual and collective behavior, ways of perceiving, thought patterns, and values" (1999, p. 14). It follows that, if leaders strive to create more efficient organizations (or nations), then they have to understand the role of culture in the context of that organization (or nation).

Therefore, if practitioners were to do work on the assessment and development of EI levels within a country like South Africa, they would need to fully understand the culture before any meaning can be attached to the EI concepts and their expression in that particular culture. Leaders such as Nelson Mandela seemed to be able to create a synergy between their leadership style and the positive beliefs of Ubuntu, generating hope and optimism in the people. Given the significant culture change that South Africa experienced in the last decade, it is important to understand the psychological, sociological, and emotional impact of the change on its people. Although practitioners of EI need to focus on the individual, group, and team level, their work would be meaningless without understanding the forces within the South African culture.

Nelson Mandela, as an African icon, was able to illustrate the impact that an emotionally intelligent leader can have in bringing hope to millions and dramatically changing the future of a country. His emotional and interpersonal insights are well-reflected in a quote from his autobiography.

> It was during those long and lonely years that my hunger for the freedom of my own people became a hunger for the freedom of all people, white and black. I knew as well as I knew anything that the oppressor must be liberated just as surely as the oppressed. A man who takes away another man's freedom is a prisoner of hatred, he is locked behind the bars of prejudice and narrow-mindedness. I am not truly free if I am taking away someone else's freedom, just as surely as I am not free when my freedom is taken from me. The oppressed and the oppressor alike are robbed of their humanity. (Mandela, 1994, p. 617)

Africa has much that it can learn from the rest of the world, but it also has much to share. The field of EI provides a unique opportunity to combine the best of African wisdom with scientific insights from the Western world.

REFERENCES

American Friends Service Committee. (n.d.). *The African continent*. Retrieved January 15, 2008, from http://afsc.org/africa-debt/learn-about-africa/African-Continent.htm.

Barnard, A., & Herbst, R. (2005, Autumn). The relationship between emotional intelligence and self-actualization. *South African Journal of Labour Relations*, pp. 54–73.

Bar-On, R. (1997). *BarOn emotional quotient inventory: User's manual*. Toronto, ON: Multi-Health Systems Inc.

Bar-On, R., Maree, J.G., & Elias, M.J. (2006). *Educating people to be emotionally intelligent*. Sandton, South Africa: Heinemann.

Biko, S. (1978). *I write what I like*. London: The Bowerdean Press.

Broodryk, J. (2005). *Ubuntu: Management philosophy*. Randburg: Knowres Publishing.

Broodryk, J. (2007). *Understanding South Africa–the ubuntu way of living*. Waterkloof, South Africa: Ubuntu School of Philosophy.

Coetzee, D., Large, D., & Smith, P. (2008). Africa in the world: The new great game. *The Africa Report, 9*, 56–62.

Daniel, J., Lutchman, J., & Comninos, A. (2007). South Africa in Africa: Trends and forecasts in a changing political economy. In S. Buhlungu, J. Daniel, R. Southall, & J. Lutchman (Eds.), *State of the nation. South Africa 2007* (pp. 508–532). Cape Town: HSRC Press.

Gallant, S. (2005a). *EQ-i South African norms* (MHS Technical Report #0035). Toronto, ON: Multi-Health Systems Inc.

Gallant, S. (2005b). MSCEIT South African norms (MHS Technical Report #0029). Toronto, ON: Multi-Health Systems Inc.

Government Gazette. (1998). Employment Equity Act no 55 of 1998. Cape Town: South African Government.

Herbst, H.H., Maree, J.G., & Sibanda, E. (2006). Emotional intelligence and leadership abilities. *SAJHE, 20*, 592–612.

Jopie van Rooyen & Partners. (2006). Test-retest scores on the EQ-I youth version. Unpublished raw data.

Klaasen, E.G. (2004). *An evaluation of the emotional intelligence of secondary school learners from the Somerset East District of the Eastern Cape*. University of Stellenbosch.

Kouzes, J.M., & Posner, B.Z. (2001). *The leadership practices inventory (LPI): Facilitator's guide* (2nd ed.). San Francisco: Pfeiffer.

Mandela, N. (1994). *Long walk to freedom.* London: Little, Brown and Co. Ltd., & Gauteng: Nolwazi Educational Publishers (Pty) Ltd.

Mayer, J.D., Salovey, P., & Caruso, D.R. (2002). *Mayer-Salovey-Caruso emotional intelligence test (MSCEIT): User's manual.* Toronto, ON: Multi-Health Systems Inc.

Mbigi, L. (2005). *The spirit of African leadership.* Randburg: Knowres Publishing.

Mbigi, L., & Maree, J. (2005). *Ubuntu. The spirit of African transformation management.* Randburg: Knowres Publishing.

Pakenham, T. (1991). *The scramble for Africa.* Johannesburg: Jonathan Ball Publishers.

Schein, E. G. (1999). *The corporate culture survival guide.* San Francisco: Jossey-Bass.

Sipsma, L. (2000). Emotional intelligence and team effectiveness of postgraduate management students in self-managed work teams. Unpublished mini-dissertation.

Stein, S., & MHS Staff. (2005). *Benchmark of organizational emotional intelligence: Technical manual.* Toronto, ON: Multi-Health Systems Inc.

Stuart, A.D., & Paquet, A. (2001). Emotional intelligence as a determinant of leadership potential. *Journal of Industrial Psychology, 27,* 30–34.

Swart, A. (1996). *The relationship between well-being and academic performance.* Unpublished master's thesis. South Africa: University of Pretoria.

Van Jaarsveld, P. (2003). *The heart of a winner: Developing your emotional intelligence.* Wellington: Lux Verbi.BM.

Vermeulen, S. (1999). *EQ: Emotional intelligence for everyone.* Rivonia, South Africa: Zebra Press.

Dr. Jopie de Beer is the managing director and a founder member of Jopie van Rooyen & Partners SA, a well-known test publishing and distribution company in Africa. She is a licensed clinical psychologist with extensive experience in corporate consulting. She finds much satisfaction and has achieved success in using her expertise as a consulting psychologist toward enhancing individual, team, and corporate development. As a member of the American Psychological Association, the Society of Industrial Psychology of South Africa (SIOPSA), the Psychological Society of South Africa (PsySSA), and Association of Test Publishers South Africa (ATPSA), she keeps abreast of new trends in the field of psychology. Dr de Beer regularly presents at national and international conferences.

Nicola Taylor is a licensed psychometrist. She is an associate and the head of research at Jopie van Rooyen & Partners SA, where she is responsible for conducting research on psychological assessments in the South African context. Nicola also serves on the executive committee of the Division of Research Methodology of the Psychological Society of South Africa (PsySSA), as well as the Society of Industrial and Organisational Psychology of South Africa (SIOPSA). She has co-authored articles in peer-reviewed journals and book chapters and has read a number of papers at local and international conferences. Nicola's research focus is on cross-cultural psychological assessment, particularly within the field of personality assessment, test construction, response styles, and the validation of psychometric assessments in the South African context.

Dr. Renate Scherrer is a licensed clinical psychologist. She has co-authored a number of peer-reviewed journals, read papers at South African conferences, and is an International Affiliate with the American Psychological Association. Her interest is applying positive psychology and wellness principles to ensure optimizing of human potential in organizations. As consulting psychologist and director at Jopie van Rooyen, she is involved in a wide variety of organizational consulting projects, training and workshops. She is an internationally accredited trainer on various personality and EI assessments.

Christina van der Merwe is a licensed clinical psychologist and a director at Jopie van Rooyen & Partners. As the office manager of the Cape Town branch of the company, she carries full responsibility for coordinating test publishing and consulting psychology functions and as such has specialist knowledge in applying best practice principles to the use of psychometric assessments as part of a broad spectrum of consulting psychology services. An internationally accredited trainer on personality and emotional intelligence assessments, she is regarded as an expert resource in the field. She has consulted nationally and internationally and is driven by a passion for evidence-based psychological interventions that really make a difference to the lives of people. She is an affiliate member of the American Psychological Association.

PART THREE

Multiple Perspectives: Combining Wisdom

CHAPTER 11

Personality Type and Emotional Intelligence

Pragmatic Tools for the Effective Practitioner

Roger R. Pearman

INTRODUCTION: INTERPERSONAL NECESSITIES

The role of constructive interpersonal relationships is without doubt among the most important dimensions of effective leadership. In every dimension of leader or manager effectiveness, from decision making to strategic execution, the role of stable, resilient relationships is paramount. Given the plethora of business literature on the cost of toxic managers or employees at all levels who lack "social intelligence" or "emotional intelligence," we have problems achieving the quality of relationships we know are so essential to effectiveness (Albrecht, 2006; Sutton, 2006).

When leaders, executives, and managers of organizations fail, it is not because they lack intelligence, business acumen, experience on the job, or an understanding of job expectations. They fail because their interpersonal behavior is at odds with the social expectations of the organization where they work (Brousseau, Driver, Hourihan, & Larsson, 2006; Leslie & Van Velsor, 1996). The intention of this chapter is to provide the practitioner with practical suggestions for working with individuals to enhance their overall emotional intelligence as it is core to interpersonal savvy and interpersonal competence so essential to effectiveness.

Fundamental to building constructive relationships is reading the emotional needs of those important to success and being able to manage emotional energies when working with them. Helping learners to read those needs and manage their emotions requires multiple strategies and tactics. A chief strategy for many practitioners is to provide appropriate assessment tools to enhance awareness of individual behavior patterns and to aid in the development of plans to enrich individual effectiveness in using emotional energies. Understanding assessment strategies is aided by putting the various domains of emotional intelligence in a framework as suggested below.

TOWARD A COHERENT FRAMEWORK

Darwin's (1872) insights into the role of the expression of emotions underscore the importance of working with emotional intelligence for practitioners who are either coaches or trainers. He wrote:

> The power of communication between the members of the same tribe by means of language has been of paramount importance in the development of man; and the force of language is much aided by the expressive movements of the face and body (Darwin, 1872, p. 1469). . . . We have seen that the expression in itself, or the language of the emotions, as it has sometimes been called, is certainly of importance for the welfare of mankind (p. 1477).

As Darwin suggests, in the final analysis, emotions are of paramount interest because they are so integral to understanding how individuals adapt, or fail to do so, in their environment. Since Darwin's carefully presented

Table 11.1.   Proposed Domains of Emotional Intelligence Research

Domains	Summary
Behavioral array related to emotionally intelligent actions and being effective with emotional energy	Specific behavior patterns that take into consideration the effects of all of the categories below.
Cognition, Experience, Patterns that influence emotional triggers and expressions	Research that looks at how emotions influence how we think and how we think reinforces emotions.
Abilities to Perceive and Manage Emotions	Fundamental capabilities of any framework related to emotional intelligence in the tradition of general intelligence research.
Emotional Literacy—naming and recognizing the information in emotions	Biological and neurological research on the nature of emotions and the connection to behavior.

analysis, researchers have explored the biological and neurological aspects of emotions, the role of emotions in cognition, the abilities related to perceiving and managing emotions, and more recently the behavior patterns that are related to how we deal with our emotions and the effect of these behaviors on our health, satisfaction, and performance. The organization of this research, shown in Table 11.1, is intended to aid the practitioner in understanding how the field is unfolding.

These domains cover the range of topics and research reports in published professional literature. Each domain has significance for the practitioner. The professional working in the field of emotional intelligence may find that, before working with clients on behavior patterns, it may be necessary to help them gain some emotional literacy. At other times, such distinctions may not matter. Nonetheless, at the root of various models of emotional intelligence is the proposition that emotions contain information, and many people have never given any thought to either naming their emotional reactions or the deep meaning within them. On the other hand, practitioners know that assessing an array of behavior patterns such as interpersonal skills, empathy, social responsibility, stress tolerance, adaptability, and so forth yields important insights for clients. Practitioners will find that approaching emotional intelligence from multiple domains as suggested in Table 11.1 will add greatly to insights and personal gains for their clients.

BASICS OF EMOTIONAL LITERACY

Each emotion serves a distinct purpose. Emotions are so integrated into behavior that it is sometimes difficult to recognize their influence until after an interaction or situation has passed. Given the ubiquitous nature of emotional energy, clients can be aided by learning about the effect of emotions on behavior, especially in complex situations.

Conversations about emotional intelligence should include some recognition of the biology of emotions. Research on how our bodies respond to emotional states and how performance is affected by emotions is conclusive, and to underestimate this importance would be folly. For example, emotions have been found to have distinct neurochemical transmitters that follow distinct pathways in our brains (Lewis & Haviland-Jones, 2004). An aspect of the affect of emotions on our bodies is related to the degree of intensity at which individuals experience emotions. Intensity is experienced in a couple of ways. Mild anger to all-out rage is a continuum. Another continuum is how the emotions *build on each other*. For example, depending on a series of events, initial *interest* may lead to *anticipation,* which results in an event that leads to *disgust* and then to *anger*.

As a practical matter, a taxonomy of the most common emotions and their psychological meaning are summarized in Table 11.2 (Pearman, 2007).

As will be explored later, the triggers for the expression of these emotions vary by personality patterns. While anger is the same experience for everyone, it is not prompted by the same events. Being interrupted during a conversation prompts some people to quick anger and others to surprise. Exploring personality type and emotional triggers provides insight into the emotional cues and the expressions of the emotions, which is covered in the next section.

But it is not enough to simply name and recognize the power of emotions. As suggested in Table 11.1 on the domains of emotional intelligence research, there are layers of information that the practitioner may consider important. One of the virtues of having multiple ways

Table 11.2. Emotions and Their Meaning

Primary Emotion	Contains Information About
Anger	Unmet expectations and perceived violations of values or agreements
Disgust	Standards that are violated
Sadness	Loss of personal sense of competence, importance, lovability, relationships
Surprise	Sudden change from what is expected
Fear	Belief about not having the personal resources and competence to respond
Acceptance	Perception of being significant and worthwhile in others' eyes, being understood
Joy	Having achieved a goal or fulfilled an expectation, feeling appreciated and loved
Anticipation	Having a "vision" or expectation of how things should be or could be

to explore aspects of emotional intelligence is that the client has the opportunity to begin to see the links between how his or her personality affects emotional perceptions and how these emotional expressions show up in important performance-related behaviors, which is the purpose of the suggestions in this chapter.

PERSONALITY TYPE

Over the last twenty years, there have been forty-eight million administrations of the Myers-Briggs Type Indicator® tool. This means that a broad range of practitioners use the tool, and clients have experienced the results. The instrument is popular for a variety of reasons. The tool provides a constructive look at personality differences, and it organizes information about individuals that often makes transparent good sense.

The MBTI® sorts results on four scales to produce a four-letter code. Table 11.3 provides a reminder of the scales and their underlying meaning.

Table 11.3. Scales of the MBTI® Tool

Energy	Information Preferences	Decision Preferences	Orientation
Extraversion—preference for stimulation by interaction, activity, participation	Sensing—preference for concrete, realistic, literal data	Thinking—preference for analytical, logical outcomes	Judging—preference for closure, order, and structure
Introversion—preference for mental stimulation by reflecting, receiving input, or imagining	Intuiting—preference for patterns, associations, concepts, theories	Feeling—preference for evaluative results based on ideals	Perceiving—preference for emerging information, exploring questions

The individual's results from the instrument produce a four-letter code, such as ENFP or ISTJ. Working synergistically together within the individual, these preferences create a personality pattern. While we will eventually look at the link between the four-letter patterns and emotional intelligence behaviors as measured by another tool, it is instructive to first look at the relationship between the preferences and emotional prompters. Because anger is so corrosive to individuals and relationships, the preferences and their prompters to anger are provided as an illustration (see Table 11.4).

It is important to note that the preferences of the client may reflect some, but not all, of these links between their preferred energy (E or I), use of information (S or N), decision strategy (T or F), or general orientation (J or P) and anger as outlined above. Some clients will resonate with these simple links and will find it useful to understand that the unconscious preference is the source of the emotional trigger. This kind of insight can lead to exploring other complex behaviors with appropriate focus on skill enhancement (Pearman, 2002). Personality type provides insight into the ways individual patterns in cognition affect how individuals interpret and react to situations. These reactions become behavior patterns that are reflected in key measures of emotional intelligence.

EMOTIONALLY INTELLIGENT BEHAVIOR ARRAY

One hundred and twenty years after Darwin's insights, Reuven Bar-On, among a small group of researchers, would provide additional evidence

Table 11.4. Type Preferences and Prompters of Anger

Preference	Behavior that sometimes prompts anger for those with the listed preference:
Extraverting	when others withdraw or are domineering
Introverting	when others are insistent on questioning reactions and will not give personal space for reflection
Sensing	when others only present concepts, theories, big ideas with no immediate practical outcome
Intuiting	when others insist on every possible detail and plan before considering the worth of an idea
Thinking	when others appear incompetent and unwilling to do anything about it
Feeling	when others are unkind, unfair, and condescending
Judging	when others insist on waiting to take action
Perceiving	when others insist on a decision and closure before all of the information is known

that the management of emotions, especially under stressful circumstances, is essential to individual effectiveness. His model includes scales related to behaviors or perspectives in these dimensions: intrapersonal, interpersonal, adaptability, stress management, and general mood (Bar-On, 1997).

Bar-On consistently produces studies that identify how our management of stress, use of strategies to deal with challenges, orientation toward optimism, and self-acceptance can enhance an array of skills and perspectives that lead to overall success. Using his instrument, the BarOn EQ-i®, Bar-On researched the relationship of various behaviors to individual effectiveness. He proposes that overall emotional effectiveness is within our grasp if we pursue development of a specific set of behaviors (Bar-On, 2005). Fortunately, these behaviors can be enriched. The practitioner who uses the assessment in individual coaching or leadership training is able to direct attention to those behaviors most in need of attention.

Bar-On's work in emotional intelligence is parallel to efforts by other researchers who have been working to further understand the nature and application of emotional intelligence. Most notable in this research arena, Mayer, Salovey, and Caruso (2002) have produced a framework for measuring the *abilities* that make up individual emotional intelligence. From their view, any proposition about intelligence must meet the academic standards for its measurement that have emerged over decades of research. While the assessment tool they have created uses an ability measurement methodology rather than a self-report inventory, the framework they have developed is the standard for understanding the basic capacities of emotional intelligence. The practitioner is encouraged to learn more about the MSCEIT® (Mayer Salovey Caruso Emotional Intelligence Test) tool. The richness of this model exceeds the focus of this chapter.

FOCUS ON DEVELOPMENT

Arguably the MSCEIT® measurement provides an insight to key abilities related to emotional intelligence. As an abilities measure, however, it also has the same limitations of all other measures of abilities—namely, the presumption that there is not much one can do about what abilities one has except learn some behavioral "work-arounds." For example, if one does not have the ability to perceive emotional expressions in the faces of others, the individual is not likely to develop this capacity. An individual might memorize certain facial cues and have an "emotional checklist," but not have enhanced the basic ability. By contrast, the Bar-On EQ-i® and the Myers-Briggs Type Indicator® (MBTI®) are self-report tools that are designed to provide insight into behavior patterns and preferences, and indicate both strengths and areas of potential enrichment. The models on which both tools are built assume development is possible and desirable once a person has clarity about current behavior patterns.

The theory of personality types on which the MBTI® tool is based assumes that having a preference implies that the other process is available to be used. For example, an individual with an Extraverted preference can learn to utilize an Introverted process should he or she seek to use it more intentionally. Type development means having clarity about preferences and knowing when to use the opposite processes when the situation requires it. Another illustration is the Introverted manager who learns to speak up more frequently when the boss is around and to share more information with peers. This demonstrates an aspect of type development. The implication of this aspect of the theory is that an individual whose preferences may facilitate the demonstration of some behaviors may learn to appropriately display other behaviors as the situation may require.

The behavioral focus of the BarOn EQ-i® inherently suggests that current patterns are open to adjustment. The presumption is that the behaviors are demonstrated in relative degrees that can be moderated. For example, the individual who is very Assertive may find that too much of this behavior is experienced by others as aggressive. Moderating Assertiveness may result in enhancing or building relationships.

The BarOn EQ-i® has five composite scales that include results across fifteen sub-scales. The five composite scales and the associated subscales are the by-product of research indicating that these behaviors are most related to performance. One of the five composite scales, General Mood, is considered a facilitator or magnifier of the behaviors in the other four dimensions. A brief summary of all of the BarOn EQ-i® scales is provided at the end of this chapter (see Table 11.10).

As noted earlier, Bar-On studied the role of behavior on individual effectiveness and health. He pursued an examination of the kinds of behaviors that produce emotional effectiveness, and as he noted:

> The findings presented have shown that emotional-social intelligence, as conceptualized by the Bar-On model, is a multi-factorial array of interrelated emotional and social competencies, skills and facilitators that influence one's ability to recognize, understand and manage emotions, to relate with others, to adapt to change and solve problems of a personal and interpersonal nature, and to efficiently cope with daily demands, challenges and pressures (Bar-On, 2005).

The significance to the practitioner is multi-faceted. Bar-On has provided an excellent road map for understanding the relationship between degrees of Adaptability and Stress Management on Intrapersonal awareness and Interpersonal efforts. For example, a client's high degree of Adaptability and Stress Tolerance may provide cover for less-than-stellar Interpersonal behavior. Or if a client's scores indicate reasonably demonstrated Intrapersonal or Interpersonal behavior, but relatively low Stress Tolerance and a generally bad Mood (not optimistic or happy), then the behavior may not be as effective as those with greater Optimism; thus, the practitioner working with this individual on Optimism and Happiness is likely to yield the best results.

The BarOn EQ-i® tool allows for specific focus on behavior, whereas the MBTI® provides insights into both the triggers of emotional responses and the trends or patterns of BarOn EQ-i® tool scores. This is useful for the practitioner for three reasons. First, this opens the door to a very positive conversation about emotional reactions and personality patterns which invites further discussion. Second, the BarOn EQ-i® scores are reflected in patterns related to the sixteen types, which suggests that an individual "is not alone" in his or her challenges. Finally, by understanding personality types and BarOn EQ-i® patterns, the practitioner is more likely to coach with a more complete strategy for dealing with behaviors to increase emotional effectiveness.

LINKING AND LEVERAGING THE DATA POINTS

Because the BarOn EQ-i® and MBTI® tools provide a focus on development, the linkages between the personality types (sorted by the MBTI®) and the scores on BarOn EQ-i® scales provide useful clues for coaches and trainers. Table 11.5 provides the typical highs of the types on the Bar-On tool results. Coaches are encouraged to review these patterns and the suggested best learning strategy for working with the types (Table 11.6) as they select their coaching and training strategies.

Practitioners may use these patterns in a couple of ways. A client's higher scores in various BarOn EQ-i® sub-scales may be a reflection of the personality type. When this occurs, it makes sense to explore how an individual's preferences may also relate to the BarOn EQ-i® behaviors. For example, five of the eight Extraverted (E) types have Assertiveness as a high score. Exploring how the Extraversion and Assertive behaviors are related invites insight as to the development of the behavior and consideration of when these may not work effectively. This naturally leads to identifying how to flex the behavior as an Extravert, which may be quite different from the flex for an Introvert (I) who scores high in Assertiveness. The Extravert—with a natural initiating response—may need to be attentive to the urge to share an opinion, while the Introvert—with a natural reflective response—may need

Table 11.5. Highest BarOn EQ-i® Scale Scores for Each of the Sixteen Types

ISTJ	ISFJ	INFJ	INTJ
Assertiveness	Impulse Control	Emotionally Self-Aware	Self-Regard
Impulse Control	Reality Testing	Empathy	Independence
Reality Testing		Flexibility	Stress Tolerance
Problem Solving			Optimism

ISTP	ISFP	INFP	INTP
Stress Tolerance	Emotionally Self-Aware	Emotionally Self-Aware	Independence
Reality Testing	Social Responsibility	Independence	Stress Tolerance
		Flexibility	Reality Testing

ESTP	ESFP	ENFP	ENTP
Self-Regard	Emotionally Self-Aware	Emotionally Self-Aware	Assertiveness
Assertiveness	Interpersonal Relationship	Independence	Independence
Interpersonal Relationship	Flexibility	Social Responsibility	Flexibility
	Happiness	Flexibility	
		Optimism	

ESTJ	ESFJ	ENFJ	ENTJ
Assertiveness	Empathy	Self-Regard	Assertiveness
Stress Tolerance	Social Responsibility	Assertiveness	Independence
Impulse Control	Reality Testing	Empathy	Stress Tolerance
Problem Solving	Happiness	Interpersonal Relationship	Optimism
Happiness			

N = 1,127

Table 11.6. Questions for Exploration when the BarOn EQ-i® Scores are High

If the preference is . . .	Then ask . . .
Extraversion	When does this behavior get "overplayed" or "overused"?
Introversion	When do you pause to reflect on the impact of this behavior on others?
Sensing	How does your eagerness for specificity and concrete experience influence how you express this behavior?
Intuiting	How does your conceptual, idea-oriented perspective influence how you show this behavior?
Thinking	How does your analytical and logical approach color the language or perspective related to this behavior?
Feeling	How do your values and ideals influence your efforts related to this behavior?
Judging	How does the drive for closure affect your interest in action related to this behavior?
Perceiving	How is your drive for more information and exploration reflected in this behavior?

to be more aware of what he or she is being Assertive about. The Assertive ISTJ may sound bossy and critical while the Assertive ENFP may appear fussy, self-centered, and righteous. An effective coach will help the Assertive ISTJ pay more attention to his or her interpersonal style and will help the ENFP focus on content during an interaction.

The practitioner has much to gain by carefully exploring the link between the personality type preferences and the emotional intelligence behaviors of clients. To explore how preferences play out in the EQ-related dimensions, consider the questions in Table 11.6.

Behavior is expressed on a continuum. In recognition of this fact, the BarOn EQ-i® tool reports results from a low of 55 to a high of 145. As instructive as it appears when looking at the high scores, there may be more developmental opportunities when looking at scores on the low end. High-end scores present the potential of behavior being overplayed, while lower-end scores indicate an infrequent display or outright lack of know-how related to the behavior. Note that the two tables are reporting the patterns of scores that were high or low for the given type. In some cases, a low score for a given type may be at the mean for the general population or a high score may be at a standard deviation above the mean on the scales that are listed. Nonetheless, the importance of patterns of lower or higher scores for a given type reveals important trends. The peaks and valleys of scale scores, regardless of the scale number, are being summarized here. Practitioners can use the patterns in Table 11.7 to explore the role type preferences may have in the way these behaviors are grouped and expressed.

These patterns provide hints or trends to keep in mind when practitioners are coaching others. A client's low scores in various BarOn EQ-i® sub-scales may be a reflection of aspects of the personality type that are not

Table 11.7. Lowest EQ-i® Scale Scores for Each of the Sixteen Types

ISTJ	ISFJ	INFJ	INTJ
Emotional Self-Awareness	Independence	Self-Actualization	Emotional Self-Awareness
Empathy	Flexibility	Reality Testing	Empathy
ISTP	**ISFP**	**INFP**	**INTP**
Emotional Self-Awareness	Self-Regard	Self-Actualization	Emotional Self-Awareness
Impulse Control	Stress Tolerance	Interpersonal Skill	Happiness
ESTP	**ESFP**	**ENFP**	**ENTP**
Impulse Control	Independence	Impulse Control	Social Responsibility
Problem Solving	Problem Solving	Reality Testing	Reality Testing
		Problem Solving	
ESTJ	**ESFJ**	**ENFJ**	**ENTJ**
Emotional Self-Awareness	Independence	Impulse Control	Emotional Self-Awareness
Flexibility	Flexibility	Problem Solving	Social Responsibility

N = 1,127

preferences. For example, most of the types with an Intuitive (N) preference have among their low scores Reality Testing or Problem Solving. This is in part the result of how the BarOn EQ-i® defines these two sets of behavior. Both have elements of a focus on concrete, pragmatic information, which would be more reflective of a Sensing (S) type. Another illustration is that most of the individuals with a Thinking (T) preference report among their low scores Emotional Self-Control. This is likely a reflection of having less immediate use of the Feeling (F) process, which usually has quicker access to internal emotional reactions due to a values-based decision strategy. In these two examples, exploring how the Intuiting and Reality Testing behaviors are related or the Thinking and Emotional Self-Awareness behaviors are expressed invites insight as to the development of the behavior needed to increase effectiveness. This naturally leads to identifying how to accommodate concrete details as an Intuitive or identify emotional cues as a Thinking type.

Carefully exploring the link between the personality type preferences and the emotional intelligence behaviors among those scales with lower scores for each of the types will allow great insight as to the interplay of preference and the BarOn EQ-i® dimensions. For this exploration use the questions in Table 11.8.

The suggested questions in Tables 11.6 and 11.8 give practical guidance for helping a client or program participant gain a deeper sense of his or her behavior related to high and low scores for that type. A broader question is how to help the type tackle whatever EQ development challenge has emerged. With this in mind, Table 11.9 summarizes the key aspects of the sixteen types with an additional suggestion for a learning tactic question the practitioner might use when dealing with this type in areas related to emotional intelligence.

As illustrated above, the links between the behaviors measured by the BarOn EQ-i® and MBTI® tools provide additional information to use in interpreting the meaning of scores. Importantly, the practitioner has a way to invite the client to identify how to consider the role of personality patterns in emotional triggers as well as in the expression of specific EQ-related behaviors such as Assertiveness, Interpersonal Skill, Empathy, and so forth. In short, the individual has an opportunity at deeper understanding of the patterns and the ways to enhance the behavior in question.

Table 11.8. Questions for Exploration when the BarOn EQ-i® Scores are Low

If the preference is . . .	Then ask . . .
Extraversion	What are the ways that your tendency for initiating can be also applied to your areas of low scores?
Introversion	How can you clarify when to use this behavior by reflecting on what it looks like and when you actively display it?
Sensing	In what ways does your focus on pragmatic and concrete information inhibit your expression of this behavior?
Intuiting	How does your preference for patterns and big trends affect your display of this behavior?
Thinking	How does your analytical and logical approach redirect attention from more personal disclosure or interpersonal behaviors?
Feeling	How does the presence or lack of the manifestation of your values inhibit your expression of this behavior?
Judging	How might your tendency for quick closure affect your willingness to explore this behavior?
Perceiving	How might your preference for going with the flow of a situation reflect your display of this behavior?

Isabel Myers, the developer of the MBTI® tool, noted that the purpose of development is to make perceptions clearer and judgments more sound (Myers, 1981). With the use of the MBTI® and BarOn EQ-i® assessments, individuals have an extraordinary opportunity to achieve both: comprehensive insight into behavior patterns and better understanding of what to do about them when adjustments are needed.

CONCLUSIONS

There is little doubt about the importance of emotional intelligence in enhancing individual effectiveness in self-management and interpersonal skills. Further, due to the complexity of the behaviors involved,

Table 11.9. Brief Descriptions and Learning Tactics of the Sixteen Types

ISTJ

Realistic, matter-of-fact, fastidious and orderly, loyal. Enjoys finding concrete solutions to problems.

Tactic: Prepare a case study of the behavior that includes five specific steps to address the issues in the case.

ISFJ

Pragmatic, hands-on individuals who are conscientious. Enjoy finding helpful and immediate personal actions.

Tactic: Ask how the behavior in question (for development or moderation) can improve the quality of the life of those important to the type.

INFJ

Sees inter-relationships and seeks to serve common good. Pursues ideas that serve trusted values.

Tactic: Explore how the behavior in question serves one's values or mission.

INTJ

Independent minded, prefers dealing with ideas, driven to be competent. Enjoys finding systems-related solutions.

Tactic: Ask how the behavior in question is related to providing a strategic advantage in working with others.

ISTP

Tackles practical problems, takes quick action, driven for efficiency.

Tactic: Use a video clip to illustrate the behavior in question.

ISFP

Friendly and values-oriented, sensitive to the needs of others. Loyal and very private.

Tactic: Explore how the behavior in question affects family and friends.

INFP

Driven toward ideals, seeks congruence between values and external life.

Tactic: Ask how the behavior in question can serve the personal mission.

INTP

Analytical, driven to find underlying logic in situations, often theoretical. Driven to be precise.

Tactic: Ask for the logical and working principle that is advanced by developing or moderating the behavior in question.

ESTP

Has an action-oriented, "here and now" approach, uses pragmatic strategies.

Tactic: Video the actual person and deconstruct the behavior and its consequences.

ESFP

Energetic in approaching others, accepting, likes to find specific, constructive solutions.

Tactic: Ask how the behavior in question can enrich helping others find more satisfying activities.

ENFP

Spontaneous and imaginative, seeks connections and patterns, often will find synthesis.

Tactic: Ask how the behavior in question can enrich creativity and enhance relationships.

ENTP

Enjoys complex problems, often resourceful with making ideas useful, often critical.

Tactic: Ask to explore the "deltas" between what is desired and the current behavior and how to bridge the gap.

ESTJ

Likes to take action, organize, analyze, systematically implement plans, often seen as driven.

Tactic: Prepare a thirty-day action plan on how to test the outcomes of moderating behavior.

ESFJ

Seen as cooperative and conscientious, likes working with teams, attends to basic interpersonal needs.

Tactic: Ask the individual to assist you in looking at how the behavior affects his or her team.

(Continued)

Table 11.9. *(Continued)*

ENFJ

Often social and warm, seen as "attuned" to others, responsive and thoughtful toward others' needs.

Tactic: Explore how moderating the behavior in question will boost overall engagement with others.

ENTJ

Likes to think long-term, tackles comprehensive approaches to problems, decisive and forceful.

Tactic: Ask how organizational performance and personal competence is enhanced by dealing with the behavior in question.

practitioners may need a number of approaches to the topic to aid clients in gaining an understanding of how to explore their behaviors in deep and more meaningful ways. To achieve this exploration, several perspectives have been outlined to aid the practitioner. First, a framing of EQ research reveals the layers of exploration that are possible, from the basics of the taxonomy of emotions to the richness of behavior patterns. Secondly, an exploration of how to use two important models—the MBTI® for looking at how people see and think about life and the BarOn EQ-i® for exploring EQ behavior patterns—facilitates understanding and action. Finally, pragmatic questions and suggestions are provided to aid in providing feedback and facilitating clarity about the meaning of behavior in everyday life. Development is driven by appropriate assessment of behavior, clarification of the goal, and appropriate support while striving to reach a new level of performance. The aim in this chapter has been to give the practitioner prompts and observations to assist in this privileged work and to create a psychological space for an individual to reach his or her heart's desires and greater satisfaction in all areas of life.

Table 11.10. Scale Definitions of the BarOn EQ-i® Assessment Tool

Scale	Implications of Reporting More (M) & Less (L) than Most
Intrapersonal	
Self-Regard	M: self-assured, confident, poised, good opinion of self
	L: unsure, self-doubting, sees others as "better"
Emotional Self-Awareness	M: easily identifies and expresses emotional feelings
	L: denying of emotions, cannot verbalize feelings
Assertiveness	M: forthright, candid, seeks "win-win", defends rights
	L: passive, shy, over-controlled, self-denying
Independence	M: self-sufficient, resourceful, detached, relies on own ideas
	L: relies on others to make decisions, follower, "clings"
Self-Actualization	M: energized, passionate in efforts, involved, active
	L: unsure, directionless, disinterested, appears bored
Interpersonal	
Empathy	M: sensitive to others' feelings, understands others' reactions
	L: insensitive, unable to identify feelings or reactions
Social Responsibility	M: reasonable, takes roles seriously, helps others
	L: careless, lazy, unresponsive to others' needs
Interpersonal Relationship	M: spontaneous, easy talker, sociable, comfortable with emotions
	L: uncomfortable with others, hesitant, cautious, difficult to be with
Stress Management	
Stress Tolerance	M: resilient, tackles challenges with confidence, calm
	L: anxious, distressed, upset when things change

(Continued)

Table 11.10. *(Continued)*

Scale	Implications of Reporting More (M) & Less (L) than Most
Impulse Control	M: self-disciplined, controls energy toward constructive ends
	L: impulsive, often angry and annoyed, impatient, quick temper
Adaptability	
Reality Testing	M: pragmatic, realistic, attuned to specifics, focused, grounded
	L: dreamy, exaggerates, unfocused, unaware
Flexibility	M: enjoys change, variety; easily adjusts to new situations, open
	L: stubborn, prefers consistency and routine, uncomfortable with change
Problem Solving	M: takes perspective, systematic and methodical, problem-focused
	L: short-term thinking, scattered approaches, "stuck"
General Mood	
Optimism	M: positive, confident, resourceful, self-assured, motivated
	L: pessimistic, catastrophizing, often fearful, unsure of choices
Happiness	M: content, enjoys others, actively engaged with interests
	L: negative, dissatisfied with life, bored, avoids others, disengaged

(M refers to higher scores and L refers to lower scores on the scales).

REFERENCES

Albrecht, K. (2006). *Social intelligence: The new science of success.* San Francisco: Jossey-Bass.

Bar-On, R. (1997). *Manual: BarOn EQ-i.* Toronto: MHS, Inc. pp. 13–18.

Bar-On, R. (2005). The Bar-On model of emotional-social intelligence. In P. Fernández-Berrocal and N. Extremera (Guest Editors), Special Issue on Emotional Intelligence. *Psicothema, 17.*

Brousseau, K., Driver, M., Hourihan, G., & Larsson, R. (2006). The seasoned executive's decision-making style. *Harvard Business Review, 85*(2), pp. 111–121.

Darwin, C. (1872). *The expression of the emotions in man and animals*. In E. Wilson, E. (2006). *From so simple a beginning: The four great books of Charles Darwin*. New York: Norton.

Leslie, J., & Van Velsor, E. (1996). *A look at derailment today: North America and Europe*. Greensboro, NC: CCL Press.

Lewis, M., & Haviland-Jones, J. (Eds.). (2004). *The handbook of emotions*. New York: The Guilford Press.

Mayer, J., Salovey, P., & Caruso, D. (2002). *Manual: MSCEIT*. Toronto, MHS, Inc. p. 8.

Myers, I.B. (1981). *Gifts differing*. Mountain View, CA: CPP, Inc.

Pearman, R. (2002). *Introduction to type and emotional intelligence*. Mountain View, CA: CPP, Inc.

Pearman, R. (2007). *Understanding emotions*. Winston-Salem, NC: Leadership Performance Systems, Inc.

Sutton, R. (2006). *The no asshole rule*. New York: Warner Books.

Roger R. Pearman, Ed.D., researches, writes about, and coaches leaders. Combining his experience as a corporate vice president, entrepreneur, researcher, and author of nine publications, his work is focused on enhancing individual effectiveness. As president and CEO of Leadership Performance Systems, Inc., and Qualifying.org®, Inc., Roger works relentlessly to prepare pragmatic developmental experiences for his clients. Leadership Performance Systems, Inc., provides coaching and training for managers and executives. Qualifying.org®, Inc., provides blended and e-learning options for professionals seeking certification on the use of psychological tools. Dr. Pearman has been honored with the Myers Research Award and the McCaulley Lifetime Achievement Award by the Association for Psychological Type International.

CHAPTER 12

Using the EQ-i® and MSCEIT® in Tandem

Henry L. Thompson

The study of emotional and social intelligence (ESI) is in its second decade. Even so, ESI remains controversial around at least three issues. The primary issue is whether ESI is actually a new construct or just a compilation of psychological constructs, such as personality and interpersonal interaction styles, studied for over a century (Murphy, 2006). A second issue is whether ESI is an actual intelligence, that is, an internal, hard-wired neurological process/ability that facilitates emotional decision making and actions in a particular domain, or whether it is a skill that can be learned. A third issue, assuming that ESI is a valid construct, is whether it can be measured and, if so, how?

This chapter will not attempt to resolve the ESI debate, but will make the assumptions that ESI is a viable construct and that it can be measured, at least to some degree, with the currently available ESI instruments, such as the BarOn Emotional Quotient Inventory® (EQ-i®) and the Mayer-Salovey-Caruso Emotional Intelligence Test® (MSCEIT®).

For the research presented in this chapter, these two particular instruments were chosen for their different theoretical and methodological approaches to the measurement and understanding of ESI and because, when used together, they negate some of the ESI issues. The characteristics of each instrument will be described in more detail later, including how they provide a solution to the ability-versus-mixed-model debate.

The ESI literature is replete with rigorous debates over which type of model—ability (MSCEIT®) or mixed (EQ-i®)—provides the "real" measure of ESI. This chapter adds another layer of complexity to the debate by presenting evidence that true ESI might be situationally dependent. That is, ESI might not be the total score produced by an ESI instrument, but rather a particular blend of ESI components, and this blend may vary by situation (for example, job, role level, company). The situational ESI concept will be elucidated in more detail below.

Much of the data and many of the techniques discussed in this chapter come from a leadership study involving over 250 leaders. All leaders were participating in a leader development program that involved completing several assessments, including the EQ-i® and MSCEIT®, receiving feedback, and creating a personal leader developmental plan. Numerous types of additional data were collected on these leaders, including performance data, which allowed for a data-centric approach that goes beyond most ESI studies.

This chapter also addresses, to some degree, the utility of ability-based models versus mixed models for ESI assessment and use in leader development programs. A process will be shown for how these two approaches (MSCEIT® and EQ-i®) may be used in *Tandem* to provide a complementary approach to working with ESI.

Data are presented that show that the EQ-i®, which tends to accurately predict observable behaviors, and the MSCEIT®, which tends to be good at predicting one's ability to do emotional problem solving, actually complement each other. Using the EQ-i® and MSCEIT® in Tandem refers to administering the two instruments in close proximity and providing integrated feedback. Practitioners can be trained to use the two instruments in Tandem, especially in situations where the data may have a significant impact on an individual's career. Each instrument brings a unique perspective to the measurement of ESI.

Table 12.1. A Common Two-by-Two EI Model

	Self	Others
Awareness	Self-Awareness	Other-Awareness
Management	Self-Management	Relationship Management

EMOTIONAL INTELLIGENCE: ITS DEFINITION AND MEASUREMENT

The ESI literature reveals numerous, but somewhat similar, approaches to defining ESI (Bar-On, 2002; Goleman, 1995; Salovey & Mayer, 1990; Thompson, 2005). Most researchers and authors tend to agree that behaving in an emotionally and socially intelligent manner involves some degree of emotional and social awareness and management of self and others. That is, an emotionally intelligent person must have some level of awareness about his or her own emotional state, that of the person he or she is engaging, and the ability to manage both his own actions and those of the other person. Table 12.1 shows a basic two-by-two depiction of this simple model. According to this model, ESI consists of four basic processes: being aware of one's emotions, managing one's emotions, being aware of others' emotions, and managing one's relationship with others.

I view ESI as a dynamical system, and on a macro level, it can be described as *a person's innate ability to perceive and manage his/her own emotions in a manner that results in successful interactions with the environment, and if others are present, to also perceive and manage their emotions in a manner that results in successful interpersonal interactions* (Thompson, 2006).

Note that this definition involves managing/controlling the Awareness and Appraising of emotions and the resulting Action Patterns in a manner that produces successful outcomes whether in the presence or absence of others. When others are present and interpersonal interactions occur, the ESI process of managing outcomes becomes several orders of magnitude more complex. Managing the perceiving and appraising of one's own internal dynamic emotions and the dynamic emotions of other people involved in the interaction is a very complex process.

Managing the perception of my emotions and the emotions of others, Awareness, provides the foundation for being able to manage the Appraisal and Action Patterns. ESI begins by managing/controlling emotions, then extends to awareness of emotions. ESI is based on a recursive cognitive and emotional Appraisal and the blending of emotions, Motivational Complexes, and Action Patterns (see Chapter Six on Catastrophic Leadership Failure™ for more information on this model). Intelligent responses to situations require appropriate management of the emotional system in a manner that produces the highest probability of successful interactions with the environment and others, if present.

ESI models, and their associated instruments, tend to be categorized as either an *ability* model or a *mixed* model. The MSCEIT® falls into the ability model classification because of its focus on identifying and measuring the actual abilities required to use emotion to solve emotional problems. Mixed models, such as the EQ-i®, get their name as a result of incorporating a broad set of factors ranging from empathy to problem solving. The Tandem approach espoused in this chapter combines the best of both worlds by using the two most prominent ESI instruments in an integrated manner.

ABILITY MODEL CONCEPT

Proponents of ability models of ESI suggest that if ESI is actually an intelligence, then by definition ESI refers to a set of abilities, such as perceiving, using, understanding, and managing emotions to solve emotional problems. As used here, ability also implies some degree of innateness. That is, a person's neurological wiring impacts his or her ability to be "emotionally and socially intelligent." A strong argument can be made that emotional and cognitive abilities grow from birth to adulthood and that this growth is regulated or constrained by neurological development. The expression and use of emotions in infants unfolds in a particular sequence that coincides with cognitive development in the brain. For example, infants do not experience the "self-conscious emotions" of embarrassment, empathy, and envy until around eighteen to twenty-four months because the brain's cognitive capacity of self-referential behavior must be developed before these emotions can be experienced. Self-conscious evaluative emotions, such as pride, shame, and guilt, require the cognitive capacity that allows for the comparison of personal behavior to a behavioral standard. This tends to occur for most children around the age of thirty to thirty-six months. Emotions develop as part of a neurological system that includes cognitive ability.

Having ESI ability does not ensure that a person will behave in an emotionally intelligent manner. Numerous factors can prevent the use of ESI ability (see Chapter Six on Catastrophic Leadership Failure). This is similar to other skills; Grandma Moses, the legendary folk artist, was seventy-six years old before she began using her artistic ability. The Mayer-Salovey-Caruso Emotional Intelligence Test® (MSCEIT®) is an assessment based on an ability model.

Mayer-Salovey-Caruso Emotional Intelligence Test® (MSCEIT®) Overview

Peter Salovey and John Mayer (1990) are given credit for coining the term "emotional intelligence." Their approach to ESI was to identify what they believed to be the necessary abilities people need to be emotionally and socially intelligent.

Mayer, Salovey, and Caruso (2002) defined emotional intelligence as *The ability to perceive emotions, to assess and generate emotions so as to assist thought, to understand emotions and emotional meanings, and to reflectively regulate emotions in ways that promote emotional and intellectual growth* (p. 17).

To this end, Mayer and Salovey, with their colleague David Caruso, designed a test (MSCEIT®) to measure ESI ability. The MSCEIT® is constructed with a 1-2-4-8 hierarchical structure such that there is a MSCEIT® total score, two Area scores, four Branch scores, and eight Task scores (see Table 12.2). The basic premise is that to be emotionally intelligent, a person must have the ability to perceive, use, understand, and manage emotions to solve emotional problems. The MSCEIT® uses a variety of methods, such as, faces, pictures and emotional scenarios, to measure each of these abilities (see Mayer, Salovey, & Caruso, 2002). This is a knowledge-based test that relies heavily on the person's emotional vocabulary, understanding of the "rules" emotions follow, recognition of emotions in faces and pictures, and how to use emotions to facilitate intra and interpersonal interactions. MSCEIT® scores tend to represent ESI potential, not necessarily application.

Table 12.2. MSCEIT® Structural Components

MSCEIT® Areas, Branches, and Tasks	
Experiential	**Strategic**
Perceiving	**Understanding**
Faces	Changes
Pictures	Blends
Using	**Managing**
Facilitation	Emotional Management
Sensations	Emotional Relations

The MSCEIT® consists of 141 questions with a scoring system (for all scales) that has been standardized to a mean of 100 and a standard deviation of 15. Interpretation of MSCEIT® results provides an indication of the person's ESI ability, balance of ESI ability components (Tasks), emotional problem solving potential, and emotional knowledge.

MIXED MODEL CONCEPT

Proponents of mixed models of ESI, such as the BarOn EQ-i®, suggest that ESI is a "learned" intelligence, and by definition can be improved through training and practice. This has been cited as part of the lure of ESI and has contributed to its phenomenal growth in popularity. Some believe that ESI is an "intelligence" that everyone can have if they read the books or go to ESI training.

BarOn Emotional Quotient-Inventory (EQ-i)®

The Bar-On model of ESI was developed by Reuven Bar-On in the early 1980s and was based on the premise that people who function effectively at the emotional and social level should experience greater psychological well-being than those who do not. From this original work, Bar-On developed the BarOn EQ-i® for measuring specific ESI factors found to be predictive of psychological well-being (Bar-On, 2002).

Table 12.3. EQ-i® Structural Components

EQ-i® Composite and Subscales

Intrapersonal	**Interpersonal**
Self-Regard	Empathy
Emotional Self-Awareness	Social Responsibility
Assertiveness	Interpersonal Relationships
Independence	
Self-Actualization	
Stress Management	**Adaptability**
Stress Tolerance	Reality Testing
Impulse Control	Flexibility
	Problem Solving
General Mood	
Optimism	
Happiness	

Bar-On coined the term "emotional quotient" and is credited with being first to use the term emotional and social intelligence. He defines ESI as *a cross-section of interrelated emotional and social competencies, skills and facilitators that determine how effectively we understand and express ourselves, understand others and relate with them, and cope with daily demands* (Bar-On, 2006).

The Bar-On model uses a 1-5-15 hierarchical structure such that there is a Total score, five Composite scales and fifteen subscales (see Table 12.3). The EQ-i® is a self-report instrument that relies heavily on the respondent to honestly and accurately answer the questions. It is not a test and does not require an extensive knowledge of emotions, facial recognition, or emotional problem solving.

Self-report instruments always provide an opportunity for misrepresentation. The EQ-i®, however, has several validity indicators and adjustment algorithms built into the scoring to reduce deception. The EQ-i® scores tend to represent observable ESI application, not necessarily the intellectual knowledge of emotions.

The EQ-i® consists of 133 questions with a scoring system (for all scales) that has been standardized to a mean of 100 and a standard deviation of 15. Interpretation of EQ-i® results provides an indication of the person's ESI behavior, balance of ESI components (subscales) and ESI talents and skills. The EQ-i® tends to be very predictive of actual observed behavior.

ESI AS A SITUATIONALLY DEPENDENT CONCEPT

ESI, like IQ, is most often discussed as if it is a single score on an instrument, such as the EQ-i® total score or the MSCEIT® total score. This total score is a meta-view of ESI as measured by the instrument and is not a very good predictor of behavior or success. As discussed above, at its micro-level, the EQ-i® is composed of fifteen subscales and the MSCEIT® of eight subscales. These scales seem to be where most of the ESI predictive power lies.

Diana Durek describes Multi-Health Systems' Star Performer profile (see Chapter Nine) and how she finds not only clusters of EQ-i® subscales, but also specific weightings for the subscales that together account for a high percentage of variance in the success profile. A substantial body of work has been done in this area with the EQ-i®. The MSCEIT® produces similar results.

The examples above indicate two important points. The first is that blends of ESI subscales are the best predictors of success. Second, that the blends of subscales are specific to particular jobs and that the ESI requirements of these jobs can vary from one organization to another—ESI success profiles (blends) are situationally specific. Even with a particular person, job, and organization, the "blend" will be in a dynamic flux.

GOODNESS OF FIT

In Chapter Five, Rich Handley talks about the importance of drag or balance in the EQ-i® profile. A person with high Assertiveness needs relatively high Empathy to help prevent the person from being aggressive. Howard Book in Chapter Four talks about leadership derailment—when certain subscales are overused and become a liability rather than an asset.

Table 12.4. MSCEIT® and EQ-i® Goodness of Fit Means and Ranges

	Sample Size	Mean	Minimum	Maximum	Standard Deviation
EQ-(Subscale)	13.4	8.7	2.9	26.6	3.0
MSCEIT (Branch)	542	12.0	1.6	33.0	5.6
MSCEIT (Task)	542	13.4	5.0	29.3	4.5

In my work I use the term Goodness of Fit to indicate how "balanced" a person's ESI subscales are in relation to the dispersion of subscale scores. Computing a simple standard deviation of the subscale scores gives a mathematical measure of the dispersion. The smaller the standard deviation, the more even the bars on the subscale graph will be and, consequently, more balanced. Table 12.4 shows that the mean standard deviation for the EQ-i® (8.7) is much smaller than for the MSCEIT® Branch (12.0) and MSCEIT Task (13.4). Goodness of Fit scores are like golf scores—the lower the better.

Goodness of Fit can also be applied to success profiles, but this process is beyond the scope of this chapter.

EQ-I® AND MSCEIT® INTEGRATION

This section examines the relationship of the EQ-i® and MSCEIT® to each other as well as to other instruments. Knowledge of these relationships may assist the practitioner as he or she works with the two instruments. Table 12.5 shows some of the benefits that each instrument has when used for measuring ESI.

EQ-i® and MSCEIT® Combinations

An ESI assessment, such as the EQ-i® or MSCEIT®, can be viewed metaphorically as a method of making ESI psychometrically visible. That is, taking an assessment produces an ESI "score." In fact, everyone has ESI scores as well

Table 12.5.   Benefits of EQ-i® and MSCEIT®

Predicts observable EI behaviors	Measures ability to solve emotional problems
High internal validity measures	Good inter-scale reliability for Branch scales
High inter-scale reliability	
Abundant supporting research	Provides an emotions knowledge test
Predictive of numerous behaviors	Difficult to fake "good/smart/intelligent"
Fifteen scales allow for many patterns	Academic/professional group receptivity
Easy to teach/train	A "test," not a self-report
Strong practitioner following	Focuses on "using" emotions
Large "EQ family" of products	
Receptivity of feedback	

as "scores" on all other assessments. They just don't become visible until one takes the particular assessment. The point is, an ESI practitioner who uses the EQ-i® must realize that his clients also have an invisible MSCEIT® score and that this score influences the client's behavior, response to feedback and general functioning—even if he doesn't measure it.

Table 12.6 shows a breakout of different combinations of EQ-i® and MSCEIT® and leader performance scores in a sample leader population.

Several observations can be made from the data in Table 12.6. One is that scores on the two ESI instruments appear to have a nonlinear distribution and, thus, are not expected to correlate, or at best to have a very low correlation. That is, people who score high on the EQ-i® do not necessarily score high on the MSCEIT®.

A second observation is that leader performance also seems to be nonlinear such that leaders who scored the highest on performance fell into the ESI combination of low for both instruments (<95) or scored in the midrange (≥95 and <115) on both instruments. The combination that produced the lowest leader performance score was a high ESI score (>115) on both instruments. Some of this variation may be an artifact of using total ESI scores as discussed above.

Table 12.6. EQ-i® and MSCEIT® Combination
Versus Performance Scores

Combination	Percent of Sample	Performance Scores	SD
L $_{EQ-i}$ L $_{MSCEIT}$	13%	2.7	.78
L $_{EQ-i}$ M $_{MSCEIT}$	11%	2.4	.52
L $_{EQ-i}$ H $_{MSCEIT}$	1%	3.0	–
M $_{EQ-i}$ L $_{MSCEIT}$	22%	2.5	.83
M $_{EQ-i}$ M $_{MSCEIT}$	14%	2.7	.75
M $_{EQ-i}$ H $_{MSCEIT}$	8%	2.6	.98
H $_{EQ-i}$ L $_{MSCEIT}$	10%	2.4	1.0
H $_{EQ-i}$ M $_{MSCEIT}$	14%	2.6	.77
H $_{EQ-i}$ H $_{MSCEIT}$	6%	2.4	.55

Note: The first letter represents the EQ-i® total score category and the second letter is the MSCEIT® total score category; Low <95; Middle ≥95 <115; High ≥115. Performance is based on a 4-point scale with "4" being the highest score and "1" the lowest.

© 2008 by Henry L. Thompson, Ph.D. Reproduced with permission.

EQ-i® and MSCEIT® Correlations

Understanding how the two instruments correlate is valuable when using them in Tandem. Table 12.7 shows EQ-i® and MSCEIT® correlations for the leadership sample. The correlation of total scores of the two instruments, although very low, is statistically significant.

EQ-i® and MSCEIT® Relationship to Other Instruments

One of the major criticisms of ESI instruments in general, and the EQ-i® in particular, is overlap with other instruments. Thus, it is important that practitioners who plan to use the two instruments in Tandem understand how the EQ-i® and MSCEIT® relate to other instruments as well as to each other.

Table 12.7. EQ-i® and MSCEIT® Correlations

	FAC	FACI	CHA	EMA	PIC	SEN	BLE	SMA	PER	USE	UND	MGT	MSCEIT
TEI	0.11*	0.11*	−0.05	0.19*	0.09*	0.14*	0.00	0.19*	0.16*	0.16*	−0.03	0.23*	0.18*
SR	0.04	0.04	−0.06	0.09	0.07	0.06	−0.10*	0.12*	0.06	0.03	0.10*	0.13*	0.02
ES	0.05	−0.01	−0.05	0.09	0.04	0.06	0.04	0.07	0.10*	0.05	−0.01	0.09	0.10*
AS	0.16*	0.12*	−0.01	0.17*	0.12*	0.08	0.01	0.15*	0.21*	0.13*	0.00	0.21*	0.18*
IN	0.08	0.13*	−0.04	0.11*	0.03	0.06	−0.01	0.09	0.10*	0.12*	−0.04	0.12*	0.11*
SA	0.08	−0.01	−0.05	0.09*	0.04	0.08	−0.04	0.13*	0.13*	0.05	−0.05	0.12*	0.11*
EM	0.06	0.08	0.02	0.14*	0.01	0.15*	0.14*	0.12*	0.09*	0.16*	0.09	0.13*	0.19*
RE	0.09	0.10*	0.01	0.13*	0.04	0.14*	0.07	0.14*	0.12*	0.15*	0.04	0.14*	0.18*
IR	0.02	0.00	−0.05	0.18*	0.04	0.05	−0.01	0.12*	0.06	0.03	−0.04	0.16*	0.07
ST	0.09*	0.11*	0.00	0.19*	0.12*	0.14*	0.05	0.13*	0.16*	0.16*	0.02	0.20*	0.19*
IC	0.02	0.08	−0.02	0.06	0.11*	0.12*	−0.00	0.12*	0.07	0.13*	−0.02	0.10*	0.12*
RT	0.15*	0.12*	−0.03	0.12*	0.08	0.11*	0.01	0.15*	0.18*	0.14*	−0.02	0.17*	0.17*
FL	0.08	0.15*	−0.09	0.16*	0.10*	0.06	−0.01	0.22*	0.13*	0.12*	−0.06	0.24*	0.13*
PS	0.10*	0.16*	−0.06	0.18*	0.00	0.18*	−0.03	0.18*	0.11*	0.21*	−0.06	0.20*	0.15*
OP	0.12*	0.09	−0.01	0.13*	0.03	0.15*	0.05	0.14*	0.15*	0.15*	0.01	0.16*	0.17*
HA	0.02	−0.05	−0.02	0.12*	0.03	0.04	−0.06	0.11*	0.05	0.01	−0.05	0.12*	0.05

*$P<.05$; N = 470.

This section shows the relationship of EQ-i® and MSCEIT® with personality (Myers-Briggs Type Indicator®), interpersonal interaction (FIRO Element B™), and cognitive ability (Wonderlic Personnel Test™).

Personality (Myers-Briggs Type Indicator®)

The Myers-Briggs Type Indicator® instrument, with millions of administrations each year and the focus of over 1,500 theses and dissertations and thousands of research articles, is one of the most validated and widely used personality instruments. Table 12.8 shows a macro-view of the relationship of the MBTI® instrument, the EQ-i® and MSCEIT®.

Note that the EQ-i® scores in Table 12.8 are consistent with the findings of Roger Pearman in Chapter Eleven of this book. (For a more detailed analysis of the EQ-i® and MBTI® instruments, including how the EQ-i® scales relate to the MBTI® Form Q Facets, see Thompson, 2007b.)

The data show that there is a variation among MBTI® types in terms of how they score on the EQ-i® and MSCEIT®. The results in Table 12.8

Table 12.8. EQ-i® and MSCEIT® Average Scores by MBTI Type

	ISTJ	ISFJ	INFJ	INTJ
EQ-i	101	105	103	107
MSCEIT	96	98	107	106
	ISTP	ISFP	INFP	INTP
EQ-i	97	98	104	104
MSCEIT	110	84	1029	104
	ESTP	ESFP	ENFP	ENTP
EQ-i	108	108	112	109
MSCEIT	99	99	104	102
	ESTJ	ESFJ	ENFJ	ENTJ
EQ-i	111	106	111	112
MSCEIT	96	100	104	104

EQ-i = 1225; MSCEIT = 550.

© 2007 by Henry L. Thompson, Ph.D. Reproduced with permission.

are consistent with the findings of other ESI instruments—people with an extraverted preference tend to have higher ESI total scores. (For a more in-depth analysis of the MSCEIT® scales and the MBTI® instrument, see Thompson, 2008c.)

Interpersonal Interaction (FIRO Element B™)

FIRO Element B® was created by Will Schutz in the early 1980s as the next generation of FIRO-B® and contains numerous enhancements over the original FIRO-B® instrument. FIRO® theory is about interpersonal interaction and, thus, is related to ESI. Table 12.9 gives an overview of this relationship with EQ-i® and MSCEIT®.

Table 12.9. FIRO Element B™ Scale Scores by High and Low EQ-i® & MSCEIT® Scores

FIRO Element B Scale (High scores are >114; Low scores are <95)	EQ-i		MSCEIT	
	High (N = 269)	Low (N = 79)	High (N = 81)	Low (N = 164)
Inclusion I include people.	6.6*	3.8	5.9	5.3
I want to include people.	6.6*	3.8	5.8	4.9
People include me.	8.1*	4.1	7.0	6.7
I want people to include me.	6.6*	3.8	5.9	4.8
Control I control people.	6.0*	3.8	5.2	5.0
I want to control people.	4.7*	3.2	4.1	3.8
People control me.	2.7*	4.7	3.0	3.9
I want people to control me.	2.2*	3.1	2.2	2.9
Openness I am open with people.	5.3*	3.3	4.93	4.3
I want to be open with people.	5.2*	3.43	5.16	4.2
People are open with me.	7.7*	5.1	7.1	6.5
I want people to be open with me.	6.9*	5.1	6.95	5.8

Note: An *indicates High and Low scores are significant at $p<.05$.
EQ-i® = 348; MSCEIT® = 245.

FIRO Element B™, like the EQ-i®, is very predictive of observable behavior. People who score high on Total EQ-i® tend to score higher on FIRO Element B™ scales, like, *I include people,* than people who score low on Total EQ-i®.

FIRO Element B™ scores (Table 12.9) show a much smaller difference between high and low MSCEIT® Total scores than do EQ-i® scores. This might be explained by MSCEIT® scores representing potential ability, not necessarily application. MSCEIT® does not seem to be as predictive of actual interpersonal behavior as the EQ-i®.

Cognitive Ability (IQ)

IQ, like ESI, is defined several ways, but most researchers tend to agree that IQ describes an innate cognitive ability to rapidly process information and make decisions in a logical and analytical manner. This ability to process information and make decisions involves several components such as working memory, processing speed, verbal comprehension, perceptual organization and abstract reasoning. Several recognized IQ tests include the Wechsler Adult Intelligence Scale™, Raven's Progressive Matrices™ and the Wonderlic Personnel Test™.

IQ is an important factor in coaching, training, selection, and working with clients in general. It is still one of the most important factors in predicting job performance, especially in professional jobs (Schmidt, 2002; Schmidt & Hunter, 1998). People don't have much of a chance of becoming a medical doctor, lawyer or rocket scientist without a substantial IQ. At the same time, having a high IQ will not necessarily assure success even if someone obtains professional credentials.

For the purposes of this chapter, the Wonderlic Personnel Test™ (WPT) was chosen as the measure of IQ. Table 12.10 shows that the EQ-i® subscale of Self-Regard produced the only statistically significant correlation with the

Table 12.10. EQ-i® Significant Correlations with Wonderlic Personnel Test™

EQ-i	Self-Regard
WPT	−.1

$p < .05$; N = 485.

© 2007 by Henry L. Thompson, Ph.D. Reproduced with permission.

Table 12.11. MSCEIT® Significant Correlations with Wonderlic Personnel Test™

MSCEIT®	Facilitation	Change	Blends	Understanding	Total MSCEIT®
WPT	.11	.26	.28	.32	.23

© 2007 by Henry L. Thompson, Ph.D. Reproduced with permission.

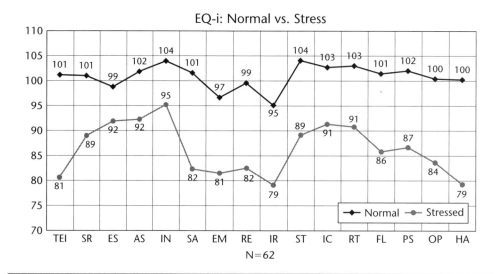

Figure 12.1. EQ-i® Normal vs. Stressed Scores

© 2005 Henry L. Thompson, Ph.D. Reproduced with permission.

WPT, and it is extremely low. These results suggest that IQ, as measured by the WPT, is of little relevance when using the EQ-i®.

Table 12.11 shows that the MSCEIT® seems to be tapping into some aspect of IQ, perhaps crystallized intelligence, more than the EQ-i®. This might explain why there is a low but significant correlation between IQ and MSCEIT®. Although the correlations are low to moderate, they are statistically significant and suggest that practitioners should be aware of this relationship.

Stress

Research suggests that both the EQ-i® (Thompson, 2005) and MSCEIT® scores (Thompson, 2008b) are influenced by the respondent's stress level. Figure 12.1

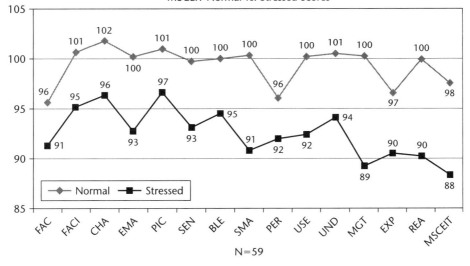

Figure 12.2. MSCEIT® Normal vs. Stressed Scores

shows that a "stressed" mindset degraded the Total EQ-i® score more than a standard deviation below the "normal" mindset average. All fifteen EQ-i® subscales experienced significant degradation under the "stressed" condition.

Even though Mayer, Salovey, and Caruso (2002, p. 1) state that [MSCEIT] scores are relatively unaffected by self-concept, response set, emotional state, and other confounds, Figure 12.2 shows that all MSCEIT® scores experienced degradation under the "stressed" mindset.

The results of these two studies on the impact of stress on EQ-i® and MSCEIT® scores suggest that practitioners should be particularly sensitive to the respondent's stress level when completing an ESI instrument. Stress has been shown to degrade both cognitive ability and ESI (Thompson, 2005, 2008b). For a more detailed discussion of the impact of stress on ESI and leader performance, see Chapter Six on Catastrophic Leadership Failure.

THE TANDEM PROCESS

The Tandem process provides a multi-lens approach to assessment, interpretation, and feedback with the end result being a more robust assessment. Each instrument unveils its own unique insights about the respondent.

When to Use the Tandem Method

If ESI results are going to be used to influence a career decision—or other important life decisions—using the EQ-i® and MSCEIT® in Tandem is recommended. The multiple lens view obtained with the Tandem approach provides a much more comprehensive measure of ESI.

One consideration is the amount of time required to complete both instruments and to give feedback with this level of complexity. Surprisingly, feedback on the results of these two instruments can be integrated relatively easily in a manner that does not require two separate feedback sessions.

Tandem Feedback

Tandem feedback is different from "normal" feedback in that the feedback recipient is exposed to two different ESI models, each with its own language, complexity, and theoretical perspective. This alone can be daunting. When the actual feedback data is added to the mix, especially if results do not match what the recipient expects to see, it can be overwhelming. Some factors that influence the success of the feedback session include the following:

- The recipient's actual ESI
- The recipient's stress level/emotional state
- Amount of risk involved with what will happen based on the results
- The recipient's history with feedback sessions
- How positively the person perceives the results
- Other factors such as personality, cognitive ability, interpersonal interaction style, and motivation

A technique that seems to work well is to begin the feedback session with the MSCEIT® results, laying a foundation for ESI ability and potential, then integrating the EQ-i® results from an action/behavior perspective. MSCEIT® provides the ability and EQ-i® provides the current application. The following case study shows how the results can be used in an important career decision.

Case Study

Bob, a forty-five-year-old senior manager in a large private company, was one of several candidates being considered for promotion into a newly vacant executive position. Each candidate participated in a rigorous executive evaluation process that included a battery of psychological assessments.

During Bob's ten years with the company, he has demonstrated that he is very bright (IQ of 120), has excellent analytical and problem-solving skills, and is very technically proficient. He also has an MBA with a concentration in mergers and acquisitions from a well-known business school.

This executive position requires building strong interpersonal, collaborative relationships with other executives and senior managers across the company, extensive communication with peers and business units, and a forceful but transformational style of leadership. Transformational leaders must have charisma, be able to inspire followers, and provide individualized coaching and mentoring for key leaders. In other words, one of the critical requirements for this executive position is a high level of emotional and social intelligence.

Three members of the five-member executive selection committee questioned whether Bob had enough ESI to be successful in this role. One of the

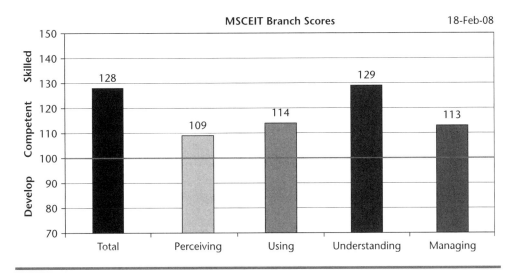

Figure 12.3. Bob's MSCEIT® Total and Branch Scores

instruments included in the assessment battery was the MSCEIT®. An examination of Bob's MSCEIT® Total (128) and Branch scores (Perceiving = 109; Using = 114; Understanding = 129; Managing = 113) in Figure 12.3 reveals that Bob scored well above the mean of 100 on all branches and almost two standard deviations above the mean on Total score and Understanding. At this level of analysis of the MSCEIT® scores it would appear that Bob should have the ESI ability required for this particular job. These scores, however, seemed to be in conflict with actual behaviors observed by some committee members.

Although the Branch scores tend to be the most statistically reliable scores for the MSCEIT®, additional hypotheses can be generated by reviewing the Task scores (Figure 12.4). In the case of Bob, it makes sense to dig more deeply into the data because some committee members doubt his ESI.

MSCEIT® Task scores typically show considerable variability (SD = 13.8) Thompson, 2008a). Bob's "Goodness of Fit" (SD = 16.7), although in the average range, is still on the high side of average and indicates a lack of balance at the Task level of ability, which may lead to less-than-desired applied ESI.

Bob also completed the EQ-i® with a Total score of 86 and Composite scale scores as follows: Intrapersonal = 86, Interpersonal = 89, Stress Management = 99, Adaptability = 106, and General Mood = 108. Figure 12.5

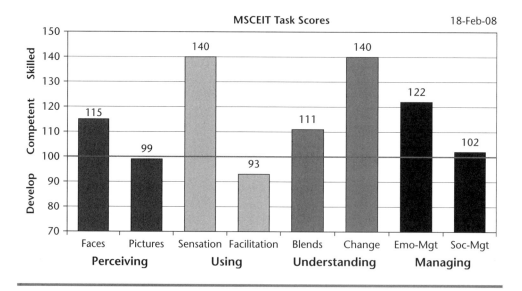

Figure 12.4. Bob's MSCEIT® Task Scores by Branch

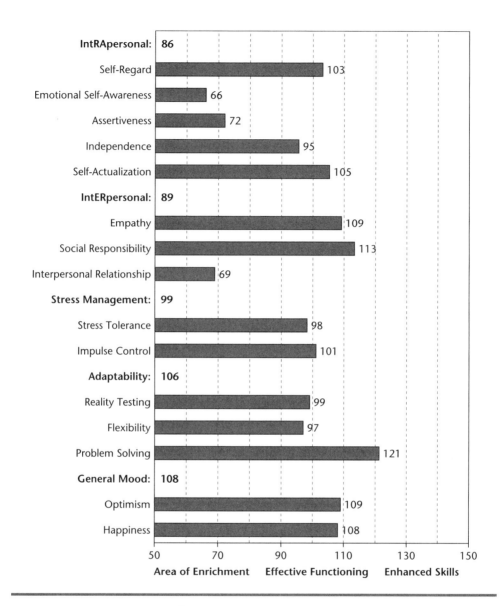

Figure 12.5. Bob's EQ-i® Scores

shows Bob's subscale scores, which seem to be significantly out of balance. Bob's EQ-i® Goodness of Fit score is 16.7, which is 2.7 standard deviations above the norm of 8.7.

Subscale scores are validated by Bob's behavior. He is a very analytical problem solver, empathetic, socially responsible, optimistic, happy, and feels good about himself. He also has a strong preference for working alone, does not build collaborative relationships, is independent, and is not assertive. Bob tends to stay in the background when in leadership roles.

Using the Tandem process, ESI assessment results suggested that Bob might not be the best candidate for this particular position. A set of questions was generated for the committee to use in an additional interview to explore Bob's ESI challenges. Bob became the committee's third choice for the job and was not promoted. He confessed during a feedback session on his Tandem results that he was relieved to be able to stay in his current job and not have to make a drastic increase in interpersonal interaction.

This is just one of many examples during this leadership project where the Tandem approach provided a more accurate picture of the leader's ESI drawing on both an ability and behavioral skills perspective.

Preparing the Practitioner to Use the Tandem Method

The Tandem method provides a more comprehensive and complex assessment and feedback process than either instrument alone. The increased complexity of the process brings with it the necessity of additional practitioner skills. This section describes how to use the Tandem method effectively.

If practitioners are going to use the Tandem method, three phases of training are recommended. (*Note:* It does not make a difference which instrument comes first in the certification process, so the order of Phases I and II can be flipped.):

- **Phase I: EQ-i® certification and in-depth training.** Phase I consists of becoming certified to use the EQ-i®. After certification, the practitioner should gain additional experience and training on the instrument.
- **Phase II: MSCEIT® certification and in-depth training.** Phase II consists of becoming certified to use the MSCEIT®. After certification, the practitioner should gain additional experience and training on the instrument.

- **Phase III: Tandem use training.** The third phase involves being trained on and gaining experience using the instruments in Tandem.

Cross-over practitioners (those who have a lot of experience with one of the assessments) sometimes find it difficult in the beginning to adapt and integrate a second ESI model. With time and experience, the benefits of using the Tandem process will become visible.

Administration

It is not unusual for senior-level leaders, particularly high performers, to resist questionnaires such as the EQ-i® and MSCEIT®. Getting busy leaders to complete two emotional intelligence assessments tends to be difficult, even with good justification.

The participants referred to in this chapter were asked to complete both the EQ-i® and the MSCEIT® as part of a leader development program. The rationale for taking both instruments was presented as a way of collecting more comprehensive information about their use of emotional intelligence and, further, that one of the questionnaires would be assessing actual ESI ability while the other would be assessing application. A few leaders did complain about the amount of time required to complete the two instruments and questioned the relevance of some of the items, for example, pictures on the MSCEIT® and the "weird" questions on the EQ-i®. All leaders in the study completed both instruments.

One question that arises when using the two instruments in Tandem is, "Does it make a difference which instrument is administered first and, if so, which one should be first?" The answer is, "It depends." If there will be several weeks between administrations, it does not seem to make a difference which is administered first. When administering the two instruments in close proximity, having participants complete the EQ-i®, then the MSCEIT®, tends to give the best overall results. The EQ-i® typically seems easier and less threatening, making it a better first instrument. It is also a self-report instrument, which might make it more susceptible to the influence of the MSCEIT®. The MSCEIT® is a test and, as such, the person either knows the answers or he doesn't.

CONCLUSIONS

This chapter has focused on preparing the ESI practitioner to use the EQ-i® and MSCEIT® in Tandem. To this end, an overview of ESI was presented along with basic supporting conceptual models for the EQ-i® and MSCEIT®.

Evidence was presented that ESI might be a situationally dependent, dynamic process rather than a single entity. This tends to be borne out in research with ESI success profiles. Approaching ESI as a blend of various components that are situationally dependent provides support for using a more robust approach to assessment and feedback, such as the Tandem process.

When using instruments in Tandem, the relationship of the instruments to each other and to other key psychological constructs, such as personality, interpersonal relationships and cognitive ability, should be part of the practitioner's knowledge base. Many factors can influence ESI scores and feedback receptivity.

The EQ-i® and MSCEIT® are valid and reliable ESI instruments with a variety of uses and, in the hands of a skilled Tandem practitioner, can be powerful tools for facilitating personal growth, job selection, leader development, and career pathing.

REFERENCES

Bar-On, R. (2006). The Bar-On model of emotional-social intelligence (ESI). *Psicothema, 18*, 3–25.

Bar-On, R. (2002). *BarOn emotional quotient inventory: A measure of emotional intelligence.* (Technical Manual). Toronto, Canada: Multi-Health Systems, Inc.

Goleman, D. (1995). *Emotional intelligence: Why it can matter more than IQ.* New York: Bantam Books.

Mayer, J.D., Salovey, P., & Caruso, D.R. (2002). *Mayer-Salovey-Caruso emotional intelligence test (MSCEIT®): User's manual.* Toronto, Ontario: Multi-Health Systems, Inc.

Murphy, K. (Ed.). (2006). *Critique of emotional intelligence: What are the problems and how can they be fixed?* Mahwah, NJ: Lawrence Erlbaum Associates.

Salovey, P., & Mayer, J. (1990). Emotional intelligence. *Imagination, Cognition, and Personality, 9*, 185–211.

Schmidt, F.L. (2002). The role of general cognitive ability and job performance: Why there cannot be a debate. *Human Performance*, *15*, 187–210.

Schmidt, F.L., & Hunter, J.E. (1998). The validity and utility of selection methods in personnel psychology: Practical and theoretical implications for 85 years of research findings. *Psychological Bulletin*, *124*, 262–274.

Thompson, H. (2005). The impact of stress on the BarOn EQ-i® reported scores and a proposed model of inquiry. High Performing Systems, Inc., Technical Report 15–5.

Thompson, H. (2006). Exploring the interface of type and emotional intelligence landscapes. *Bulletin of Psychological Type*, *29*(3), 14–19.

Thompson, H. (2007a). A summary analysis of IQ and EQ by leader level. High Performing Systems, Inc., Technical Report 5–07.

Thompson, H. (2007b). The relationship among the BarOn EQ-i® scales and the Myers-Briggs Type Indicator Form Q preferences and facets. High Performing Systems, Inc., Technical Report 6–07.

Thompson, H. (2008a). A statistical exploration of the properties of the EQ-i® and MSCEIT® instruments. High Performing Systems, Inc., Research Report 1–08.

Thompson, H. (2008b). How stress impacts the Mayer-Salovey-Caruso Emotional Intelligence Test scores. Watkinsville, GA: High Performing Systems, Inc., Research Report 2–08.

Thompson, H. (2008c). The relationship among the MSCEIT® scales and the Myers-Briggs Type Indicator™. High Performing Systems, Inc., Research Report 3–08.

Thompson, H. (2008d). The relationship among the EQ-i®, MSCEIT® and FIRO Element B™ scales. High Performing Systems, Inc., Research Report 4–08.

Henry L. (Dick) Thompson, Ph.D., is president and CEO of High Performing Systems Inc., an international management consulting and training firm he founded in 1984. Over the last thirty years, he has gained valuable experience developing and leading teams—from the battlefield to the boardroom. He is an internationally recognized consultant, researcher, speaker, and author. His areas of expertise and research include leadership, emotional intelligence, FIRO, stress, psychological type theory, chaos and complexity, and teams.

CHAPTER 13

Integrating Appreciative Inquiry and Emotional Intelligence for Optimal Coaching Results

G. Lee Salmon and James Bradford Terrell*

I n companies, teams, and governmental organizations around the world, the reality remodeling strategy known as Appreciative Inquiry is proving itself to be an exceptionally useful method for improving personal and group performance through helping individuals more effectively implement their emotional intelligence. In order to increase

---

*The views expressed are those of the author and do not necessarily reflect the positions of the Bureau of Public Debt, the Treasury Franchise Fund, or the U.S. Departments of Treasury and Interior.

their own and their clients' emotional and social effectiveness, coaches are now implementing the principles of Appreciative Inquiry, positive psychology, strength-based change, somatic awareness, and emotional intelligence in order to expand and enhance the effectiveness of their practices.

This innovation and creativity influences a number of practices and approaches in ways that complement and transcend many of the current coaching models. In this chapter we present a number of the methods consultants and coaches are using to help clients develop emotionally effective behavior in their organizations through building relationship skills that give their clients more influence and power. We also seek to provide a better understanding of the many areas of intersection, as well as the distinctions between appreciative inquiry and the topics more typically associated with emotional intelligence.

ABOUT EMOTIONAL INTELLIGENCE

In general, the field of emotional intelligence is devoted to assessing and developing the skills and competencies that help us accurately sense and identify emotions, manage our own emotions, and respond effectively to the emotions of others. It provides us with a glimpse into the deeper, more ancient realm of limbic processes, where the emotional energies that give meaning, direction, and value to our lives are transmitted, received, and evaluated nonverbally.

As members of an increasingly global, information-driven society, we are continually called upon to solve more and more problems that only become more complex. In order to succeed we must spontaneously recognize, evaluate, and respond effectively to a myriad of object- and process-oriented relationships. Because we give it such preeminence, the demands of business often require us to concentrate the majority of our attention on the objective challenges that reside "outside" us at the cost of attending to the subjective relationships that engage our more internal concerns.

In high-tech economies where measuring the quantifiable value of the bottom line has been so intensely promoted and enjoyed, the qualitative dynamics of emotional relationships have been easier to neglect. Our faith in ourselves and our neighbors has been overtaken by our faith in the distant invisible systems of production and distribution that consistently deliver the flood of consumer goods upon which we now rely for our comfort, meaning, and life support. The costs of this reliance are similar to those of a deferred maintenance strategy that allows a manager to achieve short-term budgetary savings that eventually lead to significant maintenance failures and much greater costs and problems later on. Coaches often work with their clients to help them expand their perspectives and appreciate their co-workers on the basis of the emotional connections that facilitate trust, synergy, and effective conflict resolution. In the most practical sense, this turns out to add more value to the bottom line than viewing people as merely instruments of production.

Developing and promoting increased emotional intelligence throughout the fields of business, education, government, entertainment, and healthcare is one of the critical steps necessary to help our species achieve the social re-integration and conscious acknowledgment of our global interdependency. Given the signs and reports of radical change to which we are exposed on a daily basis, it is not irrational to consider such a "big picture" view. The well-being of our species, and perhaps even its survival, may hinge on this acknowledgment and reintegration. Significantly more information on emotional intelligence research and case studies can be found at the website for the EI Consortium: www.eiconsortium.org/.

WHAT APPRECIATIVE INQUIRY IS

Appreciative Inquiry (AI) is a way of being and seeing that emerges from its unique philosophy and set of principles. It is both a worldview and an organizational development process for facilitating positive change in human systems, including organizations, groups, and communities. It assumes that every human system (including the individual) has something that works right—aspects that makes it vital, effective, and successful. AI begins by identifying this positive core and connecting to it in ways that heighten energy, sharpen vision, and inspire action for change. Bernard Mohr (Watkins & Mohr, 2001, p. 2), a noted AI practitioner, says, "Problems get replaced with innovation as conversations increasingly shift toward uncovering the organization's (or group's, or community's) positive core." AI is a paradigm that chooses to view transformational change through the lens of possibilities rather than problems.

AI was pioneered in the 1980s by David Cooperrider and Suresh Srivastva (1987), two professors at the Weatherhead School of Management at Case Western Reserve University in Cleveland, Ohio. AI consultants around the world, many of whom are also coaches, are increasingly using an appreciative approach in their organization development work to bring about collaborative and strengths-based change in thousands of profit and nonprofit organizations and communities in more than one hundred countries. AI has also been used in a number of government agencies in numerous countries around the globe. More information on AI publications, research, and case studies can be found at http://appreciativeinquiry.case.edu/.

THE PRINCIPLES OF APPRECIATIVE INQUIRY

At the heart of AI are five principles that are complementary to the principles of emotional intelligence and make it a highly effective intervention in the change process (Cooperrider, Sorensen, Yaeger, & Whitney, 2001).

1. **The Positive Principle**: positive actions and outcomes are generated by positive energy and emotions. Positive emotions and the results they create form a self-reinforcing spiral in which individuals flourish and continually grow toward optimal functioning. This is the basis for the positive psychology movement and emerging research on the power of positive emotions to change our world.

2. **The Constructionist Principle**: positive futures are created (constructed) and meaning is made through conversations and interactions with people that focus on positive experiences. Positive emotions are accessed and elicited through the positive stories we tell about our relationships and experiences with other people. We can mine our positive stories of what works to discover that our strengths comprise a positive core of experience upon which we can build our vision of a preferred future. Simply said, we live in worlds that our words and conversations create.

3. **The Simultaneity Principle**: questioning our current reality is the first step to creating change. Positive questions create a positive, self-reinforcing present by shifting our conversations and interactions in a positive direction. A question not asked is a door not opened, and as soon as a question is asked, we embark on the path to a new experience.

4. **The Anticipatory Principle**: Our questions and reflections flow from the outlook we hold. If we are optimistic and anticipate a hopeful future, our conversations and experiences tend to move in that direction. It takes a specific, positive image of the future in order to impact and shift the dynamics of the present. The positive image beckons us and creates a longing for it to be real that impels us forward. Peter Drucker, noted management guru, has frequently enjoined us to remember that the best way to predict the future is to create it.

5. **The Poetic Principle**: The more we attend to seeing the positive in the moment, the more positive will be our intentions for the future. We begin to be more aware of the richness and texture of life and its potential. Poetry and art have a way of opening our awareness to what is present but unseen because we don't pay attention. This principle connects mindfulness, intention, and attention.

Appreciative coaching is a powerful adjunct in coaching to develop emotional intelligence. It is a practical approach to coaching that draws on the philosophy, principles, and practice of Appreciative Inquiry. It shows individuals how to tap into (or rediscover) their own sense of wonder and excitement about their present lives and futures. Rather than focus in limited or problem-oriented ways, appreciative coaching guides clients through a five-stage process (often referred to as the 5-D cycle model) that inspires them to an appreciative and empowering view of themselves and their future within their social system. Frank Barrett, one of the original investigators of AI with David Cooperrider, said, "Appreciative Coaching principles, like those in Appreciative Inquiry, reflect a worldview, not of a fixed and determined machinelike universe, but one that is open, dynamic, interconnected, and filled with possibilities" (Orem, Blinkert, & Clancy, 2007, p. viii). This worldview works powerfully as a coach strategy to build EI.

HOW STAGES OF AI SUPPORT THE DEVELOPMENT OF EI

The stages of the 5-D cycle are Define (Topic Choice), Discover, Dream, Design, and Destiny (Cooperrider, Sorensen, Yaeger, & Whitney, 2001). Define is the initial stage of choosing the purpose of coaching, the presenting issue or challenge as seen by the client. The second stage, Discover, is the inquiry into what works, the positive core of one's proudest accomplishments and experiences that have resulted in success in life up to the present. The third stage, Dream, calls for imagining a vision for a positive future based on one's positive core. The fourth stage, Design, calls for designing concrete actions and practices for realizing the envisioned future in stage three. The fifth stage, Destiny, is based in implementation and action to bring the design in stage four to life. You can directly incorporate these stages into your EI practice, whether or not you are working with an instrument such as the Bar-On EQ-i®, the MSCEIT®, the ESCI, or the TESI®. In this chapter we have chosen to highlight the connection with the EQ-i® for individual coaching and leadership development.

Each of these five stages tend to lend themselves to the application of one or more of the specific emotional intelligence competencies from the overall set of fifteen developed by Dr. Reuven Bar-On for the EQ-i®. The skills of *self-regard, emotional self-awareness, assertiveness, independence, and self-actualization* cluster to form the set necessary for us to achieve and express our emotional effectiveness as an individual. *Empathy, social responsibility, and interpersonal relationship* are the skills of social effectiveness that enable us to influence our social milieu. *Stress tolerance and impulse control* help us hold life's unpleasant surprises at a safe distance and maintain the level of self-control necessary to avoid the impulsive behavior that is so often destructive. *Reality testing, flexibility, and problem solving* are the emotional skills we need in order to deal with change effectively and they make up the composite scale in his assessment that Dr. Bar-On calls adaptability. *Happiness and optimism* are the two skills that enable us to take the pulse of our satisfaction level and know how good we feel about all that is happening in our life (Bar-On, 1997).

In Appreciative Inquiry, the first stage of facilitating growth and change is called Define. It is a stage that requires concreteness and specificity. Here the competency of *reality testing* is particularly crucial in order for your clients to determine the objective reality of their current situation—Where are there real opportunities? and Where are there possible pitfalls? It will also require that clients tap their *emotional self-awareness* in order to identify which relationships and situations they are inclined to move toward, which they are inclined to move away from, and those when they are inclined to move against the status quo in order to clear the blocks to their progress.

Since Discovery is the stage in which the coach helps his or her clients gather the examples of success that have proven to be the sweetest and most fulfilling, accessing the competency of *self-actualization* will prove to be especially helpful. This competency includes the drive to achieve what they desire and become the best possible version of their self that they can be. It holds their memories of the motivation and persistence they have successfully rallied to assist them in the past.

In order to Dream their most valuable dreams, your clients must connect deeply with their *optimism*. This is not so much the time for reality testing as it is the time for accessing the full measure of their hopefulness. Our dreams both rely on our *self regard* and increase it, as we entertain new visions of what we can become and test ourselves to achieve them. Our clients must believe in their ability and affirm their worthiness to create a life that is even better than the one that they enjoy today. *Independence* should also play a part in their dreaming, not without the context of other relationships, but without undue constraints from them.

The fourth stage, Design, is based on constructing the specific actions and practices needed to succeed. Here good *problem solving* will enable our clients to develop an effective sequence for taking the necessary strategic actions. *Reality testing* and *self-actualization* may be combined to help them hold themselves accountable. *Stress tolerance* and *impulse control* can support their maintaining a balanced life style while seeking growth.

Destiny, the last stage of implementation, requires that your clients apply their *assertiveness* to consistently project the energy of their intention into their behavior with enough strength to effect the desired changes. It will also require *impulse control* to ensure the persistence necessary so they don't give up when the going gets tough. The famous poem "Desiderata" counsels us, "Beyond a wholesome discipline, be gentle with yourself." This reminder can help us *and* our clients be flexible and avoid punitive self-assessments when we don't succeed at achieving our new goals right away. Exercising the skill of *flexibility* can also provide us with important support.

This model is similar to the classic organization development tool called SWOT analysis (Strengths, Weaknesses, Opportunities, Threats) used in conducting an "environmental scan." It serves as a prelude to working on an organization's mission, vision, values, goals, objectives, strategies, and measures before initiating a strategic planning process. The difference lies in starting with a positive frame of reference that is built via an interview process with people throughout the whole system to define the positive core of shared experiences and the use of dialogue to construct a preferred future. Some applications of appreciative coaching use the 5-D cycle model in a linear progression. Some allow clients more fluidity around entering the process through whatever cycle is currently most accessible to them.

For example, a coach often conducts a 360-degree survey of a client's supervisor, peers, direct reports, and customers to obtain feedback on leadership and management competencies. The questions need to be carefully crafted to ensure positive tone and to *ask for specific examples of behavior, both observed and desired.* These results can serve to identify core strengths (Discovery), suggest areas for improvement (Dream), and even provide feedback on strategies or approaches for behavioral change (Design).

If done with the client's whole social system in mind, the questions can also be used to enroll interviewees in helping to create a supportive network of allies who are willing to help the client make successful behavioral change. This can generate a deeper level of inquiry and conversation with the client, stimulate more provocative questions, and further dialogue as the client agrees to take on greater challenges, developing or improving on the emotional and social effectiveness (ESE) skills needed to achieve their vision of success. Additional strategies for developing ESE can be found in Hughes and Terrell (2005).

CASE STUDY

Lee coached a deputy director, Fran, in a large government public health organization as part of a leadership development program. He describes how he used AI and EI principles to help Fran accurately assess the situation, identify her EI strengths, and use AI principles to envision and map out a new future.

Fran had worked in the public sector for over thirty years and was a highly successful executive known to manage people and large projects well. Unfortunately, the relationship with her boss, Tim, had deteriorated over the last year and she found herself being marginalized. During the year she was asked to work through the CFO, Dave, who was also acting as the COO and running daily operations. He was a control maniac and micro-manager and seemed to mirror Tim's demeaning management style. (All the names and some details have been changed to ensure anonymity.)

Fran was increasingly excluded from important discussions and policy decisions. No matter how much she tried to please Tim and Dave, they both kept criticizing her without explanation or feedback on how she could improve. Their communication devolved into taskings by email and rare face-to-face meetings.

The prior two deputies in her position had also not fared well and left after only a short time because of the same treatment by Tim. Fran was working long hours without appreciation and this created chronic stress that was affecting her health and family life. Fran, and I talked about her current situation and her fear that she was going to lose her position, much like what had happened to her two predecessors. She was so stressed out that she was losing sight of her strengths and beginning to second-guess herself. We decided to enter the AI Discovery stage by agreeing to do a 360 survey using the Bar-On EQ-360® to get current feedback from others on her EI competencies.

In reviewing the EQ-i® individual part of the EQ 360® report with Fran, we noticed that her strengths were in emotional self-awareness, reality testing, empathy, problem solving, interpersonal relationships, and optimism. Her weaknesses were in the competencies of self-regard, stress tolerance, and happiness. These were consistent with Fran's sense of current reality and her general unhappiness. Ratings by peers and direct reports further substantiated her strengths but also showed that most raters were unaware of her pain and suffering. As might be expected, neither Dave nor Tim provided ratings.

I asked Fran to take some time to write down her vision for the type of job she would like to have and then discuss it with me. I asked her to dream the impossible dream and draw upon her experiences of work that were enlivening and brought her joy, and not to set any limits on what might be possible.

In our first sessions, I also noticed that Fran would come in bent over and complain about headaches and back pain. From a somatic point of view, I knew that Fran was carrying too much tension in her body from stress and that this could restrict her ability to think big and expansively about her future. I asked whether she would be willing to take yoga lessons again to help improve her flexibility and provide a calming, relaxing practice. She also agreed to see a chiropractor to address her back pain and body misalignment from poor posture.

As our sessions progressed, we talked about her vision for an ideal job, drawing upon her strengths of empathy, interpersonal relationships, optimism, and problem solving. She shared with me that she had been looking for another job for some time and had recently received a lot of interest from a private-sector firm. Although this job interested her and the CEO was actively trying to recruit her, she feared leaving government and didn't want to lose her retirement benefits, for which she would not be eligible for four more years. I asked her whether an early buyout was possible, and she said she'd do some research. She also began to report that the bodywork practices I had suggested were helping her relax and she was feeling less stressed out.

In our next session she reported that her whole office was being reorganized and downsized, and she was told by Dave that Tim wanted to abolish her position and move her to another position in a different part of the organization. It took us a while to work through her anger and frustration with seeming to have no power over her circumstances. She was discouraged and demoralized but wanted more than ever to leave and not be stuck in a marginalized position that didn't interest her. She agreed to step up her research on early retirement and talk more with the company that wanted her.

When we had debriefed Fran's EQ-i® report, she acknowledged that standing up for herself was difficult. It was unusual for her to have to "manage up" with her leaders because she usually figured out exactly what they needed and delivered all of that and then some. But it was obvious that accessing the strength of assertiveness she needed now would take some real effort. For homework I asked her to read the chapter on courage from *A Coach's Guide to Emotional Intelligence* (Terrell & Hughes, 2008) and to think of examples from her past when being courageous had helped her succeed in getting what she really wanted. In that book, courage is defined as "the emotion that allows us to act on what matters to us, in the presence of danger, difficulty, uncertainty, or pain, accepting that there will be consequences without necessarily knowing what those will be but acting anyway, without being stopped by fear or being sidetracked from our chosen course of action" (p. 85). The following week, she called me to report that she found out that because of her office reorganization and downsizing, she might be eligible for an early buyout that would solve the retirement eligibility problem. Now was the time she would have to summon the courage to meet with Tim, submit her formal resignation, and ask for his approval for the buyout.

She also wanted to use her accrued annual leave to work part-time and transition out gracefully without going to another position. Fran didn't think Tim would go for this and was afraid to ask. I recommended that she read an article on courage by Victoria Stafford called *The Small Work in the Great Work*, which tells an inspirational story about a fourteen-year-old girl on the Pine Ridge Reservation's girls' basketball team who faced an anti-Indian hostile crowd with courage and imagination (Loeb, 2004). This narrative and the continuing interest from the private sector CEO helped strengthen Fran's vision of the future.

Fran was eventually able to write her letter of resignation without resentment and find the courage to ask for a face-to-face meeting with Tim. She also discussed her transition plan with Dave, who was surprisingly supportive. Although she was never able to get her meeting with Tim, she was able to get what she wanted and leave government with her spirits high and with an excitement for beginning a whole new chapter in her life.

METHODS FOR APPLYING APPRECIATIVE INQUIRY

When it comes to applying the methods of AI, some coaches feel that there is a certain order in which to use the principles and stages of the 5-D model to utilize their best advantage. They see an internal logic and syntax in them that facilitate a progressive unfolding for their clients, which they accomplish through using them as both listening tools and coaching frameworks. Depending on how clients show up, their energy and mood can suggest which principles to focus on first and then a linear order for progression can ensue (Tschannen-Moran, 2007).

Other coaches believe that paying attention more specifically to the client's social system and encouraging interaction and conversation with "appropriate others" in the system is important to ensure success. The constructionist principle can be used to construct interview questions that connect a client's success to organizational success. This ensures that coaching is seen by the organization in a positive light. This constructionist approach can be applied to enroll these key players in helping to create a partnership that supports the client's goals for behavioral change while integrating the process into the organization's culture (Sloan, 2007).

Recent research by Barbara Frederickson (2003) and others shows that positive emotions can be applied as antidotes and even undo the effects of negative emotions. "In organizations, the positive emotions of employees and especially of leaders are considered to be especially contagious. . . . Such emotions as joy, interest, contentment, and love can be transformational by contributing to the expansion of a person's way of thinking and acting" (Orem, Binkert, & Clancy, 2007, pp. 46–47).

The interface of emotional intelligence and Appreciative Inquiry can create an attitudinal space, which Arnold Mindel calls "positive land." This is a place of personal and/or organizational victory, a way of being in the world that is centered in observable positive values and principles, such as clarity, compassion, competency, consultation, and deep commitment. One way to frame our individual efforts to continually increase the scope and range of this positive experience is by comparing it with its hypothetical opposite, a kind of "negative land" composed of our experiences of dysfunction, confusion, greed, judgment, jealousy, sabotage, and all the various types of oppression that seem so abundant in the "real world" of personal and organizational competition.

A variety of types of emotional and behavioral models are available to help coaches map and evaluate how skillfully their clients can create change in both the positive and shadow sides of their human experience. Our positive and negative lands turn out to be but different sides of the same life coinage, where we generally can see only one side at a time.

ANOTHER CASE EXAMPLE

In the example that follows, the coach's efforts to deal with some basic business issues rapidly lead to the discovery of long-standing behavior patterns that were undermining the client's success professionally and in her personal life. In order to be able to help her client achieve positive progress, she helped her client access background behavior patterns by directing her attention to the sensory information that contained and masked some of the emotional and cognitive data she needed to move in a new direction. Working with a client's sensory representation systems requires specialized training because they engage a deep level of processing that includes unconscious as well as conscious awareness.

The models of reality and the vocabularies that best engage this level of deep structure and its dynamics do not always lend themselves to the same degree of logical rigor that reductionist science requires (or at least prefers) to satisfy its validity claims. Nonetheless, even the most ardent advocates of the scientific method will, if they are honest, acknowledge that there are aspects of human motivation and behavior that lie beyond what their models can explain. The compassion that motivates coaching seeks to facilitate development at all levels of the human experience that impact personal growth.

This case example is based on a client from an Asian culture who was coached by Dr. Ruth Allen (2008) of the AEH Institute. This illustrates how applying such models to discover values, strengths, and what is positive in life can create a rich experience in the AI cycles of Discovery and Design that can help coaches facilitate a significant reframing of events, even when they may appear to be tragic. They show us how a coach can help her client find the way out of "negative land" by using the AI constructionist principle, creating new language, and opening the possibility for a new vision of life filled with joy and happiness and that reflects increased emotional intelligence capacities of emotional self-awareness, assertiveness, and self regard. The case also demonstrates how the 5-D cycles of AI are often iterative and how we sometimes, because of life-altering events, return to certain aspects of the Dream cycle to refocus our vision and access new possibilities for action once they have shifted from the background into the foreground.

The case involves a thirty-five-year-old businesswoman we will call SJ who worked as an on-site marketing consultant. SJ was self-employed and had two major clients whose work comprised over 80 percent of her annual revenue. They were both successful family-owned businesses and SJ's interface with each organization was through a family member at the middle management level. Both of these individuals were described as difficult to work with because they were "temperamental and arbitrary." SJ said she could never tell what she would need to do next to keep her client bosses happy with her work. She said that often she would be severely criticized for executing the very action plans they had developed together and that had been approved in earlier meetings, even when successful. One client would accuse her of "trying to run the show," and the other would delay the payment of her invoices in what appeared to be a show of control and power.

SJ's willingness to tolerate this sort of treatment raised some initial questions about her level of self-regard and assertiveness. She admitted feeling intimidated by her clients' wealth and status as well as the fact that one of them was significantly older than she. These dynamics played a more significant role in her relationship with them, given the fact that she and her clients were all of Asian descent.

Initially SJ's feelings of anger and disenfranchisement made her unable to appreciate much of anything that was going right in her life, and for the first few coaching sessions she continued exploring and owning the emotions she felt as a result of the challenges in her professional life. She began to discover similar emotions that had also been pervasive in her personal relationships, along with some new feelings, of which she was previously unaware. This was valuable new ground to cover inasmuch as she had never felt she had permission to value her own emotions. Providing her with a high degree of supportive attention and permission allowed her emotional self-awareness to begin growing rapidly. This rate of self-development was possible in part because she had been encouraged throughout her life to notice what other people were feeling and to be understanding of why they felt that way. The result was that she had a very strong foundation in the competency of empathy.

Her evolving emotional self-awareness helped her get traction and begin moving in a direction that was truly positive and motivating to her. Eventually she was willing to honestly engage the question: "What really brings energy, joy, and meaning to my life now?" and *Define* her real situation. As it turned out, the world of business had no direct routes to positive land, but when she shared her *Dreams* of adopting a child, being a mother, and starting a family, the coaching sessions began to fill and overflow with positive language, imagery, and hopefulness.

Once she had made this *Discovery*, it was an easy step to begin envisioning how her new life as a mother would look and sound and feel. As she began to engage the anticipatory principle, it enabled her to begin building a solid foundation for what her life would become through her specific visions of the playful, loving interactions with her child. The next step was to move into design and make her plan concrete. Because of her strong spiritual upbringing, the first behavioral change model used was the simple Hoffman Quadrinity model (www.quadrinity.com). This helped to conceptualize her identity in terms of the four main areas of human attention: her physical, emotional, mental, and spiritual abilities and concerns. With a little work she developed clear mental images of how each part represented itself and how it was acting in her life. (For a secularly oriented client, an alternate starting model that can be used is the integral Life Coaching Quadrant model (www.newventureswest.com; see also Flaherty, 1999).

SJ reported that she saw her physical self attired in an athletic suit, her emotional self as a five-year-old in a frilly pink frock, her mental self wearing professional business attire, and her spirit clad in an orange caftan. A major breakthrough occurred when she recognized that her emotional self (the five-year-old) was in charge of her life and her spiritual self was missing in action. As one might imagine, attempting to manage business and family interactions subjectively from this developmental level was not only unsuccessful, but often deeply painful. The first behavioral change practice she undertook was learning to develop a more detached, objective point of view that she would practice shifting into on a regular basis in order to observe these various "selves" and how they were playing out their interrelationships.

Two other components of her *Design* that were very powerful were to work as an infant babysitter and a preschool teacher. The strength of her empathy in these two activities helped her become very grounded and confident in the success of her new role because they filled in some of the experiences she was concerned she might miss out on because it appeared she would not be able to adopt an infant. This readily carried her into some of the Destiny aspects of the process wherein she was able to celebrate significant accomplishments that were very concrete, tactile, and nurturing for her.

The endeavor to adopt a child was not without challenges. The international adoption process is fraught with many unexpected delays and unpleasant surprises, but the strength and certainty of her vision sustained SJ, her husband, and her baby girl until the day on which they finally all drove home together. By then, SJ's self-regard had not only recovered, but grown to perhaps its highest level in her life. She naturally grew to be appropriately assertive on behalf of her dream of family. As with so many clients, the initial reason for coaching, business development skills, changed significantly along the way as a result of turning her attention away from what was wrong and working to thoroughly explore where the joy and energy and hope of her life truly resided.

Best Practices Summary

- AI is a powerful and well-developed worldview and organization development process that can be used to develop individual and organizational emotional and social intelligence.
- Use the five principles of AI as a method for engaging with your clients whether you are working to build self-regard, assertiveness, or optimism.
- Use the stages of AI to support the development of EI. The AI process can be used as a concrete strategy for accomplishing sustainable behavior change and, thus, growth in acting with emotional and social intelligence. The five stages are define, discovery, dream, design, and destiny.

CONCLUSION

In summary, when the language and tools of emotional intelligence and Appreciative Inquiry are applied together skillfully, they can build a tremendous synergy that strengthens every aspect of the coaching relationship. Because these two approaches are so highly complementary, integrating the AI philosophy and questioning process into your coaching will not only help your clients further develop their emotional and social intelligence skills, it can also greatly enhance the opportunity for mutual success.

REFERENCES

Allen, R.H. (2008). Unpublished case study. AEH Institute, www.aehinstitute.com.

Bar-On, R. (1997). *The emotional quotient inventory (EQ-i®): Technical manual* (pp. 15–18). Toronto: Multi-Health Systems.

Cooperrider, D., Sorenson P., Yaeger, T., & Whitney, D. (2001). *Appreciative inquiry: An emerging direction for organization development.* Champaign, IL: Stipes.

Cooperrider, D., & Srivastva, S. (1987). Appreciative inquiry in organizational life. In W. Passmore & R. Woodman (Eds.), *Research in organization change and development* (Vol. 1, pp. 129–169), Greenwich, CT: JAI Press.

Flaherty, J. (1999). *Coaching: Evoking excellence in others.* Boston, MA: Butterworth Heinemann.

Frederickson, B. (2003). Positive emotions and upward spirals in organizations. In K.S. Cameron, J.E. Dutton, & R.E. Quinn (Eds.), *Positive organizational scholarship: Foundations of a new discipline* (pp. 163–175). San Francisco: Berrett-Koehler.

Hughes, M., Patterson, B., & Terrell, J. (2005), *Emotional intelligence in action: Training and coaching activities for leaders and managers.* San Francisco: Pfeiffer.

Loeb, P. (Ed.). (2004). *The impossible will take a little while.* New York: Basic Books.

Orem, S., Binkert, J., & Clancy, A. (2007). *Appreciative coaching: A positive process for change.* San Francisco: Jossey-Bass.

Sloan, B. (2007, May). Social construction in appreciative inquiry coaching. *AI Practitioner: The International Journal of AI Best Practice.*

Terrell, J., & Hughes, M. (2008). *A coach's guide for emotional intelligence.* San Francisco: Pfeiffer.

Tschannen-Moran, B. (2007, May). Five-principle coaching. *AI Practitioner: The International Journal of AI Best Practice.*

Watkins, J., & Mohr, B. (2001). *Appreciative inquiry: Change at the speed of imagination.* San Francisco: Pfeiffer.

G. Lee Salmon is the practice leader for executive coaching, mentoring, and leadership development with the Federal Consulting Group, U. S. Department of Interior. Lee is an executive consultant, certified executive coach with the International Coach Federation, and has more than forty years of leadership and management experience working in the public and private sectors. For the past twelve years Lee has coached political appointees, executives, and senior managers in the executive branch of the federal government. He also has a private coaching practice, Learning for Living, where he works with executives in the private sector. He has degrees and certificates in physics, change management, and leadership development and specializes in working with scientific and technical organizations. Currently, he is on the board of directors for the International Consortium of Coaching in Organizations and is the author of numerous articles and publications on coaching and leadership. Lee contributed a chapter to *A Coach's Guide to Emotional Intelligence* (2008).

James Bradford Terrell is vice president of Collaborative Growth® where he applies his expertise in interpersonal communication to help a variety of public and private sector clients anticipate change and respond to it resiliently. Co-author of *A Coach's Guide to Emotional Intelligence* (2008), *The Emotionally Intelligent Team* (2007), *The TESI® Short Facilitator's Guide Set* (2009), and *Emotional Intelligence in Action (2005),* James coaches leaders, teams in transition, and senior management, using the Bar-On EQ-i®, the EQ-360®, and other assessments. He is co-creator of the Team Emotional and Social Intelligence Survey® (TESI®), which supports team growth worldwide. James provides train-the-trainer workshops and educates coaches on how to develop the insightful interpretation and application of EQ results.

Practical Perspectives on the "Social" Within Emotional Intelligence

Carina Fiedeldey-Van Dijk

INTRODUCTION

Regardless of the EQ model followed or assessment tool used, emotional intelligence (EI) encompasses a social element that has again come under the spotlight. While definitions of emotional intelligence vary, each is sure to mention the relationship with "others." Half of Daniel Goleman, Hay/McBer, and Richard Boyatzis' ECI scales are devoted to *social awareness* and *social relationship management*. Jack Mayer, Peter Salovey, and David Caruso address *social management* in their MSCEIT®, while Reuven Bar-On emphasizes this aspect in the EQ-i® under a composite scale called the *interpersonal domain*.

Reuven Bar-On has expanded his earlier thinking on EI to now speak of emotional-social intelligence (Bar-On, 2007).

By comparison, Dan Goleman's book, *Social Intelligence,* published in 2007 as a follow-up to his best-seller on emotional intelligence, represents a shift from a one-person to a two-person perspective, underscoring the distinction drawn between EI and social intelligence.

The purpose of this writing is fourfold: (1) to give readers a basic understanding of the underpinnings of social intelligence (SI) within a framework of EI, (2) to clear up two myths around SI, (3) to share new learning of SI, and (4) to lead EQ users to practical ways to assess and develop SI as needed.

HISTORICAL APPROACHES TO SOCIAL INTELLIGENCE

To date there are two major approaches to SI. A brief knowledge of each helps us understand the meaning and value of SI as a concept in everyday practice. Those who are interested in more comprehensive reading can download a white paper on the major approaches to SI (see Fiedeldey-Van Dijk, 2008b).

The SET Approach

Many of us prefer to capture SI and constructs such as EI, personality type and style, motivation, and aptitude by using psychometric assessments, which essentially rely on experimental and statistical methods. These means include efforts to accurately measure the dynamics between people in different scenarios.

Goleman's (2007) new book rests upon the discovery by social neuroscientists that we, as individuals, are wired to connect. Although Kihlstrom and Cantor (2000) point out that research on the neurological underpinnings of social cognition and behavior is highly impressionistic and speculative, our brain's evolutionary design makes it sociable (Knecht, 2004). It enables us to interact and engage with others in desirable and undesirable ways. Essentially this happens through neural linkups, aptly described in Goleman's book as a dance of feelings. Neurologically our interpersonal capabilities gauge our every move by acting like a choreographer whereby we continually reset key parts of our brain function, steering and re-steering the dance among a multitude of consequential possibilities.

It is extremely complex to accurately measure the dynamics between two people using psychometric means, even if it is perhaps the most widely used method, because the focus is on individual and social interactions from the perspective of an individual. This characteristic distinguishes the first approach to SI, which I term the SET Approach.

Thus, within the SET Approach, an individual's perception of interactions is often measured by responses to some assessment with validated psychometric properties. These responses remain a mere snapshot in time, that is, the individual's perception at the time of the assessment, or at best several repeated snapshots. Hence the temptation to infer from collective individual perspectives on the dynamics of what is really going on when people interact and then ultimately anchoring it as a form of intelligence may easily be seen as a bit of a stretch by some. Our focus on the individual, albeit in the context of interaction, is fundamental to the SET Approach.

The Venn diagram, introduced by John Venn in 1881, gives practitioners a palatable way to explain the approaches to SI. A basic Venn diagram consists of two partially overlapping sets or circles (persons A and B) (see Figure 14.1). Within the SET Approach our attention is focused on person A in interaction with person B (and perhaps with other people, in which case we can introduce more overlapping sets or circles to the Venn diagram). Our attention on person A may manifest in the form of coaching, development, therapy, selection, and so forth.

We can also choose to focus on person B, in which case our attention shifts from person A to person B. Even when we look at persons A and B in a comparative fashion by pairing or contrasting characteristics and qualities, our focus remains at the individual level within the SET Approach.

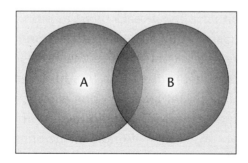

Figure 14.1. A Basic Venn Diagram

The INTERSECT Approach

There is a second approach to SI that captures the attention of scientists and practitioners alike. A social-intelligence view of personality (as traits) as it manifests in everyday behavior is distinct from the psychometric perspective that defines SI as a concept that can be measured as a group of traits. The point of departure of this approach is that social behavior *is* intelligent (Kihlstrom & Cantor, 2000). This is akin to saying that intelligence lies in the interaction between two people, rather than in the people by themselves.

From the psychometric viewpoint it's about *how much* SI people possess. By comparison, from the social-intelligence view of personality it's about *what* SI people have when interacting. The latter is attractive by itself in studying and applying SI. Borrowing from Venn again, this time the focus is on the intersection of A and B (the overlapping portion of the circles) when both are present; hence I term it the INTERSECT Approach.

According to this approach, SI is the product of regulated cognitive processes that people bring to each other *and* their individual and collective capability to act upon these processes (Byrne & Whiten, 1988; Mischel, 1973; Worden, 1996). Followers of this approach argue that it makes no sense to try and measure it, as it is not a frequency, but a quality. Thus the overlap in the two circles represents the interaction between two people, rather than the people themselves. Our focus on the interaction is characteristic of the INTERSECT Approach, which may manifest in the provision of various professional services, such as relationship counseling, family therapy, and team building.

CALLING FOR A UNIFIED APPROACH IN STUDYING SI

The 21st century has seen steady refinement and diversity of ideas on the concept of SI. When criticism of each approach becomes fierce, it seems that the SET approach and the INTERSECT approach stand as opposites to each other. No wonder that the two approaches are still at it after some eighty years of research—today the term SI is fast approaching the century mark!

The SI repertoire of studies largely consists of multiple categorizations of the perceptions of people's behavior in different contexts (Cantor & Kihlstrom, 1987). Its complexity tempts us to include within it all positive human attributes within an interactive context and risk being over-inclusive. The studies together denote diligence, result in an initial understanding of SI (Greenspan, 1979, 1997) and each helps to narrow the definition of SI.

Hopefully, future research on SI will focus less on just the SET approach or the INTERSECT approach, but dare to unite both. This may result in a new perspective, the UNIFIED Approach. Recalling the Venn diagram from Figure 14.1, this approach encompasses both A and B as individuals, their overlap, and the surrounding area, which includes all the possible factors that can impact on people and their interaction.

SHAPING SI IN THE UNIFIED APPROACH

We can ask both how socially intelligent the person is compared to some norm (the SET Approach) *and* what SI a person has (the INTERSECT Approach). While the concept is still being developed, it is possible to empirically explore the "social" within EI by addressing both approaches. We recognize three major models of EI as acknowledged by the *Encyclopedia of Applied Psychology* (Spielberger, 2004). These are the ability model of Jack Mayer, Peter Salovey, and David Caruso that assesses EI with the MSCEIT®, the performance model of Daniel Goleman and the Hay Group measuring EI with the ECI, and the trait model of Reuven Bar-On that is reflected in the EQ-i® assessment.

Out of these three, the Bar-On model seemed appropriate to draw upon for this purpose for reasons offered below. Those not familiar with this model may appreciate learning that it comprises a 1-5-15 structure (Bar-On, 2007), which is labeled and abbreviated as shown in Table 14.1.

The appropriateness of the Bar-On model and accompanying Emotional Quotient Inventory (EQ-i®) for scoring SI lies in the following reasons:

- It endorses a personality (trait) model of EI. Emotional-Social Intelligence is defined on Bar-On's personal website as "a cross-section of interrelated emotional and social competencies, skills and facilitators that determine how well we understand and express ourselves, understand others and relate with them, and cope with daily demands, challenges and pressures" (Bar-On, 2007).
- It has a distinct composite scale that measures the social domain within EI. The interpersonal domain at the second level of the Bar-On

Table 14.1. List of EQ-i® Scales

Total EQ				
Intrapersonal	**Interpersonal**	**Stress Management**	**Adaptability**	**General Mood**
SR Self-regard	EM Empathy	ST Stress tolerance	RT Reality-testing	OP Optimism
ES Emotional self-awareness	RE Social responsibility	IC Impulse control	FL Flexibility	HA Happiness
AS Assertiveness	IR Interpersonal relationship		PS Problem solving	
IN Independence				
SA Self-actualization				

structure is specifically designed to deal with social awareness, as well as the establishment and maintenance of relationships with people (Bar-On, 2007). From a psychometric perspective via the EQ-i® assessment, the interpersonal domain forms one of five domains at the composite level, and includes three of the fifteen scales at the scale level at the bottom of the Bar-On structure. These are empathy (EM), defined as the ability to have others sense that we are aware of and understand how they feel, social responsibility (RE), identifying with and socially feeling part of the group, and interpersonal relationship (IR), establishing and maintaining mutually satisfying relationships with others.

- Its survey items sometimes address the individual, other times the interaction. A careful analysis of the 130 items counted in scale score calculations of the EQ-i® revealed that fifty-five items (thirty-nine items directly and sixteen items indirectly) refer to some form of behavior specifically in relation to another person. The remaining seventy-five items refer to behavioral aspects pertaining to the individual outside of an interactive context. (When thirteen double items in the scoring algorithm are taken out of the equation to leave 117 unique items used to calculate scale scores, forty-six items belong to the socially oriented group, and seventy-one items belong to the personally oriented group.)

These three aspects are thought to make the Bar-On model, with accompanying EQ-i® assessment, suitable for empirically studying the dynamics of SI within the UNIFIED Approach.

SUBJECTING THE EQ-I® TO THE UNIFIED APPROACH

Together the three interpersonal scales of the EQ-i® make up twenty-four (of 117) unique items (excluding double items at the composite level) that are used to specifically calculate the fifteen scale scores. Roughly speaking, the *inter*personal domain makes up about one-fifth (20 percent) of the total EQ score. By comparison, the *intra*personal domain takes up about 32 percent with the other three domains covering the remaining 48 percent of the total EQ score.

Focusing on the interpersonal domain of the EQ-i® and zooming in at the scale level, the empathy (EM), social responsibility (RE) and interpersonal relationship (IR) scales contribute eight, ten, and eleven items respectively (twenty-nine items in total). Three of the twenty-nine interpersonal items serve a double purpose in measuring scales belonging to the other four EQ domains. In addition, EM shares one of its eight items with IR and four of the eight with RE. (The high inter-correlation between EM and RE reported in the *EQ-i® Technical Manual* (Multi-Health Systems, 2002) can partially be attributed to this fact.) Due to the degree of overlap between at least two of the three interpersonal scales, for the purpose of this writing we will only empirically look at interpersonal scores at the domain, or larger composite level.

We should acknowledge that the double use of items within the interpersonal domain may not so much be a product of its design on a conceptual level, as that it is guided by the construct and predictive statistical validation analyses performed on the composite norm base. This may reflect that we have yet more to learn with regard to fully grasping and distinctly expressing the subtleties that exist in social interaction and engagement. It may also signal that there is still room for increasing sophistication in how we recognize and cope with daily demands and pressures on a social level.

Thorndike (1920) noted presciently that while SI is easily observable, a valid measurement of this concept is a different ball game. A good measure of SI perhaps still lies some time in the future, because existing assessments that claim to measure the concept largely focus on people's conscious awareness and knowledge about how they behave in social situations, which does not necessarily reflect that which is automatic and which lies in the subconscious (Ahuja, 2006).

In using the EQ-i® in everyday research and consulting, in reading and re-reading published work on the model and assessment, and in personal conversation with its author and survey developers, we are making the assumption that Bar-On and his team focused on the psychometric approach when formulating his theory of emotional SI. That is, when thinking through and testing the theoretical structure of factors and meta-factors, they very much had the purity of each scale in mind when formulating the survey items.

It is very tempting for researchers and scientists to stay within the known, the psychometric SET Approach, partially because it is powerful and provides definite advantages. Already we are wiser about employees' EQ profiles in the interpersonal domain compared to the other four EQ-i® domains at different job levels in organizations, between males and females, across different age categories, against job performance criteria, and so forth.

Several studies on leadership and management show that the greatest performers sometimes lack interpersonal skills such as empathy and empathic listening, trust, modesty, and attunement to others that can be a significant predictor of work success (Andrews & Kiessling, 1980; Fiedeldey-Van Dijk & Freedman, 2007; George, 2000; Miller, 1999; Rock, 2003). The Center for Creative Leadership found that one of the most important factors derailing executives was poor relationships (Leslie & Van Velsor, 1996). New research continues to be published in this regard. From a SET Approach then, these findings may lead to an early hypothesis that:

1. *Overall, people score lower in the interpersonal domain and its scales than in other EQ-i® domains.*

Note how our focus here is on the characteristics and qualities within the person; comparatively *how much* of these there are. The EQ-i® not only accommodates the SET Approach, but also the INTERSECT Approach. During the development of the EQ-i®, the SI of the developers' collective personality is automatically and perhaps subconsciously embedded in all the survey items viewed together. Without consciously controlling the item generation this way, 42 percent of the items are interactive or social (i.e., referring to a person in relation to others) and 58 percent are personal (i.e., referring to a person without any mention of, or implication to, others). In other words, the EQ-i® appears to be a fitting assessment with the UNIFIED Approach.

It is possible to calculate and standardize two factors, Social EQ (SEQ) versus Personal EQ (PEQ) from this balance in items, just as is done for total EQ, the interpersonal domain, and other scales. The former factor, SEQ, represents the SI view on personality. While our focus will be on SEQ rather than PEQ, it is important to view SEQ in relation to PEQ, as interaction between people is influenced by what each brings to the table as well.

We need to exercise caution in not equating SEQ with interpersonal competence and PEQ with intrapersonal competence in the SET Approach. In fact, two intrapersonal scales of the EQ-i, namely assertiveness and independence, contribute strongly to SEQ, while only about half (twenty-one out of forty-six) of the items—doubles excluded—come from the interpersonal domain. The concepts of SEQ and PEQ are created purely on the basis of whether survey items are referring to a relational component with others, or not, to stay true to the definition of SI.

Further investigation reveals that twenty-three out of the fifty-five SEQ items (42 percent) are phrased in the negative, compared with thirty-nine out of the seventy-five PEQ items (52 percent), which scores are reversed during calculations. Out of the thirteen items used twice in scoring, nine are SEQ items and four are PEQ items. Readers experienced in the intricacies of test development and validation may deduct from these comparative figures that they further underscore the thinking that currently we are better at finely distinguishing between personal emotions than we are at social emotions. This can have practical implications for how practitioners plan intervention strategies. It can also lead to a second early hypothesis that:

2. *Overall, people will score higher in PEQ than SEQ.*

Note how our focus here is on the *what*, whether the nature of the interaction resembles PEQ or SEQ (or a combination of both). These two hypotheses will be addressed starting with a description of the sample that was used for this writing.

SAMPLE CHARACTERISTICS

The empirical study draws from a large database of EQ-i® profiles of 1,179 individuals that was accumulated over several years. Approximately eight out of ten people completed the "133-item" version of the EQ-i®, while the remainder completed the "125-item" version. (For those not familiar with the EQ-i®, currently two versions of the assessment are offered to certified users, depending on the number of validity indicators (and hence survey items) they prefer to include with the 117 unique scale items during test administration.) The average inconsistency index, positive impression and negative impression scores (the major validity indicators) all lie within normal range. The individuals displayed varying response styles that together revealed desirable item behavior when the responses of the assessment are investigated from a methodological perspective.

The sample group is very composite in nature, meaning that EQ profiles of employees are pooled from numerous smaller client projects for different purposes, spanning across a range of industry sectors and several countries across the world. A total of 42 percent in the group are male and 58 percent are female. Almost two-thirds are in their thirties and forties, with the average age being thirty-nine years and ten months and ranging from seventeen to sixty-five years. The group represents a large distribution of work sectors, such as education, finance, consulting, retail, HR, health, insurance, IT, business administration and others. The job levels of the sample group are categorized as shown in Figure 14.2.

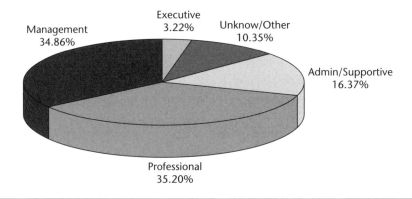

Figure 14.2. Job Level

The job level composition displayed in Figure 14.2 mirrors the general target market for consulting, training, coaching, development, and recruitment within the realm of EI initiatives. The growing EQ-i® norm population against which scale scores are standardized will also be increasingly loaded with individuals at managerial levels. Hence sporadic updates in the norm group are needed.

For a group of this size one would expect all the scale scores to lie at the standardized average of 100 with a standard deviation score of 15. In reality, this group's total EQ score (unadjusted) was found to be 104.78 (SD = 12.90, compared to 15) with the lowest score being 101.77 for self-regard (SR——accepting and respecting ourselves) and the highest scores being 105.44 for reality testing (RT—validating our feelings and thinking with external reality) and 105.43 for stress tolerance (ST—coping and withstanding adverse events without falling apart). The standard deviation scores for the fifteen scales vary between 12.77 and 14.34. These scores can be explained on the basis of the demographic characteristics of the sample, as well as the growing suspicion that the professional community at large has shifted slightly in their EQ competence over the last twenty years and that the figures used to standardize EQ-i® scores are in need of an update.

Moving away from the fifteen scales to the five EQ domains and to our first hypothesis stated above, out of the five EQ-i® domains, the interpersonal domain scored the second lowest, followed only by the general mood domain. The reader needs to exercise extreme caution in drawing conclusions, however, as the difference in scores between the highest and lowest scored domain is negligibly small (1.31 points). A calculation of the statistical significance of these average domain score differences may be inflated due to the large sample size, while the practical significance is minor.

These figures are unable to confirm the first hypothesis, and hence it is a myth that overall people score lower in the interpersonal domain than in the other EQ-i® domains. This is important for practitioners because, when the contrary is found for a particular individual or group of individuals within an organization, for example, this is telling, as it goes beyond that of the norm population and is not an artifact of the assessment itself. A person or group scoring low in the interpersonal domain will indeed benefit from further development.

NEW SI LEARNING

One would expect to see a fairly strong correlation between people's total EQ and their interpersonal EQ as measured by one of the five EQ-i® domains. The correlation of 0.72 for this sample (see Table 14.2) forms a solid baseline for further associative comparisons. The higher linear associations between the total EQ and PEQ and also between the total EQ and SEQ are expected within the associative and commutative nature of the UNIFIED Approach and because these outcomes are artifacts of roughly half of the items shared between them. One is best off by saying that if half of the items between the two variables (and about 20 percent in the case of the interpersonal domain) are shared and hence perfectly correlated, then the correlation between the remaining items is pretty strong.

The second column of the correlation matrix is informative, as it gives a sense of the association between the interpersonal domain and SEQ versus PEQ. All interpersonal domain items form part of the SEQ items; the 0.16 that is lost in the correlation is of interest. None of the interpersonal domain items form part of the PEQ items, which makes the correlation of 0.61 between PEQ and the interpersonal domain satisfactory. Bear in mind that the interpersonal domain is designed to show individual capability as represented by the SET Approach, while PEQ is the basis against which SEQ is viewed in the INTERSECT Approach. It makes sense then that the correlation between PEQ and SEQ is comparatively higher at 0.83, because it points to overall healthy functioning of the individuals that spills over to beneficial interactions with other people. At the same time, the deviation from a perfect correlation (i.e., r = 1.00) shows that we're not living in a perfect world either.

Table 14.2. Linear Association Between SI Perspectives

	Total EQ	Interpersonal	SEQ	PEQ
Total EQ	1.00			
Interpersonal domain	0.72	1.00		
SEQ	0.93	0.84	1.00	
PEQ	0.97	0.61	0.83	1.00

Setting the Standard for SI

Our current understanding of SI within the UNIFIED Approach positions us well for considering the difference in standardized scores between SEQ and PEQ. These are displayed in Figure 14.3. For the mathematically curious, the SEQ and PEQ scores are standardized in identical fashion to the standardization of Total EQ, the interpersonal domain, and other EQ-i® scales using the population norms reported in the technical manual of the EQ-i® (Multi-Health Systems, 2002), whereby 100 is used as the mean and 15 as the standard deviation. Using the same standardization procedure and leaving these scores unadjusted enable us to make direct comparisons between the bars in Figure 14.3.

We already mentioned that overall people's competence in the interpersonal domain is right on par with their total EQ when viewed from a psychometric perspective (see hypothesis 1). This implies that overall people have what it takes to interact with others. The important message from Figure 14.3 is that a statistically significant difference ($p < 0.01$) exists between SEQ and PEQ, as there is about a 4-point difference between the two. Moreover, this does not occur just for the group as a whole, but on average also when SEQ

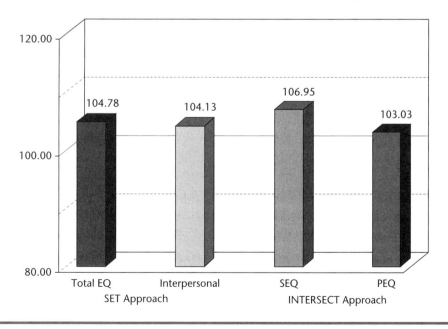

Figure 14.3. The UNIFIED Approach to SI Based on the EQ-i®

and PEQ are compared at an individual level. *This means that we can reject the second hypothesis as well—in fact, overall people's SEQ is higher than their PEQ.*

In practice this means that, when assessed with the EQ-i®, people perceive themselves to have a richer quality of performance when interacting with others than when just by themselves. While it is still an open question whether superiors, peers, and subordinates will echo this, it points to the importance of teamwork and collaboration, minimized hierarchical structures, and open-source arrangements where partnerships are sought in the modern work environment. Generally people see themselves as behaving more desirably when in the public eye than when they are on their own.

Another application for practitioners is to insist on a good balance among the four aspects depicted in Figure 14.3 as a base for further development, counseling, and coaching, as well as for selection, classification, and recruitment initiatives. This would be true at the individual level, where a person's SEQ and PEQ scores are ideally standardized against that of the population norm. An imbalance between any of the scores would indicate a follow-up. Individual SI comparisons are graphed and described for EQ-i® users in the AIR-Social, one of the Advanced Interpretation Report Series published by ePsy Consultancy (Fiedeldey-Van Dijk, 2008a). Those interested in example copies of the AIR-Social can download it from www.epsyconsultancy.com/rcentre/examples.com.

To illustrate the importance of balance between the four aspects in Figure 14.3 further, I divided the sample described here into three equal-sized groups of marginal, standard, and top performance overall for each of SEQ and PEQ. The three groups can be described as follows:

- *Marginal*—average scores for each ranging from the low 80s to the low 90s
- *Standard*—average scores for each ranging from the high 90s to low 100s
- *Top*—average scores for each ranging from the high 100s to high 110s

Because the scores in SEQ and PEQ differ with about 4 points on average, the cut-offs used to group each of the SEQ and PEQ scores into the equal-sized groups differ slightly within each of the above descriptive boundaries. In any event, on average there is a sizable difference in standardized scores between the three groups.

A two-dimensional comparison between the two in Table 14.3 reveals that approximately two-thirds of the people have their SEQ and PEQ in fair

Table 14.3. Categorization of SI

Key to read each cell:	Frequency Percentage Row Pct Column Pct	SEQ			Total
		Marginal	Standard	Top	
	Marginal	220	11	0	231
		20.04	1.00	0.00	21.04
		95.24	4.76	0.00	
		44.27	3.64	0.00	
	Standard	219	142	23	384
PEQ		19.95	12.93	2.09	34.97
		57.03	36.98	5.99	
		44.06	47.02	7.69	
	Top	58	149	276	483
		5.28	13.57	25.14	43.99
		12.01	30.85	57.14	
		11.67	49.34	92.31	
	Total	497	302	299	1,098
		45.26	27.50	27.23	100.00

To read the table, consider as example the cell showing top PEQ and top SEQ people:

276	Number of people belonging to that category; a total of 276 (out of 1,098) people were both top PEQ and SEQ performers
25.14	Percentage of people belonging to that category; they form 25.14 percent of the group, with the rest of the people belonging to one of the remaining eight categories
57.14	Focus on one PEQ category only; a little more than half of the top PEQ performers were top SEQ performers also, with the rest of the top PEQ people belonging to one of the remaining two SEQ categories
92.31	Focus on one SEQ category only; the majority of top SEQ performers were top PEQ performers also, with only about 8 percent belonging to the remaining two PEQ categories.

alignment, as indicated by the shaded cells in the table. This then also means that for a third of the group their social and personal EQ are disconnected (and statistically significant, at that). A misalignment of the magnitude of this categorization (the closest difference between the categories being 10 points on average!) deserves our attention.

The direction of the difference, indicated by the higher numbers toward the bottom left cells in Table 14.3, confirms that while the balance between SEQ and PEQ (in the grey cells) looks good overall, 42 percent of the people in the sample see themselves as having at the very least a 10-point difference on average between SEQ and PEQ. This finding is highly significant. One wonders to what extent SEQ serves as a coping strategy in the presence of others when PEQ reveals underlying personal challenges.

Going back to the SET Approach, multivariate statistics show several significant differences ($p < 0,05$) when we compare people with dominance in SEQ with those showing a dominance in PEQ. SEQ dominance is particularly evident in empathy (EM), social responsibility (RE), and the interpersonal domain, while PEQ dominance is marked in self-regard (SR), optimism (OP—having a positive attitude and looking at the brighter side of life), and the intrapersonal domain.

Given the consistency in performance of the interpersonal scales, no wonder then that today the workplace sees itself taking action on mental health challenges such as stress, depression and anxiety, which cause incremental absence from and cost to organizations (Canada Safety Council, 2005), by supporting social and physical activity within and around the workplace. The findings also emphasize the important role of SR and OP, which are both acknowledged in the first cluster of seven offered in the AIR Series from ePsy Consultancy for their role in how individual well-being radiates toward others (Fiedeldey-Van Dijk, 2008a).

Interestingly, the five EQ-i® scales that showed no statistically significant differences between SEQ and PEQ are emotional self-awareness (ES—recognizing, being aware of, and understanding our emotions), assertiveness (AS—expressing and defending our feelings and ourselves nondestructively), independence (IN—being self-reliant and free of emotional dependency on others), problem solving (PS—generating effective solutions to emotional and social problems), and happiness (HA—feeling content with and seeing the joy in ourselves, others, and life in general). Three of these scales (IN, AS, and PS) com bine with SR and RT to contribute to Cluster 3, the first of three clusters on leadership measured in the AIR Series. This cluster speaks to people's drive toward tangible output. It makes sense then that dominantly-SEQ people will use different means than dominantly PEQ people to be productive.

SI and Gender

Let us further explore the findings in Figure 14.3 with regard to different sample demographics. Note that the stereotype of females as more caring and empathic than males fits with the SET Approach and is statistically significant ($p < 0.01$), but is far less prominent within the INTERSECT Approach (although still significantly different ($p < 0.01$), see Figure 14.4). Men (in the left bars) and women (right bars) scored lower in PEQ than in SEQ, although the difference is more noticeable among women.

These results are important for practitioners working in fields such as development, coaching, and selection. When working with women, one could focus on PEQ when a good balance between SEQ and PEQ is

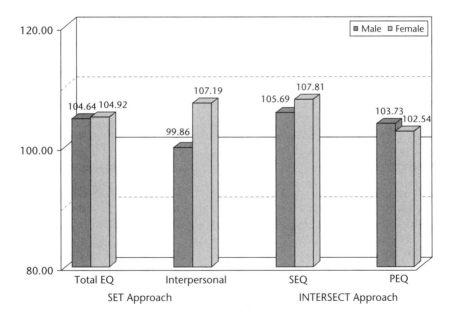

Figure 14.4. Gender-Based SI

sought. Women with a distinct strength in SEQ above PEQ working in a male-dominated or high-PEQ environment may do well in a leadership role in which facilitation and inspiration of teams are needed. With men, one could focus on strengthening both SEQ and PEQ in relation to one another. Men who are strong in PEQ can partner with those who are strong in SEQ to form role models for each other, and to men and women who are not as strong in either.

A final observation from Figure 14.4 is that men in particular scored lower than women in both the interpersonal domain and SEQ comparative to PEQ, although not ineffectively by any means. This may indicate that, in general, men tend to draw from other means than their interpersonal capabilities *per se*. This does not mean that men are less socially intelligent than women. Staying true to the UNIFIED Approach, ultimately SI depends on interpersonal strength (where women generally do well) *and* on a good balance between SEQ and PEQ (where men do well).

SI and Age

Age group differences in SI are shown in Figure 14.5. Only age groups with sample sizes of more than 160 people each are shown, reading from left

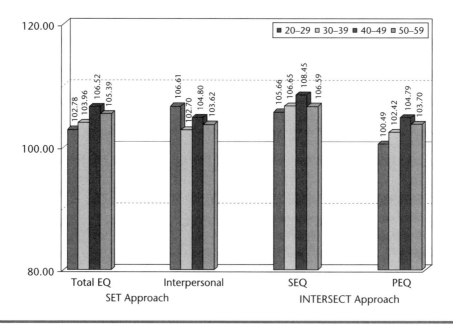

Figure 14.5. Age-Based SI

to right in each cluster of bars as people in their twenties, thirties, forties, and fifties. Similar to the EQ-i® norm population, the findings lean toward peaking in the forties (Multi-Health Systems, 2002). However, the difference in scores between the age groups found here is statistically non-significant with one exception, namely those in their forties scored significantly higher in PEQ than those in their twenties.

A comparison of SEQ against the baseline of PEQ for each of the age groups reveals that an alignment of SEQ and PEQ seems to develop slightly with age. In other words, the strive for near-balance between SEQ and PEQ seems to naturally move in the desired direction over time for people in general, yet not to the extent that PEQ is ever on par with SEQ.

By contrast, the interpersonal domain (representing the SET Approach, where it matters *how much* SI we have) seems to peak in the twenties, dips somewhat in the thirties, and thereafter holds relatively steady over time. One wonders whether this pattern reflects the life stages when long-term relationships typically are formed in the personal and work lives of people, with some of these relationships failing some time later. Within the INTERSECT Approach (where we look at *what* SI people have), it appears that overall not just EI, but also SI, manifests only somewhat later in life—in the forties—as the kind of optimal SI state that is currently achievable by people.

SI and Job Level

Another perspective on SI lies with the job level of people in the workplace. Figure 14.6 shows that measured total EQ tends to increase with job level, confirming research based on a different EQ model published by Fiedeldey-Van Dijk and Freedman (2007). People in the upper echelons of organizations may give a silent sigh of relief (many still assume that a high score in a personality, EI, or SI measure must be better than a low score across the scale range). This needs some careful interpretation, as the climbing total EQ bars do not take into account other factors (such as age and gender) that may be at play: senior people in most organizations tend to represent the older age categories, while they remain male dominant. However, the effects of age and gender on job level appear to neutralize one another, leaving Figure 14.6 with a pattern of scores that are reliable.

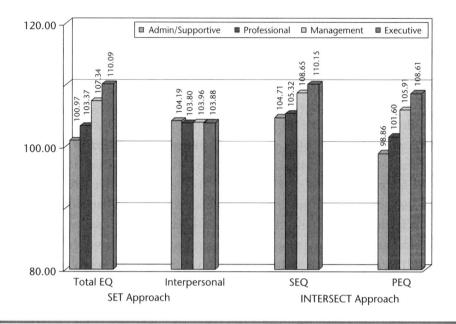

Figure 14.6. Role-Based SI

From the perspective of the SET Approach, it is encouraging to see that, on average, people at any given job level have the same interpersonal capability—all of us have what it takes interpersonally to do well on our own home turfs. The INTERSECT Approach reveals how PEQ tends to catch up with SEQ as job level increases, until the two are in fair balance. Apart from relatively high total EQ, the near-balance between SEQ and PEQ is another distinguishing quality of managers and executives versus professionals and administrative or supportive employees ($p < 0.05$). In practice this may be an important job requirement when employees are recruited or groomed for a managerial position.

Drawing from the UNIFIED Approach, when we compare the interpersonal domain scores with that of the SEQ-PEQ balance, on average, administrative or supportive employees and professionals seem to depend comparatively little on their personal strength and rely more on their social strength in order to be effective. By contrast, executives, and to some extent managers, function well both when interacting with other people and especially when by themselves, but they draw from means beyond their interpersonal capabilities. It seems that at the managerial levels, currently the *what* of SI matters more than the *how much*. Therefore it is insufficient to infer from people's performance in the interpersonal domain only whether they are socially intelligent. The playoff between the components of the two approaches at different demographic categorizations paves the way for deeper, unified understanding and working with SI going forward.

In summary, when working with an individual or group SI profile we can use a checklist to account for known demographic effects. In general, we can expect to find the following tendencies:

- People have similar interpersonal domain scores at all job levels.
- Interpersonal domain scores peak in the twenties and dip somewhat in the thirties.
- Women score higher in the interpersonal domain than men.
- Men score higher in their total EQ (and SEQ) than in their interpersonal domains.
- People in executive levels score higher in total EQ than in their interpersonal domains.
- Total EQ, SEQ, and PEQ scores increase with job level.
- PEQ scores are lowest in the twenties and peak in the forties.
- A near-balance in SEQ-PEQ scores is more achievable with age.
- Men have near-balance between their SEQ and PEQ scores.
- Women score higher in SEQ (and the interpersonal domain) than in PEQ.
- People in non-managerial levels score higher in SEQ than in PEQ.
- A near-balance in SEQ-PEQ scores is more achievable with an increase in job level.

These pointers can bring hope and focus to intervention strategies that practitioners may offer clients. Undesirable exceptions to the above guidelines are worthy of follow-up.

SI AND EQ PROFILING: GROUNDING THE ACTION STEPS FOR PRACTITIONERS

Taken together, what constitutes SI from the perspective of an EI assessment? We now know that within the UNIFIED Approach SI comprises two aspects, namely (1) a score in the interpersonal domain on the EQ-i® that indicates high-effective functioning, and (2) a good balance between Social EQ (SEQ) and Personal EQ (PEQ). From a practitioner's standpoint, we are interested in instances when (and how) individuals and groups deviate from this scenario, as this is where our value and contribution lie. In other words, practitioners interested in SI stand on alert when any one or more of the following occurs:

- The interpersonal domain is low and/or distinctly lower than the total EQ.
- SEQ is distinctly larger than PEQ.
- PEQ is larger than SEQ.
- Both SEQ and PEQ are distinctly smaller than the interpersonal domain.

What do individuals reveal through their EI to qualify their SI as less than ideal? Contrasting SEQ and PEQ sheds some light as this goes beyond mere total EQ and the interpersonal domain from the EQ-i® profile, which many are fixated on when addressing SI. Figure 14.7 serves as our window from which we can observe the combined EQ profile of 1,099 people for whom data were available. A total of 752 people (68.43 percent) had a larger SEQ score than PEQ score; for 347 people (31.57 percent) the opposite was true or the two scores were the same. The skew in numbers toward SEQ is to be expected, because all the previous figures show that SEQ > PEQ. Out of the latter group, only thirty-four people had a smaller SEQ score than a PEQ score, comprising 3.09 percent of the total sample group.

Figure 14.7 is based on the premise that for the light grey bars PEQ is significantly larger than SEQ, while for the dark grey bars it is the opposite. The asterisks indicate that the SEQ and PEQ profiles are significantly different for all the EQ-i scales ($p < 0.05$), except for ES and IN. For the sake of fluency, scale abbreviations (generally the first letters of the scale names) will be used in the profile interpretation of Figure 14.7 below. Readers are referred to Table 14.1 for the complete list of EQ-i® scales where needed.

The EQ-i® profile reveals that people with dominant SEQ scores (in the dark grey bars) can be described as being intent on and belonging to their audience (SR) and recognizing, understanding, and owning their emotions (emotional self-awareness). These people are very focused on what is mutually shared: they establish and maintain a relationship with their addressees (IR), and are adept in having their listeners sense that they are aware of and understand how others feel (EM). SEQ-dominant people are least characteristic of always being positive (OP). They tend to contain strong emotions such as aggression,

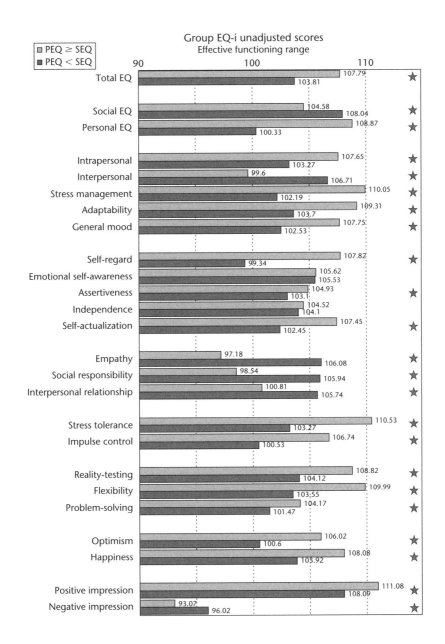

Figure 14.7. PEQ- Versus SEQ-Dominant EQ Profiling

$p < 0.05$

EQ-i® scales. Copyright © 2002 Multi-Health Systems Inc. All rights reserved.

Personal EQ (PEQ) & Social EQ (SEQ). Copyright © 2008 ePsy Consultancy. All rights reserved.

or reacting on the spur of the moment (IC), and are fairly critical of themselves (SR). Last, they have well-developed social awareness (interpersonal domain).

By contrast, people with dominant PEQ scores (in the light grey bars in Figure 14.7) can be described as capable of holding together in a controlled manner and handling themselves well (ST), adjusting to changes as they occur (FL), and looking strategically—being prepared for what comes next rather than being focused on the immediate (RT). These people are not very intent on others: they don't put in a large effort to have others sense that they are aware of and understand how they feel (EM) and don't exercise great care to identify with and socially feel part of the group (RE). Their relationships with others (IR) come second to their own acceptance of and respect for themselves (SR), yet they are not fully self-reliant and free of emotional dependency on others (IN). Note that the difference between the SEQ and PEQ scores are smaller for these people (light grey bars) than for those who are SEQ-dominant (dark grey bars). Their display of SI also relies on factors outside of interpersonal capability.

Observe also how the scale range (that is, the gap between the highest and lowest scores) in the PEQ profile (light grey bars) is much larger than that of the SEQ profile (dark grey bars). This underscores that dominant-PEQ people rely heavily on strengths in ST, FL, and RT in the absence of strong interpersonal capability.

These two EQ-i® profiles form the two sides of the social-intelligence coin. An individual's profile will likely lie somewhere in between these two profiles. From Figure 14.7 we learn that there are at least two different ways (SEQ or PEQ) and combinations thereof to plan further development of individual or group SI.

CONCLUSION

An individual's (or group's) SI can be numerically expressed and graphed in the form of a total SQ score. Similarly, his or her EQ-i® profile can be matched against each of the SEQ and PEQ profiles. This is conveniently available to EQ-i® users in the form of a report, called the AIR-Social. (See Fiedeldey-Van Dijk, 2008a, to download sample reports.) Depending on the match percentages and on what side of the SEQ and PEQ profiles the individual profile lies, practitioners can use either or a combination of both profile descriptions to plan and direct development and selection initiatives against the backdrop of an AIR-Social for that individual or group.

From the two profiles in Figure 14.7 it is clear that neither the SEQ nor the PEQ profile alone is optimal for SI. Although it appears that both types of people with either profile can be rather sophisticated in how they display SI (after all, overall their EQ-i® profile lies mostly in the high-effective functioning range), they can learn from one another. Ultimately, from a practitioner's perspective, SI lies in a combination of both profiles that is displayed strongly. Clearly, SI entails more than mere development of our interpersonal competence. While our social awareness and skill in establishing and maintaining interpersonal relationships matter, a too simplistic focus will neither ensure, nor fully explain success in the workplace and elsewhere. From Figure 14.7 it is conspicuous that at least thirteen of the fifteen EQ-i® scales in dynamic interplay are at stake when dealing with SI. We can draw a lot from EI alone when done effectively in our pursuit of being or becoming socially intelligent.

REFERENCES

Ahuja, A. (2006, September 18). Socially superior. *The Times.* Available: www.timesonline.co.uk/article/0,,7-2360480.html.

Andrews, D.A., & Kiessling, J.J. (1980). Program structure and effective correctional practices: A summary of CaVIC research. In P. Gendreau & R.R. Ross (Eds.), *Effective correctional treatment.* Toronto, ON: Butterworth.

Bar-On, R. (2007, April 18). The Bar-On model of emotional-social intelligence. Available: www.reuvenbaron.org/bar-on-model/essay.php?i=2.

Byrne, R., & Whiten, A. (Eds.). (1988). *Machiavellian intelligence: Social expertise and the evolution of intellect in monkeys, apes, and humans.* Oxford, UK: Clarendon Press.

Canada Safety Council. (2005). *Mental health and the workplace.* Available: www.safety-council.org/info/OSH/mentalhealth.html.

Cantor, N., & Kihlstrom, J.F. (1987). *Personality and social intelligence.* Englewood Cliffs, NJ: Prentice-Hall.

Fiedeldey-Van Dijk, C. (2008a, May). Advanced interpretation reports (AIR). Available: www.epsyconsultancy.com/rcentre/examples.htm.

Fiedeldey-Van Dijk, C. (2008b, August). White paper: A critical perspective on the "social" within emotional intelligence. Available: www.epsyconsultancy.com/rcentre/white.htm.

Fiedeldey-Van Dijk, C., & Freedman, J. (2007). Differentiating emotional intelligence in leadership. *Journal of Leadership Studies*, 1(2), 8–20.

George, J.M. (2000). Emotions and leadership: The role of emotional intelligence. *Human Relations*, *53*, 1027–1055.

Greenspan, S.I. (1979). Intelligence and adaptation: An integration of psychoanalytic and Piagetian developmental psychology. *Psychological Issues*, *12*(3–4), 1–408.

Greenspan, S.I. (1997). *Twin studies, heritability, and intelligence*. MA: Addison-Wesley.

Kihlstrom, J.F., & Cantor, N. (2000). Social intelligence. In R.J. Sternberg (Ed.), *Handbook of intelligence* (2nd ed.) (pp. 359–379). Cambridge, UK: Cambridge University Press.

Klein, S.B., & Kihlstrom, J.F. (1998). On bridging the gap between social-personality psychology and neuropsychology. *Personality & Social Psychology Review*, *11*(2), 228–242.

Knecht, T. (2004). What is Machiavellian intelligence? Views on a little appreciated side of the psyche. *Der Nervenarzt*, *75*(1), 1–5.

Leslie, J.B., & Van Velsor, E. (1996). *A look at derailment today: North America and Europe*. Greensboro, NC: Center for Creative Leadership.

Miller, M. (1999). Emotional intelligence helps managers succeed. *Credit UNIFIED Magazine*, *56*(7), 25–26.

Mischel, W. (1973). Toward a cognitive social learning reconceptualization of personality. *Psychological Review*, *80*, 252–283.

Multi-Health Systems Inc. (2002). *BarOn Emotional Quotient Inventory. Technical manual*. Toronto, ON: Author.

Rock, M. (2003). *EQ goes to work* (3rd ed.). Toronto: Self-Development Dimensions Inc.

Spielberger, C. (Ed.). (2004). *The encyclopedia of applied psychology* (Vol. 1–3). New York: Academic Press.

Thorndike, E.L. (1920). Intelligence and its use. *Harper's Magazine*, *140*, 227–235.

Worden, R.P. (1996). Primate social intelligence. *Cognitive Science*, *20*(4), 579–616.

Dr. Carina Fiedeldey-Van Dijk, president of ePsy Consultancy, helps organizations foster a healthy work climate, achieve top performance, display leadership, and attract valued employees and customers. Using assessment results and supporting data from surveys and job performance measures, she focuses on the bottom line with custom research, targeted consulting, and individual/group coaching.

Being accredited in several emotional intelligence assessments and a seasoned speaker, Carina facilitates advanced EQ interpretation workshops. She authored the Advanced Interpretation Report (AIR) Series and the Group Dynamics Report (GDR), both based on the EQ-i®, and co-authored the SEI-Youth Version, the Organizational Weather Report (OWR), and the Multi-Rater Leadership Inventory (MRLI), among other assessments.

Education: Leaders and Students

CHAPTER 15

A Sustainable, Skill-Based Approach to Building Emotionally Literate Schools

Marc A. Brackett, Janet Patti, Robin Stern, Susan E. Rivers, Nicole A. Elbertson, Christian Chisholm, and Peter Salovey

"Educating the mind without educating the heart is no education at all." These words, spoken by Aristotle, are, at long last, being taken seriously by educators, academics, and policymakers. Education in its best form is more than science, history, and arithmetic, and students are driven by more than their natural aptitude to acquire knowledge or perform well on standardized tests. As Aristotle acknowledged, humans are social and emotional animals, and, by extension, social and emotional learners (Kristjánsson, 2007). Rather than denying that reality, the ancient Greeks capitalized on it to guide the acquisition of knowledge and to integrate students into the community. This system of tutelage in many ways foreshadowed what is referred to today as social and emotional learning (SEL).

SEL refers to the acquisition of skills such as self- and social awareness, self-regulation, responsible decision making and problem solving, and relationship management (Elias, Zins, Weissberg, Frey, Greenberg, Haynes, et al., 1997; Kress & Elias, 2006). These skills impact significantly academic performance, classroom behavior, social interactions, mental and physical health, and lifelong effectiveness (Brackett & Rivers, 2008; Payton, Graczyk, Wardlaw, Bloodworth, Tompsett, & Weissberg, 2000; Zins, Weissberg, Want, & Walberg, 2004). In fact, a *systematic process* for promoting SEL is the common element among schools reporting a decrease in problem behavior and an increase in academic success and quality of relationships (Greenberg, Weissberg, O'Brien, Zins, Fredericks, Resnik, & Elias, 2003). The evidence is so convincing that states such as Illinois and Alaska are creating learning standards for SEL (similar to learning standards for traditional subjects).

In this chapter, we describe our district-wide implementation plan for creating schools that foster SEL. Our programs, *Emotionally Literate Schools*, which have been adopted by school districts throughout the United States and England, represent the collective expertise of psychologists, educators, and school administrators. The programs address the underlying emotional skills that foster well-being, improved academic and work performance, and healthy social interaction. The assertion is that, for children to thrive, it is necessary both to integrate the teaching of emotional skills into the academic curriculum and provide training and opportunities for students and all stakeholders—school leaders, teachers, staff, and family members—to apply these skills in their daily interactions.

Incorporating SEL programming into a school or district can be challenging, however (Zins, Weissberg, Wang, & Walberg, 2004). In the past, many schools have implemented one prevention initiative after another, resulting in a succession of disjointed efforts. Moreover, while most SEL programs teach important concepts, few integrate easily into existing curricula using straightforward, effective teaching techniques that have enduring benefits beyond the classroom (Kress & Elias, 2006). Finally, without institutionalizing SEL practices by garnering support from all stakeholders, even the best programs eventually fail.

According to the Collaborative for Academic, Social, and Emotional Learning (CASEL)—an organization providing guidance to researchers, educators, and policy makers on school-based SEL programs—initiatives to integrate SEL into schools are most effective when they provide training to all stakeholders. Additionally, the best programs are field-tested, evidenced-based, and rooted in sound psychological and educational theory (Elias et al., 1997; Zins, Weissberg, Want, & Walberg, 2004). Optimal SEL programs (a) teach how to apply SEL skills both in and out of school; (b) build connections to school by creating caring and engaging learning environments; (c) provide developmentally and culturally appropriate instruction; (d) enhance school performance by addressing the cognitive, affective, and social dimensions of learning; (e) encourage family and school partnerships; and (f) include continuous evaluation and improvement. *Emotionally Literate Schools* is a set of programs that fulfills these requirements and aligns with CASEL's sustainable schoolwide plan (Devaney, O'Brien, Resnik, Keister, & Weissberg, 2006).

To acquaint the reader with the theory and rationale underlying *Emotionally Literate Schools*, we begin with an overview of our emotional literacy model and review research that shows the importance of emotional skills in all areas of life. We then describe our three-phase plan designed to ensure successful implementation of our programs.

WHAT IS EMOTIONAL LITERACY?

The programs comprising *Emotionally Literate Schools* are anchored in our model of emotional literacy, which posits that personal, social, and intellectual functioning improves by teaching children and adults how to recognize, understand, label, express, and regulate emotions (Brackett & Rivers, 2008). We use the acronym RULER to refer to this set of skills. Table 15.1 provides a definition of each component of RULER and illustrates examples for two emotions: amusement and sadness. The RULER model is an outgrowth of decades of research on emotional intelligence (Mayer & Salovey, 1997; Salovey & Mayer, 1990) and has deep roots in both cognitive and affective science. The RULER model is distinguishable from conceptions of emotional

Table 15.1. The Five Components of Emotional Literacy: RULER Definitions and Examples

	Definition	Examples	
		Sadness	**Amusement**
Recognize	Identifying and interpreting the experience of emotion from nonverbal cues, including facial expressions, gait, posture, voice, gesture, touch, and physiological changes	Corners of lips pulled down, lips may be turned downward, upper eyelids puffy, crying, slow movement and speech, slouched posture	Smile, raised cheeks, wrinkles at outer corners of eyes, laughter, feelings of arousal
Understand	Being aware of the causes and consequences of emotion, involving the situations that cause emotions, the transition and progression between emotions, and how emotions influence thinking and behavior	Occurs in response to that object, physical or psychological feelings; something being left behind, an excitement cancelled; thinking becomes negative, helpless, thoughts return to bad relationships; may withdraw interactions	Occurs in response to something humorous or entertaining; thinking becomes expansive and more creative; thoughts about self and others become more positive; willingness to help others increases
Label	Developing a diverse vocabulary of terms to describe the full range of emotions	Disappointed, blue, disconsolate, depressed, unhappy, distressed	Charmed, entertained, pleased

Express		
Knowing multiple modes of emotional expression, including spoken, written, and nonverbal, as well as appreciating that there are more and less appropriate modes of and times for emotional expression, depending, in part, on the person's audience and context	Expressing amusement entails knowing appropriate times to laugh or smile at something amusing (e.g., it is not socially appropriate to laugh or smile when the person who did something amusing did not do so intentionally and got physically hurt)	Expressing sadness involves knowing how best to let others know that help or support is needed, or that the loss is meaningful and significant. Some expressions of sadness may bring about negative social consequences, like ridicule (e.g., being called a *cry baby*). Thus, appropriate expression involves knowing when and how much sadness to express to garner social support
Regulate		
Accumulating strategies to change emotional states: preventing, enhancing, reducing, and initiating in oneself and others to fit the situation	Regulating amusement may involve engaging in behaviors to prolong the experience, such as doing something fun, laughing with others, telling others about the amusing event; When it is necessary to reduce or prevent this emotion, an effective strategy is cognitive reappraisal whereby one thinks about the situation in a different way (focusing on the person's injury that occurred as a consequence of the event, for example)	Regulating sadness may involve attempts to reduce the emotion. This may be done by obtaining support through physical comfort (like a hug) or help at replacing the lost object (e.g., if an object is lost, having others help to look for it). Sadness also can be reduced through distraction strategies such as watching a funny movie, playing with friends, or exercising

intelligence, "EQ," and emotional literacy depicted in the popular media, which tend to use these terms to represent an array of perceived competencies, personality traits and attitudes related to character and self-esteem, among other constructs (Brackett & Geher, 2006). We assert that keeping emotional literacy constrained to a set of emotional skills (i.e., RULER) provides a firm foundation for both developing programs to enhance such skills and assessing learning (see Mayer, Salovey, & Caruso, in press).

Emotional literacy capitalizes on three important advances in psychological science. The first pertains to shifting views about the importance of emotions. Historically, emotions were seen as disruptive and intrusive to rational thought and decision-making capabilities. We now know that emotions drive attention, motivation, and memory, helping us to learn, make wise decisions, and maintain positive social relationships (Damasio, 1994; Ekman, 1973; Izard, Fine, Mostow, Trentacosta, & Campbell, 2002; Keltner & Haidt, 2001; Lazarus, 1991; Mayer & Salovey, 1997). The second advance is the broadening view of what it means to be intelligent and "successful" to a diverse set of mental abilities, including emotional skills (Gardner, 1983/1993; Mayer & Salovey, 1997; Salovey & Mayer, 1990; Sternberg, 1985). The final advance is the growing need for schools to prevent problematic behavior and to promote prosocial behavior among students. The idea that developing students' emotional skills can decrease school violence and other maladaptive behaviors such as substance abuse and bullying comes from years of research documenting links between poor emotional skills and problematic behavior (Eisenberg, Fabes, Guthrie, & Reiser, 2000; Halberstadt, Denham, & Dunsmore, 2001; Kindlon & Thompson, 2000; Underwood, 2003).

THE IMPORTANCE OF EMOTIONAL LITERACY FOR STUDENTS, TEACHERS, AND SCHOOL LEADERS

Students encounter a gamut of emotions at school, each of which calls upon their emotional skills. To name a few, they feel pride when they accomplish a difficult task, anxiety about taking tests, fear when victimized by a bully, and anger when treated unfairly by a peer. Given the myriad emotions students experience, emotional literacy is central to their success. Consider, for example, a student who feels apprehensive about an impending math test. The emotionally literate student *recognizes* and *labels* his feelings of anxiety about the test (by noticing his racing heart and constant thoughts about it), *understands* that he feels this way because he both didn't do well on the previous test and is afraid he will fail the next one, *expresses* his feelings to his parents and his teacher, and *regulates* his feelings by taking a deep breath and deciding to skip soccer practice the night before the test to spend extra time studying with a parent. As a result, this student will secure the attention and support he needs, be more psychologically healthy, and perform better on the test.

Considerable research shows that emotionally skilled children and adolescents tend to flourish (Denham, 1998; Fine, Izard, Mostow, Trentacosta, & Ackerman, 2003; Rivers, Brackett, & Salovey, 2007; Saarni, 1999). These youth have more positive relationships, are less likely to engage in risk-taking behaviors such as using drugs and alcohol, experience fewer emotional symptoms (e.g., stress, anxiety, and depression), and perform better academically (Brackett, Mayer, & Warner, 2004; Brackett, Rivers, Shiffman, Lerner, & Salovey, 2006). In addition, teachers perceive emotionally skilled youth as more socially competent and non-aggressive; less hyperactive, depressed, and anxious; and relatively popular, prosocial, and self-confident (Agostin & Bain, 1997; Eisenberg, Fabes, Guthrie, & Reiser, 2000; Gil-Olarte Marquez, Palomera Martin, & Brackett, 2006; Halberstadt, Denham, & Dunsmore, 2001; Saarni, 1999).

When the adults in students' lives also have the abilities to recognize, understand, label, express, and regulate emotions, they can provide students with positive role models and the resources needed to thrive. For example, emotionally skilled teachers are likely to demonstrate empathic behavior, encourage healthy communication, and create more open and effective learning environments where students feel safe and valued (Brackett, Katulak, Kremenitzer, Alster, & Caruso, 2008). The emotional skills of teachers also influence student conduct, engagement, attachment to school, and academic performance (Baker, 1999; Hawkins, 1999; Schaps, Battistich, & Solomon, 1997; Sutton & Wheatley, 2003; Wentzel, 2002).

Teachers' emotional skills are critical to their own effectiveness and success as their work involves a significant potential for emotionally draining situations (Dorman, 2003; Maslach & Leiter, 1999). Compared to people working in other professions, a greater percentage of teachers report work as a source of stress (Cox & Brockley, 1984). Teachers who are stressed and burnt out offer less information and praise to students, are less accepting of student ideas, and interact less frequently with students (Travers & Cooper, 1996). However, teachers who are more skilled at regulating their emotions tend to report less burnout and greater job satisfaction; they also experience greater positive affect while teaching and receive more support from the principals with whom they work (Brackett, Mojsa, Palomera, Reyes, & Salovey, 2008).

Emotional literacy also is at the core of the ability of school leaders to build and maintain positive and trusting relationships, as they spend more time on average dealing with people "issues" and problems than on any other work task (Patti & Tobin, 2006). For example, a principal who accurately *recognizes* a teacher's mild irritation during a meeting and *understands* the significance of that emotion will be better able both to predict the teacher's subsequent actions and respond appropriately to the teacher (Elfenbein & Ambady, 2002). How well the principal *expresses* and *regulates* emotions also is critical to the relationship with the teacher, as these two skills help individuals behave in socially appropriate ways (Gross, 1998). One angry outburst can destroy a teacher-principal relationship forever. Moreover, when implementing emotional literacy programs, these skills can help school leaders move trainings forward by supporting and being open to teachers' feelings about the programs, exhibiting resiliency in the face of challenges, and helping all stakeholders work through potential roadblocks (Hoy & Hoy, 2003).

The programs of *Emotionally Literate Schools* consider the emotional skills of all stakeholders involved in the education of children—school leaders, teachers, staff, parents, and, of course, the children themselves. The curricula and interactive workshops provide skills training to these stakeholders to promote their emotional literacy and create positive learning and working communities. Our plan for successful implementation and enduring sustainability of the programs lays the groundwork for achieving these objectives.

IMPLEMENTATION PLAN FOR EMOTIONALLY LITERATE SCHOOLS

In this section, we describe the purpose and action steps for each phase of the implementation plan for *Emotionally Literate Schools*. The three phases are

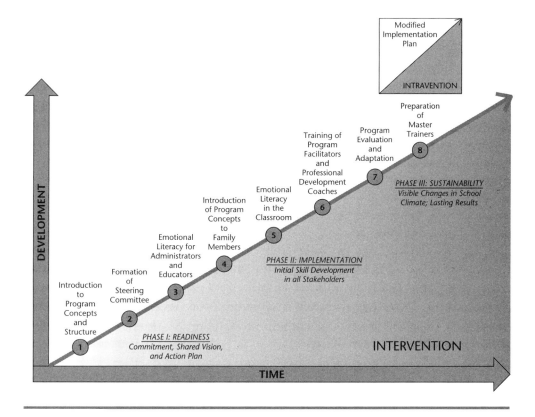

Figure 15.1. Implementation Plan for *Emotionally Literate Schools*

Readiness, Implementation, and Sustainability. Figure 15.1 depicts graphically the phases and the action steps.

Readiness Phase

The Readiness Phase is comprised of the first two action steps in our implementation plan: (1) Introduction to Program Concepts and Structure and (2) Formation of the Steering Committee. The goal of this phase is to gain commitment from key stakeholders, to build a shared vision between the school or district and program developers, and to create an action plan for program implementation.

Introduction to Program Concepts and Structure

The objective of *Emotionally Literate Schools* is to enhance the emotional skills of all stakeholders in the school or district with the eventual goal of creating more satisfying, caring, productive, and engaging learning and working environments. It is essential to the success of our programs that schools faithfully implement all phases. To do so, school leaders need to secure commitment from all stakeholders. Board members, building-level administrators, and teachers are more likely to champion the initiative and to help make it successful when they are included in the planning phase. Securing their support must take place prior to adopting the programs.

When introducing emotional literacy to a school, we typically work with school leaders (usually the principal or superintendent) to make a professional presentation to key stakeholders. The goal of the presentation is to:

- Describe the theoretical model foundational to the programs.
- Make explicit the links between our model and the philosophy, policies, and current practices of that school.
- Illustrate how the programs can help the school achieve its desired goals, emphasizing the social, emotional, and academic growth of students and staff.
- Develop a preliminary budget and resource allocation plan (e.g., equipment, venues for trainings, professional development hours).

After deciding to adopt *Emotionally Literate Schools*, but before implementing the programs, we recommend that schools conduct a needs and resource assessment to evaluate how the new programming fits with the existing practices and culture of the school. Schools often need to make changes to accommodate the emotional literacy programs (e.g., allocating professional development days to the program, integrating this initiative with instructional programming). This evaluation effort typically falls under the responsibility of a steering committee, which needs to occur early in the adoption of the programs.

Formation of the Steering Committee

Central to successful implementation of *Emotionally Literate Schools* is the judicious pre-planning to select and develop the steering committee whose primary objective is to spearhead the adoption and implementation of the initiative. Depending on the size of the school or district, the school principal usually is instrumental in forming the committee and recruits members from every part of the school community. Members should include administrators, teachers from all subject areas, parents, school aides, support staff such as counselors, social workers, and psychologists, and even students (in the upper grades). Often, a community member might be integral to the team, particularly if providing financial support. For example, in one school with which we have worked, the steering committee was comprised of an assistant principal, a school counselor, and one teacher from each subject area (language arts, math, science, etc.). In larger districts, it may be necessary to create multiple steering committees that are overseen by selected individuals in the district office.

Each member of the steering committee needs to be knowledgeable of both the curricula constituting *Emotionally Literate Schools* and other initiatives in the school. When members already have this knowledge, they will be able to assist in the larger thinking needed to move emotional literacy forward. If they do not, part of the implementation will require developing this team so they can assume the much needed leadership.

The steering committee needs a coordinator to be the group's leader. The ideal coordinator is someone whom the committee trusts and respects and someone with whom stakeholders are comfortable interacting. Ideally, the coordinator is an experienced teacher or administrator who has the time to devote to the initiative.

Equally important to the selection of the coordinator is the delineation of roles for each committee member, which must be underlined by the school principal. The steering committee exists to assure consistency of implementation, accountability, and long-term sustainability. Carefully planned action steps led by these members, with needed support from the program developers or external providers of the program, ensures that the implementation is being well-received by key stakeholders and that the effects of the programs are evident in the behaviors and social, emotional, and academic achievement of all students, teachers, and administrators. Table 15.2 includes some of the responsibilities assumed by the steering committee. Expectations for the committee and member roles differ across schools and districts, as well as across time (e.g., the tasks required to establish the program differ from those needed to sustain it).

The mission statement of the steering committee, updated yearly, should articulate clearly the purpose of the committee and the expectations for each

Table 15.2. Assuring Implementation, Accountability, and Long-Term Sustainability: Examples of Steering Committee Responsibilities

a. Conducting an initial needs and resources assessment of current SEL practices and programs, school readiness to implement the curricula, and possible barriers to implementation

b. Working with the principal or superintendent to allocate resources such as funding, professional development days, and personnel

c. Scheduling all program-related trainings

d. Coordinating seamlessly the components of *Emotionally Literate Schools* with other school initiatives and in all subject areas

e. Assuring that the emotional literacy work is evident in the school culture, including the upkeep and design of the school, and ensuring that components of the curricula are employed throughout the system (e.g., during recess and at lunchtime)

f. Participating in various subcommittees of the steering committee so as to streamline information to the full committee about the initiative. For example, some members may assist classroom teachers with instruction of *Emotional Literacy in the Classroom*. In this capacity, they would work as program facilitators who are able to provide teachers with support for teaching the program

g. Meeting regularly with teachers and school leaders to discuss how the programs are being implemented and to problem solve about any unexpected occurrences during instruction

h. Monitoring and recording details of the initiative to evaluate practices and to create a modified implementation plan, if necessary

i. Developing a plan to respond to the questions and concerns of all stakeholders

j. Producing a long-term sustainability plan

member. The steering committee needs to set its goals in the context of the larger school vision. Actions of the committee should be based upon evidence of the programs' efficacy. This evidence also informs the larger community about school-wide needs and outcomes of the programming, as they occur.

Each school principal needs to be aware of the mission and responsibilities of the steering committee and support the efforts of its members. Financial resources should support the committee's efforts, which adds credibility and importance to the implementation process and ensures consistency over time. Mistakenly, some school leaders separate emotional literacy programming from the essential components of instruction, jeopardizing the perceived importance and sustainability of the programs.

Implementation Phase

The Implementation Phase is comprised of Action Steps 3 through 6 in our plan and involves (3) skills training for administrators and educators, (4) an introduction of program concepts to family members, (5) launching of emotional literacy classroom programs, and, finally, (6) training of program coaches and professional development coaches. In this phase, initial skill-building takes place for all stakeholders.

Emotional Literacy for Administrators and Educators

School leaders, teachers, and other school personnel who interact with students are instrumental in the execution of *Emotionally Literate Schools*. The presence of a supportive leader, for instance, is one of the most powerful predictors of a school's ability to sustain new programming (Elias & Kamarinos Galiotos, 2004). Teachers, like school leaders, are central to the success of the initiative because they are the primary implementers of the student programs. Many "educator-level" factors influence the success of the initiative, including educators' own emotional literacy, their beliefs about the importance of the program, their willingness to participate actively and enthusiastically in its roll out, and their confidence in teaching and modeling program components (Greenberg, Domitrovich, Graczyk, & Zins, 2005). Modeling of emotional literacy is one of the most powerful tools as it gives leaders and teachers credibility in promoting the initiative. For example, each time the teacher responds positively to a student's emotions in class, the teacher is modeling emotional literacy and reinforcing its relevance and importance. On the other hand, when students notice that their teachers are not "practicing" what they are "preaching," they are more likely to mimic what they see versus what they are told to do (Mize & Ladd, 1990).

Although many school leaders and teachers are naturally gifted in dealing with their own emotions and those of others, a majority do not have a foundational background in emotional literacy. We assert that the knowledge and skills of emotional literacy (i.e., RULER) are accumulated best in a structured and systematic way (Brackett & Geher, 2006; Mills, 2003; Stronge, 2002; Wentzel, 2002). For these reasons, prior to launching the classroom program, administrators and educators participate in their own workshops, *Emotional Literacy for Administrators* and *Emotional Literacy for Educators*, respectively. The curricula for each workshop provide the tools and training necessary to ensure successful implementation.

The *Emotional Literacy for Administrators* programs (Brackett & Caruso, 2007a) inform school administrators how emotions impact individuals, relationships, and organizational climate, as well as how they can harness the wisdom of emotions to become more effective team and school leaders and create optimal learning climates. A healthy and open school climate generates high levels of trust, collegiality, support for school improvement, as well as commitment to the initiative (Hoy & Tarter, 1997). The *Emotional Literacy for Educators* programs (Brackett & Caruso, 2007b) teach educators and other school staff about the role and importance of emotional skills in building quality relationships with students, stress management, making informed decisions, managing and leading classrooms, and student engagement and performance.

These highly interactive workshops provide participants with specific tools both to enhance and apply all five components of RULER and create an effective learning community. Participants learn the importance of self- and other-awareness; how emotions influence attention, memory, learning, and relationships; the benefits of expressing the full range of emotions; the costs of suppressing and hiding emotions; the emotion regulation strategies that are effective in reducing negative emotions and enhancing positive ones; and how to listen empathically and provide constructive feedback, among other skills. A message emphasized throughout the workshops is that it is normal to experience *all* emotions, and both children and adults should feel safe sharing, discussing, and problem-solving about their emotions in school.

In the workshops, both administrators and educators learn how to leverage the RULER skills using two tools—the Mood Meter and the

Emotional Literacy Blueprint. The Mood Meter requires individuals to consider two important dimensions related to mood states: valence (unpleasantness/pleasantness) and arousal (low/high energy levels). In schools that have adopted our programs, Mood Meters are posted in every classroom and office, as well as throughout the school building. Administrators, teachers, and students regularly plot their moods and discussions take place to help students identify whether they are in the right frame of mind for learning and to determine what strategy would be useful to maintain, enhance, or reduce their current emotion, taking into consideration each child's personal circumstances (Brackett, Katulak, Kremenitzer, Alster, & Caruso, 2008). The Blueprint integrates scientific theory on emotional literacy with its practical applications. The function of the Blueprint is to help individuals engage in effective problem solving about past, present, and future emotion-laden experiences and challenging situations using the RULER framework. Ultimately, the Blueprint helps individuals enhance interpersonal interactions and decision making (see also Caruso & Salovey, 2004).

In summary, the design and curricula of the administrator and educator workshops achieve four primary goals for participants: (a) understand the importance of emotional literacy in everyone's lives; (b) learn the RULER model; (c) develop and apply emotional literacy skills and the program tools; and (d) gain sufficient background information and excitement about the launching of the student programs. Importantly, the learning for administrators and educators continues after participating in the initial workshops. In schools that adopt our full implementation plan, all administrators and educators attend advanced workshops involving personalized assessments and feedback and training on complex topics such as conflict management. The most progressive schools allocate a professional development coach to teachers and administrators, which maximizes one's emotional literacy development. Later in the chapter, we describe the coaching component in more detail.

Introduction of Program Concepts to Family Members

It is important to involve students' families as early as possible. The success of our emotional literacy programs is dependent, in part, on parents and other caregivers being active participants and collaborators in the program (Christenson & Harvey, 2004; Patrikakou & Weissberg, 2007). The extent to which family members are involved in their child's education from early childhood through high school strongly predicts student academic achievement (Henderson & Berla, 1994). Thus, effective programming needs to include efforts to foster the development of school-family partnerships to support and extend classroom learning to the home.

In most schools, a public meeting with parents is held just before the launching of the student programs. (Some schools opt to present the program to parents and family during parent-teacher conferences.) In this meeting, teachers or school leaders inform family members about emotional literacy, ask them to consider how the program relates to their family values, and provide guidance about how they can support the program at home. During this meeting, parents also are notified that the school is committed to developing students' emotional skills systematically, in a manner similar to the teaching of other academic topics such as math, science, and reading. Like school administrators and educators, parents learn about each of the RULER skills and the role and importance of these skills in building healthy relationships, academic performance, managing stress, and effective problem solving. Parents also are introduced to the Mood Meter and the Blueprint and are provided with materials for use in the home.

Because each of the student programs has a family component, family members also are introduced to aspects of the program that require their involvement. In the family component of the classroom programs, students become "teachers" as they introduce to family members the "feeling" words (i.e., the emotion terms they are learning as part of the lesson). The goal is for students and family members to learn about each other by sharing personal experiences related to the feeling word. The benefits to families are numerous and include family members being engaged in student learning, regular opportunities for students to have quality time with family members while reinforcing content from school lessons, and greater bonding among family members while gaining insight and understanding about the significance of each person's feelings.

Emotional Literacy in the Classroom

The next step in our implementation plan is to launch emotional literacy instruction in the classroom. Emotional literacy is foundational to academic performance and facilitates the achievement of the more distal goals of education by equipping students for life, allowing them to develop to their full potential, not only as students, but also as citizens and professionals in a fast changing society (Rivers, Lord, McLaughlin, Sandoval, Carpenter, & Brackett, 2008). Designed to enhance existing school curricula without taking time and focus from other academic areas, *Emotional Literacy in the Classroom (ELC)* programs are both field-tested and evidence-based (Brackett, Rivers, & Salovey, 2008).

ELC programs are available for students in lower elementary grades (Wilson, Brackett, DeRosier, & Rivers, 2008), upper elementary grades (Brackett, Kremenitzer, Mauer, Carpenter, Rivers, & Katulak, 2008), and middle school (Maurer & Brackett, 2004). A high school program and intensive intervention to address at-risk children are under development. Teacher training includes a one-day workshop on program concepts and pedagogy, followed by attendance at onsite modeling of program lessons by trained staff, "booster" sessions to review key elements of the program, and one-on-one meetings with program facilitators who observe lessons, provide feedback, and address questions teachers may have.

The ELC curricula aim to both enhance children's emotional literacy (i.e., RULER skills) and create an optimal learning environment that promotes academic, social, and personal effectiveness. All of the curricula are language-based and designed to integrate seamlessly into all subject areas such as history, language arts, science, math, art, and music. Teachers introduce students to an array of feeling words using a series of steps that encourage differentiation of instruction and address each student's unique thinking and learning style. (In all programs, the teacher introduces a new feeling word every other week throughout the school year.) The feeling words were selected from a systematic and exhaustive review of research on basic emotions (e.g., joy, sadness, anger), more complex, self-evaluative emotions (e.g., shame, pride, embarrassment), and other, emotion-laden terms that describe motivational and relationship states (e.g., empowerment, loneliness, alienation).

The activities represented by the steps are highly interactive and engage students in a creative, multifaceted approach that incorporates multiple modes of instruction, including personalized and integrated learning, divergent thinking, active problem-solving, parent-student interactions, and creative writing. The complexity and number of steps in each program vary as a function of students' cognitive, emotional, and social development. Below is a brief description of the five steps in the upper elementary program (Brackett, Maurer, Rivers, Carpenter, Elbertson, et al., 2008):

- *Step 1: Personal Association.* Teachers introduce feeling words in a way that relates to each student's existing knowledge base.
- *Step 2: Academic and Real World Link.* Teachers use feeling words to facilitate students' understanding of course materials and current events, as well as students' abilities to evaluate how emotions influence the way people and groups think and behave.
- *Step 3: School-Home Partnership.* Students become teachers as they introduce feeling words to their family members with the goal of sharing personal experiences.
- *Step 4: Creative Connection.* Students move away from a literal interpretation of emotions by portraying feeling words (and their relation to school subjects and real-world situations) through artistic drawings and dramatic performances.
- *Step 5: Strategy-Building Session.* Student-driven discussions take place which revolve around effective strategies that students and their peers can use to express and regulate emotions in order to achieve their goals.

Special content teachers support the implementation of ELC by exploring ways emotional literacy can be extended into art, music, and physical education classes, among other subject areas such as design and technology. In art, students discuss how the feeling of *elation* might be expressed using color, shape, and texture and then create sculptures or drawings to represent the word. Students also could design a key chain that resembles a particular emotion. In music, students might create or find a melody that elicits a particular feeling such as *fearlessness* or write the lyrics to a song to emphasize that feeling. Emotions also influence performance in sports. Unregulated anger often leads to violent outbursts and player penalties, whereas joy resulting from winning a game tends to promote team cohesion. Thus, the very nature of a physical education teacher's job offers "teachable moments" for emotional literacy skill development.

With time and practice, emotional literacy becomes part of the daily routine of the classroom and the school. Morning meetings using the Mood

Meter help teachers and students to identify the feelings they are bringing to the classroom and to select effective strategies to modify these feelings in order to achieve the learning goals for the day. The Blueprint is employed to enhance students' and teachers' ability to handle specific emotionally charged incidents, including bullying and problems associated with personal responsibility. The ELC program, therefore, is the vehicle by which students:

- Learn to recognize and label their own and others' emotions and behavior;
- Understand and analyze the causes and consequences of their own emotions as well as those of historical figures, literary characters, friends, and family members;
- Express and communicate emotional experiences effectively in their writing and in social situations; and
- Develop self-regulation strategies to lead a productive and purposeful life, build trusting relationships, and resolve conflict successfully.

In these ways, emotional literacy helps schools to simultaneously meet national educational goals and educate the "whole child."

Training of Program Coaches and Professional Development Coaches

Our classroom programs will have the intended impact only when implemented properly. Initial training on the programs provides teachers with a review of the RULER model of emotional literacy, knowledge of how emotional literacy impacts student development, and initial instruction on how to integrate the program steps into existing curricula.

Learning a new program within the scope of a single day does not provide sufficient training for long-lasting sustainable results, however (cf. Miller, 1998). According to the National Staff Development Council (NSDC, 2001), the best professional development is on-going, collaborative, and reflective. Yet, schools provide limited days for professional development and offer few opportunities for accountability and assessing the quality of implementation for most initiatives. For these reasons, Emotionally Literate Schools incorporates into its implementation plan program coaches and professional development coaches.

Program Coaches. Trained experts in the delivery of our programs, program coaches ensure that teachers receive the support they need to teach the ELC curricula as designed. Program coaches provide classroom teachers with observation-based, individualized coaching sessions to support the proper instruction of the ELC programs in a private, non-evaluative manner. Based on evidence-based coaching techniques, Program coaches work with teachers to identify and leverage implementation successes (rather than failures) and to enhance enthusiasm for and commitment to the ELC programs (Biswas-Diener & Dean, 2007). Generally, program coaches are usually trained within schools to build capacity.

In our model (Holzer, Brackett, & Katulak, 2008), program coaches meet with teachers five times throughout the school year. In the sessions, they provide teachers with constructive feedback, resources, and tools to ensure proper program implementation. The first session focuses primarily on relationship building, allowing the program coach and teacher to get to know one another and to establish trust. In the following sessions, program coaches observe small portions of lessons, review lesson sheets and student work, and offer constructive feedback. Teachers also have the opportunity to reflect on and express their successes and frustrations with various aspects of the program, including its theoretical underpinnings, the program steps, the Mood Meter, and use of the Blueprint. The final session provides closure to the relationship and allows teachers to both evaluate the process and reflect on the experience of the program as a whole.

In between regular contacts with program coaches, teachers can access online resources through the website developed by the program developers (www.ei-schools.org). The website offers up-to-date resources and online professional learning communities for the effective implementation of the ELC programs. For example, teachers have the opportunity to share lesson plan ideas, organized by grade level and word categories. The website also features examples of stellar student work, sample teacher lesson plans, and video clips of veteran teachers and program developers conducting model lessons.

Professional Development Coaches. Schools that adopt the full Emotionally Literate Schools model recognize that professional development for teachers and administrators requires consistent commitment and ongoing support. Our Emotional Literacy Coaching Program provides this support by meeting educators at their individual readiness stage (Patti, Stern, Brackett,

Caruso, & Martin, 2008). In the program, certified coaches work with administrators and teachers ("coachees") to both develop and apply emotional literacy skills as they relate to each individual's professional goals.

The coaching model draws from well-established coaching practices (e.g., Ting & Scisco, 2006) and several theories, including emotional intelligence (Mayer & Salovey, 1997), emotional literacy (Brackett & Rivers, 2008), motivational theory (Herzberg, 2003; Thomas, 2002), choice theory (Glasser & Dotson, 1998), intentional change theory (Boyatzis, 2006), and self-psychology (Kohut, 1971). Each session harnesses the coachee's intrinsic motivation to achieve personal goals, feel competent, and find meaning in work. The importance of taking personal responsibility for change to occur is at the core of the model, as is the development of emotional literacy.

The coaching process includes six sessions, at regular intervals, lasting approximately four months. A series of assessments, including emotional literacy, personality, and school climate, taken in advance of the first session, serve as the anchor for the coaching program. Initial sessions focus on developing the relationship of coach and client, and helping the client to create a professional vision—a way to look forward in her career with meaning and purpose. Throughout the process, the coach helps the client create and pursue short-term and long-term career goals by using personally-tailored strategies developed in the sessions. The Mood Meter and Blueprint also serve as connecting threads through all sessions.

The overarching goal of the coaching program is to help teachers and leaders achieve their vision and enhance their professional practice through goal setting and skill building. Ultimately, educators who both develop emotional literacy skills and take responsibility to grow professionally positively support the school community—they create a peaceful and emotionally safe space for adults to teach and children to learn.

Sustainability Phase

The Sustainability Phase is comprised of the last two action steps in our implementation plan: (7) Program Evaluation and Adaptation and (8) Preparation of Master Trainers. In this phase, visible changes in school climate are expected, schools gradually become independent from the program developers, and sustainable, positive effects are expected.

Program Evaluation and Adaptation

Monitoring the progress and impact of the programs in a school or district is an integral part of the implementation process. This can be done informally or formally, depending on the goals of the school or district. Recall, *Emotionally Literate Schools* is designed to be a multi-year initiative, and effects are expected to be more evident over time as the programs become integrated into all aspects of school culture.

Informal Evaluations. Feedback from administrators, teachers, staff, parents, students, and outside observers throughout the implementation of the programs provides important information to assess the attitudes and perceived quality of the programs, as well as to guide modifications to ensure continuous improvement and positive effects. This can be accomplished by administering surveys, as well as by conducting interviews with these stakeholders. For example, changes in students' attitudes, behaviors, and engagement are excellent sources of data about the progress and impact of the programs. Each program also has its own quality assurance measures that examine both implementation quality and impact of the programs.

Formal Evaluations. Another way of monitoring the implementation of the programs is through scientific research. To conduct this type of evaluation, a school or district generally works with a team of researchers from a university. The purpose of a formal evaluation is to obtain empirical evidence that the program is having the intended impact. Formal evaluation provides specific feedback on program delivery and what changes are produced in various stakeholders.

In our own formal evaluations, we employ a multi-method approach, including surveys, observer ratings, academic records, attendance records, and assessments of emotional literacy skills. For example, in one experimental study conducted in our laboratory, students in fifth- and sixth-grade classrooms randomly assigned to integrate our emotional literacy programs into existing curricula had higher academic grades in writing and science, and better work habits (e.g., followed directions) than students in the standard-of-care classrooms (Brackett, Rivers, & Salovey, 2008). This research provided empirical support for the theory underlying the program—emotional literacy instruction contributes to academic and social effectiveness. Currently, we are studying the effectiveness of *Emotionally Literate Schools* in changing the culture of seventy schools in one large district using a cluster-randomized control design.

Preparation of Master Trainers

Schools ultimately want to develop the internal capacity to sustain and enhance effective program implementation. For this reason, *Emotionally Literate Schools* has a series of Master Training Programs. Master trainings generally occur after all of the programs have been implemented and evaluated, and adaptations have been made. However, in larger districts, master trainings may occur earlier in the implementation process to expedite rollout of the programs.

Master trainers are a select group of individuals from each school or district who receive additional training to become proficient at delivering one or more of our programs. These individuals work with the program developers, steering committee, and classroom teachers to maintain the initiative and provide ongoing professional development. We look for individuals who model emotional literacy skills, possess leadership skills, and who are recommended highly by colleagues.

Each Master Training Program involves multiple days of advanced training followed by an apprenticeship, internship, and supervision period. The procedures and criteria for certification vary from program to program, but generally entail live or videotaped observations, performance evaluations, and recommendations from colleagues. It is in this phase that the *inter*vention transitions gradually into an *intra*vention, such that the school or district sustains the programs independent of the program developer team. Full integration of *Emotionally Literate Schools* typically requires eighteen to thirty-six months or more (Hord, Rutherford, Huling-Austin, & Hall, 1987).

CONCLUSION

Psychologists and educators have discovered scientifically what Aristotle and Dewey knew instinctively: emotional skills impact our success at home, in school, and in society. *Emotionally Literate Schools* offers a comprehensive approach to a "whole" child and adult education by offering a set of theoretically grounded programs and curricula for all stakeholders involved in the education of children, including a three-phase implementation plan to ensure lasting results and sustainability.

In the *Readiness Phase*, the entire school community prepares for implementation. Here, school leaders and stakeholders are introduced to program concepts and the benefits that can be expected, an initial commitment is made, and a steering committee is formed to help drive the initiative. The *Implementation Phase* begins with the professional development training for all school leaders, educators, and staff. Next, parents are informed of the new program, they learn how it will affect their child and community, and they are invited to help their child by reinforcing emotional literacy concepts at home. Teachers then introduce the classroom programs to students. Bearing in mind future sustainability, program coaches and professional development coaches are trained to help students and educators get the maximum benefits from the programs—and to turn these new emotional techniques into classroom reinforced habits.

Finally, the *Sustainability Phase* involves an evaluation of all programs to determine if any adaptations are necessary to improve implementation, and the preparation of master trainers who work with the program developers, steering committee, and classroom teachers to both maintain the initiative and provide ongoing professional development.

Traditionally, policy makers have indoctrinated educators to separate emotion from academics, yet in doing so schools have done a disservice to students and educators. While the scientific evidence supporting emotional literacy is new and quickly accumulating, the ideas behind it are shared wisdom among our nation's best educators. Both Aristotle (nearly three millennia ago) and John Dewey (last century) made eloquent pleas for the education of the whole child (Kristjánsson, 2007). *Emotionally Literate Schools* takes the best aspects of classical education and combines it with rigorous scientific evidence. The result, when applied as proposed, is a whole-school approach that will help children and educators maximize their potential socially, emotionally, and academically.

REFERENCES

Agostin, R.M., & Bain, S.K. (1997). Predicting early school success with development and social skills screeners. *Psychology in the Schools, 34*, 219–228.

Baker, J.A. (1999). Teacher-student interaction in urban at-risk classrooms: Differential behavior, relationship quality, and student satisfaction with school. *Elementary School Journal, 100*, 57–70.

Biswas-Diener, R., & Dean, B. (2007). *Positive psychology coaching: Putting the science of happiness to work for your clients*. Hoboken, NJ: John Wiley & Sons.

Boyatzis, R.E. (2006). An overview of intentional change from a complexity perspective. *Journal of Management Development, 25,* 607–623.

Brackett, M.A., & Caruso, D.R. (2007a). *Emotional literacy for administrators.* Cary, NC: SELmedia, Inc.

Brackett, M.A., & Caruso, D.R. (2007b). *Emotional literacy for educators.* Cary, NC: SELmedia, Inc.

Brackett, M.A., & Geher, G. (2006). Measuring emotional intelligence: Paradigmatic shifts and common ground. In J. Ciarrochi, J.P. Forgas, & J.D. Mayer (Eds.), *Emotional intelligence and everyday life* (2nd ed.) (pp. 27–50). New York: Psychology Press.

Brackett, M.A., Katulak, N.A., Kremenitzer, J P., Alster, B., & Caruso, D.R. (2008). Emotionally literate teaching. In M.A. Brackett, J.P. Kremenitzer, M. Maurer, M.D. Carpenter, S.E. Rivers, & N.A. Katulak (Eds.), *Emotional literacy in the classroom: Upper elementary.* Port Chester, NY: National Professional Resources.

Brackett, M.A., Kremenitzer, J.P., Maurer, M., Carpenter, M.D., Rivers, S.E., & Katulak, N.A. (Eds.). (2008). *Emotional literacy in the classroom: Upper elementary.* Port Chester, NY: National Professional Resources.

Brackett, M. A., Maurer, M., Rivers, S. E., Carpenter, M. D., & Elbertson, N. et al. (2008). Emotional literacy in the classroom: Upper elementary curriculum. In M. A. Brackett, J. P. Kremenitzer, M. Maurer, M. D. Carpenter, S. E. Rivers, & N. A. Katulak (Eds.), *Emotional literacy in the classroom: Upper elementary.* Port Chester, NY: National Professional Resources.

Brackett, M.A., Mayer, J.D., & Warner, R.M. (2004). Emotional intelligence and its relation to everyday behavior. *Personality and Individual Differences, 36,* 1387–1402.

Brackett, M.A., Mojsa, J., Palomera, R, Reyes, R., & Salovey, P. (2008). *Emotion regulation ability, burnout, and job satisfaction among secondary school teachers.* Manuscript submitted for publication, Yale University, New Haven, CT.

Brackett, M.A., & Rivers, S.E. (in press). *Creating emotionally literate schools: How teaching emotion knowledge and skills can improve school climate and performance.* Port Chester, NY: National Professional Resources.

Brackett, M.A., Rivers, S.E., & Salovey, P. (2008). *Enhancing academic performance and social and emotional competence with emotional literacy training.* Manuscript submitted for publication, Yale University, New Haven, CT.

Brackett, M.A., Rivers, S., Shiffman, S., Lerner, N., & Salovey, P. (2006). Relating emotional abilities to social functioning: A comparison of performance and self-report measures of emotional intelligence. *Journal of Personality and Social Psychology, 91,* 780–795.

Caruso, D.R., & Salovey, P. (2004). *The emotionally intelligent manager.* San Francisco: Jossey-Bass.

Christenson, S.L., & Harvey, L.H. (2004). Family-school-peer relationships: Significance for social-emotional and academic learning. In J.E. Zins,

R.P. Weissberg, M.C. Wang, & H.J. Walberg (Eds.), *Building academic success on social and emotional learning: What does the research say?* (pp. 59–75). New York: Teachers College Press.

Cox, T., & Brockley, T. (1984). The experience and effects of stress in teachers. *British Educational Research Journal, 10,* 83–87.

Damasio, A.R. (1994). *Descartes' error: Emotion, reason, and the human brain.* New York: Grosset/Putnam.

Denham, S.A. (1998). *Emotional development in young children.* New York: Guilford Press.

Devaney, E., O'Brien, M.U., Resnik, H., Keister, S., & Weissberg, R.P. (2006). *Sustainable schoolwide social and emotional learning (SEL).* Chicago, IL: CASEL.

Dorman, J. (2003). Testing a model for teacher burnout. *Australian Journal of Educational and Developmental Psychology, 3,* 35–47.

Eisenberg, N., Fabes, R.A., Guthrie, I.K., & Reiser, M. (2000). Dispositional emotionality and regulation: Their role in predicting quality of social functioning. *Journal of Personality and Social Psychology, 78,* 136–157.

Ekman, P. (1973). *Darwin and facial expression: A century of research in review.* Oxford, England: Academic Press.

Elfenbein, H.A., & Ambady, N. (2002). Predicting workplace outcomes from the ability to eavesdrop on feelings. *Journal of Applied Psychology, 87,* 963–971.

Elias, M.J., & Kamarinos Galiotos, P. (2004). *Sustaining social-emotional learning programs: A study of the developmental course of model/flagship SEL sites.* Unpublished manuscript, Rutgers University, Piscataway, NJ.

Elias, M.J., Zins, J.E., Weissberg, R.P., Frey, K.S., Greenberg, M.T., Haynes, N.M., et al. (1997). *Promoting social and emotional learning: Guidelines for educators.* Alexandria, VA: Association for Supervision and Curriculum Development.

Fine, S.E., Izard, C.E., Mostow, A.J., Trentacosta, C.J., & Ackerman, B.P. (2003). First grade emotion knowledge as a predictor of fifth grade self-reported internalizing behaviors in children from economically disadvantaged families. *Development and Psychopathology, 15,* 331–342.

Gardner, H. (1983/1993). *Frames of mind: The theory of multiple intelligences* (10th anniversary edition). New York: Basic Books.

Gil-Olarte Marquez, P., Palomera Martin, R., & Brackett, M.A. (2006). Relating emotional intelligence to social competence and academic achievement in high school students. *Psicothema, 18,* 118–123.

Glasser, W., & Dotson, K. (1998). *Choice theory in the classroom.* New York: HarperCollins.

Greenberg, M.T., Domitrovich, C.E., Graczyk, P.A., & Zins, J.E. (2005). *The study of implementation in school-based preventive interventions: Theory, research, and practice (Volume 3).* Rockville, MD: Center for Mental Health Services, Substance Abuse and Mental Health Services Administration.

Greenberg, M.T., Weissberg, R.P., O'Brien, M.U., Zins, J.E., Fredericks, L., Resnik, H., & Elias, M.J. (2003). Enhancing school-based prevention and youth development through coordinated social, emotional, and academic learning. *American Psychologist, 58*, 466–474.

Gross, J.J. (1998). The emerging field of emotion regulation: An integrative review. *Review of General Psychology, 2*, 271–299.

Halberstadt, A.G., Denham, S.A., & Dunsmore, J.C. (2001). Affective social competence. *Social Development, 10*, 79–119.

Hawkins, J.D. (1999). Academic performance and school success: Sources and consequences. In R.P. Weissberg, T.P. Gullotta, R.L. Hampton, B.A. Ryan, & G.R. Adams (Eds.), *Enhancing children's wellness* (pp. 276–305). Thousand Oaks, CA: Sage.

Henderson, A.T., & Berla, N. (Eds.). (1994). *A new generation of evidence: The family is critical to academic achievement.* Washington, DC: Center for Law and Education.

Herzberg, F. (2003). One more time: How do you motivate employees? *Harvard Business Review, 81*, 86–96.

Holzer, A., & Brackett, M.A. (2008). *Emotional literacy in the classroom: Program coach manual.* Health, Emotion, and Behavior Laboratory, Department of Psychology, Yale University, New Haven, CT.

Hord, S.M., Rutherford, W.L., Huling-Austin, L., & Hall, G.E. (1987). *Taking charge of change.* Alexandria, VA: ASCD.

Hoy, A.W., & Hoy, W.K. (2003). *Instructional leadership: A learning centered guide.* Boston: Allyn & Bacon.

Hoy, W.K., & Tarter, C.J. (1997). *The road to open and healthy schools: A handbook for change* (Elementary ed.). Thousand Oaks, CA: Corwin Press.

Izard, C.E., Fine, S., Mostow, A., Trentacosta, C., & Campbell, J. (2002). Emotion processes in normal and abnormal development and preventive intervention. *Development and Psychopathology, 14*, 761–787.

Keltner, D., & Haidt, J. (2001). Social functions of emotions. In T.J. Mayne & G.A. Bonanno (Eds.), *Emotions: Current issues and future directions* (pp. 192–213). New York: Guilford Press.

Kindlon, D., & Thompson, M. (2000). *Raising Cain: Protecting the emotional life of boys.* New York: Ballantine Books.

Kohut, H. (1971). *The analysis of the self.* New York: International Universities Press.

Kress, J.S., & Elias, M.J. (2006). School-based social and emotional learning programs. In K.A. Renninger & I.E. Sigel (Eds.), *Handbook of child psychology* (6th ed., Vol. 4, pp. 592–618). Hoboken, NJ: John Wiley & Sons.

Kristjánsson, K. (2007). *Aristotle, emotions, and education.* Aldershot, UK: Ashgate Publishing, Limited.

Lazarus, R.S. (1991). *Emotion and adaptation.* New York: Oxford University Press.

Maslach, C., & Leiter, M.P. (1999). Teacher burnout: A research agenda. In R. Vandenberghe, A.M. Huberman, & R. Huberman (Eds.), *Understanding and preventing teacher burnout: A sourcebook of international research and practice* (pp. 295–303). Cambridge, UK: Cambridge University Press.

Maurer, M., & Brackett, M.A. (2004). *Emotional literacy in the middle school: A 6-step program to promote social, emotional, & academic learning.* Port Chester, NY: National Professional Resources.

Mayer, J.D., & Salovey, P. (1997). What is emotional intelligence? In P. Salovey & D.J. Sluyter (Eds.), *Emotional development and emotional intelligence: Educational implications* (pp. 3–34). New York: Basic Books.

Mayer, J.D., Salovey, P., & Caruso, D.R. (in press). Emotional intelligence: New ability or eclectic traits? *American Psychologist.*

Miller, E. (1998). The old model of staff development survives in a world where everything has changed. In R. Tovey (Ed.), *Professional development: Harvard education letter focus series* (Vol. 4, pp. 1–3). Cambridge, MA: Harvard College.

Mills, C.J. (2003). Characteristics of effective teachers of gifted students: Teacher background and personality styles of students. *Gifted Child Quarterly, 47,* 272–281.

Mize, J., & Ladd, G.W. (1990). A cognitive-social learning approach to skill training with low-status preschool children. *Social Competence, 26,* 388–297.

National Staff Development Council (NSCD). (2001). *Standards for staff development, revised.* Oxford, OH: NSDC.

Patrikakou, E.N., & Weissberg, R.P. (2007). School-family partnerships and children's social, emotional, and academic learning. In R. Bar-On, J.G. Maree, & M.J. Elias (Eds.), *Educating people to be emotionally intelligent* (pp. 49–61). Rondebosch, South Africa: Heinemann Educational Publishers.

Patti, J., & Tobin, J. (2006). *Smart school leaders: Leading with emotional intelligence.* Dubuque, IA: Kendall Hunt.

Patti, J., Stern, R., Brackett, M.A., Caruso, & Martin, C. (2008). *The start factor emotional literacy coaching model.* New York: Star Factor, LLC.

Payton, J.W., Graczyk, P.A., Wardlaw, D M., Bloodworth, M., Tompsett, C J., & Weissberg, R P. (2000). Social and emotional learning: A framework for promoting mental health and reducing risk behavior in children and youth. *Journal of School Health, 70,* 179–185.

Rivers, S.E., Brackett, M.A., & Salovey, P. (2007). *Emotional intelligence and its relation to social, emotional, and academic outcomes among adolescents.* Unpublished data, Yale University, New Haven, CT.

Rivers, S.E., Lord, H., McLaughlin, K.A., Sandoval, R.F., Carpenter, M.D., & Brackett, M A. (2008). Educating the whole child with emotional literacy: Promoting academic, social, and emotional competence. In M.A. Brackett, J.P. Kremenitzer, M. Maurer, M.D. Carpenter, S.E. Rivers, & N.A. Katulak (Eds.), *Emotional literacy in the classroom: Upper elementary.* Port Chester, NY: National Professional Resources.

Saarni, C. (1999). *The development of emotional competence*. New York: Guilford Press.

Salovey, P., & Mayer, J.D. (1990). Emotional intelligence. *Imagination, Cognition and Personality, 9*, 185–211.

Schaps, E., Battistich, V., & Solomon, D. (1997). School as a caring community: A key to character education. In A. Molnar (Ed.), *Ninety-sixth yearbook of the National Society for the Study of Education* (pp. 127–139). Chicago: University of Chicago Press.

Sternberg, R.J. (1985). *The triarchic mind: A new theory of human intelligence*. New York: Penguin.

Stronge, J.H. (2002). Qualities of effective teachers. *Adolescence, 37*, 868.

Sutton, R.E., & Wheatley, K.F. (2003). Teachers' emotions and teaching: A review of the literature and directions for future research. *Educational Psychology Review, 15*, 327–358.

Thomas, K.W. (2002). *Intrinsic motivation at work: Building energy and commitment*. San Francisco: Berrett-Koehler.

Ting, S., & Scisco, P. (Eds.). (2006). *The Center for Creative Leadership (CCL) handbook of coaching: A guide for the leader coach*. San Francisco: Jossey Bass.

Travers, C.J., & Cooper, C.L. (1996). *Teachers under pressure: Stress in the teaching profession*. London: Routledge.

Underwood, M.K. (2003). *Social aggression among girls*. New York: Guilford Press.

Wentzel, K.R. (2002). Are effective teachers like good parents? Teaching styles and student adjustment in early adolescence. *Child Development, 73*, 287–301.

Wilson, M.E., Brackett, M.A., DeRosier, M.E., & Rivers, S.E. (2008). *Emotional literacy in the classroom: K to 2*. Cary, NC: SELmedia, Inc.

Zins, J.E., Weissberg, R.P., Wang, M.C., & Walberg, H.J. (Eds.). (2004). *Building academic success on social and emotional learning: What does the research say?* New York: Teachers College Press.

Marc Brackett is the deputy director of the Health, Emotion, and Behavior Laboratory and head of the Emotional Intelligence Unit in the Edward Zigler Center in Child Development and Social Policy at Yale University. He is the co-developer of the RULER model of emotional literacy and the author of more than fifty scholarly publications.

Janet Patti is a former public school teacher, counselor, and administrator. Currently, she is a professor in the Department of Curriculum and Teaching at Hunter College. Dr. Patti is the author or co-author of many articles and books, including *Smart School Leaders: Leading with Emotional Intelligence* (2006) and *The Star Factor Coaching Model* (2005).

Robin Stern is a licensed psychoanalyst with twenty years' experience developing programs for personal and professional growth. She is on the faculty of the Summer Principals Academy, Teachers College, Columbia University, and is the co-author of many books and articles, including *The Star Factor Coaching Model*. Her recent book, *The Gaslight Effect*, is about psychological manipulation.

Susan E. Rivers is an associate research scientist at Yale University. Her research focuses on emotional literacy and its role in optimal functioning. In addition to publishing several articles and chapters on these topics, she is the co-author of school-based emotional literacy curricula and conducts research to evaluate their effectiveness.

Nicole A. Elbertson is a research associate and the coordinator of the Health, Emotion, and Behavior Laboratory in the Department of Psychology at Yale University. Nicole works primarily on the development and implementation of emotional literacy programs and the dissemination of information and research related to the programs.

Christian Chisholm is a sophomore in Davenport College at Yale University. His interests include education policy, evolutionary biology, and international development. At Yale, he is a member of two debating societies, tutors at a local elementary school, rows with Lightweight Crew, and works in the Health, Emotion, and Behavior Laboratory.

Peter Salovey, Dean of Yale College at Yale University, is professor of psychology, management, and of epidemiology and public health at Yale. As director of the Health, Emotion, and Behavior Laboratory, his research has focused on the psychological significance and function of human emotions and the application of social psychological principles to promote healthy behavior.

CHAPTER 16

Developing Emotional, Social, and Cognitive Intelligence Competencies in Managers and Leaders in Educational Settings

Richard E. Boyatzis

Various combinations of emotional, social, and cognitive intelligence competencies have been shown to predict effectiveness in leadership and management throughout the world (Boyatzis, 2008). Although billions of dollars are spent each year in attempts to develop these competencies, and in graduate management education to prepare people for these roles, little systematic research of the actual changes resulting has been done to show what works and what does not. In this chapter I will address this gap by offering a model that has been tested in more than twenty-two studies of twenty-five to sixty-five year-olds. The model will illustrate that sustained improvement in these competencies, which are so important to effective leadership and management, can occur, but it involves a change in how we think about sustained, desired change and a modification in our methods.

Specifically, using twenty years of longitudinal studies of people twenty-five to sixty-five at the Weatherhead School of Management (Boyatzis, Stubbs, & Taylor, 2002), supported by other Model Programs from the Consortium for Research on Emotional Intelligence in Organizations (Cherniss & Adler, 2000), and a review of other published, longitudinal, multi-trait studies, I will show that (1) most approaches to training or management education do not affect these vital competencies; (2) some studies show significant improvements in competencies that sustain at least seven years; and (3) to understand the change process that works requires both Intentional Change Theory and concepts from complexity theory.

While billions are spent trying to develop competencies each year, the results have been less than satisfactory. This does not even measure the millions of person hours spent in pursuit of competency development through performance reviews, training programs, coaching sessions, or workshops and courses in graduate or executive education. Some conclude from all this that effective leaders, managers, and professionals cannot be developed. This conclusion leads to a belief that effective leaders, managers, and professionals are either born that way or that people should just focus on their current, evident strengths and find jobs, careers, and organizational settings in which they will be effective (Buckingham, 2002).

This chapter will bring a message of hope, by building on earlier longitudinal studies (Boyatzis, Cowen, & Kolb, 1995; Boyatzis, Stubbs, & Taylor, 2002). The competencies related to effective leaders, managers, and professionals can be developed in adults, but it is not easy. As the many longitudinal studies reviewed and reported here show, even dramatic success in developing these competencies can be eroded by destructive organizational practices.

WHAT DO PEOPLE NEED TO BE EFFECTIVE?

To be an effective leader, manager, or professional, a person needs the ability to use knowledge and to make things happen. These can be called competencies, which Boyatzis defines as, "the underlying characteristics of a person that lead to or cause effective and outstanding performance" (1982, p. 14). A set of competencies has been shown to cause or predict outstanding leader, manager, or professional performance in the literature (Boyatzis, 1982; Druskat, Mount, & Sala, 2005; Howard & Bray, 1988; *Journal of Management Development*, 2008, 2009; Kotter, 1982; Luthans, Hodgetts, & Rosenkrantz, 1988). Several conceptual integrations or meta-analytic syntheses have provided a summary of other studies (Goleman, 1998; Spencer & Spencer, 1993). Compiling these findings and summaries, it can be said that the important competencies fall into three clusters: (1) cognitive intelligence competencies, such as systems thinking or pattern recognition; (2) emotional intelligence competencies, or intrapersonal abilities, such as adaptability, emotional self-control, emotional self-awareness, positive outlook, and achievement orientation; and (3) social intelligence competencies, or interpersonal abilities, such as empathy, organizational awareness, inspirational leadership, influence, coaching and mentoring, conflict management, and teamwork. In addition, there are several cognitive capabilities that appear to be threshold competencies from the research cited above. That is, they are needed to be adequate in performance, but using more of them does not necessarily lead to outstanding or effective performance. Given research to date, these would include knowledge (technical and functional), deductive reasoning, and quantitative reasoning.

DO PEOPLE DEVELOP COMPETENCIES?

Decades of research on the effects of psychotherapy (Hubble, Duncan, & Miller, 1999), self-help programs (Kanfer & Goldstein, 1991), cognitive behavior therapy (Barlow, 1988), training programs (Morrow, Jarrett, & Rupinski, 1997), and education (Pascarella & Terenzini, 1991) have shown that people can change their behavior, moods, and self-image. But most of the studies focused on a single characteristic, such as maintenance of sobriety or reduction in a specific anxiety. But few studies show sustained improvements in the sets of desirable behavior that lead to outstanding performance.

In companies or government agencies, the development of competencies is often relegated to the HR department. Executives all too often are willing to send people to programs, but not necessarily to focus on their development. In graduate management schools, there is a comparable disavowal of responsibility for development. Many faculty members still see competency development as the responsibility of the career placement office or adjuncts hired to conduct non-credit workshops. So in universities, there is a double challenge. First, there is the question as to whether or not the methods yield graduates who can and will use the competencies to be effective. Second, are these competencies integrated into the curriculum? Is it a main element in the program or school's mission? If faculty adopt the challenge of developing "the whole person," competency development would be as fundamental to objectives and methods as accounting (Boyatzis, Cowen, & Kolb, 1995).

Outcome assessment in higher education asks, "What are our students learning?" The early results from such studies were sobering, with only one clear conclusion—students graduating from our colleges were older than they were when they entered. Evidence was reported of knowledge acquisition, improvement in competencies, including critical thinking, and shifts in motivation, but these were far less frequent than was predicted or expected (Mentkowski & Associates, 2000; Pascarella & Terenzini, 1991).

As of the early 1990s, only a few management schools had conducted student-change outcome studies that compared their graduates to their students at the time of entry into the program. Today, many schools have conducted other types of outcome studies, namely studies of their alumni or studies with employers and prospective employers. Some schools have examined the student-change from specific courses (Bigelow, 1991). Student-change outcome studies have been a focus in undergraduate programs (Astin, 1993; Mentkowski & Associates, 2000; Pascarella & Terenzini, 1991), but still relatively little has been documented about the effects of graduate programs on experienced managers and leaders.

This leaves the major question: Can MBAs and participants in executive education develop competencies that are related to outstanding managerial, leadership, and professional performance? And the related question is, Can people engaged in management training develop the competencies related to outstanding leadership, management, and professional performance?

IMPACT OF MANAGEMENT EDUCATION AND TRAINING

The "honeymoon effect" of typical training programs might start with improvement immediately following the program, but within months it drops precipitously (Campbell, Dunnette, Lawler, & Weick, 1970). Only fifteen programs were found in a global search of the literature by the Consortium on Research on Emotional Intelligence in Organizations to improve emotional intelligence (Cherniss & Adler, 2000). Surprisingly, only five of them are still being offered or delivered. Most of them showed impact on job outcomes, such as number of new businesses started, or life outcomes, such as finding a job or satisfaction, which are the ultimate purpose of development efforts. But showing an impact on outcomes, while desired, may also blur *how* the change actually occurs. Furthermore, when a change has been noted, a question about the sustainability of the changes is raised because of the relatively short time periods studied.

The few published studies examining improvement of more than one of these competencies show an overall improvement of about 10 percent in emotional intelligence abilities three to eighteen months following training (cited in Boyatzis, 2008). More recent meta-analytic studies and utility analyses confirm that significant changes can and do occur, but not with the impact that the level of investment would lead us to expect, nor with many types of training (Morrow, Jarrett, & Rupinski, 1997). The author does not claim this is an exhaustive review, but suggestive of the percentage improvement as a rough approximation of the real impact.

The results appear no better from standard MBA programs, where there is no attempt to enhance emotional intelligence abilities. Even before the humbling Porter and McKibbin (1988) report showed that MBA graduates were not fulfilling the needs of employers or the promise of the schools, the American Assembly of Collegiate Schools of Business started a series of outcome assessment studies in 1978. They showed faculty to be effective in producing significant improvement of students with regard to some abilities (Boyatzis, Stubbs, & Taylor, 2002). Studies reviewed in Boyatzis (2008) and Boyatzis, Stubbs, and Taylor (2002) showed that students had significantly increased on 40 to 50 percent of the competencies assessed in two MBA programs, while another study reviewed reported that students in the two MBA programs in their sample had significantly increased on 44 percent of the variables assessed.

But they also decreased significantly on 10 percent of the variables in these studies. When the overall degree of improvement in these abilities was calculated (Goleman, Boyatzis, & McKee, 2002), these studies showed about a 2 percent increase in emotional and social intelligence competencies in the one to two

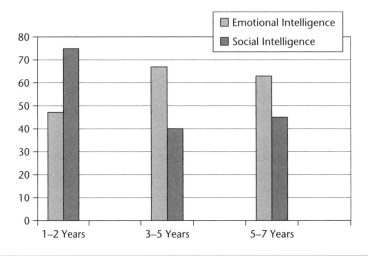

Figure 16.1. Percentage Improvement of Emotional and Social Intelligence Competencies from Behavioral Measurement of Different Groups of MBA Graduates Taking the LEAD Course[1]

NOTE: The first bar in each case indicates impact of company and government training programs three to eighteen months after training on multiple emotional intelligence competencies.

The second bar indicates impact of a variety of above average MBA programs

[1]For "n" and description of measures, see Boyatzis, Stubbs, and Taylor (2002) AMLE article; comparison references are listed in Goleman, Boyatzis, and McKee (2002). This figure first appeared in Goleman, Boyatzis, & McKee, *Primal Leadership* (2002).

years students were in the MBA programs. In fact, they showed a gain of 4 percent in emotional intelligence (i.e., self-awareness and self-management abilities), but a *decrease* of 3 percent in social intelligence (i.e., social awareness and relationship management) (Boyatzis, Renio-McKee, & Thompson, 1995). Studies from another two highly ranked business schools behavior showed similar results, only improvements of 2 percent in the skills of emotional intelligence.

To test the possibility of competency development, a series of longitudinal studies underway at the Weatherhead School of Management of Case Western Reserve University have shown that people can change on this complex set of competencies that distinguish outstanding leaders, managers, and professionals. And the improvement lasted for years. A visual comparison of the percentage improvement in behavioral measures of emotional intelligence from different samples is shown in Figure 16.1. The one- to two-year data was from the full-time MBA cohorts. The three- to five-year data was from the part-time MBA cohorts. The five- to seven-year data was from two-thirds of the part-time MBA cohorts (the same as assessed for the years three to five sample). The latter were interviewed two years following their graduation. Again, critical incident interviews were conducted to solicit work samples. The audiotapes were coded by the same reliable coders as the other samples. The behavioral code used for all of these samples, from 1990 through 1996, and the two-year follow-up sample, were the same. When coders were coding the graduating samples (or the two-year follow-up sample), they had to recode the entering (or in the case of the two-year follow-up, recoding was done on the entering and graduating interviews) to ensure minimal interference from coder interpretation drift, that is, a shift over time in interpretation of the codebook. Again, inter-rater reliability was calculated each year of these longitudinal studies.

MBA students (average age twenty-seven at entry into the program) showed dramatic changes on videotaped and audiotaped behavioral samples and questionnaire measures of these competencies as a result of the competency-based, outcome oriented MBA program implemented in 1990 (Boyatzis, Stubbs, & Taylor, 2002). The coding of these audiotapes of work samples through critical incidents and videotapes of simulations were accomplished by advanced doctoral students with an average inter-rater reliability of 89 percent on a behavioral code for the competencies (Boyatzis, 1998). The code was developed from earlier inductive studies of the behavioral indicators that distinguished outstanding from average performing managers (Boyatzis, 1982; Goleman, 1998; Spencer & Spencer, 1993).

The positive effects of this program were not limited to MBAs. In a longitudinal study of four classes completing the Professional Fellows Program (i.e., an executive education program at the Weatherhead School of Management), Ballou, Bowers, Boyatzis, and Kolb (1999) showed that these forty-five to fifty-five year-old professionals and executives improved on Self-Confidence, Leadership, Helping, Goal Setting, and Action skills. These were 67 percent of the emotional intelligence competencies assessed in this study.

In the case of the MBAs, the entire program was organized around the competencies and values in 1990. Most courses required experiential activity in the form of team projects or field work. Career development activities, clubs, service work, and other program design changes contributed to the reinforcement of the message about competency development.

For the Professional Fellows Program, the leadership course was one-fourth of the program activity. In addition, the remaining program components were all designed to reinforce their group formation and exploration of their Learning Plan. Once the year-long formal program was over, they all were inducted into the Society of Fellows. This was a self-directed learning society. Approximately two-thirds of the Fellows ending the program continued to be involved in development activities in the following years through the Fellows Society. About one-third of the Fellows were heavily involved in the years following their completion of the program.

SUSTAINED DESIRED CHANGE IS INTENTIONAL

What the studies referred to above have shown is that adults learn what they want to. While this sounds trite, the important distinction is that often people engage in learning or development activities for other reasons. That is, they attend a program to get a degree, not necessarily to learn something. They attend a training program because they think their boss wants them to do it or it is expected by the corporate human resources department. In this way, it appears that most, if not all, sustainable behavioral change is intentional. *Sustained desired change is an intentional change in an aspect of who you are (for example, the Real) or who you want to be (for example, the Ideal), or both.*

Another feature of this theory is that most change is best understood through complexity theory (Boyatzis, 2006). A preliminary concept is that most of the time the process of sustained, desired change unfolds in discontinuous and non-linear ways. This was called punctuated equilibrium by Gersick (1991). The nature of the non-linear change and the suddenness of the emergence of the various stages may be easier to notice when observing sustained, desired change through Intentional Change Theory (ICT) on changes in teams, organizations, or communities (Amis, Slack, & Hinings, 2004).

The process of intentional change is graphically shown in Figure 16.2 (Boyatzis, 2006; Boyatzis & McKee, 2005; Goleman, Boyatzis, & McKee, 2002). The description and explanation of the process in this chapter is organized around five points of discovery. A person might begin intentional change at any point in the process, but it will often begin when the person

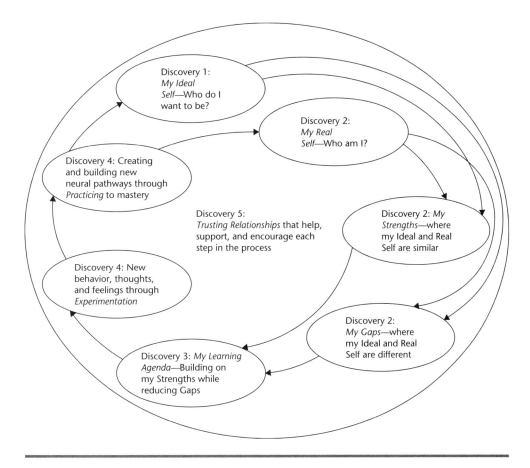

Figure 16.2. Boyatzis' Intentional Change Theory (Boyatzis, 2001, 2006)

experiences a discontinuity, the associated epiphany or a moment of awareness and a sense of urgency. This theory first was described in several articles in the late 1960s (Kolb & Boyatzis, 1970).

This model was used to design a course used as part of the degree, non-degree, and company-specific programs at the Weatherhead School of Management. Although experimentation and research into the various components have resulted in refinement of these components and the model as discussed in this paper, a detailed description of the course can be found in Boyatzis (1994). Again, the course was the stimulus and source of the students' learning plans. But it took the remainder of the program to enable them to work on the learning plans and practice the desired changes. Without the surrounding system of the program (including both formal program requirements and informal in-school and out-of-school activities), the desired changes could not be practiced and internalized. This course was taught by twenty-three different faculty over the eighteen years of the research studies. It is believed, therefore, that the results could not be attributed to one faculty member, which is often a problem with developmental programs. In addition, the same course is now a required part of most of the degree programs at ESADE in Barcelona, Spain. Although they have not completed sufficient outcome studies to date to show the comparable impact, they are underway. ESADE has a dramatically different student base than Weatherhead School of Management has, consisting mostly of Spanish and Latin American students with some Europeans currently working in Spanish companies. At least seven different faculty are teaching the course at ESADE. Faculty from other universities in the United States, Europe, and Malaysia have used this course design.

The First Discovery: My Personal Vision

The last twenty years has revealed literature supporting the power of positive imaging or visioning in sports psychology (Loehr & Schwartz, 2003), meditation, and biofeedback research, and other psycho-physiological research. It is believed that the potency of focusing one's thoughts on the desired end-state or condition is driven by the emotional components of the brain (Boyatzis & McKee, 2005). Visioning or positive imagery works through creating new neural circuits that the person can then use later when wanting to engage the related actions (Bennis & Nanus, 1985). They also work by arousing hope (Curry, Snyder, Cook, Ruby, & Rehm, 1997), which in turn stimulates the parasympathetic nervous system (PSNS) and its resulting increase in cognitive openness, cognitive power, and flexibility. In this aroused state, a person can grow new neural tissue, referred to earlier as neurogenesis (Erikson, Perfilieva, Bjork-Eriksson, Alborn, Nordburg, Peterson, & Gage, 1998), and improve the healing powers of engaging a person's immune system (Manniz, Chadukar, Rybicki, Tusek, & Solomon, 1999).

This research indicates that we can access and engage deep emotional commitment and psychic energy if we engage our passions and conceptually catch our dreams in our Ideal Self-image. It is an anomaly that we know the importance of consideration of the Ideal Self, and yet often, when engaged in a change or learning process, we skip over the clear formulation or articulation of our Ideal Self-Image. If a parent, spouse, boss, or teacher tells us something that should be different, he or she is telling us about the person *he or she* wants us to be. As adults, we often allow ourselves to be anesthetized to our dreams and lose sight of our deeply felt Ideal Self.

The Second Discovery: My Personal Balance Sheet

The awareness of the current self, the person others see and with whom they interact, is elusive. For normal reasons, the human psyche protects itself from the automatic "intake" and conscious realization of all information about ourselves. These ego-defense mechanisms serve to protect us. They also conspire to delude us into an image of who we are that feeds on itself, becomes self-perpetuating, and eventually may become dysfunctional (Goleman, 1985).

For a person to truly consider changing a part of himself or herself, he or she must have a sense of what he or she values and wants to keep. These areas in which your Real Self and Ideal Self are consistent or congruent can be considered Strengths. Likewise, to consider what you want to preserve about yourself involves admitting aspects of yourself that you wish to change or adapt in some manner. Areas in which your Real Self and Ideal Self are not consistent can be considered Weaknesses.

The sources of increased awareness often come from developing the comparison of the Ideal and Real selves (Higgins, 1991). Acknowledging discrepancies can be a powerful motivator for change. But as this line of research by Higgins has shown, the distinction between the person's Ideal Self and his or her "Ought" Self become an important additional discovery. The Ought Self is the accumulation of the Ideal Self for a person that others around him or her impose.

All too often, people explore growth or development by focusing on the "gaps" or weaknesses. Organizational training programs and managers conducting annual reviews often make the same mistake. There is an assumption that we can "leave well enough alone" and get to the areas that need work. It is no wonder that many of these programs or procedures intended to help a person develop result in the individual feeling battered, beleaguered, and bruised, not helped, encouraged, motivated, or guided.

The second discovery can be achieved by finding and using multiple sources for feedback about your Ideal Self, Real Self, Strengths, and Weaknesses (Taylor, 2006). The sources of insight into your Real Self can include systematically collecting information from others, such as 360-degree feedback, currently considered fashionable in organizations. Other sources of insight into your Real Self, Strengths, and Weaknesses may come from behavioral feedback through videotaped or audiotaped interactions, such as collected in assessment centers. Various psychological tests can help you determine or make explicit inner aspects of your Real Self, such as values, philosophy, traits, motives, and such.

Sources for insight into your Ideal Self are more personal and more elusive than those for the Real Self. Various exercises and tests can help by making explicit various dreams or aspirations you have for the future (Boyatzis & McKee, 2005; McKee, Boyatzis, & Johnston, 2008). Talking with close friends or mentors can help. Allowing yourself to think about your desired future, not merely your prediction of your most likely future, is the biggest obstacle. These conversations and explorations must take place in psychologically safe surroundings.

The Third Discovery: Mindfulness Through a Learning Agenda

The third discovery in intentional change is development of an agenda and focusing on the desired future (Boyatzis & McKee, 2005; McKee, Boyatzis, & Johnston, 2008). While performance at work or happiness in life may be the eventual consequence of our efforts, a learning agenda focuses on development. A learning orientation arouses a positive belief in one's capability and the hope of improvement. This results in people setting personal standards of performance, rather than "normative" standards that merely mimic what others have done. Meanwhile, a performance orientation evokes anxiety and doubts about whether or not we can change (Chen et al, 2000).

As part of one of the longitudinal studies at the Weatherhead School of Management, Leonard (2008) showed that MBAs who set goals desiring to change on certain competencies, changed significantly on those competencies as compared to other MBAs. Previous goal-setting literature had shown how goals affected certain changes on specific competencies

(Locke & Latham, 1990), but has not established evidence of behavioral change on a comprehensive set of competencies that constitute emotional intelligence.

A major threat to effective goal setting and planning is that people are already busy and cannot add anything else to their lives. In such cases, the only success with self-directed change and learning occurs if people can determine what to say "no" to and stop some current activities in their lives to make room for new activities.

Another potential challenge or threat is the development of a plan that calls for a person to engage in activities different from his or her preferred learning style or learning flexibility (Kolb, 1984). In such cases, a person commits to action steps in a plan that requires a learning style that is not his or her preference or not within his or her flexibility. When this occurs, a person becomes demotivated and often stops the activities, or becomes impatient and decides that the goals are not worth the effort.

The Fourth Discovery: Metamorphosis

The fourth discovery is to experiment and practice desired changes. Acting on the plan and toward the goals involves numerous activities. These are often made in the context of experimenting with new behavior. Typically following a period of experimentation, the person practices the new behaviors in actual settings within which he or she wishes to use them, such as at work or at home. During this part of the process, self-directed change and learning begin to look like a "continuous improvement" process.

To develop or learn new behavior, the person must find ways to learn more from current or ongoing experiences. That is, the experimentation and practice do not always require attending "courses" or a new activity. It may involve trying something different in a current setting, reflecting on what occurs, and experimenting further in this setting. Sometimes, this part of the process requires finding and using opportunities to learn and change. People may not even think they have changed until they have tried new behavior in a work or "real-world" setting.

Dreyfus (2008) studied managers of scientists and engineers who were considered superior performers. Once she documented that they used considerably more of certain competencies than did their less-effective counterparts, she pursued how they developed some of those competencies. One of the distinguishing competencies was Group Management, also called Team Building or Teamwork. She found that many of these middle-aged managers had first experimented with team building in high school and college, in sports, clubs, and living groups. Later, when they became "bench scientists and engineers" working on problems in relative isolation, they still pursued the use and practice of this competency in activities outside of work. They practiced team building and group management in social and community organizations, such as 4-H Clubs and professional associations in planning conferences and such.

The experimentation and practice are most effective when they occur in conditions in which the person feels safe (Kolb & Boyatzis, 1970). This sense of psychological safety creates an atmosphere in which the person can try new behavior, perceptions, and thoughts with relatively less risk of shame, embarrassment, or serious consequences of failure.

The Fifth Discovery: Resonant Relationships

Our relationships are an essential part of our environment. The most crucial relationships are those in which we feel trust and safety in conversation. These are called "resonant relationships" (Boyatzis & McKee, 2005; Goleman, Boyatzis, & McKee, 2002). They are often a part of groups that have particular importance to us. These relationships and groups give us a sense of identity, guide us as to what is appropriate and "good" behavior, and provide feedback on our behavior. In sociology, they are called reference groups. These relationships create a "context" within which we interpret our progress on desired changes, the utility of new learning, and even contribute significant input to formulation of the Ideal (Kram, 1996).

In this sense, our relationships are mediators, moderators, interpreters, sources of feedback, sources of support and permission of change and learning (Boyatzis & McKee, 2005; Boyatzis, Smith, & Blaize, 2006). They may also be the most important source of protection from relapses or returning to our earlier forms of behavior. Wheeler (2008) analyzed the extent to which the MBA graduates worked on their goals in multiple "life spheres" (for example, work, family, recreational groups, etc.). In a two-year follow-up study of two of the graduating classes of part-time MBA students, she found that those who worked on their goals and plans in multiple sets of relationships improved the most and more than those working on goals in only one setting, such as work or within one relationship.

In a study of the impact of the year-long executive development program for doctors, lawyers, professors, engineers, and other professionals mentioned earlier, Ballou, Bowers, Boyatzis, and Kolb (1999) found that participants gained self-confidence during the program. Even at the beginning of the program, others would say that these participants were very high in self-confidence. It was a curious finding. The best explanation came from follow-up questions to the graduates of the program. They explained the evident increase in Self-Confidence as an increase in the confidence to change. Their existing reference groups (i.e., family, groups at work, professional groups, community groups) all had an investment in them staying the same; meanwhile, the person wanted to change. The Professional Fellows Program allowed them to develop a new reference group that encouraged change.

Based on social identity, reference group, and now relational theories, our relationships both mediate and moderate our sense of who we are and who we want to be. We develop or elaborate our Ideal Self from these contexts. We label and interpret our Real Self from these contexts. We interpret and value Strengths (i.e., aspects considered our core that we wish to preserve) from these contexts. We interpret and value Weaknesses (i.e., aspects we wish to change) from these contexts.

WHAT IF LEARNING WERE THE PURPOSE OF EDUCATION OR TRAINING?

Borrowing from the title of Chapter 10 of Boyatzis, Cowen, and Kolb's (1995) book for the subtitle of the implications section of this chapter, we can offer a promising answer. An MBA education or management training *can* help people develop cognitive, emotional, and social intelligence competencies needed to be outstanding managers, leaders, and professionals. But we cannot use the typical lecture and discussion methods with their focus on knowledge acquisition only in education. Nor can we use the "data dump and run" approach typical of assessment and feedback processes in training. A more holistic approach can help dramatically to improve our impact and the relevance of education or training to their future work organizations.

For practitioners or educators, the major implications lie in the design of the training or developmental assessment programs. Designing and conducting outcome research may be humbling, but it keeps you honest. When you offer a development program, you could have the outcome data to know what participants are learning and how much of it is sustained. If you do, it is likely that you will find the impact will be improved by following the discoveries and sequence described in Intentional Change Theory.

REFERENCES

Amis, J., Slack, T., & Hinings, C.R. (2004). The pace, sequence, and linearity of radical change. *Academy of Management Journal, 47*(1), 15–39.

Astin, A.W. (1993). *What matters in college? Four critical years.* San Francisco: Jossey-Bass.

Ballou, R., Bowers, D., Boyatzis, R.E., & Kolb, D.A. (1999). Fellowship in lifelong learning: An executive development program for advanced professionals. *Journal of Management Education, 23*(4), 338–354.

Barlow, D.H. (1988). *Anxiety and disorders: The nature and treatment of anxiety and panic.* New York: The Guilford Press.

Bennis, W., & Nanus, B. (1985). *Leaders: Strategies for taking charge,* New York: Harper and Row.

Bigelow, J.D. (Ed.). (1991). *Managerial skills: Explorations in practical knowledge.* Thousand Oaks, CA: Sage.

Boyatzis, R.E. (1982). *The competent manager: A model for effective performance.* Hoboken, NJ: John Wiley & Sons.

Boyatzis, R.E. (1994). Stimulating self-directed change: A required MBA course called Managerial Assessment and Development. *Journal of Management Education, 18*(3), 304–323.

Boyatzis, R.E. (1998). *Transforming qualitative information: Thematic analysis and code development.* Thousand Oaks, CA: Sage.

Boyatzis, R.E. (2006). Intentional change theory from a complexity perspective. *Journal of Management Development, 25*(7), 607–623.

Boyatzis, R.E. (2008). Competencies in the 21st century. *Journal of Management Development, 27*(1), 5–12.

Boyatzis, R.E., & Akrivou, K. (2006). The ideal self as a driver of change. *Journal of Management Development, 25*(7), 624–642.

Boyatzis, R.E., Cowen, S.S., & Kolb, D.A. (1995). *Innovation in professional education: Steps on a journey from teaching to learning.* San Francisco: Jossey-Bass.

Boyatzis, R., & McKee, A. (2005). *Resonant leadership: Renewing yourself and connecting with others through mindfulness, hope, and compassion.* Boston, MA: Harvard Business School Press.

Boyatzis, R.E., Renio-McKee, A., & Thompson, L. (1995). Past accomplishments: Establishing the impact and baseline of earlier programs. In R.E. Boyatzis, S.S. Cowen, & D.A. Kolb (Eds.), *Innovation in professional education: Steps on a journey from teaching to learning*. San Francisco: Jossey-Bass.

Boyatzis, R.E., & Saatcioglu, A. (2008). A twenty year view of trying to develop emotional, social and cognitive intelligence competencies in graduate management education. *Journal of Management Development, 27*(1), 92–108.

Boyatzis, R.E., & Sala, F. (2004). Assessing emotional intelligence competencies. In G. Geher (Ed.), *The measurement of emotional intelligence* (pp. 147–180). Hauppauge, NY: Novas Science Publishers.

Boyatzis, R.E., Smith, M., & Blaize, N. (2006). Developing sustainable leaders through coaching and compassion. *Academy of Management Journal on Learning and Education, 5*(1), 8–24.

Boyatzis, R.E., Stubbs, E.C., & Taylor, S.N. (2002). Learning cognitive and emotional intelligence competencies through graduate management education. *Academy of Management Journal on Learning and Education, 1*(2), 150–162.

Buckingham, M. (2000). *Now find your strengths.* New York: HarperCollins.

Campbell, J.P., Dunnette, M.D., Lawler, E.E. III, & Weick, K.E. (1970). *Managerial behavior, performance, and effectiveness.* New York: McGraw-Hill.

Chen, G., Gully, S.M., Whiteman, J.A., & Kilcullen, R.N. (2000). Examination of relationships among trait-like individual differences, state-like individual differences, and learning performance. *Journal of Applied Psychology, 85*(6), 835–847.

Cherniss, C., & Adler, M.(2000). *Promoting emotional intelligence in organizations: Make training in emotional intelligence effective.* Alexandria, VA: American Society for Training and Development.

Curry, L., Snyder, C.R., Cook, D., Ruby, B., & Rehm, M. (1997). The role of hope in academic and sport achievement. *Journal of Personality and Social Psychology, 73,* 1257–1267.

Dreyfus, C. (2008). Identifying competencies that predict effectiveness of R&D managers. *Journal of Management Development, 27*(1), 76–91.

Druskat, V., Mount, G., and Sala, F. (Eds.). (2005). *Emotional intelligence and work performance.* Mahwah, NJ: Lawrence Erlbaum Associates.

Erikson, P.S., Perfilieva, E., Bjork-Eriksson, T., Alborn, A-M, Nordburg, C., Peterson, D.A., & Gage, F.H. (1998). Neurogenesis in the adult human hippocampus. *Nature Medicine, 4,* 1313–1317.

Gersick, C.J. (1991). Revolutionary change theories: A multilevel exploration of the punctuated equilibrium paradigm. *Academy of Management Review, 16,* 274–309.

Goleman, D. (1985). *Vital lies, simple truths: The psychology of self-deception.* New York: Simon and Schuster.

Goleman, D. (1998). *Working with emotional intelligence*. New York: Bantam.

Goleman, D., Boyatzis, R.E., & McKee, A. (2002). *Primal leadership: Realizing the power of emotional intelligence*. Boston, MA: Harvard Business School Press.

Higgins, E.T. (1991). Development of self-regulatory and self-evaluative processes: Costs, benefits and tradeoffs. In M. Gunnar & L.A. Sroufe (Eds.), *Self-processes and development: The Minnesota symposium on child psychology, vol. 23* (pp. 125–165). Mahwah, NJ: Lawrence Erlbaum Associates.

Howard, A., & Bray, D. (1988). *Managerial lives in transition: Advancing age and changing times*. New York: Guilford Press.

Hubble, M.A., Duncan, B.L., & Miller, S.D. (Eds.). (1999). *The heart and soul of change: What works in therapy*. Washington DC: American Psychological Association.

Kanfer, F.H., & Goldstein, A.P. (Eds.). (1991). *Helping people change: A textbook of methods* (4th ed.). Boston, MA: Allyn and Bacon.

Kolb, D.A. (1984). *Experiential learning: Experience as the source of learning and development*. Englewood Cliffs, NJ: Prentice-Hall.

Kolb, D.A., & Boyatzis, R.E. (1970). Goal-setting and self-directed behavior change. *Human Relations, 23*(5), 439–457.

Kotter, J.P. (1982). *The general managers*. New York: Free Press.

Kram, K.E. (1996). A relational approach to careers. In D.T. Hall (Ed.), *The career is dead: Long live the career* (pp. 132–157). San Francisco: Jossey-Bass.

Kreiman, G, Koch, C., & Fried, I. (2000). Imagery neurons in the human brain. *Nature, 408*, 357–361.

Leonard, D. (2008). The impact of learning goals on emotional, social, and cognitive intelligence competency development. *Journal of Management Development, 27*(1), 109–128.

Locke, E.A., & Latham, G.P. (1990). *A theory of goal setting and task performance*. Englewood Cliffs, NJ: Prentice Hall.

Loehr, J., & Schwartz, T. (2003). *The power of full engagement: Managing energy, not time, is the key to high performance and personal renewal*. New York: Free Press.

Luthans, F., Hodgetts, R.M., & Rosenkrantz, S.A. (1988). *Real managers*. Cambridge, MA: Ballinger Press.

Manniz, L., Chadukar, R., Rybicki, L., Tusek, D., & Solomon, O. (1999). The effect of guided imagery on quality of life for patients with chronic tension-type headaches. *Headache: Journal of Head and Face Pain, 39*, 326–324.

McKee, A., Boyatzis, R.E., & Johnston, F. (2008). *Becoming a resonant leader and renewing yourself and others*. Boston, MA: Harvard Business School Press.

Mentkowski, M., & Associates. (2000). *Learning that lasts: Integrating learning, development, and performance in college and beyond*. San Francisco: Jossey-Bass.

Morrow, C.C., Jarrett, M.Q., & Rupinski, M.T. (1997). An investigation of the effect and economic utility of corporate-wide training. *Personnel Psychology, 50*, 91–119.

Pascarella, E.T., & Terenzini, P.T. (1991). *How college affects students: Findings and insights from twenty years of research*. San Francisco: Jossey-Bass.

Porter, L. & McKibbin, L. (1988). *Management education and development: Drift or thrust into the 21st century?* New York: McGraw-Hill.

Spencer, L.M., Jr., & Spencer, S.M. (1993). *Competence at work: Models for superior performance*. Hoboken, NJ: John Wiley & Sons.

Taylor, S. (2006). A conceptual framework and empirical test of leader attunement: Toward a theory of leader self-awareness. Unpublished doctoral dissertation. Case Western Reserve University, Cleveland, Ohio.

Wheeler, J.V. (2008). The impact of social environments on emotional, social, and cognitive competency development. *Journal of Management Development*, 27(1), 129–145.

Richard E. Boyatzis is a professor in the Departments of Organizational Behavior, Psychology, and Cognitive Science at Case Western Reserve University and Human Resources at ESADE. He is the author of more than one hundred articles on leadership, competencies, emotional intelligence, management education, and thematic analysis and six books, including The Competent Manager; the international best-seller, Primal Leadership with Daniel Goleman and Annie McKee; Resonant Leadership, with Annie McKee; and Becoming a Resonant Leader (with Annie McKee and Fran Johnston). Professor Boyatzis has a BS in aeronautics and astronautics from MIT and a MS and Ph.D. degrees in social psychology from Harvard University.

CHAPTER 17

Emotional Intelligence, Leadership, and the School Administrator

James D.A. Parker, Howard E. Stone, and Laura M. Wood

INTRODUCTION

There is a growing body of research indicating that the type of social and emotional abilities linked with emotional intelligence are strongly related to one's ability to cope with life's demands and stressors (Mayer, Caruso, & Salovey, 1999). Emotional intelligence, not surprisingly, has come to be viewed as an essential factor in the quality of one's general emotional and social well-being (Taylor, Parker & Bagby, 1999), as well as an important predictor of an individual's ability to succeed on the job or in the classroom (Parker, Summerfeldt, Hogan, & Majeski, 2004; Zeidner, Matthews, & Roberts, 2004). For example, recent studies have found a link between academic success and emotional intelligence in both secondary and post-secondary students (Parker, Creque, Barnhart, Irons, Majeski, Wood, Bond, & Hogan, 2004; Parker, Duffy, Wood, Bond, & Hogan, 2005; Parker, Summerfeldt, Hogan, & Majeski, 2004).

Early on, there was a strong interest in examining the relationship between EI and leadership in a variety of workplace environments. Although popular discussions of EI and workplace success (e.g., Goleman, 1995) often focus on the top leadership level (e.g., what makes a good CEO), there is growing empirical evidence to suggest that EI abilities are linked with positive leadership behaviors at various levels within an organization (George, 2000).

Trends in the recent literature on successful leadership suggest that EI appears to contribute to positive leadership behavior in several basic ways. Individuals with above average levels of EI tend to have advanced communication skills (often in both verbal and non-verbal forms). This is an essential skill for leaders who need to communicate goals and objectives to subordinates on an ongoing basis. Individuals who have above average levels of emotional and social competency often have above average coping abilities (Parker, Taylor, & Bagby, 1998). The ability to cope with stress is very important for successful leadership; this is the skill that helps a leader generate and maintain enthusiasm, confidence, and cooperation in the workplace. Stress is an inevitable part of any workplace, but over the long term, people are more optimistic and trusting if they work around or for individuals who cope well under pressure (George, 2000).

With respect to leadership and managing stress in the workplace, school administrators have a large and challenging role to play in most communities. In Canada, there are over fifteen thousand elementary and secondary schools (Statistics Canada, 2006); the number for the United States is slightly more than ten times that number (U.S. Department of Labor, 2006–2007). Each one of these institutions is headed by a school principal who has a plethora of tasks and responsibilities. The school principals not only have the primary leadership role for the school's teaching and support staff, but they are often responsible for the counseling and discipline of students. They have primary responsibility at the school for implementing school board or government initiatives, but are also on the front line for managing staff-to-staff conflict, as well as the most problematic school-parent problems and concerns. At the same time, school principals are also charged with managing budgets that can match those associated with medium-sized businesses.

Given the demanding work environment linked with school administration, it is not surprising that most boards have invested considerable time and attention to the recruitment and training process for principals. A review of the current preparation programs for principals in both the United States and Canada would seem to indicate a growing awareness of the importance of various emotional and social competencies for successful school leadership (Begley & Zaretsky, 2004; Fullan, 2003). Missing in the recent school leadership literature, however, has been a clear indication of exactly what competencies are important for successful school leadership.

Recently, a study funded by the Ontario Ministry of Education and Training was conducted to explore the relationship between emotional intelligence and school leadership. Specifically, the Ontario Principals' Council (OPC) leadership study (Stone, Parker, & Wood, 2005) sought to identify critical emotional and social skills required by school administrators (principals and vice-principals) to successfully fulfill their roles and responsibilities. It was hoped that the information gathered from this project could be used to guide the development of professional development activities for current and future principals and vice-principals.

OPC LEADERSHIP STUDY

Four hundred and sixty-four principals or vice-principals (187 men and 277 women) from nine school boards in Ontario, representing the social, economic, cultural and geographic diversity of the province, participated in the study. Two-hundred and twenty six participants were elementary school principals, eighty-four were elementary school vice-principals, forty-three were secondary school principals, and fifty-seven were secondary school vice-principals (fifty-four did not indicate their current position). The mean age of all participants was forty-seven.

Measuring Emotional Intelligence

Information was gathered about participants' emotional intelligence by having participating principals and vice-principals complete the Emotional

Quotient Inventory® (EQ-i®) (Bar-On, 1997) online. The EQ-i®, one of the most widely used measures of EI, is a 125-item self-report instrument designed to measure the core features of emotional intelligence as described by the Bar-On model of emotional and social intelligence. The EQ-i® generates four main scales, which make up total emotional intelligence: intrapersonal (measuring one's ability to recognize and label one's feelings), interpersonal (measuring one's ability to recognize and appropriately react to the feelings of others), adaptability (measuring one's ability to adjust his/her emotions and behaviors to changing situations), and stress management (measuring one's ability to effectively manage stressful situations). The four main scales are further broken down into subscales. The intrapersonal scale consists of the subscales self-regard, emotional self-awareness, assertiveness, independence, and self-actualization. The interpersonal scale consists of the subscales empathy, social responsibility, and interpersonal relationship. The adaptability scale consists of the subscales reality testing, flexibility, and problem solving. The stress management scale consists of the subscales stress tolerance, and impulse control. The EQ-i® also includes a general mood scale (consisting of the subscales optimism and happiness).

Measuring Leadership Ability

Participants in the OPC study were also requested to ask their immediate supervisor s(superintendent if the participant was a principal and the principal if the participant was a vice-principal) to complete a questionnaire about the participants' leadership abilities. Principals and vice-principals were also requested to ask three staff members to rate the individuals' leadership abilities. The supervisors completed a supervisor-rated leadership questionnaire and the staff members completed a staff-rated leadership questionnaire, all of which were returned directly to the researchers by the supervisors and staff members. The mean of all completed staff rated forms for each participant was calculated. Both the supervisor-rated and staff-rated leadership questionnaires included twenty-one items related to leadership abilities. The participants also completed the twenty-one-item leadership questionnaire about themselves. The factor structure of the leadership questionnaire was examined for all rater groups; analyses revealed two broad leadership dimensions: a task-oriented leadership dimension (e.g., "comes well prepared for meetings") and a relationship-oriented leadership dimension (e.g., "seeks consensus among staff members"). The former dimension related to skills like managing resources, delegating tasks, and planning for the future; while the latter dimension related to skills like motivating others and communicating one-on-one as well as in small groups. This two-dimensional model of leadership is similar to one identified by Humphrey (2002). Each of the leadership questionnaires also included an overall indicator of leadership ability using a 10-point scale, ranging from "0" for "No leadership ability" to "9" for "Highest level possible."

Key Research Findings

No differences were found between individuals working in an elementary school versus a secondary school on any of the EQ-i® scales; the same was true when comparing principals and vice-principals on the EQ-i® scales. With regard to leadership ratings (supervisor and staff), individuals employed by an elementary school did not differ from those employed at a secondary school. However, when comparing principals and vice-principals on leadership ratings, principals were rated higher than vice-principals on task-oriented leadership, relationship-oriented leadership, and total leadership by their supervisors. On the other hand, vice-principals were rated higher on relationship-oriented leadership by their staff. These findings suggest that the overall results of the study with respect to the relationship between EI and leadership ability can be generalized to principals and vice-principals working in both elementary and secondary environments.

A positive relationship was found between the leadership ratings from supervisors and staff; however, the association was weak and revealed substantial divergence between raters. Due to this low association, a combination of both supervisor and staff ratings for total leadership scores were calculated for each individual. Individuals rated at the 20th percentile or lower on leadership ability according to both the supervisor and staff ratings were categorized as having below average leadership ability; while those individuals who were rated at the 80th percentile or higher on leadership ability by both the supervisor and staff ratings were categorized as having above average leadership ability. The above average leadership group scored higher on total EI and all four broad dimensions (intrapersonal, interpersonal, adaptability, and stress management) of the EQ-i® than the below average leadership group. The two groups did not, however, differ on the general mood scale of the EQ-i®. These results were consistent regardless of gender, whether the individual worked in an elementary or secondary school, or whether the individual was a principal or vice-principal. Table 17.1 presents the means and standard deviations for the two leadership groups on the five dimensions of the EQ-i®, as well as for the fifteen subscales.

The above-average and below-average leadership groups were also compared on the subscales on the EQ-i®. For the intrapersonal abilities, the above-average leadership group scored significantly higher on the emotional self-awareness and self-actualization subscales than the below-average leadership group did. The above-average leadership group also scored higher than the below-average leadership group on the empathy and interpersonal relationship subscales, but not on the social responsibility subscale of the interpersonal dimension. Examination of the adaptability skills revealed that the above-average leadership group scored higher than the below-average leadership group on the flexibility and problem-solving subscales. Finally, when looking at the two stress management subscales, the above-average leadership group scored higher than the below-average leadership group on the impulse control subscale, but not on the stress tolerance subscale.

The findings from the OPC study support prior research on effective leadership. Prior research has found, for example, that the most effective leaders have a combination of both task-oriented and relationship-oriented leadership skills (Humphrey, 2002). When it comes to task-oriented leadership, behaviors similar to emotional self-awareness, self-actualization, and impulse control have been found to be important (Humphrey, 2002). Empathy is likely a critical skill for relationship-oriented leadership, but it has also been shown to contribute to cognitive skills necessary for task-oriented leadership (Humphrey, 2002; Wolff, Pescosolido, & Druskat, 2002). In addition to empathy, the ability to establish mutually satisfying interpersonal relationships is necessary to facilitate relationship-oriented leadership (George, 2000). Leadership positions are often changing and the demands of the job continually shift; effective leaders need to be flexible in the way in which they behave and use their emotions to approach problems and new situations (George, 2000). Additionally, skills similar to flexibility and problem

Table 17.1. Means and Standard Deviations (SD) for the EQ-i® Scales and Subscales by Above- and Below-Average Groups (Based on Combined Supervisor and Staff-Rated Leadership Ability)

	Below Average (N = 77) Mean (SD)	Above Average (N = 78) Mean (SD)
Intrapersonal	105.0 (10.97)	108.6 (10.67) *
Self-Regard	101.5 (11.82)	103.2 (10.17)
Self-Awareness	104.4 (13.52)	109.9 (13.11) *
Assertiveness	104.4 (11.62)	105.9 (11.56)
Independence	105.8 (9.68)	107.7 (10.44)
Self-Actualization	103.9 (9.95)	107.3 (10.49) *
Interpersonal	102.5 (11.32)	107.9 (10.17)*
Empathy	105.0 (11.56)	111.1 (10.15) *
Social Responsibility	104.0 (9.80)	106.7 (8.99)
Interpersonal Relation	99.7 (12.70)	105.3 (12.01)*
Adaptability	105.7 (10.13)	109.5 (9.50)*
Reality Testing	106.9 (9.98)	108.9 (9.65)
Flexibility	102.5 (12.71)	106.0 (11.30)*
Problem Solving	104.5 (11.45)	108.5 (9.28)*
Stress Management	105.6 (9.28)	109.8 (9.42)*
Stress Tolerance	105.9 (10.11)	109.3 (11.00)
Impulse Control	104.2 (10.33)	108.2 (10.86)*
General Mood	104.5 (9.25)	107.2 (8.83)
Optimism	105.7 (9.13)	107.1 (8.94)
Happiness	103.6 (9.90)	107.2 (8.83)
Total EI	105.6 (9.99)	110.2 (10.03)*

Note: * $p < .05$

solving have been suggested to be important for both task- and relationship-oriented leadership (George, 2000).

Although total emotional intelligence was found to be a significant predictor of successful school administration, some dimensions of emotional intelligence were found to be better predictors than others. Specifically, the results of the OPC study suggested that professional development programs would be wise to focus on promoting or developing a very specific set of abilities:

- Emotional self-awareness (the ability to recognize and understand one's feelings and emotions);
- Self-actualization (the ability to tap potential capacities and skills in order to improve oneself);
- Empathy (the ability to be attentive to, understand, and appreciate the feelings of others);
- Interpersonal relationships (the ability to establish and maintain mutually satisfying relationships);
- Flexibility (the ability to adjust one's emotions, thoughts, and behaviors to changing situations and conditions);
- Problem solving (the ability to identify and define problems as well as to generate potentially effective solutions); and
- Impulse control (to the ability to resist or delay emotional behaviors).

As was noted earlier, there were no differences on any of the EQ-i® scales when principals and vice-principals were compared, as well as when individuals working in an elementary school were compared with individuals working in a secondary school. Thus, professional development programs that promote and develop core EI abilities can be used with a broad range of school administrators.

TEACHING SCHOOL ADMINISTRATORS TO BE MORE EMOTIONALLY INTELLIGENT

This section of the chapter describes the EI training program developed based on the results from the OPC study to assist principals and vice-principals to develop the skills necessary to effectively do their jobs.

The development, delivery, and assessment of the program represented a joint venture among four school boards in Ontario, Trent University, and Learning Ways Inc.

This program, originally called At the Heart of School Leadership, was designed as a four-module training program based on the seven key emotional and social competencies identified in the OPC leadership study. The training program was developed to recognize the pivotal role that school leaders play in mobilizing members of the education community to lead school improvement efforts that focus on student learning. This leadership position is at the *heart* of the action, the source of accountability for literacy and numeracy targets and the required capacity building to reach these standards. School leaders' success will depend on their ability to cultivate an inspired, collaborative learning culture within their school community. The OPC leadership study, which examined the connection between emotional intelligence and principal/vice-principal performance, demonstrated that specific emotional and social competencies are prerequisite characteristics for effective leadership. School leaders lacking in these abilities will find a challenge to lead and sustain professional learning communities—the agreed-on signature of high-performing schools. Building leadership capacity in emotional and social competencies is at the foundation of school improvement efforts. These competencies need to be at the forefront of professional development programs for principals and vice-principals.

The purpose of the emotional and social competency training program was to provide support for the ongoing development of effective school leaders in fulfilling their leadership purpose and responsibilities in order to achieve the results that promote student learning. It focused on the key emotional and social competencies identified in the OPC leadership study: emotional self-awareness, self-actualization, interpersonal relationships, empathy, problem solving, flexibility, and impulse control. Effective school leaders who are emotionally and socially competent will have a strong sense of self and the ability to understand and manage emotions both in themselves and others. They will engage the *heart* (emotions) and then the *mind* of key stakeholders as the gateway to gaining support for school improvement initiatives. Effective, high-performing leaders will have the ability to develop collaborative learning environments that focus on student learning and will empower new leaders within their educational community to assist in the pursuit of provincial and system goals and standards. They will demonstrate repeatedly the ability to solve problems, to adapt to change, and to overcome obstacles. High-performing leaders will balance the increasing demands and complexities of the role with a positive, optimistic outlook.

Each of the four modules was developed to explore leadership practices, ideas, and strategies that reflect the previously mentioned seven distinguishing emotional and social competencies. The content of the program represented concepts that repeatedly appear in the literature describing the actions and attributes of effective leaders, and therefore represent informed, current educational research and thinking. The workshop activities attempted to translate these concepts to fit the world of the school administrator.

As mentioned previously, four school boards sponsored the implementation of the program for their respective school administrators. The program consisted of four five-hour modules delivered over a period of two years to each district. Each five-hour workshop was designed as an interactive session invoking participant discussion and input of the presented concepts. Each module included a feedback session that helped the presenters revise the content in order to enhance the practicality and application of the workshop concepts. The content and delivery of each module evolved over time as each module was presented four times. The team of individuals who developed and presented the program included Howard Stone, one of the authors of this chapter, Mark Schinkel, superintendent with the Waterloo Region District School Board, Gerry Watts, secondary school principal with the Grand Erie District School Board, and Sharon and Brad Robertson, elementary school principals from the Waterloo Region District School Board. Each member of the team was certified in the use of the assessment instruments used for the OPC leadership study. Their involvement was critical because they, at the time of developing the program, were living the role due to their positions in school districts.

Module One: Intrapersonal

Each module dealt with one area of emotional intelligence and the related key competencies identified by the OPC leadership study. Module One focused on the intrapersonal dimension and specifically self-actualization and emotional self-awareness. In this session participants worked through a number of activities but concentrated on the development and articulation of their purpose in life and as leaders. Most educators who pursue the role of principal and vice-principal want to enhance and expand their contributions to the education environment. They view this leadership role as an opportunity to influence the behaviors of a greater number of educators and stakeholders in the education community in order to support the achievement of students in this larger context. This internal drive, to maximize their current and potential competencies, abilities, and talents with the intention of making a positive difference in their chosen role, characterizes *self-actualization* in school leaders.

Emotional self-awareness is considered by many to be the foundation of emotional intelligence and was also the primary topic of this module. For school leaders, it represents the ability to understand feelings and what is generating them. It helps individuals understand and 'control the gap between a challenging event and their mental, physical, and emotional response to the situation. Leaders make the connection by developing a clear understanding of their underlying beliefs, values, and assumptions. They understand how these beliefs and values influence their decision making and responses to situations. The leader's ability to "tune into" this information paves the way for a more productive response to any situation, especially those that are emotionally challenging. A leader's ability to communicate his or her emotions and feelings in an appropriate and timely fashion is dependent on his or her own emotional self-awareness. To support the development of this competency, the participants experienced a number of activities that helped them identify emotions. They also learned to pay attention to their own internal dialogue to be more mindful of the emotions being triggered by the events and experiences they encounter.

Module Two: Interpersonal

In Module Two, the content reflected the interpersonal domain and specific competencies of interpersonal relationship and empathy. The discussion for interpersonal relationship focused on building relationships in the school community and developing and maintaining effective teams, whereas the section on empathy considered empathic behavior and actions of effective leaders.

The participants spent considerable time exploring and sharing the strategies they used to build and strengthen relationships with members of their school community. Time was also devoted to a discussion of some of the key attributes required to build and maintain relationship as identified in the leadership literature. The participants were also afforded the time to practice empathic communication using scenarios they would experience on the job. This activity reminded participants of the importance of taking time to understand the perspective of others before advancing one's own ideas. It also emphasized one of the important building blocks of building and maintaining effective relationships.

Module Three: Adaptability

Module Three paid attention to the adaptability domain by examining best practice activities related to problem solving and flexibility. In this module, we decided to dwell on encounters with hostile people. How do school administrators manage their emotions and those of others when confronted with this difficult scenario—a hostile person? How does one manage emotions and preserve relationships to get permission to engage in problem solving? This focus seemed welcomed by many participants, as it reflected one of the difficult challenges faced in their position. The session also examined the need to have a framework for problem solving readily available especially during trying circumstances when emotions are running high. Again, a leader's empathic skills were seen as necessary to determine when it is appropriate to move into a problem-solving mode. If this appears to be the right decision, and there is general agreement to proceed, then the leader must be able to recall and apply a problem-solving process that fits the situation. The leader who cannot bring a framework to this type of situation, which is clouded with emotions, will undoubtedly cause friction among the group members and lose permission to proceed as the leader. Time was also devoted to an examination of the influence emotions have in negotiations. School leaders are continually negotiating as part of their jobs. Since most negotiations deal with issues of personal significance, emotions will be involved and contribute to the outcome, positively or negatively. Leaders who understand this concept and have the knowledge and skill to manage this aspect of negotiations have a better chance of reaching an outcome that benefits all parties.

Module Four: Stress Management

Module Four concentrated on the stress management domain and the impulse control competency. The decision made by the program developers and presenters was to focus on stress tolerance. Our belief was that impulse control would be stronger in individuals who can better tolerate the stress encountered on the job. Our discussions with the participants also reinforced this focus and related to their current experiences and needs. The demands being placed on school leaders in this high-stakes accountability environment increased the stress encountered on the job. Not only were the principals and vice-principals facing more scrutiny over student achievement results, but they were also experiencing an increasingly agitated education environment. The unsettled relationship with teachers' unions due to recent contract agreements and resulting implementation requirements was adding to the demands and challenges faced on a daily bases. The content in Module Four, accordingly, examined the stressful situations encountered in the role of principal and vice-principal. Many situations were examined to assist the participants in understanding how these challenging situations related to their own stress levels. Additional time was spent on reviewing appropriate stress protectors and then allowing participants to review their own status. They completed a gap analysis examining their current stress protectors and then considered new habits that could assist them in coping with the demand placed on them.

Program Evaluation

As noted earlier, the training program for promoting EI originated from the findings of the OPC leadership study. The development of the program occurred only because four school districts committed to the training program after the OPC leadership study was completed and the results distributed to members of the organization. Leaders in the four districts believed that emotional intelligence and especially the seven identified competencies were integral to the effective functioning of their school leaders. These school boards, Waterloo Region District School Board, Grand Erie District School Board, District School Board of Niagara, and Rainy River District School Board, took the risk of committing their administrators to a training program that was developed as it was being implemented.

Intuitively, the leaders in each of these districts knew the importance of these abilities and were willing to move forward and support the development of this training program. As mentioned earlier, the program evolved during the delivery of each workshop as the presenters received valuable feedback from the participants.

Each district approached the implementation of the program differently. Two districts had very specific groups participate in the sessions. One district selected principals and vice-principals new to their position, while a second board selected administrators who were part of their internal leadership team. The two other districts enrolled all their principals and vice-principals. This decision worked well in one situation, in which there were only about thirty-five administrators in the district. In the other case, the size of the group, approaching one hundred, proved to be a challenge in the initial delivery of the program. This district eventually divided the group into two sections, which reduced the time available for the workshop but made the format more conducive to the content and interactive style of the presentation.

The EI program was delivered over a two-year period. This decision was made for a number of reasons. The content of the program, as mentioned, was being developed at the same time. The sessions, for the most part, were organized for the fall and spring terms, which provided time to develop each workshop and react to the feedback regarding delivery style. This gap also provided time for individual boards to complement the training program with their own in-house professional development initiatives. The two-year period also helped the districts budget for the program as the expenses were spread over two fiscal years. The two-year period did prove problematic in maintaining the participation of all administrators who started the program. Retirements, new appointments, job conflicts, and an individual's commitment to the program affected the consistency of the attendees.

Questions that we continue to explore deal with the length of the program given the time administrators are required to be out of the school for professional development and other meetings related to their role. Other questions are: Have we focused in on the best practices that relate to the key competencies identified in the research? Who should be the intended audience? In this case our position leans to the aspiring school leader or those new to the position as the most appropriate audience for this program or one of a similar focus. In recent years the turnover of school administrators has escalated as many experienced principals have reached retirement age. It seems that the new appointees are younger and have had less leadership experience in other capacities before assuming the role of vice-principal. Many superintendents from districts involved in this initiative indicate that this lack of prior leadership opportunities negatively impacts the growth of EI abilities. These new administrators, usually vice-principals, have not experienced situations as leaders that demand the emotional investment and abilities required in their role. Accordingly, the EI training program must be based on the core competencies discovered in our research, address the challenging everyday situations new vice-principals will face on the job and identify strategies and best practices that will assist new administrators in performing their duties. The training program used for this endeavor attempted to encompass these three factors in order to be directly applicable to the events encountered in the schools by vice-principals and principals.

Most theorists assume that emotional and social competencies or abilities, no matter what model is being used, are quite malleable (Bar-On, 2000; Mayer, Caruso, & Salovey, 1999); that is, it is suggested that emotional and social skills can be developed and enhanced via appropriate interventions (Bar-On & Parker, 2000). The preliminary results from the data collected to examine the OPC training program support this idea. Data from forty-three principals and vice principals was collected to examine the efficacy of the program. The forty-three participants completed the EQ-i® at the beginning of the program and again at the end of the program (approximately twenty-four months apart). The principals and vice principals who participated in the program had higher scores on the intrapersonal, interpersonal, and adaptability composite scales and total EI score on the EQ-i® at the end of the program than at the beginning of the program.

FUTURE DIRECTIONS

Along with further examination of the benefits of the OPC training program, other research needs to be conducted on the role emotional and social competencies play in successful school leadership. Another project is currently under way to examine the relationship between EI and leadership in a related group of school administrators. In the new project, the EI and leadership abilities of a diverse group of supervisory officers (superintendents) from a variety of public school boards in Ontario are being examined. For this project, leadership abilities are linked to the nine critical skills identified by the Ontario Public Supervisory Officials' Association (OPSOA) as core skills for functioning as an effective supervisory officer: acquiring broad-based knowledge of education issues, modelling lifelong learning, developing a vision for "strategic doing," taking and accepting responsibility, building emotional resilience to sustain integrity, ensuring quality and excellence, demonstrating effective communication, fostering positive relationships with all stakeholders, and building and nurturing relationships. Similar to the OPC project, the participants will complete the EQ-i® and will have their leadership abilities evaluated by three to five independent raters (who report to the supervisor). Similar procedures will be used as with the OPC leadership study and results from this new project will be used to assist with professional development training of existing and new supervisory officers. Additional research will need to be conducted to examine efficacy of any program developed out of the results.

BEST PRACTICE SUMMARY

Our work with the participating school districts and the follow-up dialogue with the research and program participants (principals, vice-principals, and superintendents) has provided valuable insight into what needs to be considered when developing and implementing an EI leadership program within a school district.

1. The school district clearly articulates the emotional intelligence competencies valued in its leaders. This information is published in documents that are used to describe what is expected in its leaders.
2. The emotional intelligence competencies articulated by the school district, as core attributes for its leaders, are reflected in its succession planning and leadership development practices. This includes the selection process for leaders.

3. Senior leaders within the district are knowledgeable about emotional intelligence and embrace it as integral to the success of all leaders in the system.

4. The senior leaders in the district are role models in understanding their EI profile and in using this information to enhance their leadership practices. It should not be perceived as only valuable for those other than the senior leaders within the district.

5. Senior leaders within the district take an active role in the training programs offered to its aspiring and current leaders. Having superintendents and senior principals as part of the delivery team provides a powerful message regarding the importance of the emotional intelligence to the effectiveness and success of its leaders.

REFERENCES

Bar-On, R. (1997). *Bar-On emotional quotient inventory: Technical manual.* Toronto: Multi-Health Systems.

Bar-On, R. (2000). Emotional and social intelligence: Insights from the emotional quotient inventory (EQ-i®). In R. Bar-On & J.D.A. Parker (Eds.), *Handbook of emotional intelligence.* San Francisco: Jossey-Bass.

Bar-On, R., & Parker, J.D.A. (2000). *Handbook of emotional intelligence.* San Francisco: Jossey-Bass.

Begley, P.T., & Zaretsky, L. (2004). Democratic school leadership in Canada's public school systems: Professional value and social ethic. *The Journal of Educational Administration, 42,* 640–655.

Fullan, M. (2003). *The moral imperative of school leadership.* London: Sage Publications.

George, J.M. (2000). Emotions and leadership: The role of emotional intelligence. *Human Relations, 53,* 1027–1055.

Goleman, D. (1995). *Emotional intelligence.* New York: Bantam Books.

Humphrey, R.H. (2002). The many faces of emotional leadership. *The Leadership Quarterly, 13,* 493–504.

Mayer, J.D., Caruso, D.R., & Salovey, P. (1999). Emotional intelligence meets traditional standards for an intelligence. *Intelligence, 27,* 267–298.

Parker, J.D.A., Creque, R.E., Barnhart, D.L., Harris Irons, J., Majeski, S.A., Wood, L.M., Bond, B.J., & Hogan, M.J. (2004). Academic achievement in high school: Does emotional intelligence matter? *Personality and Individual Differences, 37,* 1321–1330.

Parker, J.D.A., Duffy, J., Wood, L.M., Bond, B.J., & Hogan, M.J. (2005). Academic achievement and emotional intelligence: Predicting the successful transition from high school to university. *Journal of the First-Year Experience and Students in Transition*, *17*, 67–78.

Parker, J.D.A., Summerfeldt, L.J., Hogan, M.J., & Majeski, S. (2004). Emotional intelligence and academic success: Examining the transition from high school to university. *Personality and Individual Differences*, *36*, 163–172.

Parker, J.D.A., Taylor, J.G., & Bagby, R.M. (1998). Alexithymia: Relationship with ego defence and coping styles. *Contemporary Psychiatry*, *39*, 91–98.

Statistics Canada (2006). A profile of elementary and secondary school principals in Canada: First results from the 2004–2005 Survey of Principals. *Insights on education: Learning and training in Canada* (Vol. 3, No. 2).

Stone, H., Parker, J.D.A., & Wood, L.M. (2005, February). OPC leadership study: Exploring the relationship between school leadership and emotional intelligence. Presented at the Ontario Principals' Council executive meeting, Toronto, Ontario.

Taylor, G.J., Parker, J.D.A., & Bagby, R.M. (1999). Emotional intelligence and the emotional brain: Points of convergence and implications for psychoanalysis. *Journal of the American Academy of Psychoanalysis*, *27*, 339–354.

U.S. Department of Labor (2006–2007). *Occupational outlook handbook*. Washington, DC: Bureau of Labor Statistics.

Wolff, S.B., Pescosolido, A.T., & Druskat, V.U. (2002). Emotional intelligence as the basis of leadership emergence in self-managing teams. *The Leadership Quarterly*, *13*, 505–522.

Zeidner, M., Matthews, G.M., & Roberts, R. (2004). Emotional intelligence in the workplace: A critical review. *Applied Psychology: An International Review*, *53*, 371–399.

Dr. James D.A. Parker is a professor in the Department of Psychology at Trent University (Ontario, Canada) where he also holds a Canada Research Chair (Tier II) in Emotion and Health. Dr. Parker has published over one hundred articles and chapters, mostly in the areas of emotion and health. Dr. Parker co-developed the *Coping Inventory for Successful Situations* (*CISS*; published in 1990), as well as the youth version of the BarOn Emotional Quotient Inventory (EQ-i:YV, published in 2000). Dr. Parker was also the co-editor (with Reuven Bar-On) of *The Handbook of Emotional Intelligence*, published in 2000 by Jossey-Bass.

Howard E. Stone is a former superintendent with the Waterloo Region District School Board and holds a master's of education degree from the University of Toronto, Ontario Institute for Studies in Education.

He is currently the provincial coordinator for the Supervisory Officer's Qualification Program provided by the Ontario Principals' Council in partnership with the Ontario Public Supervisory Officials' Association. He also manages his own leadership consulting business, Learning Ways Inc., which provides learning opportunities in emotional intelligence for the education sector. He has provided workshops and training programs on emotional intelligence to a variety of school districts and educational organizations.

Laura M. Wood graduated from Trent University with her master's degree in 2006 and is currently the research coordinator of the Emotion and Health Research Laboratory and a part-time instructor in the Department of Psychology at Trent University. Laura has written a dozen peer-reviewed publications and has given over twenty peer-reviewed presentations at a variety of annual conferences. One of her major research interests is the study of affect-regulation abilities, particularly the relationship between emotional and social competency and success across the life-span, including academic success and workplace performance. Additional research interests include scale development and assessment.

Conclusion

What a pleasure it has been to be able to work with all of the exceptionally talented and devoted contributors to this volume. Even if you only sampled a few of the rich offerings here, it must certainly be apparent how the power of this work can increase the quality and depth of engagement that human beings can achieve. Now we can learn how to operate the currents and fields of emotional energy that enable us to meaningfully engage each other with respect, creativity, and collaboration.

Our heartfelt thanks to all of you who shared your inspiring work, to all of you who will apply it to improve your practice and thus your clients' results, and to everyone who will be open and diligent enough to try it until you fully accomplish the changes you desire.

Marcia Hughes, J.D., M.A.
Henry L. (Dick) Thompson, Ph.D.
James Bradford Terrell

Name Index

A

Aberman, R., 74
Ackerman, B. P., 335
Adler, M., 4, 360, 363
Agostin, R. M., 335
Ahuja, A., 308
Alborn, A.-M., 368
Albrecht, K., 235
Allen, R., 295
Alster, B., 335, 343
Ambady, N., 336
Amis, J., 366
Andrews, D. A., 308
Annan, K., 210
Arnsten, A., 115

B

Bachman, J., 183
Bagby, R. M., 379, 380
Bain, S. K., 335
Baker, J. A., 335
Ballou, R., 373
Bandler, R., 16
Bane, K. D., 36
Barker, L., 35
Barling, J., 184
Barlow, D. H., 361
Barnard, A., 226
Barnhart, D. L., 380
Bar-On, R., 6, 23, 75, 97, 104, 166, 213, 214, 221, 240, 241, 243, 259, 262, 263, 288, 301, 305, 306, 393
Barrett, F., 287

Barsade, S., 54, 157
Battistich, V., 335
Begley, P. T., 381
Bennis, W., 368
Berla, N., 344
Bharwaney, G., 21, 22, 23, 37, 39, 43, 47
Biko, S., 209, 210–212, 220
Binkert, J., 294
Bion, W. R., 86, 92
Biswas-Diener, R., 348
Bjork-Eriksson, T., 368
Blaize, N., 372
Blinkert, J., 287
Bloodworth, M., 330
Bond, B. J., 380
Book, H., 5, 73, 95, 166, 184, 199, 264
Bowers, D., 373
Bowlby, D., 78
Boyatzis, R. E., 6, 51, 53, 65, 301, 359, 360, 361, 362, 363, 364, 365, 366, 367, 368, 370, 372, 373, 377
Brackett, M. A., 329, 330, 331, 334, 335, 336, 342, 343, 345, 346, 348, 350, 357
Bray, D., 361
Brockley, T., 336
Brookryk, J., 206, 207, 208, 209
Brousseau, K., 236
Buckingham, M., 360
Byrne, R., 304

C

Campbell, J. P., 334, 363
Campbell, K., 183

Gordon, W., 183, 203
Graczyk, P. A., 330, 341
Gray, T. M., 111
Greenberg, M. T., 330, 341
Grinder, J., 16
Gross, J. J., 336
Guthrie, I. K., 334, 335

H

Haidt, J., 334
Halberstadt, A. G., 334, 335
Hall, G. E., 351
Handley, R., 5, 6, 97, 110, 199, 264
Harris Irons, J., 380
Harvey, L. H., 343
Haviland-Jones, J., 238
Hawkins, J. D., 335
Haynes, N. M., 330
Henderson, A. T., 344
Herbst, H. H., 224
Herbst, R., 226
Herzberg, F., 349
Higgins, E. T., 369
Hinings, C. R., 366
Hodgetts, R. M., 361
Hogan, M. J., 379, 380
Holzer, A., 348
Hord, S. M., 351
Hourihan, G., 236
Howard, A., 361
Hoy, A. W., 336
Hoy, W. K., 336, 342
Hubble, M. A., 361
Hughes, M., 1–2, 3, 9, 16, 141, 142, 145, 147, 164, 290, 292, 399
Huling-Austin, L., 351
Humphrey, R. H., 383, 384
Hunter, J. E., 116, 271

I

Izard, C. E., 334, 335

J

Jae, J. H., 183
Janis, I., 87, 147
Jarrett, M. Q., 361, 363

Johnston, F., 49, 51, 71, 370
Jones, G., 26, 35, 39, 75

K

Kamarinos Galiotos, P., 341
Kanfer, F. H., 361
Katulak, N. A., 335, 343, 345, 348
Keister, S., 331
Kelloway, E. K., 184
Kelly, J.R., 54
Keltner, D., 334
Kernberg, O. F., 86, 92
Kiessling, J. J., 308
Kihlstrom, J. F., 302, 304
Kindlon, D., 334
Klaasen, E. G., 220
Knecht, T., 302
Kohut, H., 349
Kolb, D. A., 360, 362, 367, 371, 372, 373
Kopelman, R. E., 36
Kotter, J. P., 75, 361
Kouzes, J. M., 224
Kram, K. E., 372
Kremenitzer, J. P., 335, 343, 345
Kress, J. S., 330
Kristjánsson, K., 330, 352

L

Lad, G. W., 341
Langhorn, S., 23
Large, D., 206
Larsson, R., 236
Latham, G. P., 371
Lawler, E. E., III, 363
Lazarus, R. S., 113, 334
LeDoux, J. E., 120
Legge, D., 197
Leiter, M. P., 335
Leonard, D., 370
Lerner, N., 335
Leslie, J., 236, 308
Lewis, M., 238
Lindemann, M., 35
Livingston, D., 205, 206
Locke, E. A., 371
Loeb, P., 293
Lord, H., 345
Luskin, F., 74

Lutchman, J., 206
Luthans, F., 361
Lynn, R., 116

M

MacKinlay, A., 23
Majeski, S., 379
Majeski, S. A., 380
Makhetha, M., 49
Maltz, M., 73
Mandela, N., 207, 210, 212, 220, 228
Manniz, L., 368
Maree, J. G., 208, 209, 212, 213, 221, 224
Martin, C., 349
Maslach, C., 335
Matthews, G. M., 379
Maurer, M., 346
Mayer, J. D., 6, 74, 166, 216, 242, 259, 261, 273, 301, 305, 331, 334, 335, 349, 379, 393
Mbigi, L., 208, 209, 212
McAdams, D. A., 49
McGovern, J., 35
Mckee, A., 49, 51, 53, 56, 65, 70, 363, 366, 368, 370, 372
McKibbin, L., 363
McLaughlin, K. A., 345
McMillen, C., 56
Mentkowski, M., 362
Miller, E., 347
Miller, M., 308
Miller, S. D., 361
Mills, C. J., 342
Mindel, A., 294
Mischel, W., 304
Mize, J., 341
Mohr, B., 285
Mojsa, J., 336
Morrow, C. C., 361, 363
Moss, M. C., 133
Mostow, A., 334, 335
Mount, G., 361
Murphy, J., 74
Murphy, K., 118, 257
Murphy, S., 35
Mwelwa, E., 49, 71
Myers, I., 249

N

Noel, J. L., 60
Nordburg, C., 368

O

O'Brien, M. U., 330, 331
Olivero, G., 36
Orem, S., 287, 294

P

Pakenham, T., 205
Palomera Martin, R., 335, 336
Paquet, A., 223
Parker, J.D.A., 74, 201, 379, 380, 393, 396
Pascarella, E. T., 361, 362
Patrikakou, E. N., 343
Patti, J., 329, 336, 348, 357
Payton, J. W., 330
Peale, N. V., 73
Pearman, R. R., 5, 14, 235, 238, 240, 255
Pepermans, R., 124
Perfilieva, E., 368
Pescosolido, A. T., 384
Peterson, D. A., 368
Porter, L., 363
Posner, B. Z., 224

R

Rath, T., 171
Rehm, M., 368
Reiser, M., 334, 335
Renio-McKee, A., 364
Resnik, H., 330, 331
Reyes, R., 336
Richardson, D., 114, 121
Rivers, S. E., 329, 330, 331, 335, 345, 346, 350, 358
Rizzolatti, G., 54
Robertson, B., 388
Robertson, S., 388
Roberts, R., 379
Rock, M., 308
Rosenkrantz, S. A., 361
Rosti, R. T., 36
Rotondo, S., 49, 71
Ruby, B., 368
Ruderman, M., 23

Vergara, M., 35
Vermeulen, S., 213

W

Walberg, H. J., 330, 331
Walsh, P., 122
Want, M. C., 330, 331
Wardlaw, D. M., 330
Warner, R. M., 335
Warrenfeltz, R., 35
Watkins, J., 285
Weick, K. E., 363
Weissberg, R. P., 330, 331, 343
Wentzel, K. R., 335, 342
Wheatley, K. F., 335
Wheeler, J. V., 372
Whiten, A., 304

Whitney, D., 286
Wilson, M. E., 345
Wolff, S. B., 384
Wood, L. M., 74, 201, 379, 380, 397

Y

Yaeger, T., 286
Yerkes, R. M., 115

Z

Zagorsky, R., 116
Zaretsky, L., 381
Zeidner, M., 379
Zillman, D., 114
Zins, J. E., 330, 331, 341

Subject Index

Page references followed by *fig* indicate an illustrated figure; followed by *t* indicate a table.

Behavior: difficult emotions and related passive aggressive, 160–161; emotionally intelligent array of personality types and, 240–242; MBTI insights into patterns and preferences of, 242–244; perception-appraisal-motivation-action model of, 118–119*fig*, 120; personality differences and, 161, 242–254*t*. *See also* Intentional change

Black Consciousness movement (Africa), 210–211, 220

BOEI (Benchmark of Organizational Emotional Intelligence): comparison of work settings using, 173–180; EI measured using, 172–173*t*; organizational development application of, 226; South African EI research using, 218–219

Bullies, 161–162

C

Cambodia: Resonant Leadership for Results Program conducted in, 55–63; Resonant Leadership for Results Program lessons learned in, 63–69

Canada: Ontario Ministry of Education and Training, 381; Ontario Principals' Council (OPC) leadership study, 201, 381–395; Ontario Public Supervisory Officials' Association (OPSOA), 394

Canadian Imperial Bank of Commerce (CIBC), 200–201

Career coaching. *See* Coaching

CASEL (Collaborative for Academic, Social, and Emotional Learning), 331

Center for Creative Leadership, 308

Choice theory, 349

CLF (Catastrophic Leadership Failure): decision-making characteristics, 126; examining the causes of, 111–112, 125–126; stress as compromising EI, 112–116; three key factors for bolstering resistance to, 112, 126–135, *See also* Leadership derailment

CLF (Catastrophic Leadership Failure) prevention: ARSENAL best practices for, 112, 127*fig*, 130–135; Cognitive Resilience (CR), 112, 126–129; Stress Management Capacity (SMC) for, 112, 126–129; Stress Resilient EI (SREI), 112, 127*fig*–130

Coaching: as emotional intelligence application, 226–227; Emotional Literacy Coaching Program for, 348–349; 5-D cycle model for Appreciative Inquiry, 287–297; value of emotional intelligence (EI), 284–285. *See also* Management education & training

A Coach's Guide to Emotional Intelligence (Hughes and Terrell), 15, 292

Cognitive intelligence (IQ): comparing EQ-i and MSCEIT to tests of, 271*t*–272; correlation between leadership performance and, 116–117; description of, 116; stress as compromising, 112, 115–116

Cognitive Resilience (CR): description and building of, 129; as key factor for resisting CLF, 112, 126–127*fig*, 128

Collaborative Growth model, 4, 147

Collaborative Intelligence, 147

Competency: EQ-i scores for Telplus leader competency, 193*t*; EQ-i scores of Telplus leaders by rating, 192*fig*; Heart of School leadership program to build leader, 386–390; impact of management education and training on, 362–366; leader competency model on, 186–187, 195–199; need for, 360–361; Telplus goal attainment criteria for, 187*t*; total EQ of Telplus by rating leader, 191*fig*

Conflict: difficult emotions and, 159–163; difficult people or bullies and, 161–162; fear of scarcity of resources and, 162; passive aggressive behavior and, 160–161; personality differences and, 161

Conflict resolution: using emotional and social intelligence (ESI) skills, 141–142; team skills in, 144*fig*–145; TESI research on divergent thinking and, 148–156; tips on managing team's difficult emotions for, 163

Consortium for Research on Emotional Intelligence in Organizations, 4, 201, 360

Constructionist Principle (Appreciative Inquiry), 286

Courage: chunking strategy for, 16–17; as ESE building strategy, 15–17; measuring, 8*t*; reality check strategy for, 17

D

Decision-making: CLF (Catastrophic Leadership Failure), 126; examples of poor leadership, 111

Deloitte, 201

Dependency assumption, 86, 87–88, 91

Difficult emotions: conflict-adverse leaders and, 159–160; description of, 159; passive aggressive behavior related to, 160–161

Difficult people (or bullies), 161–162

DISC: gathering information through, 14; personality differences measured by, 161

District School Board of Niagara, 391

Divergent thinking (DT): effective team emotional and social intelligence and, 146–148; measuring levels of, 151–156; TESI research on conflict resolution skills and, 148–156

Drag: examining the EQ-i concept of, 98–103; high drag profile, 100*fig*; high drag profile with personal mean, 102*fig*; as limiting human potential, 98; low drag profile with personal mean, 103*fig*

Dynamic Inquiry (DI) process: description of, 56–57; Resonant Leadership for Results Program use of, 57–59

E

ECI 2.0 (Emotional Competency Inventory), 6

Educational settings: Emotionally Literate Schools program in, 330, 331–352; management education and training, 362–366, 362–374; South African IQ research application to, 219–221. *See also* Schools

EI-Stress Effect, 120–124*fig*

ELC. *See* Emotionally Literate Schools (ELC) program

Emergenetics: gathering information through, 14; personality differences measured by, 161

Emotional and social effectiveness (ESE): examining different approach to building, 4–5; experiential ideas for building, 3–4; five key areas of, 4; measuring emotional intelligence (EI) and, 5–9; strategies for building, 7*t*–9*t*, 10–18

Emotional and social effectiveness (ESE) strategies: authentic success, 8*t*–9*t*, 17–18; courage, 8*t*, 15–17; responsive awareness, 7*t*, 15; valuing others, 7*t*, 13–14; valuing self, 7*t*, 10–13

Emotional and social intelligence (ESI): ability models of, 260–262; conflict resolution using skills of, 141–142; divergent thinking essential to effective team, 146–148; focusing on conflict resolution and team, 144*fig*–145; impact of LEAD course on improving, 364*fig*–365; impact of management education and training on, 362–366; measures of individual, 145–146; mixed models of, 262–264; as situationally dependent concept, 264; team context of, 142–144. *See also* Interpersonal domain (EQ-i); Social intelligence (SI)

Emotional intelligence (EI): coaching development of, 284–285; comparing high achievers to other achievers,' 24*t*; definition of, 22, 259–260, 284; examining South African perspective on, 205–229; five key areas of effectiveness for, 4; general emotional and social well-being related to, 379–381; the human brain and, 54–55; impact of LEAD course on improving, 364*fig*–365; impact of management education and training on, 362–366; leadership and, 187*t*, 191*fig*–196*fig*, 380–381; leadership derailment through too much, 75–82; "living," 65; measuring ESE and, 5–9; organizational leadership through, 53–54*fig*; personality type and, 235–254*t*; relationship between leadership and, 124; relationship of organization EI and individual, 166–167; star performance five-step process and role of, 183–202; stress as compromising, 112–116; U.S. Air Force study (1996) on, 199–200. *See also* EQ-i (BarOn Emotional Quotient Inventory)

Emotional intelligence (EI) assessment tools: comparing EQ-i and MSCEIT to other, 267, 269–273; debate over use of, 257–258; EQ-i and MSCEIT integration for, 265–279; ESCI (Emotional and Social Competency Inventory), 6, 7*t*–9*t*. *See also* EQ-i (Bar-On Emotional Quotient Inventory); MSCEIT (Mayer, Salovey,

Caruso Emotional Intelligence Test);
Psychological testing

Emotional intelligence (EI) models:
ability, 261–262; Bar-On, 6, 75–76*fig*,
213–216; Collaborative Growth, 4, 147;
components of the, 53–54*fig*; excitation transfer, 114*fig*; 5-D cycle model of
Appreciative Inquiry, 287–290; Goleman,
6; leader competency, 186–187, 195–199;
Life Coaching Quadrant, 297; mixed ESI,
262–264; perception-appraisal-motivation-
action, 118–119*fig*, 120; RULER, 331–334,
342–343, 346–347, 348, 349; Salovey-
Mayer, 6; three major conceptual, 6;
two-by-two, 118*t*, 119

Emotional intelligence (EI) research:
Emotionally Literate Schools program,
330, 331–352; Ontario Principals' Council
(OPC) leadership study, 201, 381–395;
proposed domains of, 237*t*–238; South
African, 213–227; TESI (Team Emotional
Social Intelligence Survey), 143–144,
148–156

Emotional Intelligence (Goleman), 74

Emotional intelligence organizations: BOEI
comparisons of two workplace settings of,
173–177; description of, 167–168; relationship of individual EI to, 166–167; summary of best practice options for, 181; as
truly great workplace, 168–172; underlying mood of, 177–180

Emotional intelligence workshops: characteristics of effective, 224–225; Emotional
Literacy for Administrations workshops,
342; Emotional Literacy for Educators
workshops, 341

Emotional literacy: basics of, 238–239;
importance for students, teachers, and
school leaders, 334–336; RULER model
for teaching, 331–334, 342–343, 346–347,
348, 349

Emotional Literacy Blueprint tool (RULER
model), 343, 349

Emotional Literacy for Administrations
workshops, 342

Emotional Literacy for Educators workshops, 341

The Emotionally Intelligent Team (Hughes and
Terrell), 142, 145, 147

Emotionally Literate Schools (ELC) program: description of, 330, 331; Emotional
Literacy Coaching Program as part of,
348–349; emotional literacy RULER
model followed by, 331–334, 342–343,
346–347, 348, 349; implementation plan
for, 336–351

Emotionally Literate Schools program
implementation: implementation phase
of, 341–349; overview of, 336–337*fig*;
readiness phase of, 337–341; sustainability
phase of, 349–351

Emotional Quotient Inventory. *See* EQ-i
(BarOn Emotional Quotient Inventory)

Emotions: awareness of, 156–163, 260;
coherent framework of interpersonal relationships and, 236–238; contagious nature
of, 54; control as core of EI competencies,
55; difficult, 159–163; fear of scarcity of
resources and, 162; positive, 157–159;
understanding purpose and meaning of,
238–239*t*

Empathy, 15, 146, 306

Encyclopedia of Applied Psychology
(Spielberger), 6, 305

EQ-360, 145, 290, 291

*The EQ Edge: Emotional Intelligence and Your
Success* (Stein and Book), 166

EQ-i and MSCEIT integration: benefits
of, 266*t*; correlations of, 268*t*; EQ-i and
MSCEIT combinations used for, 265–266;
performance scores vs. combination of,
267*t*; tandem approach to, 273–279. *See
also* EQ-i (BarOn Emotional Quotient
Inventory); MSCEIT (Mayer, Salovey,
Caruso Emotional Intelligence Test)

EQ-i and MSCEIT tandem case study: EQ-i
scores for, 277*fig*; MSCEIT task scores by
branch, 276*fig*; MSCEIT total and branch
scores for, 275*fig*; overview of, 275–278

EQ-i and MSCEIT tandem process: administration role in, 279; case study on using,
275–278; comparing "normal" feedback
to, 274; description of, 273; preparing the
practitioner to use, 278–279; when to use
the, 274

EQ-i (BarOn Emotional Quotient
Inventory): balance concept of, 103–107,
108*t*; comparing cognitive ability (IQ)

and, 271t–272; comparing FIRO Element B and, 270t–271; comparing MBTI types with, 269t–270; data analysis of measurements of, 190–195; data analysis of personality type information provided by, 244–254t; debate over using MSCEIT versus, 257–258; description of, 213; drag concept of, 98–103*fig*; EI measured using, 145, 170; ESE measured using, 6, 7t–9t; examining combining Myers-Briggs Type Indicator with, 5; Goodness of Fit means and ranges, 264–265t; interpersonal domain of, 301–325; leverage concept of, 107–110; measuring impact of stress, 122–123*fig*; as mixed model, 262–264; OPC leadership study use of, 381, 385t; origins and development of, 97; potential scope of EQ-i scale integration, 200*fig*; relationship to other instruments, 267, 269; respondent's stress level affecting, 272t–273; scale definitions of the, 253t–254t; scores of sales directors by executive performance rating, 194*fig*; self actualization skills in, 17; South African norms published for, 213–216; star performance process and measuring, 187–189t; structural components of, 263t; subjected to the UNIFIED Approach, 307–309. *See also* Bar-On model; Emotional intelligence (EI); Emotional intelligence (EI) assessment tools; EQ-i and MSCEIT integration

EQ-i Technical Manual (Multi-Health Systems): balancers listed in the, 104–107, 108t; drag measures in, 98–103*fig*; EM and RE inter-correlation reported in, 307; leverage measures in the, 107–110

ESADE, 368

ESCI (Emotional and Social Competency Inventory), 6, 7t–9t

Excitation transfer model, 114*fig*

Exercise (ARSENAL practice), 133

F

Fears, 162

Fight-flight assumption, 89–91

FIRO Element B (interpersonal interaction), 270t–271

5-D cycle model: case study application of, 295–297; overview of, 287–290

"Foot-in-the-mouth disease," 121

G

The Game of Life and How to Play It (Shinn), 73

Gardner's multiple intelligences, 3

Gender differences: social intelligence (SI) and, 317*fig*–318; South African and North American EQ-i scale on, 215t

Goleman model, 6

Goodness of Fit, 264–265t

Government Gazette, 222

Grand Erie District School Board, 391

Groupthink: description of, 87; social intelligence for counteracting, 148; sources of, 147

H

Hay Group, 305

Health self-talk, 11–12

Heart of School leadership program: description of, 386–387; evaluation of, 391–393; module one: intrapersonal, 388–389; module two: interpersonal, 389–390; module three: adaptability, 390; module four: stress management, 391

High achievers: case study interventions for, 25–45; comparing to other achievers, 23–25; context of, 23; description of, 23

High achievers EI interventions: buddying used in, 43; business imperative of, 35; designing considerations for, 25–26; development plans used in, 42; focused coaching as part of, 43; format of program for, 35–38; leading components of, 38–39; length of program for, 38; Manchester Inc. study on, 35–36; results achieved by, 43–45; senior sponsors of, 40, 41t, 42; structuring used in, 26–27, 28t–31t; support mechanisms as part of, 39–40*fig*

High achievers Group A (Potential Leaders): description of, 22–23, 35; main support mechanisms implemented for, 41t; profile of, 32*fig*; split between coaching and training for, 37t; summary of EI programs for, 28t–31t, 35–45

High achievers Group B (Official Leaders): description of, 22–23, 27; main support mechanisms implemented for, 41*t*; profile of, 33*fig*; split between coaching and training for, 37*t*; summary of EI programs for, 28*t*–31*t*, 35–45

High achievers Group C (Official and Unofficial Leaders): description of, 22–23, 27; main support mechanisms implemented for, 41*t*; profile of, 33*fig*; split between coaching and training for, 37*t*; summary of EI programs for, 28*t*–31*t*, 35–45

HIV/AIDS crisis: African experience with, 210, 212, 222; emotional intelligence as part of solution for, 69–70; Teleos Institute's Resonant Leadership for Results Program for, 52–69

How to Win Friends and Influence People (Carnegie), 73

Human brain, 54–55

Human capital strategy, 198*fig*

I

Ideal Self-image, 368–369

Impulse control: balance between assertiveness and, 104, 106, 108*t*; definition of, 76; leadership derailment from lack of, 76–79; measuring individual, 146

Individual development, 226–227

Infrastructure deficits: dependency assumption as, 86, 87–88, 91; fight-flight assumption as, 89–91; identifying impact on leader's EI, 91–92; issues related to, 86–87

Intentional change: creating personal vision of, 368–369; effective practices for sustainable, 4–5; metamorphosis of, 371–372; mindfulness through a learning agenda, 370–371; personal balance sheet kept for, 369–370; process of, 366–368, 367*fig*; resonant relationships and, 372–373. *See also* Behavior

Intentional change theory, 349, 360

Interpersonal domain (EQ-i): appropriateness of EQ-i scoring of, 305–307; description of, 301; sample group used in study of, 310*fig*–311; unified approach to the, 307–309. *See also* Emotional and social intelligence (ESI); Social intelligence (SI)

Interpersonal interaction (FIRO Element B), 270*t*–271

Interpersonal relationships: coherent framework of emotions and, 236–238; Heart of School Leadership program focus on, 389–390; intentional change and resonant, 372–373; leadership and role of constructive, 235–236. *See also* Personality types

INTERSECT Approach, 304

Intrapersonal module (Heart of School Leadership), 388–389

IQ. *See* Cognitive intelligence (IQ)

"I-We" continuum, 65–66

J

Job level-social intelligence relationship, 319–321

Jopie van Rooyen & Partners, 221

Journal of Management Development, 361

L

LEAD course, 364*fig*–365

Leader competency: emotional leadership relationship to, 380–381; EQ-i scores for Telplus, 193*t*; EQ-i scores of Telplus, 192*fig*; Ontario Principals' Council (OPC) study on, 201, 381–395; predictors for Telplus leaders, 196*fig*; Telplus goal attainment criteria for, 187*t*; total EQ of Telplus by rating, 191*fig*. *See also* Competency

Leader competency model: applying the, 195–199; description of, 186–187

Leadership: correlation between IQ and successful, 116–117; examples of poor decisions by, 111; Heart of School leadership program to build school, 386–390; infrastructure deficits affecting, 86–92; Ontario Principals' Council (OPC) study on, 201, 381–395; relationship between emotional intelligence and, 124; role of constructive interpersonal relationships to, 235–236; South African EI research application to developing, 223–224; strengths/weaknesses affecting, 75–86; stress of, 112–116

Leadership derailment: using BarOn model to examine, 75–76*fig*; exploring strengths as weaknesses to prevent, 83–84; identifying strengths that are causing, 82–83*t*; impulse control leading to, 76–79; optimism leading to, 80–82; repairing weakened strengths to prevent, 84–86. *See also* CLF (Catastrophic Leadership Failure)

Leadership strengths: explored as weaknesses, 83–84; identifying strengths becoming weaknesses, 82–83*t*; repairing weakened, 84–86; which become weaknesses, 75–82

Learning: as ARSENAL practice, 134*t*–135; as education and training purpose, 373–374

Learning exercises, 1334*t*

Life Coaching Quadrant model, 297

Life College Programme (South Africa), 220

Life's 2Solution (Hughes), 12

M

Management education & training: impact of, 362–366; learning as purpose of, 373–374; process of intentional change through, 366–373. *See also* Coaching

Manchester Inc. study (2001), 35–36

Marcus Aurelius, 73

MBTI. *See* Myers-Briggs Type Indicator (MBTI)

Meditations (Marcus Aurelius), 73

MHS Staff, 218

Mixed models: description of, 262; EQ-i (BarOn Emotional Quotient Inventory) as, 262–264

Models. *See* Emotional intelligence (EI) models

Mood Meter tool (RULER model), 342–343, 346–347, 348, 349

Moses, Grandma, 261

Motivational theory, 349

MSCEIT (Mayer, Salovey, Caruso Emotional Intelligence Test): ability model basis of, 261–262*t*; comparing FIRO Element B and, 270*t*–271; debate over using EQ-i versus, 257–258; Goodness of Fit means and ranges, 264–265*t*; insight to abilities related to emotional intelligence by,

242; measurements of, 6, 7*t*–9*t*, 170; measuring impact of stress, 123–124*fig*; respondent's stress level affecting, 273*fig*; South African EI measured using, 216–218; structural components of, 262*t*. *See also* Emotional intelligence (EI) assessment tools; EQ-i and MSCEIT integration

Multi-Health Systems (MHS): *EQ-i Technical Manual* published by, 98–110, 307; Star performance profile of, 183–201, 264

Multiple intelligences theory, 3

Myers-Briggs Type Indicator (MBTI): behavior patterns and preferences insights by, 242–244; brief descriptions of personality types of the, 250*t*–252*t*; comparing EQ-i and MSCEIT to, 269*t*–270; data analysis of personality types of, 244–254*t*; examining EQ-i combination with, 5; gathering information through, 14; personality differences measures by, 161, 239–240*t*; scales of the, 240*t*

N

National Staff Development Council (NSDC), 347

NLP (neuro-linguistic programming), 16

Nutrition (ARSENAL practice), 133–134

O

Ontario Ministry of Education and Training, 381

Ontario Principals' Council (OPC) leadership study: best practice summary learned from, 394–395; description of, 201, 381; future directions for expanding research of, 393–394; on Heart of School leadership program, 386–390; key research findings of, 383–386; measuring emotional intelligence, 381–382; measuring leadership ability, 382–383; on teaching school administrators to build EI, 386–393

Ontario Public Supervisory Officials' Association (OPSOA), 394

Optimal performance curve, 115*fig*

Optimism: description of, 80; leadership derailment from enhanced, 80–82; measuring individual, 146

Organizations: BOEI applications to developing, 226; coaching programs by, 226–227, 284–297, 348–349; emotional intelligence, 166–181; infrastructure deficits affecting leadership, 86–92; management education and training by, 362–374. *See also* Workplace

P

Perception-appraisal-motivation-action model of behavior, 118–119*fig*, 120

Personal EQ (PEQ) profile, 309, 323*fig*–324

Personality types: conflict, difficult emotions, and, 161; emotionally intelligent array of behavior and, 240–242; EQ-i data analysis of, 244–254*t*; MBTI measures of differences in, 161, 239–240*t. See also* Interpersonal relationships

Poetic Principle (Appreciative Inquiry), 287

Positive Principle (Appreciative Inquiry), 286

The Power of Positive Thinking (Peale), 73

The Power of Your Subconscious Mind (Murphy), 74

Practitioners: preparing for EQ-i and MSCEIT tandem process, 278–279; SI and EQ profiling by, 321–324

Prefrontal cortex (PFC), 115, 117, 120, 121

Psycho Cybernetics (Maltz), 73

Psychological testing, 222. *See also* Emotional intelligence (EI) assessment tools

R

Rainy River District School Board, 391

Raven's Progressive Matrices, 271

Reality testing, 146

Real Self, 369

Research. *See* Emotional intelligence (EI) research

Resonant Leadership for Results Program lessons: 1. develop EI in yourself before teaching it, 63–65; 2. the "I-We" continuum, 65–66; 3. creating Resonant Facilitator Group is essential, 66–67; 4. eliminate jargon and manage translation, 67–69

Resonant Leadership for Results Program (Teleos Institute): Dynamic Inquiry used in, 56–59; identifying diverse participants, 56; launching the, 60–61; lessons learned from, 63–69; overview of the, 55–56*fig*; program enrollment meetings and customization of, 59; program facilitators, 61–62; Regional Change Group of, 60–61; systems approach used in, 62–63

Responsive awareness: as ESE building strategy, 15; measuring, 7*t*; observing and practicing empathy for, 15

Rest (ARFSENAL component), 132

Rooster Effect, 121–122

RULER model: emotional literacy taught using, 331, 334; five components of, 332*t*–333*t*; Mood Meter and Emotional Literacy Blueprint tools of, 342–343, 346–347, 348, 349

S

Salovey-Mayer model, 6

School administrators: best practices for implementing EI program for, 394–395; Emotional Literacy Coaching Program for, 348–349; Heart of School leadership program for, 386–390; Ontario Principals' Council (OPC) study on leadership of, 201, 381–395

Schools: Emotionally Literate Schools program in, 330, 331–352; Emotionally Literate Schools program steering committee of, 338–341; importance of emotional literacy for, 334–336. *See also* Educational settings

Self-actualization, 389

Self-awareness. *See* Awareness

Self Help (Smiles), 73

Self-regard, 145–146

Self Reliance (Emerson), 73

SET Approach, 302–303*fig*

Simultaneity Principle (Appreciative Inquiry), 286

The Small Work in the Great Work (Stafford), 293

Social and emotional learning (SEL): CASEL on school-based programs for, 331; challenge of incorporating into school curriculum, 330–331; description of, 330; Emotionally Literate Schools program for, 330, 331–352; a systematic process for promoting, 330

Social EQ (SEQ) profile, 309, 323*fig*–324

Social Intelligence (Goleman), 302

Social intelligence (SI): age-based, 318*fig*–319; gender-based, 317*fig*–318; impact of LEAD course on improving, 364*fig*–365; impact of management education and training on, 362–366; INTERSECT Approach to, 304; job level and, 319–321; personal EQ (PEQ) profile of, 309, 323*fig*–324; SET Approach to, 302–303*fig*; setting standard for, 313*fig*–317; social EQ (SEQ) profile of, 309, 323*fig*–324; UNIFIED approach to study of, 305–309, 312*t*, 313*fig*–324. *See also* Emotional and social intelligence (ESI); Interpersonal domain (EQ-i)

Social responsibility, 105–106, 108*t*, 306

South Africa: African role models in, 210–212; apartheid of, 211; emotional intelligence in today's, 212–213; emotional intelligence measures and studies in, 213–219; emotional intelligence research applications in, 219–227; Life College Programme of, 220; Resonant Leadership for Results Program conducted in, 55–63; Resonant Leadership for Results Program lessons learned in, 63–69; Ubuntu philosophy practiced in, 207–210, 227. *See also* African continent

South African Employment Equity Act 55 (1998), 222

South African IQ research: BOEI used for, 218–219; EQ-i (BarOn Emotional Quotient Inventory) used for, 213–216; MSCEIT used for, 216–218

South African IQ research applications: educational, 219–221; individual development, 226–227; organizational, 221–226; sporting context of, 227; TV reality shows, 222–223

Sports development (South Africa), 227

Star performance: examining emotional intelligence role in, 183–184; five-step process of, 185*fig*–201, 264

Star performance steps: 1. examine your performance metrics, 185–187; 2. measure emotional intelligence, 187–189*t*; 3. analyze the data, 190–195; 4. apply the model, 195–199; 5. implement and evaluate your system, 199–201

Statistics Canada, 380

Stress: affecting MSCEIT and EQ-i scores, 272*fig*–273*fig*; as compromising cognitive intelligence (IQ), 115–116, 1112; as compromising emotional intelligence (EI), 112–116, 120–124*fig*; EQ-i normal vs. stressed scores on, 123*fig*; excitation transfer model on, 114*fig*; Heart of School Leadership program on managing, 391; physical response to long-term, 113–116; prefrontal cortex (PFC) and, 115, 117, 120, 121; redefined as body's non-specific response to demands, 113

Stress Management Capacity (SMC): description and building of, 128–129; Heart of School Leadership module on building, 391; as key factor for resisting CLF, 112, 126–127*fig*, 128

Stress Resilient EI (SREI): description and building of, 129–130; as key factor for resisting CLF, 112, 127*fig*, 128

Students: Emotionally Literate Schools program role of, 330, 331–352; importance of emotional literacy for, 334–336

Support (ARSENAL practice), 132–133

SWOT analysis, 289

Systems theory: Resonant Leadership for Results Program approach using, 62–63; as Teleos Leadership Institute basis, 50–51

T

Teachers: Emotionally Literate Schools program role of, 330, 331–352; importance of emotional literacy for, 334–336

Team emotional and social intelligence (ESI): conflict resolution and, 144*fig*–145; description of, 143; divergent thinking and effective, 146–148; measuring individual EI in, 145–146

Team Emotional and Social Intelligence Survey (TESI) [Hughes, Thompson, and Terrell], 142

Teams: awareness regarding emotions of team, 156–163; definition of, 143; difficult emotions and, 159–163; difficult people or bullies in the, 161–162; individual scale results compared to overall effectiveness rating of, 150*fig*; passive aggressive behavior in, 160–161; positive emotions of, 157–159; South African EI applications to developing, 225–226; TESI (Team Emotional Social Intelligence Survey) of, 143–144

Teleos Leadership Institute: EI and systems theory basis of, 50–51; HIV/AIDS leadership challenge of, 52–53; leadership development programs conducted by, 49–50; lessons learned from, 63–69; making change sustainable, 62–63; origins of the, 51–52; Resonant Leadership for Results Program of, 55–69

Telplus (pseudonym): description of, 185–186; star performer five-step process used by, 185–201

TESI (Team Emotional Social Intelligence Survey): description and functions of, 143–144; research on conflict resolution and divergent thinking, 148–156

360-degree survey, 145, 290, 291

TV reality shows (South Africa), 223

2Solution, 12–13

Two-by-two emotional intelligence model, 118*t*, 119

U

Ubuntu philosophy, 207–210, 227

UNIFIED Approach: calling for study of social intelligence, 304–305; to social intelligence based on EQ-i, 305–309, 312*t*, 313*fig*–324

U.S. Air Force QI study (1996), 199–200

U.S. Department of Labor, 380

V

Valuing others: acknowledge others as, 14; enhancing awareness of diversity in personalities, 14; as ESE building strategy, 13–14; measuring, 7*t*

Valuing self: as ESE building strategy, 10–13; health self-talk as, 11–12; *Life's 2Solution* action plan for, 12–13; measuring, 7*t*

Venn diagram, 303*fig*

W

Walden (Thoreau), 73

Waterloo Region District School Board, 388, 391

Weatherhead School of Management, 360, 364–365, 367, 370

Websites: Appreciative Inquiry, 286; Bar-On model, 6; Collaborative Growth team model, 147; Consortium for Research on Emotional Intelligence in Organizations, 4; Life Coaching Quadrant model, 297

Wechsler Adult Intelligence Scale, 271

Wonderlic Personnel Test (WPT), 271

Work/life balance, 18

Workplace: BOEI comparisons of two settings of, 173–180; characteristics of a truly great, 168–172; relationships and purpose in the, 171–172. *See also* Organizations

Workshops. *See* Emotional intelligence workshops

About the Editors

Marcia Hughes, J.D., M.A., is president of Collaborative Growth®, L.L.C., and serves as a strategic communications partner for teams and their leaders in organizations that value high performers. She weaves her expertise in emotional intelligence throughout her consulting work, facilitation, team building, and workshops to help people motivate themselves and communicate more effectively with others. Her keynotes are built around powerful stories of how success can grow when people work collaboratively. Businesses, government agencies, and nonprofits have all benefited in such areas as team and leadership development, strategic design, and conflict resolution from her proven formula for success. She is co-author of *A Facilitator's Guide to Team Emotional and Social Intelligence* (2009), *A Coach's Guide for Emotional Intelligence* (2008), *The Emotionally Intelligent Team* (2007), *Emotional Intelligence in Action (2005),* and author of *Life's 2% Solution.* Marcia and her partner, James Terrell, are authors of The Team Emotional & Social Intelligence Survey® (TESI®), an online team assessment. Marcia and James Terrell have worked with many diverse clients, including American Express, Medtronic, the World Bank, the Central Intelligence Agency, the United States Environmental Protection Agency, and the Department of Agriculture.

Marcia is a certified trainer in the Bar-On EQ-i® and EQ 360®. She provides train-the-trainer training and coaching in powerful EQ delivery. Her efforts to improve productivity in the workplace through strategic communication grew out of a distinguished career in law, where her firm specialized in complex public policy matters. There again, her leadership and communication skills enabled her team to effectively address controversial environmental, land use, and water development matters involving numerous stakeholders, which included federal, state, and local governments, along with the general public. As an assistant attorney general, she served the Department of Public Health and the Environment. She clerked on the 10th Circuit Court of Appeals for the Honorable William E. Doyle.

Henry L. (Dick) Thompson, Ph.D., is an internationally recognized consultant, educator, speaker and author. Over the past 30 years, he has gained valuable experience developing and leading teams—from the battlefield to the boardroom. He uses his vast experience and knowledge to help leaders and organizations improve performance. Dick is president and CEO of High Performing Systems, Inc., an international management consulting and training firm he founded in 1984 to help leaders, teams, and organizations achieve high performance. The philosophy of HPS is based on a systems approach to performance improvement. Clients are Fortune 500 companies, government agencies, and a diverse group of public, private, and international firms. These include AT&T, Georgia-Pacific Corporation, Shell Oil Company, Johnson & Johnson, General Mills, Mohawk Industries, U.S. Forest Department, and Owens-Corning.

Numerous command and staff positions during his twenty-one-year military service have resulted in exceptional management insight and expertise. During that time, he trained and led some of the most elite teams in the world. He served as an officer with the U.S. Army Special Forces Group (Green Berets) in Vietnam. Dick has published numerous articles, training manuals, and several books, including *The CommunicationWheel®: A Resource Book, Jung's Function-Attitudes Explained, Introduction to the CommunicationWheel®*, and *Introduction to FIRO Element B® in Organizations*. Dick is well known for his innovative use of emotional intelligence (EI) with his clients. He conducts leading-edge research in EI and continues to integrate results into the Leadership

Potential Assessment process. He is also a certifying instructor for the BarOn Emotional Quotient Inventory® (EQ-i®).

James Bradford Terrell is vice president of Collaborative Growth®, L.L.C., where he applies his expertise in interpersonal communication to help a variety of public- and private-sector clients anticipate change and respond to it resiliently.

Co-author of *A Facilitator's Guide to Team Emotional and Social Intelligence,* (2009), *A Coach's Guide for Emotional Intelligence* (2008), *The Emotionally Intelligent Team* (2007), and *Emotional Intelligence in Action (2005),* he coaches leaders, teams in transition, and senior management, using the Bar-On EQi®, the EQ 360®, and other assessments. Terrell and his partner, Marcia Hughes, are authors of The Team Emotional & Social Intelligence Survey® (TESI®), an online team assessment. James provides train-the-trainer workshops and educates coaches on how to develop insightful interpretation and application of EQ results. Marcia Hughes and James work with many diverse clients, including American Express, Medtronic, the World Bank, the Central Intelligence Agency, the United States Environmental Protection Agency, and the Department of Agriculture.

James worked as a psychotherapist in private practice for many years and served as executive director of the Syntropy Institute, a not-for-profit research organization investigating how communication training impacts human effectiveness. He also served as the director of training for the Metro-Denver Mutual Housing Association, an early developer of cooperative housing in the Denver area.

In a previous life, he was the owner/operator of Integrity Building Systems, a construction company specializing in residential and commercial renovation and served as a project coordinator on a wide variety of building projects, including Denver International Airport and the National Digital Cable Television Center. In a future life he is certain he will be a rock star.